An OPUS book

THIS STAGE-PLAY WORLD

Julia Briggs is Professor of English and Women's Studies at De Montfort University, Leicester. Her wide range of interests include ghost stories and books written for children, but she is best known for her biography of E. Nesbit and her edition of Virginia Woolf for Penguin Books. She has written on Shakespeare and Marlowe, and has edited *The Second Maiden's Tragedy* for Oxford University Press's *Complete Works of Thomas Middleton*.

THIS
STAGE-PLAY
WORLD

TEXTS AND CONTEXTS, 1580–1625

SECOND EDITION

Julia Briggs

Oxford   New York
OXFORD UNIVERSITY PRESS
1997

Oxford University Press, Great Clarendon Street, Oxford OX2 6DP
Oxford New York
Athens Auckland Bangkok Bogota Bombay
Buenos Aires Calcutta Cape Town Dar es Salaam
Delhi Florence Hong Kong Istanbul Karachi
Kuala Lumpur Madras Madrid Melbourne
Mexico City Nairobi Paris Singapore
Taipei Tokyo Toronto Warsaw
and associated companies in
Berlin Ibadan

Oxford is a trade mark of Oxford University Press

© Julia Briggs 1983, 1997

First published 1983 by Oxford University Press
Second edition published 1997 as an Oxford
University Press paperback

British Library Cataloguing in Publication Data
Data available

Library of Congress Cataloging in Publication Data
Briggs, Julia.
This stage-play world : texts and contexts, 1580–1625 / Julia
Briggs.—2nd ed.
"An Opus book."
Includes bibliographical references (p.) and index.
1. English literature—Early modern, 1500–1700—History and
criticism.   2. Literature and society—Great Britain—History—16th
century.   3. Literature and society—Great Britain—History—17th
century.   4. Great Britain—Civilization—16th century.   5. Great
Britain—Civilization—17th century.   6. Social problems in
literature.   I. Title.
PR421.B7 1997   820.9'003—dc21   97–5258
ISBN 0–19–289286–X (pb)

1 3 5 7 9 10 8 6 4 2

Typeset by Best-set Typesetter Ltd., Hong Kong
Printed in Great Britain
by Biddles Ltd.,
Guildford and King's Lynn

Preface to the Revised Edition

This Stage-Play World was originally written to introduce students of Renaissance literature to its social, political, and cultural context, and to introduce history students to a literature that gives thrilling and powerful expression to thought and life in early modern England. My chief difficulty, then and now, lay in the substantial differences between the two subjects and their different methodologies, between 'two different kinds of categorization of human experience . . . unhomologous systematic constructions put upon interpenetrating subject-matters'.[1] Since this book was first published in 1983, a great deal of critical attention has focused upon Renaissance texts and the conditions that produced them: in what follows, I have tried to give some impression of the main lines of argument.

To read Renaissance literature in the aftermath of New Criticism was to rediscover the importance of historical context, and the kind of insight it could give into the production and operation of literary texts. History offered political ideas and an engagement that had been exiled from critical practice: the radical sympathies of Christopher Hill, or the Cambridge history of ideas and political thought opened new perspectives on Shakespeare and Jacobean drama. At the same time, the history of early modern England was itself transformed in the 1970s by a series of invigorating new accounts, notably Peter Burke on popular culture (1978), Margaret Spufford on Protestantism and the reading public (1974, 1981), Quentin Skinner on political thought (1978), Lawrence Stone on education, the aristocracy and the family (1964, 1977), Sir Keith Thomas on religion and popular belief (1971), Keith Wrightson on social history (1982), and Penry Williams's overview of the Tudor regime (1979)—this list is by no means inclusive.[2] While these books reflected a range of political attitudes, they shared a sense of the period as one of dynamic change working at a variety of levels within society, change that partly resulted from the impact of the printed word, in which texts themselves were the agents as well as the products. Auden's sad sense that 'poetry makes nothing happen'[3] could be repudiated from early modern history, when the spread of ideas through writing and reading directly effected religious and political change.

The writing of history in the seventies was expansive, and eager to learn from the neighbouring disciplines of sociology and anthropology. It recorded the proselytizing passion of the Protestant revolution, its contribution to a new sense of self-hood, and its egalitarian edge, aspects sympathetic to socialist or Marxist interpretations. Since then, the wide appeal of the Reformation has been called in question. Was there really a broad-based popular Protestant movement at all? Patrick Collinson still argues forcefully for it, but Christopher Haigh and Eamon Duffy have investigated the role of the Church as it was at the moment of Henry's Reformation, when corruption and venality were supposed to be its dominant characteristics. Instead of enthusiasm for change, they have identified a sense of communal loss as the Churches' rich and colourful ornaments were torn down, and the public celebrations of saints' days and the cult of the Virgin were abandoned. Haigh has distinguished between Anglicans and Protestants, identifying the latter as a small but noisy minority.

In addition to rewriting traditional accounts, historians, and literary critics too, have opened up whole areas of research previously omitted from consideration. Interest in how the working population lived, on the one hand, and in non-canonical texts on the other, has brought a range of popular literature into view, including advice books, marriage manuals, almanacs, herbals, news pamphlets, and ballads, the range of material first surveyed in Louis B. Wright's classic *Middle-Class Culture in Elizabethan England* (1935, 1958), and now being re-examined by Peter Burke, Bernard Capp, Peter Lake, Barry Reay, and Margaret Spufford, and in its distinctive Protestant versions, by Patrick Collinson and Tessa Watt. Even more ephemeral material such as libellous rhymes are gradually being recovered from letters and commonplace books as a way of estimating popular attitudes.

Attempts to reconstruct the lives and reading of ordinary people are linked to a wider and more fundamental process of interrogating the silent exclusions made by traditionally patriarchal and Eurocentric approaches to history. Economic historians had long recognized the impact that the wealth of the New World had on old Europe; the twentieth-century collapse of colonial rule exposed the racism and exploitation that underpinned the whole process of colonization. When Columbus landed in America in 1492 he equated the unknown people of the Caribbean with 'cannibals': the New World conquerors projected their fantasies of fear and aggression on to the peoples they found there, establishing patterns of intimidation and oppression whose workings are only now beginning to be analysed and understood. Renaissance literature flourished at precisely the moment that the English set out to establish 'plantations', and to abduct Africans as slaves. The presence of black people in England increased rapidly during the seventeenth century, and from the outset they were treated with prejudice, their appearance serving to redefine European skin colour and physical features as desirable in themselves.

The ways in which the colonists demonized those they had conquered has been compared to the way a patriarchal society demonizes its women, and both have been subjected to scrutiny in recent criticism. Feminism has been the single most important influence on literary criticism in the last twenty years, providing a paradigm for considerations of difference, whether of gender, race, or class. Feminist historians and critics have contributed substantially to the reinterpretation of early modern England and its writing, impatient with accounts that are blind to the roles and activities of half the population. Historians have explored how women lived, what rights they had, and how fully they internalized the rules imposed on them. Feminist critics have considered how women are represented in canonical texts (especially Shakespeare's), and reconsidered their stereotyping both in terms of psychoanalytical theory and of the operation of market forces upon their lives. In addition, scholarly research has shown their influence as patrons, and uncovered a cache of women's writing that had been long forgotten, so that in addition to prayers, polemic, and diaries, a range of imaginative writing—the plays, lyrics, and romances of writers such as Mary Sidney, Aemilia Lanyer, and Mary Wroth—can now be read. Virginia Woolf's account, in chapter 4 of *A Room of One's Own*, in which individual women's voices did not make themselves heard until the mid-seventeenth century, has had to be revised.

The history and writings of the colonies and of women have been extensively theorized, as has the larger question of the relation of literary texts to the culture that produced them. This issue has been central to New Historicism, a critical movement originating in California and influenced by Derrida's theories of *differance* and logocentrism, and Michel Foucault's analyses of the operation of power within discourse. Stephen Greenblatt, effectively its founder, shared with contemporary historians an interest in the methodologies of anthropology, employing its structural classifications of language and symbolism as ways of reading canonical, non-canonical, and non-literary texts so as to shed light on one another. The most familiar of Renaissance texts, Shakespeare's plays, were transformed by being examined as if they were the products of a society whose symbolic language was not yet known.

Stephen Greenblatt's *Renaissance Self-Fashioning* (1980) explored the connections between state power, the self-construction of the individual in relation to authority and social practice, and the fear of 'otherness' that characterized colonial enterprise. Fellow critics such as Louis Montrose, Stephen Orgel, and Jonathan Goldberg focused their attention on the court, its ethos and influence, and the ways in which it created and reproduced images of its own power. Their work stimulated an extensive re-engagement with Renaissance texts and culture, and the reassessment of several key features including the nature of patronage, censorship (Annabel Patterson), and nationalism (Richard Helgerson), the position of the theatre (Michael Bristol, Steven Mullaney) and its conventions of cross-dressing

(Jean Howard, Stephen Orgel). New Historicism has been characterized by its exploration of texts through other texts, or cultural artefacts; it has preferred to avoid citing traditional historiography, which was often regarded as mystifying or falsifying since it had its own agendas and narrative methods, re-interpreting and generalizing from the particular, whereas New Historicism focused on the insights afforded by specific texts.

Some historians responded to post-structuralist criticisms of mainstream historiography with impatience, yet they too have been influenced by it to the extent of studying court culture alongside the less obviously eventful history of the people, drawing a wider range of material into their analyses, and producing accounts of taste and fashion, in addition to more traditional narratives: James I's use of imperial imagery has been traced out in art and architecture, as well as in literature. Roy Strong has explored the court of Prince Henry; Blair Worden has discussed the politics of Jonson's *Sejanus*, Marvell's 'Horatian Ode', and, most recently, Sidney's *Arcadia*, and Malcolm Smuts, Kevin Sharpe, and Linda Levy Peck have explored further aspects of Jacobean court culture, as have literary critics as different from one another as Jonathan Goldberg and Graham Parry. New material in the form of the texts of masques and country-house entertainments is still surfacing in county archives and great houses.

Both history and the literary and cultural criticism of early modern England have been dominated by the debate on social disorder and subversion. Fifteen years ago England in the 1590s was regarded as a country in crisis, destabilized by outbreaks of plague, dearth, and famine. The mob, the 'many-headed monster' that threatened Artegall in Book 5 of *The Faerie Queene*, the Flemings in the unperformed play-text of *Sir Thomas More*, that followed Jack Cade in *2 Henry VI* or Antony in *Julius Caesar*, were alarming because they were familiar. But increasingly enclosure and food riots have come to be interpreted as appeals for government intervention, calls for the law or the 'Book of Orders' to be implemented, rather than acts of disruption, resistance, or rebellion. London, potentially the most dangerous setting of all for mob activity, as the City Fathers' anxiety over the theatres indicates, has seemed to its recent historians, Ian Archer and Steve Rappaport, surprisingly stable and law-abiding. The attempt by the Earl of Essex and his supporters to initiate a popular rising against the ageing and childless Queen met only with disapproval: one Londoner 'marvelled that they could come in that sort in a civil government, and on a Sunday'.[4]

For the New Historicists, concerned to map the location of power, questions of disruption (or subversion) and resistance were also central, but they sought for evidence not in the analysis of events or the operation of particular social structures, but in individual texts, and what they revealed of the way the state deployed discourse to maintain its power. In its earliest phase New Historicism made exaggerated claims for the state's ability to determine discourse, influenced, perhaps, by the effectiveness of the modern state in manipulating ideology and political attitudes. Stephen Greenblatt's widely read essay on *Henry IV* and *Henry V*, 'Invisible Bullets', saw the subversion enacted by Falstaff and his companions as re-contained within the dramatic structure as a whole. His account is weighed down by a twentieth-century sense of the impossibility of historical intervention, and ends by including the reader in acknowledging defeat: 'we are free to locate and pay homage to the plays' doubts only because they no longer threaten us. There is subversion, no end of subversion, but not for us.'[5]

In spite of great theoretical sophistication, New Historicism looked in danger of repeating the mistake made by E. M. W. Tillyard in *The Elizabethan World Picture* (1943), of assuming that establishment views remained uncontested or unironized. Some critics were apparently unfamiliar with the numerous texts, both popular and religious, that questioned state policy or denounced the court, and sometimes the monarch too, as degenerate and corrupt. Such opposition had been linked with the origins of the English Civil War by Christopher Hill, and its presence as a discourse in Elizabethan and Jacobean drama had been identified by Margot Heinemann, and thereafter by 'Cultural

Materialism', an approach which drew on Hill's history and the French critic Althusser's philosophy to examine an altogether wider field of power relationships, and which traced evidence of class and gender conflicts in early modern England whose counterparts are still with us today.

Whereas New Historicism tended to take the form of in-depth studies, focused upon particular anecdotes, pictures, or objects, Cultural Materialism concerned itself rather with genre, producing reassessments of Jacobean tragedy (Jonathan Dollimore and Catherine Belsey), its treatment of ideas and of the subject within the state. It reread comedy in the light of Mikhail Bakhtin's classic analysis of carnival, *Rabelais and his World* (1965), and, unlike the new historicists, found a positive value in its celebration (Peter Stallybrass and Allon White). It has also offered 'Alternative' and 'Political' readings of Shakespeare, questioning his ascendancy in school and university curricula (as well as the 'heritage' industry), and offering its own readings of transgression and subversion in his work. Shakespeare's status as a 'popular' dramatist has been debated (Robert Weimann, Annabel Patterson), and his presentation of popular risings has been called as evidence (Richard Helgerson).

The pleasure in subversion reflected in popular literature is also common to carnival, the celebration of feast days, and other popular rituals involving role reversal: some of these were allowed and even encouraged; others were condemned or occasioned conflict between the more 'liberal' court and the less liberal 'godly folk' (as Leah Marcus has shown). Literature, especially popular literature, has a markedly subversive streak, which does not necessarily correspond to known events, at least as recent historians have interpreted them. This may be a further reflection on the disparate nature of the two disciplines. While official documents emphasize good order (or panic in its absence), imaginative writing and performance play out fantasies that may be spoken, written, and even performed on the stage, but cannot yet be put into practice.

Society and literature affect each other in very different ways: while literary texts register the nature of social conditions, their own impact is most visibly recorded upon other literary texts, although the writings of Erasmus and Luther changed the history of the Western Church, and, ultimately, how individuals thought about themselves and their lives. Literature, like painting, offers paradigms such as Foxe's Protestant martyrs, who established a new form of heroism through their passive resistance of authority. It creates fashions: the chivalry central to Sidney and Spenser's romances was revived to represent Prince Henry, implicitly criticizing his peacemaking father. On the other hand social practice and individual texts may also be at odds: transvestism was widely condemned and punishable by law, yet *The Roaring Girl* (1611) represents the cross-dresser Moll Frith as a heroine who reunites young lovers and works for the good of the community. The cony-catching pamphlets and many of the city comedies that echo them may exaggerate levels of criminal activity: they certainly take a vicarious pleasure in the skills of the criminals and tricksters that they ostensibly warn against. And though Hal must always reject Falstaff on the printed page, in many productions he comes off worse in terms of audience sympathy, so that the subversion contained by the text is valorized in performance. Representation may offer an area of safe play, an alternative to, rather than an acting out of, daily experience.

Contemporary conditions are written into texts at every level, from the vocabulary a society employs to the icons and myths it creates for itself. What Louis Montrose has termed 'a reciprocal concern with the historicity of texts and the textuality of history'[6] has been extensively discussed since this book was originally published, but their asymmetry continues to cause problems: one theory which gives full value to both terms of the equation (here redefined as 'subjectivism' and 'objectivism') is Pierre Bourdieu's concept of fields of cultural production, a theory which identifies works of art and their producers within a series of fields that exert differing degrees of influence: the complex structure of the field provides the focus of investigation, rather than individual biography or social conditions, since the field defines the nature of their interaction—as Bourdieu has said, 'what we have to do is all these things at the same time'.[7] The theory is sufficiently flexible to allow for the many distinctive factors present in language and history at any given point, but at the cost of an alarming complexity. My own approach has focused on two key aspects: first, the conditions of living and thought that shaped literature and determined the particular forms it took; and second, the ways in which individual texts articulate society's concerns in direct and often highly imaginative ways; if the first suggests the need for the student of literature to know something of history, the second suggests the rewards that Renaissance literature can offer the student of history.

This Stage-Play World has been widely read since it was first published, and in 1996 Oxford University Press invited me to update the bibliography, but registering the amount of new work in the field only seemed to draw attention to its shortcomings: if it was to retain its usefulness, it needed revision and expansion. In the end I rewrote it completely, setting it out rather differently and adding new chapters on women and the beginnings of colonization. In the process, I have been greatly helped by Ian Archer, who was kind enough to read both versions and comment on them in detail, and by Malcolm Godden, who has given help and advice at every stage. Special thanks are due to De Montfort University and its English department, and in particular to Deborah Cartmell and Imelda Whelehan, for making this revision possible.

JULIA BRIGGS

De Montfort University, Leicester

Contents

Change and Continuity

O peerless poesy, where is then thy place?

PIERS asks this question in the October Eclogue of Spenser's *Shepheardes Calender* (l. 79), expressing a doubt that momentarily holds up the movement of the verse. In 1579 the question of where poetry stood, whether it looked back to its roots, or to the judgement of modern audiences, was an urgent one. The lines that follow attempt to set poetry in a social context: it belongs by rights to the court ('princes' palace'), but if the court is not prepared to support it (and this eclogue is in part a lament for lack of patronage), and those of 'baser birth' cannot comprehend it, it must return to 'heaven', the ideal, otherworldly state from where the impulse to write poetry first descended. Yet if poetry is addressed primarily to the leisured classes, and employs a high style to match, why has Spenser used shepherds as his speakers, drawn on country dialect, and set out his sequence with woodcuts so that it resembles the almanacs and calendars consulted by real shepherds at the time?

The October Eclogue expresses the poet's fear that he is writing for an age uninterested in poetry: with Virgil, Chaucer, and Maecenas, the ideal patron, all long dead, can there be a place for poetry at the present time, in the England of 1579? Despite his misgivings, *The Shepheardes Calender* marked the opening of a new phase in the development of English literature, a phase in which questions about the nature of poetry were eagerly debated. Spenser himself, in the argument at the beginning of this eclogue, refers to his own 'Discourse on English poetry', since lost. All we know of it is what he tells us here, that it dealt with 'celestial inspiration'. Poetry was connected with the divine through the history of the word itself. George Putten-ham's *Art of English Poesy* (1589) begins: 'A poet is as much to say as a maker. And our English name well conforms with the Greek word, for of *poiein*, to make, they call a maker *poeta*. Such as (by way of resemblance and reverently) we may say of God.' Philip Sidney's *Defence of Poetry*, probably written at about the same time as *The Shepheardes Calender*, set out claims for English poetry that had not been made before, yet apart from a reference to Spenser as 'worthy the reading', his claims were inspired more by hopes for a brighter future than by the limited achievements of the past. Sidney also saw the poet as essentially a maker, possessing a power that resembled that of God; by presenting the world as it might become or ought to be, the poet could bring home to his readers how sinful they were, while instructing them to live better and delighting them by means of his ideal vision. We should

> give right honour to the heavenly Maker of that maker, who having made man to His own likeness, set him beyond and over all the works of that second nature: which in nothing he showeth so much as in poetry, when with the force of a divine breath he bringeth things forth surpassing her doings—with no small argument to the credulous of that first accursed fall of Adam, since our erected wit maketh us know what perfection is, and yet our infected will keepeth us from reaching unto it.
>
> ('A Defence of Poetry', p. 79)

Sidney's emphasis on man's fallen state is traditionally Christian, but his high claim for the role of the poet is characteristic of the Renaissance, as is Spenser's use of the pastoral mode, and his presentation of it in the October Eclogue as the trial of the poet's wings before he follows Virgil and 'soars' to the full height of epic poetry.

The Italian Renaissance took the best part of two centuries to reach England, a little offshore island outside the mainstream of European culture; its founding poets were Petrarch and Boccaccio, the Italian contemporaries of the English poet Geoffrey Chaucer. The invention of the printing-press in the mid-fifteenth century was to speed up the spread of new literature and learning. At the court of Henry VIII, Thomas Wyatt and the Earl of Surrey had imitated Petrarch's sonnets, but it was particularly through the examples of Sidney and Spenser that Renaissance poetic practices and habits of mind came to be widely adopted. These included the imitation of classical genres such as epic, pastoral, and satire, reflecting a new artistic self-consciousness, combined with an older sense that love and poetry were emotionally refining and uplifting.

By arriving so late in England, this long-lived Renaissance new wave coincided with other tides bringing intellectual and cultural change, and so was more rapidly absorbed, making a wider range of forms and modes available. But English poets continued to treat their European models with a degree of suspicion, even while they borrowed from them, so that the great achievements of the English Renaissance look distinctly odd beside their French or Italian prototypes. Spenser's *Faerie Queene* is the most idiosyncratic of epics, Shakespearean tragedy the most irregular from an Aristotelian point of view, while comedy soon abandoned its traditional comic types to focus on the local tensions of London, of Cheapside and Smithfield. English writers had grown up within the Reformed Church, under an emergent nationalism that was both political and religious, that regarded Catholic Europe with distrust and Spain and Italy with something approaching paranoia. A sense of identity as a newly forged Protestant nation fostered a desire to equal or surpass the acknowledged masterpieces of pagan Rome or of modern Catholic nations.

Such ambitions were made possible by the educational reforms inspired by humanism, the revival of classical learning, which aimed at familiarizing English schoolboys with Latin literature. Thus the grammar-school master at Stratford introduced William Shakespeare, the son of a provincial glove-maker, to the comedies of Terence and Plautus, so that he later set himself to excel them. Printing played a crucial role as a catalyst in all these developments, making Latin textbooks available and cheap enough for study in school, just as it had spread the theological arguments that resulted in the reform of the Western

Church in the first half of the sixteenth century, and had provided the drawings, diagrams, tables, and figures needed for the scientific revolution.

The term 'renaissance', literally 'rebirth', was first used by the Italian art historian Giorgio Vasari in tracing *The Lives of the Most Eminent Painters* (1550). According to his account, the plastic arts, having reached great heights in classical times, fell into decay, but then came to a second birth ('sua rinascita') in the hands of a group of modern artists. The sense of awakening from a period of artistic and intellectual darkness had been voiced two centuries earlier, when the poetry of Petrarch and Boccaccio and the painting of Giotto and Cimabue seemed to herald a recovery or rediscovery of the arts, but was renewed in the fifteenth century by the revival of classical learning. The Italian humanists represented the immediate past as barbaric, above all in its 'bad' Latin, and its misreadings of classical authors, so that an accurate knowledge of their language, philosophies, and ways of life needed to be established. Yet in turning back to classical Rome for moral and artistic authority, the Renaissance was paradoxically reaffirming its confidence in the past, though a more distant past. Humanists often found themselves pressing for reforms that set one ancient authority in conflict with another: the philosopher and jurist Francis Bacon fought a lifelong battle for the adoption of the rational, codified system of Roman law in England, but he was defeated by respect for the Common Law, based on custom and precedent, and regarded as traditionally English. Out of that debate came the first *Institutes of the Law of England*, written up by Edward Coke in his capacity as chief defender of the Common Law against Bacon's proposals.

Innovations

Bacon identified himself with the cause of rational knowledge, rationally acquired. In his entertainment *A Conference of Pleasure*, put on for the Queen by the Earl of Essex in 1592, Bacon makes 'Knowledge' announce the age's three greatest discoveries, only to dismiss them again on the grounds that they had been arrived at by accident:

Printing, a gross invention; artillery [i.e. guns and gunpowder], a thing that lay not far out of the way; the needle [i.e. the ship's compass], a thing partly known before; what a change have these three made in the world in these times; the one in state of learning, the other in state of the war, the third in the state of treasure, commodities and navigation. And those, I say, were but stumbled upon and lighted upon by chance.

(*Essays*, p. 261)

Bacon's point was that a systematic investigation of nature would have produced far more useful results: 'Now we govern nature in opinions, but we are thrall unto her in necessity; but if we would be led by her in invention, we should command her in action' (p. 262). The French essayist Michel de Montaigne (1533–92) was even less optimistic than Bacon, observing that these discoveries were essentially second-hand: 'We exclaim at the miracle of the invention of our artillery, of our printing; other men in another corner of the world, in China, enjoyed these a thousand years earlier. If we saw as much of the world as we do not see, we would perceive, it is likely, a perpetual multiplication and vicissitude of forms' ('Of Coaches', *Essays*, p. 693).

Advances in the technology of war were self-evidently destructive, with soldiers becoming mere 'food for powder' . In *Paradise Lost*, Milton represented gunpowder as the invention of Lucifer. But encounters with new continents, new methods of communication, and new facts about heavenly bodies all turned out, in their different ways, to be intellectually threatening and politically divisive. The promise and actuality of wealth from the New World aroused greed, intolerance, and brutality on an unprecedented scale. Europeans wondered why so much of the rest of the world had not received the Christian gospel, and how they came to have radically different sign-systems and modes of social interaction. The expanding universe, newly centred upon the sun, threatened to displace the sense of human centrality within it, as Robert Burton who taught the new scientific ideas at Oxford observed, quoting from the astronomer Johannes

Kepler: 'But who shall dwell in these vast bodies, earths, worlds, "if they be inhabited? rational creatures?" as Kepler demands, "or have they souls to be saved? or do they inhabit a better part of the world than we do? Are we or they the lords of the world? And how are all things made for man?"' (*The Anatomy of Melancholy*, part 2, section 2, member 3).

Printing proved to be quite as dangerous as the other discoveries, undermining religious, political, and social stability throughout Europe, as disputes over theology, government, and law, once confined within particular institutions or within academic communities, became accessible to anyone who could read. As literacy spread, more books were published in vernacular languages than in Latin, the language shared by European intellectuals, and this undermined a confidence in shared assumptions previously enjoyed by educated Christendom, and particularly by humanists such as Erasmus and Thomas More. Gradually that confidence was replaced by the recognition that some disagreements were unresolvable, some truths irreconcilable or unattainable, although intellectual leaders continued to assume that education and access to knowledge would automatically result in the adoption of their own particular point of view, or that the study of particular texts would bring readers to the same conclusions as one another—a myth that persists even to this day.

Authorities

The ultimate textual authority was the Bible, the revelation of God's word, while nature was the revelation of His works. Some way behind came the Church Fathers, particularly Augustine, and then the great classical authors. In contrast with modern attitudes, it was usually supposed that contemporary thinkers were inferior to the great intellects of the past, and that the best hope for the advancement of learning lay in the close study of their writings. Knowledge, like the world itself, was thought to be in a state of decay rather than one of active growth. Far from steadily increasing, it was always being spilled, like water from a fountain. The 'ancient wisdom', important secrets concerning the natural world, had been known to a group of sages that included Moses and Zoroaster, but had long since been lost, perhaps beyond recall. The authority of past thinkers still shaped and determined intellectual procedures, and the Renaissance itself has sometimes been described in terms of a reassessment of the ideas of the Greek philosophers Plato and Aristotle.

From an early stage in its history, Christianity had absorbed some of the main elements of Plato's thought, and in particular his notion of an ideal world of forms, of Being, to which every individual who was subject to the unstable world of Becoming was drawn through an inborn tendency to distinguish between beauty and ugliness, both physical and moral. But by emphasizing different aspects of this concept, different interpretations might result: a concentration on Plato's transcendent truths led to the rejection or withdrawal from worldly life, such as was recommended by the Church and adopted by some of the contemplative monastic orders in the Middle Ages. By contrast, the school of Florentine Neoplatonists of the fifteenth century focused upon the spiritual elements within the individual, finding them reflected in this world in the form of male beauty, capacity, and self-determining power; the question of the nature of 'man' was widely discussed, and though it notionally included all human beings, in practice women were categorized separately and usually regarded as spiritually and morally inferior. Hamlet echoes Neoplatonic arguments when he observes, 'What a piece of work is a man, how noble in reason, how infinite in faculties . . .' (II. ii. 303–4), though his conclusion, 'what is this quintessence of dust?', reverts to the alternative tradition of thought that rejected worldly existence.

In *The Republic*, Plato had used the image of the cave to demonstrate the difference between reality and illusion: the cave's inhabitants mistake the shadows cast by the firelight for reality, and refuse to believe the philosopher who has seen the actual light of the sun, which corresponds to the 'real', that is, the permanent and transcendent world of ideal forms. The deceptions of worldly existence are easily associated with the

deceptive nature of representation, as happens when Walter
Raleigh, in his *History of the World*, contrasted the reality of
Christian truth with the false attractions of the world, here
figured as the theatre:

And though Nature, according to common understanding, have made
us capable by the power of reason, and apt enough to receive this image
of God's goodness, which the sensual souls of beasts cannot perceive;
yet were that aptitude naturally more inclinable to follow and embrace
the false and dureless pleasures of this stage-play world, than to become
the shadow of God by walking after Him ...

(Book i, chapter ii; section 2)

Plato's *Republic* was a central text, not only for its metaphysics
but for its attempt to establish principles for the conduct of
an ideal state. Aristotle's contributions to political theory, his
system of logic, and his conception of the world as an elaborately
interlocking mechanism still provided the basis of Renaissance
university studies, though all were increasingly questioned. The
authority of classical teachings had to be repudiated, or invoked
in support of new departures, so that when Copernicus demonstrated that the earth was in orbit, he worked within, rather than
against the system of Aristotelian physics. Even a thinker as
subversive as Machiavelli offered his analysis of contemporary
power politics in the guise of *Discourses* or commentaries on
Livy's *History of Rome*.

   The use of the authority of the past as a way of legitimating
innovation solved one set of problems only to create another.
Once the ultimate textual authorities, the Bible and Augustine,
had been invoked to support the opposed positions of the
Catholic and Reformed Churches, a crisis of interpretation was
inevitable. Biblical texts were closely examined for accumulated
errors, but the new readings that resulted were highly divisive:
changing the translation of the Greek word *presbuteros* from
'priest' to 'elder', or that of *ecclesia* from 'church' to 'assembly'
or 'congregation' suggested that the Catholic Church had disguised the form of government of the primitive Church to
strengthen its own position. The right to decide or limit the

meanings of the Bible, who read it and in what version, who interpreted it and how, were questions that led to war and bloodshed on an international scale in Europe, and in England to the persecution, torture, and execution of thousands of people, on both sides of the religious divide.

State control over the meaning of the Bible and other religious texts, and the subject's right to resist such control thus became tragically visible, and in the course of time came to be accepted, and even regarded as legitimate. Individuals fought, died, and were driven into exile for their right to interpret the words of God, for their freedom of conscience. Yet the practices and beliefs of the Catholic and Reformed Churches were not sufficiently different from one another to explain or justify the horrors of war and persecution they occasioned. The claims and counter-claims of dogma led to doubt and aroused that sense of the relative that characterizes modern awareness. Such feelings found their most intelligent expression in the writings of Michel de Montaigne, whose *Essays*, with their comprehensive critique of human presumption, remain unparalleled. Their expression of the age's uncertainties, their sense of searching rather than finding, their recognition of the instability of personality and of the relative, partial, and transitory nature of opinion anticipated or influenced much late-Elizabethan and Jacobean writing. Montaigne's scepticism led him to reject the (ultimately Aristotelian) concept of universal laws, and to question whether it was possible to know the world, in any meaningful sense.

Montaigne was a committed Catholic, but he also accepted a number of ideas from scepticism and stoicism. These were classically derived philosophies, and stoicism was particularly well suited to survival in 'interesting times', in Montaigne's case the French Wars of Religion. Influenced by the writings of the Roman playwright and philosopher Seneca, stoicism recommended withdrawal from political involvement and the cultivation of the mind as a garden, a self-sufficient inner world that was, perhaps, a secular equivalent of the life of Christian contemplation, though the stoic's ultimate act of self-determination, suicide, had been forbidden to Christians by Augustine. Stoic thought was reworked by the Flemish political theorist Justus Lipsius (1547–1606), who also suffered in the European Wars of Religion and shared Montaigne's political quietism. In his *Six Books of Politics* (1589, translated 1594) he argued for state-imposed religious uniformity, and the punishment of dissidents for the sake of the community as a whole, urging his readers not to resist, nor to take up arms on behalf of new causes or join in civil wars, but rather to submit themselves to the existing form of government, and to obey its law and its ministers. Individuals could only take responsibility for their own lives. Peace of mind was not to be expected from the world of contingency, where all were subject not only to powers beyond their control, but also, as Montaigne had pointed out, to sudden pain, incurable sickness, and early death.

Lipsius's neo-stoicism appealed particularly to those involved in government or at court who had invested in the state yet at the same time were themselves subject to the arbitrary whims of the ruler, or the changing 'pacts and sects of great ones'. Such a philosophy recognized the limits of individual agency and the constraints imposed by 'the necessity of the times'. It discouraged the prickings of conscience that stirred people to resist tyranny and religious oppression and carried them into the dock, the fire, or the cannon's mouth. It also justified the state's use of violence against its critics, the fining and imprisoning of religious dissidents, and the public torture and execution of outspoken opponents.

While the logic and effects of political and theological debate could be identified and understood by the educated, the underground workings of economic and demographic change were virtually impossible to recognize. The late sixteenth century was a period of inflation: running at about 1 per cent, it was negligible by modern standards but severe in comparison to a previous stability. As much as half the population lived at subsistence level off the land. Unemployment rose, and crime increased when times were hard. Traditional community relations came under pressure, and class structures began to shift, creating fears of chaos and social breakdown, 'in cities, mutinies; in countries, discord; in palaces, treason; and the bond crack'd 'twixt son and father . . .' (*King Lear*, I. ii. 107–9). Writers were as vulnerable to economic pressure as everyone else, often leading lives of poverty and squalor. The playwright and pamphleteer Thomas Dekker described himself 'every hour hammering out one piece or other of this rusty iron age, since the gold and silver globes of this world are so locked up that a scholar can hardly be suffered to behold them'.[1] He and his contemporaries left unforgettable accounts of London as 'Nighttown', a surreal city in the grip of a crime wave or a visitation of the plague; its terror and alienation resemble that of the modern city.

Writers and the Age

Yet the reign of Elizabeth was celebrated as a golden age even before it was over, and the next generation looked back on it with undisguised nostalgia. In Shakespeare and Fletcher's collaboration, *Henry VIII*, performed in 1613, Cranmer prophesies over the newly born princess:

> She shall be lov'd and fear'd: her own shall bless her:
> Her foes shake like a field of beaten corn,
> And hang their head with sorrow. Good grows with her;
> In her days every man shall eat in safety
> Under his own vine what he plants, and sing
> The merry songs of peace to all his neighbours.
> God shall be truly known . . .

> (v. iv. 30–6)

For some it was a golden age, for others an age of rusty iron. Elizabeth, like her successor James I, extended patronage in one form or another to Spenser, Shakespeare, Jonson, and Donne, encouraging them to adopt the state's interests, and outlook.

For those writers whom the power, wealth, and status of the court could not win over, there were ways of deterring open criticism: control over publication was exercised through the Stationers' Company, the printers' professional association, which was held responsible for the activities of its members.

From 1586 printing presses were only allowed in London and the university towns of Oxford and Cambridge, and all presses were required to be identified. Licence to print was conferred through the Stationers' Register, and the Archbishop of Canterbury and the Bishop of London or their representatives exercised censorship over all registered texts. Punishments for publishing illegally included cutting off the right hand and hanging. By the turn of the century the court's Revels Office had taken on the task of licensing and censoring play-texts scheduled for performance but not yet in print.

The decree of 1586 reflected general anxiety over the rising number of books being published, but also more specific fears of a Spanish invasion, which resulted in the execution of the Catholic claimant, Mary Queen of Scots, in the following year, and an increase in the persecution of Catholic missionary priests, as well as a series of campaigns against the Irish (since it was thought that English Catholics and the Irish might lend their support to a Spanish invasion). The launching of the Armada in 1588 fulfilled this fear, but the fleet's destruction by storms laid it to rest. Much of the literature of the eighties celebrates national virtues or explores heroic attitudes, from the uninhibited chauvinism of Lyly's *Euphues and his England* (1580) to the critical analysis of Marlowe's *Tamburlaine* (1587); these are also present in Sidney's *Arcadia* and Spenser's *Faerie Queene*, though neither was published immediately. The nineties were to be the most difficult years of Elizabeth's long reign, when a series of bad harvests and plague outbreaks brought misery, social disruption, and civil unrest. Crime increased, food riots broke out, and the government put on shows of strength in London. The Queen's one-time favourite, the Earl of Essex, expressed his personal dissatisfactions in a futile rising in 1601.

The disillusionment and bitterness of these years is recorded in the work of pamphleteers like Dekker, Nashe, and Greene, whose precarious livelihood laid them particularly open to economic pressures, but such attitudes were becoming increasingly fashionable, perhaps as a reaction to the idealism and patriotism of an older generation of writers. The young John Donne, John

Marston (later a playwright), and Joseph Hall (later a bishop) all wrote topical verse satires, and while lyric poetry retained an idealized, formulaic imagery, experimental poets learned to twist their Petrarchan models into all kinds of unexpected arguments. Marlowe, before his premature death in 1593, translated Ovid's *Amores*, a sequence of erotic encounters, and made a titillating narrative poem out of the story of *Hero and Leander*. Both were widely imitated. In 1599 the Archbishop and the Bishop intervened, banning and burning a number of satiric and erotic poems, including Marlowe's. Satire, melancholy, and social discontent survived on the stage, where they were simultaneously exploited and laughed at.

James I, reigning from 1603 to 1625, inherited Elizabeth's troubled Church settlement, and her debts, and being far more personally extravagant than she was, soon found himself in conflict with parliament over finance. His preferred role was that of peacemaker in a Europe rocked by religious wars; he shored up a potentially precarious position by attempting to balance Catholic against Protestant European alliances, but ran into difficulties in 1618 with the onset of the Thirty Years War in Europe, when his Protestant son-in-law, the Elector Palatine, needed his support. James was a more active patron of the theatre than Elizabeth, taking Shakespeare's company under his protection. Revenge, tragedy, city comedy, and tragicomedy were all popular on stage, as written by Jonson, Middleton, Webster, Fletcher, and Chapman, several of whom also wrote pageants for the Lord Mayors of London, as well as court masques—spectacular shows that led into dances and other forms of official revels.

The social purpose of any particular type of writing was likely to determine its form and boundaries; poetry tended to distinguish between supposedly private forms of address, such as verse letters or *risqué* epigrams, and more public celebrations of great men, their houses, families, and achievements. Religious and love poetry was nominally addressed to God or the mistress, while silently assuming that it would reach a wider audience. The contrasting styles of Ben Jonson (associated with clarity, metrical smoothness, rhymed couplets, and a Horatian poise) and John

Donne (who employed rhythms shaped by the speaking voice, puns, paradoxes, and startling images and turns of thought), though by no means mutually exclusive, provided contrasting approaches for their successors. Both wrote religious poetry and hymns, composed satires, epigrams, verse letters, love lyrics, celebrated particular occasions, or complimented particular aristocrats on their life-styles, providing later poets with various points of departure.

Popular Literature

In the years from 1580 to 1625 English writers absorbed the high culture of Europe and of classical literature faster than ever before. They learned the rules for writing an epic or a pastoral romance, a satire, an ode, or a sonnet. Libraries grew rapidly; translations of the classics and of contemporary Renaissance masterpieces proliferated and were widely read, and not only by the leisured classes. Ben Jonson mocked citizens' pretensions to learning through the goldsmith Gilthead, who has named his son 'Plutarchus', because

> That year sir
> That I begot him, I bought Plutarch's lives,
> And fell so in love with the book as I called my son
> By his name; in hope he should be like him:
> And write the lives of our great men!
> (*The Devil is an Ass*, III. ii. 21–4)

Here lies the beginnings of the middle-class aspiration to culture that is still apparent today. Even so, the writing of poetry, like participating in scholarly debate or making history, were activities strictly limited to the comparatively small percentage of those who were educated and informed. These individuals occupy our attention because their ways of living, thinking, and feeling have survived when others have not. The births and deaths of the silent majority are recorded in church registers, and their misbehaviour in legal records, but their culture, the culture of the illiterate people, is irrecoverable, having been spoken rather than written. What studies have been made suggest that it was rich and complex in ways in which our own culture is poor: more immediate, verbally and visually, and less private and self-conscious than our own, it derived from an intimate knowledge of the environment and included much aural patterning of words into structures that were heard rather than seen (since language acquires its visual dimension through writing). It included weather- and nature-lore, sayings and songs, proverbs, rhymes, and folk-tales of all kinds. Rhyme was an aid to memory and was often improvised, as in modern 'rap': reading ability was not necessarily an advantage to a poet, though writing provided a record of the work. By contrast, modern readers find it difficult to distinguish reading from writing, and writing from the process of composition itself. So one answer to Piers's question concerning the place of poesy with which this chapter began, and one explanation of Spenser's use of dialect and even of the calendar form itself, lies in a recognition that rhyming and verse belonged to and were used quite as much by the lower members of the social order as the higher. By combining elements from both cultures in *The Shepheardes Calender*, Spenser may have been expressing a hope of their future synthesis in serious poetry, in terms of stylistics; a hope that the Protestant language of the people might be absorbed into the sophisticated forms of Renaissance high culture, perhaps even voicing an ideal of social integration and national unity.

The advent of print culture and a rapid increase in literacy that was one effect of the Reformation also created a market for popular reading. Single printed sheets or small books (chap-books) were sold from stalls in London and in the countryside by peddlers like Shakespeare's Autolycus (*The Winter's Tale*, IV. iii, iv). Their subject matter was wide, and they included religious tracts, almanacs and calendars giving domestic or agricultural advice, part-songs, jest-books, and all kinds of histories, romances, and tales of knightly adventures. Broadside ballads (i.e. ballads printed on a single side of paper) were sold for a penny and often pasted up on walls in alehouses; they included a range of stories and songs but also functioned as early news-papers, relating sensational murders in rhyme, or the appearance of strange prodigies, or wars and actions abroad. It was not until the mid-seventeenth century that news-sheets began to be com-posed in prose rather than verse, as the forerunners of news-papers. Broadside ballads thus performed a role equivalent to that of today's 'tabloids', and their viewpoint tended to be cor-respondingly conservative, patriotic, and moralizing, though they occasionally celebrated the fall of heroes in opposition such as the Earl of Essex or Sir Walter Raleigh.

Their subject matter, and sometimes their outlook, are strik-ingly close to that of Elizabethan drama, and possibly the drama itself might have remained just another form of popular culture, as the 'jigs' or musical dialogues with which they often ended have done, had it not been for a generation of highly educated playwrights with their aspirations firmly fixed upon court patronage: the actors complain the playwrights 'smell too much of that writer *Ovid*, and that writer *Metamorphoses*, and talk too much of Proserpina and Jupiter', in the second part of *The Return from Parnassus* (IV. iii. 1767–8). The first generation of playwrights in particular drew on the same kind of subject matter as the broadside ballads, presenting history in the form of legends from the chronicles, folk-tales, and civic myths. Peele's *Old Wives' Tale*, Dekker's *Old Fortunatus* and the legend of Simon Eyre in *The Shoemaker's Holiday*, and Greene's *Robert a Greene, the Pinner of Wakefield*, and *Friar Bacon and Friar Bungay* conform to this pattern, as do tales of popular heroes such as Sir Thomas Stukeley, or Munday's plays of Thomas More or Robin Hood, Earl of Huntingdon. Sensational crimes were dramatized in *Arden of Faversham*, Heywood's *A Woman Killed with Kindness*, and *The Yorkshire Tragedy*, recently attributed to Middleton; even Marlowe's *Dr Faustus* was the subject of a popular chapbook. Middleton and Heywood continued to write tragedies based on this kind of material well into the seventeenth century, but more sophisticated tastes developed rapidly among London audiences, and popular tales provided the occasion for knowing laughter in Beaumont's

Knight of the Burning Pestle (1611) and Jonson's *The Devil is an Ass* (1616).

Drama was the most exciting of the various encounters between high and popular culture, and in this respect resembled the age's great syncretic fictions, Rabelais's *Gargantua*, Spenser's *Faerie Queene*, and Cervantes's *Don Quixote*, though it shared with popular print a commercial motive that made it particularly responsive to the market and its changing tastes. A more calculated and less commercial foray into the market-place was made by the early reformers, who set out to reach the common people by using their plain, familiar language. Like earlier missionary movements, particularly that of the Franciscans, the reformers were concerned to spread their gospel, if necessary on the back of popular words and music. Tyndale, committed to making a translation of the Bible directly accessible to all believers, produced by far the most colloquial of the many Renaissance translations: while remaining close to the Hebrew, he found simple and telling phrases such as 'The day present hath ever enough of his own trouble' or 'The Lord was with Joseph and he was a lucky fellow', and his subsequent theological disputes with Thomas More employ a prose style heavily influenced by the spoken language, that easily accommodates proverbs, sayings, and well-worn jokes.

The 'low' style was thus established by the reformers as a way of speaking to the people, as it is in Hugh Latimer's 'Sermon of the Plowers' (1548) or in Cranmer's *Book of Homilies*, the very title of which was chosen for its associations with the people: the Greek word *homilia* means 'conversation' or 'instruction', and is derived from the word for 'crowd' or 'multitude', thus reflecting the nature of the language used by Jesus and the apostles. In Cranmer's spelling ('Certayne Sermons, or Homelies'), it picked up further 'homely' associations. But as well as being an appropriate way of speaking to ordinary people, the 'low' style also provided a way of speaking *for* them, and had been used as such in a number of Tudor petitions appealing to the king, pleas such as Simon Fish's *Supplication of Beggars* (1529) or Henry Brinkelow's *Complaynt of Roderyck Mors* (1548). John

Skelton's *Colin Clout* was the speaker of a poem that voiced the dissatisfactions of the people with their rulers, both lay and clerical. Spenser adopted the name, using it for his own poetic persona, perhaps in acknowledgement of his humble origins. In *The Shepheardes Calender* Colin Clout stands poised between the world of the shepherds and his aspiration to fly higher, both poetically and socially, while retaining something of their outlook. Piers's name was taken from that of Langland's medieval visionary, *Piers Plowman*, whose anti-clerical jibes had classified him as a proto-Protestant. Chaucer was also interpreted as a critic of the established Church, and a later attack on the Church, the fifteenth-century poem 'The Plowman's Tale', was attributed to him in the 1530s in an effort to slip it past the censor. Another of Spenser's shepherds, the day-labourer Diggon Davey, looks back to Thomas Churchyard's 'Davy Dycar's Dream' (1551), an apocalyptic vision in a direct line of descent from *Piers Plowman*. Spenser grew up within a flourishing tradition of mid-century reforming poetry, and his own earliest work contributed to it, though that tradition was later overlooked by the more courtly poetic manuals of the 1580s composed by Webbe, Puttenham, and Sidney.

The mid-century Protestant preachers and poets justified their plain style by appealing to an older poetic tradition, one that had spoken through the dissident voices of countrymen, identified by generic names that reflected their poverty or their status as labourers: Piers the Plowman, Colin Clout, Diggon or Dyker Davy voiced the complaints and dreams of the common people as a whole, while also being inspired by a higher power, according to a popular saying which identified the voice of the people with the voice of God ('Vox populi, vox Dei'). Spenser's *Shepherdes Calender* attempted to span the divide between the popular culture of the reformers and the high culture of the Renaissance.

Order and Society

Sᴜʀ Thomas Elyot opened his *Boke named the Governour* (1531) by justifying his translation of the Latin term *respublica* as 'public weal', and carefully distinguishing it from 'common' (or 'commune') 'weal' on the grounds that 'public' referred to the whole of society, while the 'commonaltie', or 'commons' (Latin *plebs*) 'signifieth only the multitude wherein be contained the base and vulgar inhabitants not advanced to any honour or dignity'. For Elyot, a proper distinction between gentles and commons was necessary 'for the discrepance of degrees, whereof proceedeth order'. If England were to be a genuine common-wealth, 'either the commoners only must be wealthy, and the gentle and noble men needy and miserable, or else, excluding gentility, all men must be of one degree and sort, and a new name provided'.

The myth of a golden age, an imaginary past characterized by peace, plenty, and social equality, when common wealth belonged to all in common, was both potent and potentially subversive. It challenged a hierarchic and inequitable society to justify its values, though only hard-headed realists like Machiavelli or Hobbes were capable of defending the *status quo* without reference to a divine order. In the proem to Book V of *The Faerie Queene*, where he is concerned with the chief threats to Elizabeth's realm, Spenser explains that contemporary political constraints impose attitudes very different from the golden-age ideals that had operated elsewhere in his epic. Simple truth may be 'of all admired', but it is no longer relevant to the modern state:

> For that which all men then did virtue call,
> Is now called vice; and that which vice was hight,
> Is now hight virtue, and so used of all;
> Right now is wrong, and wrong that was is right,
> As all things else in time are changed quite.
>
> (v. i. 4)

This confusion of values is the result of the world gradually running down, but there can be no turning the clock back. Book V reveals with unexpected candour the extent to which Spenser's government relied on coercion (here represented by Talus, the iron man) to compel its subjects to share its values and conform to its rules.

Spenser's attitude, like Sir Thomas Elyot's, sprang from a desire for what he considered to be good order. He shared with his society a belief in the value of order, and a recognition that punitive measures might be necessary to maintain it. His anxiety to preserve the *status quo*, and his consequent rejection of attempts to restore the lost harmony of the golden age, are reflected in an episode in which Artegall and his iron servant Talus come upon a giant by the seashore. The giant holds a pair of scales, the displaced emblem of Justice (who has bequeathed Artegall her sword, but not her balance), and is preaching equality. He has attracted quite a crowd, even though it mainly consists of 'fools, women and boys'. Echoing Spenser's own assertion that the world has degenerated from its former perfection, the giant concludes that the time is now ripe for all things to be restored to their former state. This will involve levelling out differences, since in the golden age all men were equal:

> Tyrants that make men subject to their law,
> I will suppress, that they no more may reign;
> And lordings curb, that commons over-awe;
> And all the wealth of rich men to the poor will draw.
>
> (v. ii. 38)

Artegall begins by pointing out that the giant cannot restore things to their former state since he does not know how they were originally distributed. Interference will merely upset the existing *status quo*, since 'all change is perilous'. He then tries to persuade him to use his balance to weigh right and wrong, but the giant will only weigh extremities, so Talus simply pushes him off the cliff (his position is literally as well as metaphorically vulnerable), and chases away the assembled crowd who have now formed an armed rebellion. Artegall looks on. It is not for noblemen to stain their hands 'In the base blood of such a rascal crew'.

In this episode Spenser voices the anxiety of the ruling class that the existing order of things might be called in question, and that rioting would result, while showing its acceptance of the necessity of force against the unarmed, but 'many-headed' mob. Spenser's society was preoccupied with maintaining order at many levels and in many forms. Social disruption in the shape of rebellion, riot, and various forms of criminal activity was a recurrent fear both in literature and public life, though such fears often exceeded the reality. Literature enacted the fears and fantasies of disorder, which could function to justify state brutality (as in the episode of the levelling giant). Sometimes these fears were so vividly recorded that their mere expression was experienced as a threat: Antony Munday's play of *Sir Thomas More* included a scene of the 'evil May Day', when More as sheriff of London dispersed a rioting crowd, but although More famously defused the situation, the recital of their complaints was apparently too much for the Master of the Revels, who ordered the scene to be cut.

Threats to Stability

From a modern perspective, the years from 1580 to 1625 were comparatively peaceful, a period of consolidation between the violent mid-century disturbances of the sixteenth and seventeenth centuries, especially in comparison with Europe, which was torn by religious wars. Though the nineties were years of major social stress, of plague, and a sequence of poor harvests, the period as a whole was marked by government efforts to relieve the poor and hungry through the collection of a rate, that could be used to give help where it was most needed. In practice, most people recognized the advantages of maintaining law and order. When individuals or groups broke the law, their actions were often unpremeditated, and usually prompted by a sense of injustice. Social hierarchy was widely accepted as a precondition of good order (as Sir Thomas Elyot had argued it was). Those who lost out most were in any case least capable of changing things or imagining an alternative. The 'better sort of people' were aware of the problems created by widespread poverty, and they were sensitive to shifts in power that might threaten their interests, while beginning to recognize that different social groups—town and country dwellers, or farm and industrial workers—might have conflicting interests.

Considering that so few enjoyed so large a share of the total resources, demands for social justice were comparatively unusual. Two-thirds of all cultivated land and all forested land was owned either by the Church, the monarch, the aristocracy, or by major landowners. The last third belonged to small owners who were under constant pressure to pay more rent, change their practices, or have their land 'improved'; smallholdings were growing fewer, while the number of landless day labourers was increasing. Claims for greater equality had been made before the Reformation, and in the mid-seventeenth century were forcefully restated by radical sectarians. The authority of the Bible itself could be invoked in support of a sense of social injustice. It was man, not God, who had created divisions of status and wealth, as the old rhyme asserted:

> When Adam delved and Eve span
> Who was then the gentleman?

All readers of the New Testament knew that Christ had condemned wealth and worldly display, had instructed the rich to give away what they had to the poor, and had himself lived as a poor man among working folk, though these truths were more often used to reconcile the humble to their lot than to encourage resentment of it. Thomas More's dialogue *Utopia* (1516) imagined an ideal society based on social equality, where all but the most learned worked and shared the fruits of labour. Its force as an argument was strengthened by its specific criticisms of contemporary English society, here voiced by Raphael Hythloday: he pointed out that people were being punished and even executed, for crimes committed from hunger and need. One cause, he suggested, anticipating a recurrent complaint of the sixteenth century, was the practice of enclosing common land for sheep pasture, and so depriving working people of their traditional right to graze their animals.

In the year after *Utopia* appeared, the German professor of theology Martin Luther nailed up his ninety-five theses, and in the chaos of theological debate that followed old questions about equality before God were reopened. Radical, apocalyptic sects sprang up, believing in individual inspiration and dominated by charismatic leaders, and a group of Anabaptists achieved a startling, though short-term, success in the North German town of Munster. Here in 1534, John of Leyden (Jan Beukelsz) briefly organized a commune based on shared property and free love. Besieged by the forces of the German princes, to whom the threat to property appeared especially unnatural, Munster fell, and John of Leyden was carted around Germany as a side-show before being executed. The episode, which made a profound impression, is re-created as black comedy by Thomas Nashe in his novel *The Unfortunate Traveller*. Thereafter extreme radical sects such as the Anabaptists were widely feared and distrusted, even by more moderate nonconformists. In Ben Jonson's *The Alchemist*, the separatist 'Amsterdam Brethren', hypocritical, dishonest, and self-serving, are referred to as 'my brace of little John Leydens' (III. iii. 24). But though the inspirational and egalitarian sects, so greatly feared by all European governments, had been decisively put down at Munster, Luther's Reformation was inextricably bound up with issues of self-determination, freedom of conscience, and the right to approach God and the Bible directly, without mediation. Significant numbers of Protestants remained convinced that God spoke directly to the heart of each individual, that Church hierarchy was a historical accretion, and that the original Church had been an altogether more democratic institution. Elizabeth's Church settlement was a compromise, retaining the authority of the bishops from the older system of Church government, and establishing the Queen as head of the Church, whereas in Scotland a more democratic system of Church government by elders was evolving. In England, attacks on Church hierarchy were regarded as subversive, and linked with threats to state hierarchy, since both were governed by the Queen.

Richard Hooker, in his extended defence of the compromise of the Anglican Settlement, *Of the Laws of Ecclesiastical Polity* (1593), presented the mutually supportive hierarchies of Church and State as figuring on the human plane the hierarchies of nature and the universe created by God; attacks on one part of the system could be regarded as attacks on another. At the 1604 Hampton Court Conference on Church government, James I reasserted this position with the formula, 'No bishop, no king'. In his writings, also, James identified the authority of God with that of monarch, bishops, magistrates, and even heads of families, defending one by analogy and association with the others. In practice, society's hierarchies were experienced as obligations of one kind or another. Family, social status, and state all had their own particular claims to make on the individual, and such obligations were increasingly liable to come into conflict as society grew more divided. The most overriding claims, those of God and the King, had been particularly affected by the Reformation: individuals found themselves torn between loyalty to their faith and to their ruler, at the point where these failed to agree. The most passionate arguments of the age centred on the nature and extent of the power of God and the King, the state and the law. History and political theory focused particularly on these questions, and by the mid-seventeenth century in England (and much earlier in Europe) they had stopped being matters for debate and became causes, fought for with swords and guns.

Popular culture often expressed fears of a total breakdown resulting from the pressure of irreconcilable needs and demands. Pamphleteers imagined or even thought they were actually witnessing disastrous scenarios in which an already weakened social order collapsed altogether, and humanity preyed upon itself, 'like monsters of the deep':

The son desiring his father's living and to be great before his time, mur-dereth him; the friend, his dearest friend; the wife, the husband and the husband, the wife; brother against sister and sister the brother; whereby the world is grown to such a pass that no friend dare commit any secret to his most nearest and dearest friend without some jealousy [i.e. suspicion] of his truth and faithfulness.[1]

The dramatists also represented such breakdowns of patriarchal control either as fears for the future or even as current realities. Shakespeare's Timon, utterly disillusioned with his society, urges it to throw off all traditional constraint:

> Matrons, turn incontinent!
> Obedience, fail in children! Slaves and fools,
> Pluck the grave wrinkled Senate from the bench,
> And minister in their steads! . . . Bound servants, steal . . .
> Degrees, observances, customs, and laws,
> Decline to your confounding contraries;
> And yet confusion live!
>
> (*Timon of Athens*, IV. i. 3–6, 10, 19–21)

Shakespeare's tragedies enact the loosening of the ties that link the individual to his society. Macbeth carefully lists the various claims that forbid his murder of Duncan: 'First, as I am his kinsman and his subject . . . then, as his host . . .' (I. vii. 13–14), while *King Lear* tests the entire range of social or familial bonds, setting child against parent, servant against master, brother against brother, subject against king. A series of irreconcilable loyalties tear individuals apart. Gloucester disobeys his 'great arch and patron', the Duke of Cornwall, to help the King, who has not formally abdicated. An unnamed servant attacks and kills Cornwall, appalled at his revenge upon Gloucester. In a comparable bid to save Lear from himself, Kent intervenes to prevent him disinheriting Cordelia, while Edgar lies to and tricks his despairing father in order to save him from committing suicide. Albany is forced to choose between opposed duties to defend the rightful king and to protect England from invasion, between confronting or supporting the wife he knows to have acted viciously. The play sets traditional notions of obedience and good service against more discriminating and morally fastidious forms of loyalty.

Tudor and Stuart society largely depended upon the relationships that Shakespearean tragedy tests to destruction, relationships of mutual obligation: squire or landlord and tenants, master and servants, artisan and apprentices, parent and child. In higher circles, an elaborate system of patronage operated. Great noblemen maintained large households of retainers, giving them 'livery' (the means to live and a recognizable uniform). Clients would pursue a powerful patron, throwing in their lot with his or hers, and hoping to receive in return some office or position from which they might continue to support their patron's interests as well as their own. The conferring of mutual benefits usually involved the exchange of money, gifts, or words of praise, though it might also take the form of bartering information or sexual favours for wealth or position. Jacobean tragedy seized upon such sleazy arrangements with horror, while comedy and satire exposed their potential absurdity. Corrupt conduct of this kind was thought of as characteristic of the metropolis, of the court and/or city, whereas the countryside was usually associated with traditional values and old-fashioned integrity. In reality, the rapid growth of the city and the court were as much a symptom of change as a cause of it, but contemporary critics often blamed urban profiteers for exploiting the countryside and undermining older values and ways of life.

Changes in Landholding

Under the ancient feudal system, landholding arrangements had been based on the assumption that tenants rendered their services and produce to a landlord who in turn offered them protection against outside threats. In practice, lords of the manor no longer maintained men-at-arms, but the expectation that they were responsible for protecting their tenants' interests re-

mained, though new men were increasingly acquiring old
lands. The dramatist Thomas Middleton often refers to the
greed and rapacity of citizens who flourished at the expense of
the countryside. Vindice in *The Revenger's Tragedy* (1606)
denounces its spoliation to pay for the extravagant fashions of
the day:

> Who'd sit at home in a neglected room,
>   . . . when those
> Poorer in face and fortune than herself
> Walk with a hundred acres on their backs,
> Fair meadows cut into green foreparts—O,
> It was the greatest blessing ever happen'd to women,
> When farmers' sons agreed, and met again,
> To wash their hands and come up gentlemen;
> The commonwealth has flourished ever since.
> Lands that were mete by the rod, that labour's spar'd,
> Tailors ride down, and measure 'em by the yard;
> Fair trees, these comely foretops of the field,
> Are cut to maintain head-tires—
>
>   (II. i. 213, 215–26)

forepart] stomacher, front portion of dress   foretop] front lock of
hair   head-tire] head-dress

Middleton recognized that sudden changes in property-holding
could be disastrous for tenants if their land fell into the hands
of tough businessmen who felt none of the traditional obligations of the landed gentry towards their dependants. Ben
Jonson's poem 'To Penshurst' celebrates the hospitality and
dignity of a great country house partly in terms of the absence
of a ruthlessness or inhumanity that was becoming all too familiar elsewhere:

> And though thy walls be of the country stone,
> They are rear'd with no man's ruin, no man's groan,
> There's none that dwell about them wish them down.
>
>   (ll. 45–7)

The underlying source of distress in the countryside, of unemployed labourers, high prices, low wages, changing patterns of

landholding, and the corresponding growth in size and wealth of towns, was one that the Elizabethans could have done little to control, even if they had understood it more clearly. The historian and Justice of the Peace William Lambarde identified it as 'the dearth of all things', adding 'that the number of our people is multiplied, it is both demonstrable to the eye and evident in reason'.[2] In his view, increased numbers threatened to outstrip the provision available. As he supposed, the root of the problem was a demographic one. The population, which had remained effectively at a standstill during the fifteenth century, began to increase steadily and substantially in the sixteenth, progressing from about two and a half million at the beginning to over four million by the end. The most likely explanation for this growth was an increasing resistance to the bubonic plague, which had struck with terrible force in the mid-fourteenth century, cutting the rising population by as much as a quarter, or even a third. Though outbreaks of plague continued to cause huge numbers of deaths in London in the bad years of the sixteenth century, it was becoming confined to towns, whereas earlier outbreaks had been more widespread. Its virulence began to diminish in overall terms, and after the epidemic of 1665 it effectively died out. Smallpox, on the other hand, the disease mainly responsible for reducing population growth in the seventeenth century, had not yet reached its peak; later marriage and higher rates of celibacy were social responses to the crisis, and they helped to slow down growth rates. Although the sixteenth century's rapid rise in population was out of line with the preceding and following centuries, it was part of a more general pattern of expansion over the millennium as a whole.

As the population grew, prices rose and food was in short supply, as Lambarde had pointed out, especially in years of poor harvests; but there was no corresponding rise in wages since the market was saturated with people looking for work. The day labourers who made up the majority of agricultural workers could not always find the casual work they needed to survive, and the cloth-making industry, which provided a large number of jobs in particular areas, could not expand indefinitely. The gap between haves and have-nots increased, between those with a surplus to sell at the new higher prices and those who could not even sell their own labour. The poor grew poorer, loss of land finally driving them to seek work elsewhere, either in other parts of the countryside that offered more varied forms of employment, or else in towns, which in any case were developing through the growth of trade and the provision of services required by those with money. The dispossessed and wretched trekked to the cities, looking for work, huddling in attics, cellars, tenements; at times of dearth or plague, they died in the streets. London grew fastest, from around 50,000 inhabitants at the beginning of the sixteenth century to four times that size by the end. Norwich and Bristol were the next largest. The concentration of people and the lack of effective sanitation made towns dirty, smelly, crowded, and unhealthy, their populations maintained by the steady influx of migrants from the countryside: burials substantially outnumbered baptisms. Some of those who found work in towns wisely left their families behind them in the country, as commuters and migrant workers do today. Shakespeare chose to do so. The less fortunate had no homes in which to leave them.

Population growth created shortages that affected the poorest first. It is more difficult to judge the effect it had on the gentry, whose numbers were rising. Landowners ought to have benefited from higher food prices (which doubled over the period 1560–1620), but sometimes tenants with fixed rents under long leases might be the gainers, and the real value of rents had in any case fallen with inflation, then running at about 1 per cent per annum. At the same time, the gentry were under pressure to increase their expenditure in order to maintain their status. The more successful embarked on spending sprees, lavishing money on houses, clothes, furniture, and, less visibly, dowries and education. Paying for such conspicuous consumption required good management, especially as the costs were not evenly spread. Even the careful found it necessary to borrow at times, while extravagant gallants and young men-about-town could fall hopelessly into debt, being forced to mortgage their land until the money-lenders finally foreclosed on their forfeited property. Reckless prodigals and grasping usurers were favourite targets of Jacobean comedy.

Plague and Famine

The full stress of demographic pressure was felt most acutely in the 1590s, when a major outbreak of the plague (1592–3) combined with a sequence of bad harvests (1593–7) to create a sense of panic, and fears of a more general breakdown in law and order. The plague's effect on a large, tightly packed city such as London was indeed nightmarish, as contemporary accounts record. Nashe's Unfortunate Traveller experiences a visitation of the plague at Rome in 1522, but his account of it would have been familiar to Londoners, seventy years later: heavy clouds hang over the city and, as the inhabitants die or flee, desperate criminals move in, raping and pillaging. Both Nashe and Dekker in his pamphlet on the 1603 visitation, *The Wonderful Year*, emphasize the suddenness of death and the unwillingness of others to console or help the stricken for fear of being infected themselves:

How often hath the amazed husband waking, found the comfort of his bed lying breathless by his side! his children at the same instant gasping for life! and his servants, mortally wounded at the heart by sickness! The distracted creature beats at death's doors, exclaims at windows, his cries are sharp enough to pierce heaven, but on earth no ear is opened to receive them.[3]

Dekker and Nashe vividly record individual terror and fear, but on the whole urban communities reacted with surprising resilience. From 1578 government orders directed that infected houses must be quarantined, and their inhabitants were supported from the poor rates and prevented from making further contacts. Plague victims died in the streets and fields, and even outside the houses of terrified countrymen who barricaded themselves in and would not give them water. Such treatment was inhumane, even though it was for the general good. The outbreak of 1625 was the worst of all: more than 40,000 died in London, one in eight of the total population.

The bad harvests of the 1590s meant that many of the workers who normally managed to maintain themselves by cultivating their own tiny plots (often no more than an acre on which to grow vegetables) and hiring out their labour, fell below subsistence level, and were forced to take to the roads in search of work. In 1598 the clergyman Thomas Bastard addressed an epigram to the Queen alerting her to their miserable plight:

> The forlorn father hanging down his head,
> His outcast company drawn up and down,
> The pining labourer doth beg his bread,
> The plowswain seeks his dinner from the town.
>   O Prince, the wrong is thine, for understand
>   Many such robb'ries will undo thy land.[4]

Landless workers were among the most vulnerable when times were hard. About a third of the male adult population were day labourers, hired on a daily basis, in the seventeenth century, and their numbers were growing, as landlords sought to expand or 'improve' their holdings, or land was divided up between several children, with one buying out the shares of the others. Typically, they lived in houses of brick or timber, usually with two main spaces, the hall and the kitchen or parlour, roofed over to create some kind of second level for stores or for sleeping. Outhouses or lean-tos provided further storage space or shelter for animals—most households had a cow, though seldom more than one. Inside walls were plastered and painted, or pasted with ballad-sheets.

The enclosure of common land and the conversion of arable land to sheep pasture (encouraged by the success of the cloth industry) were intended to improve agricultural profits, but as More had observed in *Utopia*, they could cause distress to the poorest. Labourers unable to graze their animals on common land or to pick up their usual seasonal work such as ploughing, sowing, or harvesting, might be forced off the land, to swell the ranks of the unemployed. The government had long been aware of the problems created by enclosure and was even sympathetic in some degree, since those who resisted it did so in the name of ancient rights and customs which the government was committed to defend, along with traditional methods of agriculture and food production. The commissions of enquiry had been set up as early as 1517 (in the wake of More's *Utopia*) to examine complaints about enclosure, and if necessary to prosecute individuals found carrying it out, though the issue was never a straightforward one since enclosure could be used not only to create sheep pasture, but also to increase the size and productivity of arable fields. The government was always reluctant to act against landlords, who were its natural allies and officers.

The sequence of disastrous harvests from 1593 and serious food shortages that followed prompted further legislation in 1597, authorizing the rebuilding of decayed farms, and the conversion of pasture lands to arable farming, where necessary. During the parliamentary debate on the subject, Francis Bacon pointed out that: 'Enclosure of grounds brings depopulation, which brings forth first idleness, secondly decay of tillage, thirdly subversion of houses, and decrease of charity and charge to the poor's maintenance, fourthly the impoverishing the state of the realm.'[5] Enclosure provided a convenient explanation of social distress and unrest, but it was actually part of a larger process of intensifying agricultural output that had begun long before the sixteenth century, though this did not make its particular effects any less disruptive or distressing. In those parts of the country where the population had been slow to recover from the ravages of the Black Death (the plague epidemic of the mid-fourteenth century), it had worked as a useful and constructive policy, and at its best, was achieved by mutual negotiation between tenant and landlord which might even benefit the tenant by establishing his rights on a firmer footing than before.

A sequence of bad harvests and sudden rises in food prices could result in food riots. The opening scene of *Coriolanus* gives a less than sympathetic, though not necessarily inaccurate picture of the rioters' logic. The first citizen, obviously the ring-leader, proposes that they kill Caius Martius, whom he describes as 'chief enemy to the people', concluding that then 'we'll have corn at our own price'. The citizens' claims 'For corn at their own rates, whereof they say | The city is well stor'd' (1. i. 189–90) echo the standard demand of contemporary food rioters. Like anti-enclosure riots, food riots can be interpreted as attempts to enforce the laws rather than to subvert them. They often began with petitions and appeals to local authorities, and might be conducted with restraint and even discipline, the rioters' aim being to draw attention to their plight in order to prompt effective intervention. They appealed to the authorities on the basis of shared values, making a common cause against hoarders and profiteers. The government, in turn, recognized the need to make special provision for the hungry in times of dearth. It did what it could to avert famine by holding a watching brief over grain exports, encouraging imports in times of shortage, ensuring that corn was not hoarded but reached the markets and was sold at fair prices, and by shifting grain to areas of dearth from areas of plenty. In periods of crisis like the 1590s, special powers were conferred on local Justices of the Peace through the Book of Orders, authorizing them to buy up corn and redistribute it. Such instructions were only as effective as the officers entrusted to carry them out.

Many local Justices of the Peace shared a sense of responsibility for the smaller people that was widespread among the gentry. This, coupled with a distrust of merchants and middle-men, encouraged their active interference in the grain market, and their prosecution of entrepreneurs, or 'badgers' as they were called. It was in everyone's interests to alleviate the worst deprivations if only to avoid the fearful alternative of riots. At the same time, many JPs were also substantial landlords with vested interests in maintaining high food prices; some, no doubt, carried out their instructions more energetically than others. Further conflicts of interest existed between different types of community: those dedicated to food production gained when food prices rose, while towns and communities dominated by other activities such as cloth-making or mining industries paid fixed wages that made no allowance for a sudden rise in food prices. Contemporary pamphleteers were well aware of the problem: 'Ah, would every estate but look into himself, and everyone in himself seek a reformation . . . The covetous grazier and farmer should take such reasonable prices for their corn and cattle, that their poor brethren handicraftsmen might live by them without oppression.'[6]

Contrasts between different types of community were characteristic of early modern England: these were partly geographical—there was a north-west/south-east divide, such as still exists today, but geographical variation occurs on a very small scale in England and sometimes contrasting communities would be near-neighbours. The two main types are usually referred to as 'fielden' and 'forest', fielden being nucleated, close communities, usually farming arable lands, often with a high proportion of 'enclosed' land, while forest (or open) villages were more straggling and spread out, and were dominated by sheep pasturing, cloth-making, mining, charcoal-burning, and other activities. Different patterns of law observance and religious beliefs have been recorded in them, and forest communities have sometimes been thought of as less law-abiding, or else as more radically Protestant than the more traditional 'fielden' models; there was probably no simple pattern. In bad times, the more varied types of employment in forest villages made them more adaptable, and encouraged a pattern of migration from fielden to forest communities, where newcomers were more easily absorbed.

In addition to the problems created by dearth, there was also a class of people who were permanently unable to support themselves: it included the very old, the very young, and the unemployed. The dissolution of the monasteries had ended some provision of relief for the poor, while traditional local charity depended on voluntary contributions, and so was difficult to maintain when it was most needed. Communal systems of poor relief began to be set up during the second half of the sixteenth century, in towns in the first instance, where large numbers of poor migrants were a visible problem. Local rates were levied from 1563, though the earliest poor relief had been collected since the 1530s. A statute of 1572 imposed a national poor rate, requiring parishioners to contribute a sum of money to be determined by the local Justice of the Peace, in accordance with the demands on it. By the seventeenth century about a third of any local population were contributing money for poor relief, the majority received no relief and paid no tax, and between 4 and 5 per cent received relief regularly, though the percentage went up in times of emergency. Rates were used to support widows and orphans, helpless dependants who were always a problem, but after 1576 they were also used to buy raw materials (wool, flax, hemp, or iron) on which the able-bodied unemployed were set to work, as 'outdoor' relief, while towns began to provide houses of correction or workhouses for them. Then as now, this class was suspected of skiving, of actively choosing to be idle: William Harrison's *Description of England* (1587) distinguished between three different classes of the poor: those who are 'poor by impotency, as the fatherless child, the aged, blind and lame, and the diseased person that is judged to be incurable; the second are poor by casualty, as the wounded soldier, the decayed householder, and the sick person visited with grievous and painful diseases; the third consisteth of the thriftless poor . . .'[7]

The provision of work was intended to encourage the poorest to remain in their own parish, rather than taking to the roads in search of work elsewhere. Bands of masterless men, discharged soldiers or servingmen, evicted tenants, and unemployed labourers increased as the century wore on and its economic pressures bit harder; by the 1590s there may have been as many as 12,000 on the road. In 1596, when the crisis was at its height, a Somerset JP, Edward Hext, wrote a panicky letter to Lord Burghley, in which he described 'the infinite numbers of the wicked wandering idle people of the land' as not so much resulting from the dearth, as causing it, since they wouldn't work, but sat around drinking all day.[8] In Hext's view, the professionally unemployed poisoned the minds of the decent poor, inspiring them 'to all contempt both of noblemen and gentlemen, continually buzzing into their ears that the rich men have gotten all into their hands and will starve the poor'. Vagabonds and tramps for whom wandering was a way of life had always been harshly treated, being exiled, hanged, or put in the galleys. After 1597 they were punished by being whipped and placed in a house of correction on the lines of the Bridewell in London, where they were forced to work.

Keeping Order

Once the parish had become the unit that provided for the poor, individuals were expected to stay within their own. Parish officials had a vested interest in whipping vagrants or other undesirables outside the boundaries, since any new arrivals only placed further strains on already stretched parish funds. In this way the poor law helped to reinforce existing prejudices against strangers. The government required all travelling professionals—tinkers, peddlers, and the like—to carry a licence, and discouraged any unnecessary travel. Despite their efforts, records suggest that the population as a whole was unexpectedly mobile. Mobility, both geographically and socially, was officially discouraged, and had been forbidden by the Statute of Artificers of 1563. Writers and preachers placed a high value on stability, and experienced the speed of change as alarming in itself. In practice, young wage-earners looked for work away from home, and often made marriages at some distance from where they had grown up. Social climbing (as well as loss of status) was common.

Justices of the Peace, like parish constables, were unpaid amateur officers of the law, carrying out government directives and punishing law-breakers. They administered the Common Law, hearing criminal charges and cases of disturbance of the peace at quarter sessions and assizes, and more minor charges at petty sessions. They were also responsible for overseeing the collection and distribution of poor rates (though from 1598 this was the responsibility of churchwardens and the overseers of the poor); also for maintaining orphans, local roads and markets, and granting the licenses required to keep an alehouse or build a cottage. In addition to the Common Law, there were three other forms of legislation: equity, whose business was chiefly conducted in the Court of Chancery at Westminster; local ecclesiastical courts, which granted probate and dealt with misconduct of various kinds; and the old manorial courts which had jurisdiction over local land-holding arrangements, but were now disappearing. To some extent, villages and towns were self-regulating. If immediate family were the most important ties, neighbours and neighbourliness played a much more active part in people's lives than they do today, offering one another help and support of all kinds, but also holding a degree of moral responsibility for one another's actions. Everyone took care to know each other's business, and while there were frequent denunciations to the church courts for slander, petty theft, and sexual peccadilloes, such mutual supervision discouraged serious crime, and made it more difficult to conceal. Strangers were treated with distrust, and regarded with suspicion. To some extent the informal support and surveillance systems operating within the village were carried over into town life, where different parishes or streets maintained a strong sense of community.

Elizabethan society was as violent as our own: quarrels and resentments might be settled by blows, and sometimes fights to the death. Ben Jonson killed an actor in a fight; the poet Thomas Watson died in another; while Marlowe, who was involved in the brawl that caused Watson's death in 1592, was himself killed a year later, also apparently in a fight. Larger towns, and London in particular, were prone to street riots, often started by apprentices and directed against foreigners or other unpopular groups. At times during the 1590s provosts were appointed to enforce martial law in London and the adjoining counties when the city and the roads leading out of it became alarmingly unsafe.

Everyday policing was carried out by petty constables, unpaid volunteers whose local knowledge helped them in their task. Shakespeare gives an amusing picture of the constables Dogberry and Verges organizing the watch, their little posse of men:

DOGBERRY: This is your charge: you shall comprehend all vagrom men;
    you are to bid any man stand, in the Prince's name.
2 WATCH: How if a' will not stand?
DOGBERRY: Why then take no note of him, but let him go, and presently
    call the rest of the watch together, and thank God you are rid of a
    knave . . .
2 WATCH: We will rather sleep than talk, we know what belongs to a
    watch.

(*Much Ado About Nothing*, III. iii. 24–30, 37–8)

Elbow, the constable in *Measure for Measure*, though braver and
more officious than Dogberry, is just as linguistically confused
and confusing. Having examined his indictment of the tapster
and bawd Pompey Bum, the magistrate Escalus tries to relieve
Elbow of his office without hurting his feelings. Though Shakespeare's constables are treated as a source of comedy, most constables were in fact literate and some were prepared to use their
judgement to prevent inadequate offenders from reaching the
courts at all, where punishments were unreasonably harsh.
Escalus himself also intervenes in an attempt to deflect the
newly imposed law against fornicators from punishing Claudio.
Though a Viennese magistrate, his conduct suggests ways in
which English JPs tempered government initiatives to the needs
of their particular community.

While allowing for comic stereotyping, it is difficult to imagine
that most constables, even if considerably more intelligent than
Dogberry or Elbow, would have been capable of stemming the
increase in crime that accompanied London's increase in
numbers. Certain areas outside the city walls, notably Clerkenwell, were notorious for their brothels, and these were maintained, according to Nashe, with the connivance of the city
authorities: 'London, what are thy suburbs but licensed stews?
Can it be so many brothel-houses of salary sensuality and six-
penny whoredom (the next door to the magistrates) should be
set up and maintained, if bribes did not bestir them?' (*Christ's
Teares over Jerusalem*; *Works*, ii. 148). With brothels came
bribery, pimps, and protection rackets, though in general
increases in crime corresponded closely to periods of economic

hardship. By the early seventeenth century the higher courts were hearing more cases of conspiracy, forgery, and fraud than of riot and the crimes of violence that had occupied them earlier.

Cony-catching Pamphlets and City Comedy

Criminal activity, both in London and on the roads, quickly established itself as a popular subject with the authors of pamphlets and satires as well as dramatists, combining the pleasures of vicarious rule-breaking with those of moral condemnation. As writers liked to remind their readers, familiarizing yourself with rogues and their tricks was one way to protect yourself against them. Two such exposés were published in the 1560s, John Awdeley's *Fraternity of Vagabonds* (1561) and Thomas Harman's *Caveat for Common Cursetors* (1567). Awdeley was a publisher of godly ballads. Harman, a Kentish Justice of the Peace, was obsessed by what he imagined to be a criminal inner ring. Both Harman and Awdeley described in some detail the activities of the vagabonds, sturdy beggars or tramps who wandered the countryside, peddling, begging, or stealing, dividing them into various categories, not necessarily mutually exclusive, and representing them as an alternative society, a secret fraternity with its own hierarchy and initiation ceremonies that mirrored those of the guild structure. Fantasies of this kind were projected on to other mysterious or alternative groups, most commonly in cases of witchcraft.

Both writers agreed that there was a master of the order, who could call the others to account and possess any of the women he desired, though Awdeley named him as the 'upright man', Harman as the 'ruffler'. In addition to tinkers and peddlers like Shakespeare's Autolycus (swigmen, or bawdy baskets if they were women), a vagabond might beg for alms pretending to be an old soldier (ruffler), afflicted with sores (palliard), epileptic (counterfeit crank), or a madman (the Abram man or Tom a Bedlam, Edgar's chosen disguise in *King Lear*). Petty criminals worked as prostitutes (doxies), thieves (prigmen), or horse-thieves (priggers of prancers). In addition to his nineteen different types of rogue, Awdeley included 'a quartern of knaves for Cocklorel': these were not vagabonds at all but disaffected serving-men, divided into twenty-five types according to their various unpleasant personal habits.

Harman was fascinated by their private language. Known as 'canting' or 'peddler's French', it contributed significantly to the impression that its users belonged to a secret society. Under-world languages of this type have been recorded in several European countries from the late fourteenth century. It was made up partly by adapting familiar terms: night and day became 'darkmans' and 'lightmans', horses were 'prancers', while 'cheat' (thing, from 'escheat') was compounded with various participial adjectives to make 'smelling cheat' (nose), 'grunting cheat' (pig), 'quacking cheat' (duck), and so on. Some words were borrowed from foreign languages: the kinchin cove (or mort) was a young boy (or girl) from 'Kindchen', German for a small child; 'bene' (good) came from Latin; 'vyle' (town) from French. A few words from Harman's list—'booze' for drink, 'cove' for a person (probably from Dutch and Romany respectively), still turn up as (old-fashioned) slang today. 'Canting' terms were later used on the stage, notably in Mid-dleton and Dekker's *The Roaring Girl* (1611). Whether there really was a class of professional vagabonds such as Harman imagined, and if so how many existed at any one time, no one knows. Harman lists 214 by name and type 'so that the laws may be enforced', but only eighteen of those names have ever been found in the records of the period. Harman's eagerness to expose his villains may have been no more than a publicity device, though it anticipates those Jonsonian characters who display similar obsessions, such as Sir Pertinax Surly in *The Alchemist* or Adam Overdo in *Bartholomew Fair* (like Harman, an over-officious JP).

Although Harman and Awdeley refer to Bridewell, Bedlam, and St Paul's (a favourite haunt of rogues), the vagabond fra-ternity they wrote about were on the move and as likely to be met with in a Kentish lane as in a London street. Later under-world pamphlets focused on urban crime, and urban victims, the gulls who thronged to the city and as innocent country rabbits (or conies) were skinned by the various pickpockets, card-sharpers, and footpads who made up the ranks of professional cony-catchers. The bewildering variety of their confidence tricks, as well as those of crossbiters (i.e. blackmailers) were exposed in pamphlets by Thomas Dekker and Robert Greene which represent London as an urban jungle. Once robber bands had operated from forest hideouts. Now that the great forests were disappearing, the crowded streets of London provided a cover for organized crime.

The first cony-catching pamphlets dealing with the London underworld were the work of Robert Greene, who wrote them between 1591 and 1592, the year of his death. They tell stories of different types of confidence tricks, frauds, and thefts prac-tised on the unwary (the conies). Judging from his deathbed *Repentance of Robert Greene*, their author considered their com-position an act of public benefaction. *The Defence of Cony-Catching* (1592) by one 'Cuthbert Cony-Catcher' (possibly Greene himself) ironically blames 'R.G.' for having spoilt 'so noble a science' by giving away trade secrets. When Cuthbert comes across some farmers playing cards in a remote corner of the West Country, one of them is trying to trick the others, but is firmly put down with 'What, neighbour, will you play the cony-catcher with us? No, no, we have read the book as well as you.'[9] At this discouraging news, the writer also abandons his plans for cheating them all. As well as providing supposedly useful infor-mation, Greene's pamphlets pander to vulgar curiosity about criminal life, particularly its erotic aspects. Unlike Thomas Harman, a 'gentry cove' driven by a quasi-scientific curiosity about the rogues whom he sentenced, Greene belonged to the underworld he wrote about. According to his own account he frequented whores, drank too much, and kept bad company, notably that of playwrights and players, although he adopted a primly moral tone when writing of the criminal classes.

A more radical note is struck in *The Defence of Cony-Catching*, where Greene himself is criticized for straining at gnats, and letting the real enemies of society pass uncensored, 'those caterpillers that undo the poor, ruin whole lordships, infect the commonwealth, and delight in nothing but in wrongful extorting and purloining of pelf [money], when as such be the greatest cony-catchers of all'.[10] An attack on usurers follows, and a justification is offered for fraud along Robin Hood lines, if its victim is 'a miserable miser, that either racks his tenants' rents, or sells his grain in the market at an unreasonable rate'. Beneath this piece of special pleading lies a genuine sense of social injustice: Jacobean city comedy, which catches up many of the types of trickery described in these pamphlets, often exposes apparently worthy and respectable burgesses to be as greedy and ruthless within the social system as the excluded tricksters and cony-catchers were outside it. The fact that the bourgeoisie did not run the same risks or accept such a view of themselves only showed them to be less honest and more hypocritical.

The growth of capitalism, bringing with it thriving middlemen and moneylenders, could still shock the conservative, who regarded their activities as little better than cony-catching and crossbiting. The medieval condemnation of usury (lending money and charging interest on it) survived, even after it became legal practice; indeed, it was becoming increasingly important to a society rapidly moving away from the exchange of commodities, during a period of price inflation and shortage of coin. Those who were lucky enough to have money to spare were frequently approached for loans; inflation, as well as demand, justified lenders in asking for rates of interest. The conflict between traditional disapproval and modern mercantile practice is reflected in Shakespeare's *Merchant of Venice* (1596) where usury is linked with trade, and the merchant's precarious dependence on the success of his 'ventures'. The Royal Exchange had been built to glorify and facilitate English trade but there were still critics who did not consider that mercantile speculation constituted an honest day's work, any more than lending money at interest did. So prosperous tradesmen, merchants, or lawyers might regard themselves as worthy citizens of substance and standing, while being seen by others as grasping usurers, exploiting their clients or tenants, caterpillars battening on the commonwealth.

Jacobean comedy was quite sophisticated enough to present both attitudes simultaneously.

Robert Greene's comedies were essentially romantic and folkloric, very different in tone from his pamphlet-writing, but by the turn of the century a new mode of comedy was emerging, whose subject was the London citizens that made up its audience, and whose outlook was influenced by the cony-catching pamphlets and verse satires of the 1590s. Dekker's *Shoemaker's Holiday* (1599) makes Simon Eyre a typical citizen hero, but differs from later developments in that it tends to accept him at his own valuation. Marston's *The Dutch Courtesan* (1605) is more typical, opposing the rogue Cockledemoy, whose elaborate ruses, confidence tricks, and disguises are very much in the cony-catching tradition, to the apparently virtuous alehouse-keeper Mulligrub, rising in wealth and social status at the expense of other people's indulgence in alcohol. Cockledemoy speaks in an eccentric slang which owes virtually nothing to the canting terms recorded by Harman, but establishes him as an individualist, operating outside the norms of linguistic exchange, just as his social malpractices function outside the norms of social exchange. The play's climax involves a comic reversal of expectation since it is Mulligrub, rather than Cockledemoy, who is arrested and nearly hanged for theft. The London rogue differs in status rather than kind from the man of substance—tradesman or merchant—who resembles the rogue in making a living out of other men's weaknesses.

Thomas Middleton (*c.*1580–1627) was the dramatist most closely associated with the city, and he left some of the most vivid accounts of its life and values. The city authorities commissioned Lord Mayor's pageants and entertainments from him and in 1620 appointed him City Chronologer, their official recorder of major events and transactions. Middleton's comedies often employ elaborately fantastic plots, yet their central concerns are commonplace: tension between gentry and bourgeoisie or country and city—'They're busy 'bout our wives, we 'bout their lands' (*Michaelmas Term*, i. i. 107)—profitable business deals, advantageous marriage bargains, inheriting a relative's

wealth or alternatively being cheated and losing out. Such concerns were central to the society he was portraying, and are in
turn reflected in contemporary trends in litigation. Middleton
is less concerned with rogues, and more with the wheeling
and dealing of the middle classes whose hopes, dreams, self-
deception, and illusions he exposed with a complex blend of
insight, humour, and disapproval. The deceits of Quomodo, the
shifty woollen-draper of *Michaelmas Term* (1606), are based on
those of a real broker, Howe, who had been prosecuted in Star
Chamber ten years earlier. He indulges in a self-congratulating
fantasy about a piece of land he hopes to gain as the forfeited
security for an unpaid loan. Its present owner is, naturally, a
spendthrift gallant:

Now come my golden days in.—Whither is the worshipful Master
Quomodo and his fair bedfellow rid forth?—To his land in Essex!—
Whence comes those goodly load of logs?—From his land in Essex!—
Where grows this pleasant fruit? says one citizen's wife in the Row—At
Master Quomodo's orchard in Essex—Oh, oh, does it so? I thank you
for that good news, i'faith.

(III. iv. 12–18)

Ben Jonson (1572–1637) was substantially less interested than
Middleton in the average citizen. If Middleton dressed up familiar anxieties in extravagant plotting, Jonson was more interested
in the extravagant for its own sake, and his imagination was con-
sistently drawn to extremes—the eccentric, the odd. Brilliant as
is his depiction of contemporary society, with every character
defined by an appropriate slang or jargon, his classical training
inclined him to look through current fads at the condition of self-
delusion beneath. It is not the characteristic aspirations of a
particular class that concern him, as they do Middleton, but the
permanent fantasies of humanity itself. Greed may appear to be
the driving force of society, but beneath it lies the urge to power,
to self-assertion and self-aggrandizement. So Volpone hazards
his wealth in order to gratify his desire to laugh at his clients
and see them disappointed—a typically self-destructive act of
homage to ego. Jonson's great confidence-tricksters, Brainworm,

Mosca, and Face, whose origins lie in the cony-catching tradition, find important satisfactions in the manipulation and deception of others, while Volpone admits that pulling the wool over
the eyes of the whole Venetian court was more thrilling than
the enjoyment of the beautiful Celia would have been: 'The
pleasure of all womankind's not like it' (v. ii. 11). Surly, in *The
Alchemist*, turns down the prospect of a wealthy match in the
hope of unmasking the criminals instead. Jonson's suggestion
that we reject real, available gain in favour of fantasies of self-
assertion is more inward and subtle than the simpler motives
portrayed elsewhere.

Bartholomew Fair (1614) develops this theme in a subversive
direction. Here the fair provides opportunities for a variety of
vendors and rogues, each brilliantly realized through a particular speech pattern, to sell to or take in the customers, a relationship which echoes that of actor and audience—indeed, one
of the tricksters is a puppet-master. But Jonson is less interested in the petty criminals and their victims than the quasi-
authoritarian figures who attempt to organize or control the
world about them, the officious servant Wasp, the zealous
puritan Zeal-of-the-Land Busy, but above all Adam Overdo, the
local JP, obsessed with an ambition to expose the various petty
crimes of the fair. Instead, he himself is beaten, set in the stocks,
and his drunken wife almost enrolled as a prostitute. The play
shows just how far from conventional attitudes the Jacobean
dramatists could travel in their explorations of human behaviour. Authority itself is seen as sharing the fantasies of power in
which all indulge and which lay us open to the dream-peddlers
and their get-rich-quick schemes. Elsewhere Jonson satirizes the
freebooting activities of the projectors, social climbers, rogues,
and profiteers, alongside those of the busybodies who set out to
control or expose their fellows. Nowhere does he leave room for
complacency. His writing is more concerned to analyse the permanent patterns of self-delusion than his vivid rendering of contemporary life suggests, although praise for its vividness is fully
justified—his record of London life remains unequalled in range
and energy.

The best of Jacobean comedy challenges conventional attitudes, sharply questioning the virtues of wealth and respectability, but by the 1620s more explicitly political accounts had begun
to appear: Massinger's *A New Way to Pay Old Debts* (1625–6) is
set in the country rather than the city, and matches old breeding against the new men, as caricatured in the monstrous and
villainous figure of Sir Giles Overreach. Based on the figure of
Sir Giles Mompesson, a client of Buckingham impeached in
1621 and now conveniently dead, the play voices the general
resentment of Buckingham's increasing political influence,
achieved through the careful planting of his clients and cronies.
Overreach's methods of evicting tenants by harassment, and of
accumulating land by foreclosing on mortgages were familiar
from earlier satires, but now Justice Greedy, the local JP, has
been bribed to help him, threatening the proper operation of the
law. The play's energies are invested in its villains. The prodigal
gentry lapse ineffectively into debt while retaining a humanity
that somehow entitles them to their rightful inheritance: for
Massinger, old breeding always tells. Though new money had
always propped up old names, Buckingham's acquisition of
power, and his influence over religious and state affairs was, by
the 1620s, a general source of anxiety. He, and protégés such
as Mompesson, who attempted to annex rights traditionally
belonging to the old landed gentry, looked increasingly dangerous. Massinger's comedy, with its praise of old breeding and old
decencies, looks back to an earlier time, before the competitive
city life depicted by Jonson and Middleton. During the 1620s the
golden age ceased to be located in the remote past and was more
and more closely identified with that of Elizabeth. The good
order, social unity, militant Protestantism, and community spirit
of her reign were remembered with affection, long after its more
discordant or disruptive aspects had been forgotten.

Women and the Family

'I AM the husband, and all the whole isle is my lawful wife; I am the head and it is my body',[1] James I told his first Parliament in the course of a debate on the proposed union of England and Scotland in 1603. Today, the word 'patriarchy' signifies social structures dominated by men and male interests, but in early modern England it described a specific political theory then prevailing, that the family and the state were parallel structures, governed by father and monarch respectively. James represented himself as father even oftener than as husband to his people, deriving his claims to authority, as did the father of a household, from Adam, as the father of all men: 'Not only Adam, but the succeeding patriarchs, had by right of fatherhood, royal authority over their children', wrote Robert Filmer in *Patriarcha*, his account of this theory.[2] The fifth of the ten commandments, 'Honour thy father and thy mother', was interpreted as demanding respect for those in authority more generally, from the father up to the king. For James, claims to be the husband or the father of the nation were linked with claims to absolute power, to rule, if not by divine right, then at least by the universal acceptance that his decisions were final. In the years leading up to the Civil War, patriarchal theory was much used by royalists like Robert Filmer, but by the end of the seventeenth century this particular set of analogies had lost its force, as the monarchy accepted limits on its power and John Locke distinguished the public domain from the private.

Although James spoke of himself as a husband, his writings just as often develop arguments based on the power of the father, since the role of the father within the family was the less controversial of the two relationships. While a father's rights over his children were widely accepted (he could claim credit for their very existence), a husband's rights over his wife were not strictly comparable, since she was another adult, equal in the eyes of God (according to some authorities), if not of man. The position of women in general, and within marriage in particular, was hotly contested, both in theory and in social practice. Elizabeth I had used the analogy of being married to her kingdom when responding to a request from her 1559 parliament that she should marry, but because she was a woman, her declaration had a different significance: she replied that she was already married 'to an husband, namely the kingdom of England',[3] and pointed to her coronation ring as if it were a wedding ring. For Elizabeth to make such a claim at the very moment when she was rejecting the advice of parliament, the elected representatives of her kingdom, was audacious and even paradoxical. Her words highlight her anomalous position as prince (therefore, governor) and woman (therefore governed by male authority). She exploited this position as best she could, creating around herself a cult of virginity described in Chapter 8.

Women and Marriage

The claims to authority made by the monarchy and extended to the father as head of the household had grown up at a time when the Church's authority over secular affairs was dwindling as a result of the Reformation, which also created changes in attitudes to marriage itself. For the Catholic Church, virginity and celibacy were the holiest of states, ideals that all should aspire to, while marriage was an inferior way of life, a necessary evil, improved by sexual abstinence, since St Paul had thought it better to marry than to burn (i.e. be damned). In the reformers' view, celibacy had too often concealed sexual misbehaviour, or contributed to the clergy's mystique. Marriage, in their view, was the condition ordained for man by God, as the creation of Eve for Adam demonstrated. Love-making was seen as 'one of the

most proper and essential acts of marriage', both because it produced children and because it made couples 'dearer and dearer
to each other's souls'.[4] Marriage could now be enjoyed even by
the clergy, while the traditional refuges from it, nunneries and
monasteries, no longer existed. Chastity was no longer identified
with celibacy, but rather with faithful wedded love, so that
Spenser's knight of chastity in *The Faerie Queene* is the maiden
warrior Britomart, searching for her future husband, rather than
the bright virgin Belphoebe. Protestant marriage doctrine, as
expressed in a sequence of advice books and manuals, followed
that of humanists like Erasmus in arguing that wives should be
treated with consideration and affection, as helpmeets and companions, rather than obedient servants, though such arguments
were employed to reinforce the existing patriarchal order, rather
than to cast doubt upon it.

Underpinning attitudes to women in early modern society was
the assumption that they were physically and morally inferior to
men (just as the lower classes were physically and morally inferior to the upper classes), and that such inequality justified the
marriage contract, in which women exchanged their material
production and labour for promises of love and protection
(rather as, in feudal society, tenants had rendered food and services in exchange for their landlords' protection). Contemporary
marriage manuals promoted Protestant ideals of 'companionate'
or 'affective' marriage (as it is usually referred to), and these
have been much debated, historians having initially judged them
to be empowering for women, and later read them as reasser-
tions of patriarchal power, in their allowance of wife-beating and
emphasis on wifely duties. In any case, manuals tell us less about
how people actually behaved than about how the authorities
thought they ought to behave: one London minister, William
Gouge (author of *Domestical Duties*, 1622), deeply upset
members of his Blackfriars congregation when he argued that a
wife should not dispose of 'the common goods of the family
without or against her husband's consent'.[5]

It is possible that the manuals were attempting to theorize
changes in the structure of marriage that had already taken

place: urban life and certain kinds of industry certainly gave some households a new economic independence. Though women's power was strictly limited in official ways, various different kinds of information, from ecclesiastical court records to the prevailing misogyny of much contemporary writing, suggest that at some level women were felt to possess powers that men could neither understand nor control. In part such fears resulted from men's daily dependence on women's goodwill and co-operation for life to go on at all: the servant's power over the master is experienced as a threat at the deepest and least conscious levels.

The fear of women's power and the celebration of it coexist dynamically in Shakespearean comedy, where such energies are ultimately channelled into marriage, and thus reintegrated into society and placed at its service. The mechanism used here to reconcile spirited heroines to becoming wives and mothers is romantic love, which has sometimes been thought of as linked with the Protestant marriage ethic, although it has an altogether longer history in European narratives and consciousness. Whereas Roman New Comedy focused on the young man's choice of marriage partner (often in opposition to that of his parents), Shakespeare transfers attention on to the young woman as chooser, thus establishing a tradition of romantic comedy focused on an exciting but exceptional moment of self-determination in women's lives, though his earliest comedies had already registered the limits of romance. Adriana in *The Comedy of Errors* speaks eloquently of the miseries of marriage, the disappointment as romantic love is succeeded by familiarity and the frustration of remaining neglected at home, while her husband walks abroad doing business and beginning love affairs (II. i. 87–101; ii. 110–146). Her sister Luciana has been deterred from marriage by seeing the 'troubles of the marriage bed' at such close quarters, yet she nevertheless responds as the Church would have done, by offering a short sermon on the necessity for wifely obedience (II. i. 15–25).

Luciana, like almost all of Shakespeare's heroines, later agrees to marry, but a surprisingly large number of women did not—in the seventeenth century, at least 10 per cent, and sometimes as many as 20 per cent chose not to marry, a rate that is at least twice that of today. In 1599 a quarter of the women living at Ealing (then a village of eighty-five households) were single, aged between 40 and 70, and indeed a larger proportion of the population of the late sixteenth and early seventeenth century consisted of single women than at any time since. Yet at a time when women were much less visible than men, these were the most invisible group of all, appearing seldom in either the imaginative writing or the records of the period. What evidence there is suggests that they sometimes lived with other women, sometimes in their own homes, and some of them supported themselves from smallholdings. Despite the large numbers who did not marry, women's status continued to be defined in terms of marriage, as can be seen from the last act of *Measure for Measure* where Mariana is asked whether she is maid, wife, or widow, and if none of these, 'Why, you are nothing then' (v. i. 171–7). Nothing or nought(y) implied sexual misbehaviour: by rejecting the statuses proposed, Mariana defined herself as sexually experienced, a maid who has lost the virginity she was supposed to preserve for her husband. The possibility that a maid might not be waiting to marry is exemplified in the play by Isabella, who desires to become a nun, but such an option was not open to the women of early modern England. For women, marriage was their presumed destiny, whether welcome or not. 'All are understood either married or to be married', explained a legal book of 1632;[6] women's status was defined within marriage and it was the main determinant of their lives.

Shakespeare's *The Taming of the Shrew* is centrally concerned with the conduct of women in marriage, setting off recent humanist attitudes to women's education against an older tradition of popular misogyny; but before it does so, it establishes a sharp distinction between the social milieu of the tinker, Christopher Sly, at the bottom of society, and that of the unnamed Lord at the top. Class is exposed as a significant factor in gender construction and expectation, as the alehouse wife beats Sly for refusing to pay his debts, while the upper-class wife (in fact the Lord's page in disguise) is all courtesy, consideration, and humble duty. The main action of the play takes place between these two extremes, among a mercantile bourgeoisie, with lower-class domestic violence and upper-class linguistic accomplishment both contributing to what follows. The notion that the lowest classes conducted personal relationships in terms of buffets and insults, while the upper classes did so in terms of elaborate politeness was a well-established literary convention, but in reality, too, the role of women in a leisured society, where education and accomplishments (as opposed to a capacity for hard work) were considered assets, was inevitably different from that of women lower down the social scale.

If women 'of the better sort' had more choice in other respects, as far as the choice of marriage partners went, they had less. The grander the family, the more direct influence parents expected to have over their children's choice of marriage partner. Marriages were usually arranged where significant titles, property, or wealth changed hands, as opposed to the usual 'portion' that all but the poorest women would bring. Younger sons who would not inherit might thus enjoy a freer choice, though they would be expected to listen to advice, while orphans, if propertied, would have a guardian appointed by the Master of the Wards. Only one group of women were in a position to act with any degree of freedom, and these were widows of independent means or the exceptional woman left in charge of a substantial household (as is Olivia in *Twelfth Night*). Friends might try to arrange suitable matches for them but they were free to choose for themselves, and occasionally caused scandal in this class-conscious society by marrying a social inferior, often a member of their own household. When Frances Brandon, Countess of Suffolk, married her young secretary and groom of the chamber, Queen Elizabeth demanded 'Has the woman so far forgotten herself as to marry a common groom?'[7] Some of the wealthiest widows preferred not to remarry, while those who did, often did so to improve their financial situations.

As in Islamic countries today, arranged marriages were generally accepted as a way of preserving and increasing family assets, and the upper classes had everything to gain from confining their advantages to a limited circle. Marriage was not expected to be personally fulfilling in the way it is today, since we have travelled so much further down the road of romance, but it provided mutual support of various kinds, and a nest for the rearing of children. Lower down the social scale, where there was less at stake in terms of status and wealth, young couples could take the initiative themselves, with parents on occasion advising or perhaps exercising some sort of informal veto, and the agreement of 'friends'—neighbours or the wider family—being sought. More romantic views of marriage required greater flexibility from parents, and the recognition that a child's needs and wishes played a part in the success of any marriage. The extent of parental involvement or approval in marriage has always been a contested area, but arranged marriages were not automatically likelier to fail than love matches. When a couple were genuinely mismatched, however, it was difficult to limit the damage: divorce was extremely rare, requiring an Act of Parliament, and legal separation was expensive and difficult to achieve. In practice, separation of various kinds was not uncommon: a proportion of husbands deserted their wives, while wives took refuge with their parents or other relatives; neither could legally remarry until their partner died.

A small but significant number of upper-class marriages were made without parental authority, and sometimes in the teeth of parental opposition. Before 1604 girls had been legally free to marry a partner of their own choice from the age of 12, boys from the age of 14; after that date, all children under 21 required parental consent for marriage. The drama often represented conflict over marriage choices, for example, Romeo and Juliet, or Desdemona, who deceives her father to elope with Othello. In Middleton's *Women Beware Women*, Leantio steals Bianca away from Venice to marry her. He is a factor, a poor clerk, whom Bianca's noble father would never have considered a possible son-in-law. In this case elopement was regarded as a kind of theft. It was treated as such in real life, when in 1601 Sir George More discovered that his 18-year-old daughter Anne had secretly married John Donne, private secretary to her uncle. Donne was imprisoned and Anne was pressured to declare the marriage unconsummated, and therefore not legally binding. When she refused, Donne was released, only to find he had lost his position. The couple lived in comparative poverty and frequent sickness with their young and growing family at Mitcham. Donne saw his marriage as the misfortune of his life, recognizing that he had also ruined Anne's: several of his most passionate love poems may have been written to make her some small amends. Men's superior status carried with it the onus of greater responsibility, as Milton's *Paradise Lost* registers.

Secret marriages were easier to effect at a time when marriage required witnesses, but was legally binding without the formal civil and religious sanctions it acquired after 1753. In Catholic countries the sacrament had to be administered, and in England the great majority of weddings were performed in church, preceded by the reading of banns, or, at short notice, the obtaining of a special licence. But in addition to those made before the minister, there were two further forms of formal betrothal (or 'spousal'): 'per verba de futuri' was a promise to marry which became binding with sexual consummation. According to this form, Mariana in *Measure for Measure*, and perhaps Helena in *All's Well* can claim to be married to Angelo and Bertram by the bed-tricks that consummate their promises, though both plays question the relation of action to intention in ways that are legally as well as morally problematic. Marriage 'per verba de presenti' involved an exchange of promises before witnesses. With this in mind, the Duchess of Malfi conceals her maid Cariola as witness to her coming interview with Antonio, to guarantee that any vows he makes will be binding. Betrothal, even without such a promise, was a serious step for a young couple, permitting them to call each other 'wife' and 'husband'. Late marriage and long betrothals meant that as many as 20 per cent of brides were pregnant when married (as was Shakespeare's bride, Anne). These older and more private forms of marriage had developed within more stable and parochial conditions, and were less appropriate to a more mobile society, where illegal marriages and bigamy might result. One pamphlet, *The Defence of Cony-Catching* (1592), told how a confidence-trickster who had contracted sixteen bigamous marriages was finally castrated by a vengeful conspiracy of his ex-wives.

Marriage in early modern society was characterized by its relative lateness, the small size of its families, and high rates of remarriage. Shakespeare's Juliet, a bride at 14, is an often-cited but misleading example of early marriage, though where large estates were at stake marriages were sometimes arranged for children in their early teens. In such cases the couple would spend a night together, as required by law, and then the bridegroom was sent away to be educated for a year or two, until he and his wife were ready to conceive children without risk to her health. Even so, the average age for upper-class marriages was nearer 20 than 15. Further down the social scale, the average age of marriage was high—26 for women, 27 to 29 for men, and still rising. Late marriage, as much as ten years after the onset of puberty (which itself occurred substantially later than today), was characteristic of Western European society as a whole, and is most convincingly explained in terms of economic constraints. Apprentices were indentured for at least seven years to their trade, and it might be even longer before they could practise independently. Surprisingly, in a few areas significant numbers of women were also apprenticed to guilds, usually as needle-workers or domestic workers, but very occasionally to such traditionally male occupations as printers, armourers, or bootmakers—local needs or customs played a determining part in such recruitment. In the country, a labourer would either need to inherit a home or save towards one in order to marry. The life expectancy of a man of 30 was on average another twenty-five or thirty years, so an eldest son might reasonably expect to inherit between the ages of 25 and 30. Late marriage played a part in reducing the number of children in a family: as the average age of a woman at marriage rises by two years, so she is statistically likely to bear one child less.

The Household

In superficial respects, the family resembled that of today, being nuclear in structure, parents typically having two or three children living at home, with a further one or two living away, though the size of individual families varied, of course. Large families on the Victorian scale were rare, because of the high infant-mortality rate. One in every seven babies died within the first year of its life, and thereafter mortality remained high—around a quarter of all children had died by the age of 10. Some time between the ages of 7 and 14 children would normally be sent away from home, to be apprenticed, go into service, or, among the upper classes, to join another nobleman's household or go to school or university. Noblemen, with their advantages in terms of life-style and nourishment, might have been expected to have larger families than the poor, and their children avoided some risks (certain kinds of domestic accident, for example), but only to encounter others (professional medical treatment was ill-suited to childish diseases); sudden illness and death were threats at every social level.

Broken marriages were as striking a feature of society then as they are today, but they were the result of death, rather than divorce. On average, marriages lasted twelve or fifteen years, and remarriage within two or three years was common, so many people married several times, men being more likely to remarry than women. Sometimes remarriage was undertaken for the children's sake (as was Thomas More's), though there are also many stories of the cruelty of step-parents. One long-lived and influential Elizabethan lady, Elizabeth Talbot, Countess of Shrewsbury ('Bess of Hardwick'), was married exceptionally early, and made four strategic marriages. Spenser married twice, Elizabeth Boyle (for whom he wrote the *Amoretti* and the *Epithalamion*) being his second wife. Milton married three times.

Despite the possible tensions of the parent–child relationship, the chief purpose of marriage was self-perpetuation, and, with mortality rates so high, for many it was a race against devouring time. The rich and great might leave enduring acts and monuments behind them, and artists their creations, but for most people children embodied their futurity, as well as promising care for themselves and their possessions when they could no longer look after themselves. Despite the dangers of childbirth, those who married, unless miserably poor, expected and hoped for children and might be bitterly disappointed if none came. The more a man had, the more he wanted a son, primogeniture (inheritance by the eldest son) being the usual system of property transfer. An example of frustrated fatherhood run mad, Henry VIII divorced his first wife and beheaded the second when neither managed to give birth to a live male heir. Shakespeare took a crucial step, albeit in the name of his father, when he applied for the coat of arms that qualified him as a gentleman. It must have been a disappointment to him that he had no male heir on whom to confer it, his only son having died at the age of 11. Shakespeare's property was left mainly to his two surviving daughters, and was thus legally at the disposal of their husbands, though shortly before his death he carefully secured the portion of his younger daughter, Judith, who, like her father, had married in a hurry, earlier in 1616.

It seems impossible to generalize with any confidence about parental attitudes to children. Montaigne, who was not obviously unfeeling, admitted with alarming vagueness, 'I have lost two or three [children] (but while they were still nursing), if not without grief, at least without repining' ('That the taste of good and evil depends in large part on the opinion we have of them', *Essays*, p. 42). It has been argued that high infant mortality would have discouraged strong emotional investment in those fragile little lives, yet the many denunciations of indulgent parents who 'Spare the rod and spoil the child' tell a different story, suggesting that warm affection flourished in the face of official disapproval. Montaigne's admission that he did not care to have his children brought up near him, in 'Of the Affection of Fathers for their Children' (*Essays*, p. 280) can be set against More's Latin verse epistle to his children: 'I never could endure to hear you cry. You know, for example, how often I kissed you, how seldom

I whipped you . . . Brutal and unworthy to be called father is he who does not himself weep at the tears of his child.'[8]

Literature provides many touching and even sentimental moments of concern for children. The Duchess of Malfi's dying requests, that her son should take some syrup for his cold, and the girl say her prayers (IV. ii. 203–5) being a typical example—the play is concerned throughout to present her as a devoted mother. Ben Jonson composed poignant epigrams on the death of his eldest daughter Mary, and on his son Benjamin which, within a careful framework of classical wit, bespeak deep feeling; but one should not generalize from particular examples. As some sections of society acquired greater leisure, they probably spent more of it with their children and so came to find them more rewarding than they would otherwise have done. For families struggling at subsistence level, however, a new baby was just another mouth to feed, and a certain negligence might conveniently diminish its already thin chances of survival. Convictions for infanticide were low, and in the absence of witnesses it was virtually impossible to distinguish from still-birth. Punishable by death, infanticide was regarded as a peculiarly monstrous and unnatural crime, linked in the popular imagination with sexual misbehaviour, lack of maternal feeling, and a wicked and abandoned way of life.

If parents exhibited a range of feeling towards children, children were expected to show gratitude to their parents for begetting them and bringing them up. The command to 'Honour thy father and thy mother' was treated with great seriousness, and given the analogies between the family and the state, disobedience figured as a form of treason. The cruelty and disrespect shown by Lear's daughters and Gloucester's bastard son would have seemed even more outrageous to its earliest audiences who lived at a time when upper-class society insisted on elaborate displays of deference to parents, sons doffing their hats and daughters kneeling or standing in their parents' presence. Children were expected to kneel each morning for their parents' blessing, and to do so again, on arrival or departure from the parental home, even when grown up. Such conventions made Lear's curses on his daughters seem particularly unnatural, and added a further dimension to the fourth-act reunion where the old King kneels before his daughter Cordelia to ask her blessing, in a deliberate reversal of expected patterns of behaviour. Kneeling indicates submission (parallels are to be found in animal behaviour), and children were expected to submit to parental authority at all times. If on occasion children were ungrateful, parents could be repressive or even brutal. Burton, discussing the general misery of the human condition in *The Anatomy of Melancholy*, observed that 'children live in a perpetual slavery, still under that tyrannical government of masters' (part 1, section 2, member 3, subsection 10). Lady Jane Grey gave Roger Ascham an alarming account of her parents' treatment of her, describing herself as 'so sharply taunted, so cruelly threatened, yea, presently sometimes, with pinches, nips, and bobs, and other ways which I will not name for the honour I bear them, so without measure misordered, that I think myself in hell'.[9]

Upper-class parents regularly put out their children to wet-nurses, and left them to be cared for and brought up by servants of one kind or another. Shakespeare's Juliet confides not in her mother but her old wet-nurse (who reminisces about weaning Juliet, and about Susan, the lost baby whom Juliet replaced, at Act I, Scene iii, lines 18–57). The nurse's inarticulate grief at Juliet's death contrasts with Lady Capulet's more formal lament. Servants played an important part in many households, living under the authority of its head, and usually under the same roof. A third of all households employed living-in servants, so that their presence extended well down the social scale. The majority of young girls from poor families went into service, where their relationship with their employers might be close, sometimes uncomfortably so.

In a large household the grandest servants, particularly the steward, would be gentlemen or women by birth, perhaps the younger sons or daughters of good families. People of this class occupying subservient positions in a household (as De Flores does in Middleton's *The Changeling*), might be sources of potential tension. *The Duchess of Malfi* is the story of a noblewoman who marries her gentleman steward, and since the obvious assumption would have been that she was driven by lust rather than love, Webster goes to some lengths to establish that the Duchess values Antonio for his moral qualities, and shows herself a tender mother and devoted wife. Her brothers assume the worst from her behaviour. In *Twelfth Night*, Olivia's steward Malvolio, though perhaps not quite a gentleman, fantasizes about marrying his employer. Relations between great ladies and their gentlewomen such as those between the Duchess of Malfi and Cariola, Desdemona and Emilia (in *Othello*), Hero and her waiting ladies (in *Much Ado*), are close and trustful, but a treacherous waiting woman plots her mistress's death in Middleton's *The Second Maiden's Tragedy*.

Apprentices to a trade might also share their master's house and Francis Beaumont's *The Knight of the Burning Pestle* reveals how fond a couple could grow of an amiable apprentice: the Grocer's Wife could scarcely be prouder of Ralph's talents if he had been her own son. Servants were encouraged to identify their interests with those of the household whose livery they wore (if it had one), and might on occasion be touchily proud of it. Family feuds were sometimes perpetuated by brawling servants whose aggressive gestures their masters felt obliged to support, as happens in the opening scene of *Romeo and Juliet*. Occasionally a servant might harbour a burning resentment against an employer who was thought to have acted ungenerously. In 1628 the poet Fulke Greville, already in his seventies, was stabbed to death by a servant dissatisfied with the provision made for him in his will. And no one who has read it can forget the traditional ballad of Lamkin, the unpaid mason who helps the wet-nurse to cut the throats of mother and baby while father is away from home.

'Did Women have a Renaissance?'[10]

For the majority of women, whether they worked as servants or wives, life consisted of hard physical labour, tending children, animals, and plants and washing, cleaning, fetching water, buying

food, and selling produce. Wealthier women had leisure to converse, think, and write, though their access to power or money
was limited and what influence they had was achieved through
husbands and sons. Constance in Shakespeare's *King John* and
Volumnia in *Coriolanus* destroy their sons through their high
ambitions for them. Women were not expected to act on their
own behalf. As daughters, wives, and mothers they held subservient positions, acting only as channels for male power. The
system of Common Law maintained the rights of men, particularly of the first-born through primogeniture, and of husbands
through 'coverture', the legal fiction that husband and wife were
a single unit governed by the husband. Married women thus had
no standing in Common Law, being classed with idiots, children,
and convicted criminals, and the only courts in which they regularly pleaded were the ecclesiastical courts, dealing with local
misbehaviour and the obtaining of probate. Technically speaking, a wife's possessions were the property of her husband,
including whatever assets she had brought into the marriage, as
well as whatever debts or duties she might incur; this left her
very much at his mercy, whether tender or otherwise. In fact the
situation was inevitably more complex than such a statement
allows, since there were various ways of protecting a bride's
property, and in practice most wives managed the household
finances jointly with their husbands. Though women's situation
was better than their Common Law position suggested, the
larger question of how to assess the satisfactoriness (or otherwise) of women's lives and what measures of comparison to use
at a time when women all over the world are becoming more
conscious of their legal and economic disabilities, remains a
problem.

In particular respects, early modern women resembled women
in England today in that they were (and are) paid only two-
thirds of what men earn. Women make up the majority of those
dependent on state support today in about the same proportion
as they depended on poor relief in the seventeenth century, and
among them, a similar proportion are single mothers with
children, who are still just as underfed and inadequately clothed

and housed, even though the reasons for their situation are different, and attitudes towards them have changed. This long history of women's poverty reflects their inferior status and the ultimate failure of the law to protect their interests, though the detailed ways in which the process has worked out differs from one historical moment to another. Early modern English law was particularly harsh in its treatments of widows, as compared to European law, allowing them only a third of their husbands' 'moveables' (children receiving a further third), though the ecclesiastical courts which dealt with probate seem to have recognized the urgency of their claims, interpreting the law in their favour whenever possible. It was in the general interest to do so, since widows without financial support became a burden on local ratepayers.

While inheritance technically passed through the eldest son, early modern parents generally tried to make some provision for all their children, tending to give money and 'moveables' (possessions of various kinds) to their daughters, and land to their sons. This was less unfavourable at a time when the value of land and possessions (bed-linen, furniture, pans, cutlery, domestic implements) was much closer than it is now. Legacies to unmarried daughters served as contributions towards their marriage portions or dowries, and these were important at every social level: a daughter of wealthy parents might be left a substantial sum of money, while a daughter of a poor family might inherit in kind—perhaps a two-year-old heifer, two pewter dishes (the poor ate off wooden plates), and two swarms of bees. At marriage, both partners would contribute whatever they could collect, ranging from a fortune to a few pots and pans, to the new household. Commonly a couple would come from similar backgrounds, though marriage was one way in which a young man could suddenly upgrade his financial prospects. Wealthy, well-endowed widows were much sought after (as Jonson's comedies suggest), while marriages that brought no financial benefit were attributed to love, or even to lust. When Shakespearean heroines marry penniless gentlemen (as do Portia and Imogen), the young men's virtues and good birth become part of the transaction. For a woman, virtue in the narrowly technical sense of virginity (also chastity, or honesty) was a part of the 'credit' that she brought into the marriage, and her sexual and financial assets were liable to be conflated. Popular legend had it that poor girls were sexually generous, though when virginity was all they had, it was in their interests to preserve it: Shakespeare's poor goatherd, Audrey, prays the gods to make her 'honest' (*As You Like It*, III. iii. 33–4). The (male) expectation that brides should be virgins at marriage was universal, and is dramatized in *Much Ado about Nothing*, while *The Changeling* includes a special virginity-testing kit (Act IV, Scenes i and ii).

Since a married woman lost her rights in her own property (being deemed 'covert baron', i.e. under the jurisdiction of her husband), including the right to make her own will, pre-marital settlements were essential to provide protective mechanisms for children by earlier marriages, or in the event of widowhood. These arrangements enabled a wife to retain property or wealth by special exemption, by proxy, or through a trust, thus insuring her somewhat against bad management on the part of her husband. Although such arrangements could not be made under Common Law, they were enforceable in a court of equity such as Chancery. The legal position of wives later deteriorated as the Common Law took over from other forms of law, Chancery declined into Dickensian chaos, and acts from 1670 on limited widows' claims to their husbands' property. In early modern England single women and widows possessed or recovered legal rights, and so could leave wills, and these often make particular provision for female kinsfolk, or even the female poor, as if women were particularly conscious of their own vulnerability to poverty: Agnes, the wealthy widow of Philip Henslowe, manager of the Rose Theatre, left twenty pounds plus a further forty shillings a year to eighty poor widows and women living in the liberty of the Clink, in the parish of St Saviour. Lady Anne Clifford's diary records her lifelong struggle to retain her estates in Westmoreland; in this, she was supported by her mother and various ladies at court, apparently including Queen Anne, who was herself in conflict with James as to how and where their children should be brought up.

If, in the legal context, women were scarcely answerable for themselves, in matters of religion their position was rather different. Though excluded from Church government, they were expected to have beliefs, and because these were subject to divine, rather than human, law they were treated with greater respect. Where freedom of (religious) conscience was concerned, women's rights were upheld even when they differed from those of their husbands, and during the Civil War some women would accept their 'motions of conscience' as calls to public action. It was obvious both to the reformers and to the Catholic Church that the obedience required in other spheres of activity was particularly problematic in matters of faith. Erasmus, in common with his contemporaries, took the view that a wife was not obliged to obey if she was ordered to do something 'contrary to faith or good manners' by her husband; 'if he persists in wishing to be obeyed, remember that it is better to obey God than man'.[11] Martin Luther, in a lecture on how far temporal authority should be obeyed, argued that the political subject was no more committed to unquestioning obedience to the state in matters contrary to faith than was a wife towards her husband. The political subject had a right to the same freedom to disobey as had traditionally belonged to wives.

'Resistance theory', that is, arguments for civil disobedience in defence of freedom of conscience and worship, was not regularly based on the analogous right of wives to disobey evil instructions, but such claims were suggestive, and obedience to a state began to be qualified according to its moral values, so that corrupt or oppressive regimes might or even ought, to be resisted. The domestic analogy was not developed, but a number of plays of the period focus upon women resisting sexual oppression backed up by social enforcement, on the lines of the biblical story of Susannah, falsely accused by the elders, or the Roman story of Lucretia, raped by Tarquin: Antony Munday's *Death of Robert, Earl of Huntingdon* (1598) has Matilda resisting the lecherous approaches of King John, while Isabella resists

Angelo in *Measure for Measure* (1604), and the Lady resists the Tyrant in Middleton's *The Second Maiden's Tragedy* (1611). In situations of this type, disobedience is perceived as a positive virtue, an expression of the soul's resistance to worldly oppression, taking its place within a long tradition of Christian martyrdom.

The right to self-determination, which might include the right to disobey, was conceded to wives within a religious context, but in a secular situation it was out of order: the two discourses clash dramatically in Act II, Scene iii of *The Winter's Tale*, where Paulina, acting as witness and truth-speaker, is dismissed by Leontes as an archetypal insubordinate wife, as a 'witch', 'bawd', 'crone', 'callat' (i.e. procurer), and 'gross hag' who deserves to be burned, the punishment reserved for heretics. 'Chastity, silence and obedience' were the traditional womanly virtues, and for obtrusive or repeated offences against them, women were summoned to account in the ecclesiastical courts, which also handled cases of adultery, fornication, and slander. Scolds, that is, women who disturbed the peace by publicly abusing their family or neighbours, were punished with primitive brutality, being gagged with a metal bridle or 'ducked', forced underwater on the 'ducking (or 'cucking') stool', as witches were. Women could be whipped as 'whores' or made to confess their sins before the congregation, clothed only in a sheet. Communities also resorted to unofficial action against women who beat their husbands or were unfaithful; this took the form of the 'charivari' or 'skimmington ride' (so called because the skimming ladle, used in the dairy, was regarded as an exclusively female implement, like the distaff). In such rituals a surrogate of the victim was paraded, either in effigy or acted by a next-door neighbour in drag, facing backwards on horseback through the streets, with a great deal of 'rough music'—the banging of pots and pans, gunshots, and cat-calls, sometimes ending in physical violence against the victim herself. Indeed, such incidents have only been recorded when the persecuted couple made a legal complaint.

The most poignant of society's victims were those accused of witchcraft. Like scolding, men could also be punished for this, but witches were far more often lonely or demented women, 'commonly old, lame, blear-eyed, pale, foul [ugly] and full of wrinkles; poor, sullen, superstitious . . . They are lean and deformed, showing melancholy in their faces . . . They are doting, scolds, mad, devilish', explained Reginald Scott, whose *Discoverie of Witchcraft* (1584) attempted to expose the imaginary nature of the crime; he was in turn attacked by James VI of Scotland (later King of England) in his *Demonologie* (1597). English witchcraft trials were less brutal and on an altogether smaller scale than their European equivalents, but even so there were some unpleasant episodes involving group denunciations, trials, and hangings, in addition to unrecorded, unofficial actions against suspected witches by local villagers. Witchcraft's supposed connection with the diabolic pact, a formal contract made with the devil, as set out in the *Malleus Maleficarum* of 1486, gave it a wider and more sinister significance than individual acts of harming or healing might have had: witches were believed to prevent cows or women from lactating, and butter from churning, and to be able to make people and animals sicken, sometimes to death, but their powers were often no more than the converse of the powers of healing that they were credited with. Association with diabolic power made witchcraft more frightening in a society already inclined to regard the world as a battlefield between God and the devil. Pacts with the devil were a popular subject for ballads and theological pamphlets, and were potentially highly dramatic, as the runaway success of Marlowe's *Dr Faustus* suggests. James I's obsessive interest in the topic was reflected in the sub-plot of Ben Jonson's *Masque of Queens* (1609), where the witches embody a threat to social order, as they do in Shakespeare's *Macbeth* (1606) and Middleton's *The Witch* (1612). The most complex dramatic treatment occurs in *The Witch of Edmonton* (by Dekker, Ford, and Rowley, 1621), based on the trial of one Elizabeth Sawyer. Within the play, her wretchedness exposes her to diabolic temptation and a desire for revenge that her familiar, the Dog, promises to fulfil. The play is carefully balanced between superstitious and rational explanations.

Threatening Sexuality

David Underdown has argued that there was an increase in the prosecution of women for various forms of disruptive behaviour after 1600, especially of scolds and witches, and that this reflects some kind of crisis in gender relations, perhaps resulting indirectly from the economic pressures of the 1590s, in which loud-mouthed women served as convenient scapegoats—though this interpretation has been hotly debated. Scolding or cursing were, however, ways of registering resentment or dissatisfaction open to the otherwise powerless, though in the form of curses, words might gather a degree of psychic force. Reginald Scot thought that the chief fault of witches was that they *were* scolds; evidently loud expressions of resentment laid women open to accusations. The symbolism of the skimmington ride emphasized the disorder or inversion that resulted when women beat or humiliated men: the rider was seated facing backwards on horseback, a man dressed as a woman and wielding female implements; everyone could join in the deliberately discordant 'rough music'. Such celebrations of misrule imply the reassertion of a familiar underlying order. The threat of a breakdown of social order occasioned by female misconduct is also apparent from popular literature, though here the criticism has shifted from impudent speech to impudent sexual behaviour. Like today's tabloids, popular pamphlets painted lurid portraits of adulterous wives and prostitutes who murdered or aborted their unwanted children; they were seen as agents of the devil, reduced to monstrosity by their unregulated desires. Apocalyptic visions of a chaos fuelled by women's lusts also occur in Shakespearean tragedy, as Timon denounces the Athenians at the beginning of Act IV, or King Lear equates hell with female sexuality ('there's hell, there's darkness, / There is the sulphurous pit . . .', IV. vi. 127–8), though both speakers are evidently deranged, and far from any normal state of mind. A number of independent sources in literature and public records suggest that a widespread demonization of women in general, and of female sexuality in particular, occurred in the earliest years of the seventeenth century, perhaps reflecting the recognition that women could never fully render the obedience or self-effacement called for by the patriarchal ideal.

A shift from scatological to sexual joking in the drama written between the mid- and late sixteenth century provides a further example of this preoccupation, while in no way explaining it. Unfocused paranoia about female sexuality is one staple of the cheap pamphlets that combined sensational news with moral condemnation. The scandal of Alice Arden, who in 1551 took a lover and murdered her husband, was retold by the chronicler Raphael Holinshed, reaching the stage as the tragedy of *Arden of Faversham* (1591). The treachery of adulterous wives is also central to Heywood's *A Woman Killed with Kindness* (1603), and *The Revenger's Tragedy* (1606), where the degenerate Duchess takes her own stepson as lover. Marriage acted as a focus for fears concerning women's sexual susceptibilities, since a wife's chastity was essential for a man to ensure that his children were his own. To have someone else's child palmed off on you, as Soranzo almost does in Ford's *'Tis Pity She's a Whore* and Leontes fears he has in *The Winter's Tale*, was the ultimate humiliation. Popular misogyny observed

> The blind eateth many a fly
> So doth the husband often ywis [indeed]
> Father the child that is not his.[12]

Granted the hierarchic arrangement of family life, it was important that a man's possessions should behave as such, and not make him look a fool in the eyes of the world. Disobedient children were bad enough, but a wayward wife was worse. Any man's wife might make him a laughing-stock by making him 'a cuckold', that is, by being unfaithful to him. Nothing was more surely guaranteed to raise a laugh on the Elizabethan stage than the mention of horns, the traditional invisible accompaniment of being cuckolded. Everyone, supposedly, could see a man's horns apart from himself, and the whole community might be laughing at him behind his back and making horn signs with their fingers until the scandal came out in the open—when a neighbour nailed a set of horns to his door, or started a riding in which the horse (or the neighbour) wore the horns that were rightly his. Anxiety about being cuckolded could reach pathological proportions, as is apparent from Jonson's portrait of the merchant Kitely (originally called Thorello, and a likely source for Othello's name) in *Every Man in His Humour*, and the even more alarming figure of Corvino in *Volpone*, who seems to dread and desire his horns with equal violence. Its tragic implications are explored in *Othello* and *The Winter's Tale*.

Being cuckolded was not merely painful in itself, exposing a husband to derision for failing to keep his household in good order; it also threatened the wider social order. A husband's adultery, on the other hand, did not arouse comparable resentment or disruption. If chastity was the chief virtue required of women, that of men was courage, and courage was no more to be expected in women than chastity was to be expected in men; the absence of the chief virtue of the opposite sex was a correspondingly trivial fault. Many men, including noblemen and kings, brought up illegitimate children whom they openly acknowledged and made provision for in their wills—Edmund's position in *Lear* is uncomfortable rather than unusual. A double standard operated, insisting that women should be virgins at marriage, and subsequently chaste, while attitudes to male promiscuity were more relaxed. Although the Church theoretically condemned all forms of sexual misconduct, in practice men's status and position did not depend on this aspect of their behaviour as women's did. Different expectations were enshrined in language in the narrowed meanings of 'credit', 'honesty' and 'honour', to refer specifically to women's chastity and good sexual reputation, whereas they were applied to men in more general (and more modern) senses.

Women's sexuality was both literally and metaphorically invisible, an unknown quantity, and one that might prove threatening, or even uncontrollable, if daughters were not carefully guarded by their fathers, and wives by their husbands—the supposed 'wantonness' of widows was a further indication of women's need for male authority. Women's 'frailty' is reflected in the use of 'whore' as the commonest of insults, a universal smear-word gendered as exclusively female. The corresponding male insults—'bawd', 'whoremaster', 'cuckold'—reflect rather on the conduct of the women around them than on the men thus insulted. So extensive was the assumption of women's sexual guilt that sexual charges brought against men by women, for harassment, assault, seduction, or rape, commonly foundered because women's reputations were so easily blackened, and accusations of complicity were difficult to disprove. It was often simpler for a woman to accept and admit sexual guilt in the course of bringing a charge against a man, even in circumstances where to do so was obviously inappropriate.

It is difficult to find a comprehensive explanation for the widespread fears of disorderly female sexuality, though they are likely to have been displaced from fears concerning a shift in the balance of power within marriage, perhaps registering women's increasing independence in urban or cloth-making contexts. It has been explained in terms of a reaction against feminine freedom and assertiveness in the real world, or attributed to the fear that they might reproduce their physiological disorderliness in social terms. Contemporary medical theory viewed women's sexuality as an inverted version of men's, since theories as to how the body functioned were predicated on the way male bodies worked. Women's bodies were seen as identical but less fully developed than men's, and the female sexual organs were regarded as unformed, upside-down versions of the male organs, the womb and the vagina forming an undescended, inside-out penis, with the ovaries corresponding to the testicles. A lack of vital heat was supposed to have prevented women's organs from turning outward, as they appeared in the perfectly formed body of the man. Consequently women were supposed to experience orgasms and release seed in the same way as men did, if rather more slowly, since they were altogether more watery, cold, and less complete. It was widely believed (though denied by Aristotle) that women could not conceive without the orgasm supposed to accompany the shedding of the seed, so that husbands were advised to give pleasure to their wives as an aid to con-

ception. This popular assumption may have added to the difficulties of bringing claims against sexual abusers. In practice,
cases of rape when they occurred were brought by fathers or
husbands and treated as versions of theft against property.
Women without any official male protectors were legally the
most vulnerable in society.

The emphasis on women's sexual guilt (vividly evoked in
Shakespeare's poem *The Rape of Lucrece*) produced a counter-
balancing need for women to preserve their sexual reputations
with care, and if necessary to defend themselves from slander in
the ecclesiastical courts. Talking or 'gadding abroad' could be
read as symptoms of unchastity, signs of the too open female
body, since women's place was in the home and silence was
traditionally recommended. In practice, women's work often
required them to display an assertiveness at odds with such
expectations, and many of their domestic duties could only be
performed outside the home. Sixteenth-century books of husbandry listed among women's tasks winnowing, making hay, and
going to market to sell their produce and to buy 'all manner of
necessary things belonging to a household'.[13] Such transactions
involved 'cheapening' or bargaining to get the best price. Effectiveness in the market-place might be difficult to distinguish
from 'shrewishness' or assertiveness, condemned at home. An
old proverb warned prospective husbands: 'Better [marry] a
shrew than a sheep.' Women themselves may have come to place
greater emphasis on the virtue of chastity than that of obedience, since obedience was less easily observed in the course of
carrying out their daily tasks. Shakespeare's *Merry Wives of
Windsor* (1597) suggests that middle-class wives were prepared
to police one another's sexual conduct, while refusing to lower
their spirits to submissiveness:

> Wives may be merry, and yet honest too:
> We do not act that often jest and laugh . . .
>   (IV. ii. 105–6)

Anxieties over women's sexuality are sharply reflected in
Shakespeare's plays, where sexual slander against women is life-

threatening even in comedy, and no good woman is unchaste. In the poems, Venus's unrestrained desire is characterized as 'lust' (rather than love), and contrasted with the perfect chastity of the unfortunate Lucrece. Victorian critics were grateful for Shakespeare's emphasis on the importance of chastity, the virtue still considered most proper to womanhood, and were correspondingly unhappy about his heroines' uninhibited discussions of sexuality. Apart from a small group of anomalous women like Gertrude, Cressida, and perhaps Cleopatra, it is only the monsters—Tamora, Margaret of Anjou, Goneril and Regan—who break the sexual rules, though the suspicion that there might be different ways of thinking about women's conduct occurs near the end of *Cymbeline*, when Posthumus, who has earlier rejected the 'woman's part' in himself, contemplates the fact that he has commanded the murder of the woman he loved only because he believed her unfaithful. He addresses the audience directly:

> You married ones,
> If each of you should take this course, how many
> Must murther wives much better than themselves
> For wrying but a little!
>
> (v. i. 2–5)

The notion that the unforgivable crime of adultery might be reduced to 'wrying [i.e. turning or deviating] but a little' seems a significant break with the values of the day, though Posthumus only reaches this view when he is confident that Imogen has paid for her sin with her life.

Shakespeare's plays, it has been observed, were the products of an entertainment industry from which women were excluded as actors, writers, or stage-hands, yet a recent study of playhouse wills shows that widows inherited and held shares in theatrical companies, as well as acting as gatherers (i.e. collecting admission fees) and investors, and, at the lower end of the scale, they probably sold food, made costumes, and cleaned up. But their crucial influence was as consumers: the presence of women among playhouse audiences is first mentioned in 1577, and thereafter is regularly recorded until the closure of the playhouses in 1642, as well as being reflected in the drama's representation of women and women's points of view. Within Shakespeare's work alone there is a clear and rapid development from the homilies on obedience spoken by Luciana in *The Comedy of Errors* and Kate at the end of *The Taming of the Shrew*, to the wise authority of the Princess of France in *Love's Labours Lost* or the witty disdain of Beatrice in *Much Ado about Nothing*. That shift is most easily explained in terms of a response to market forces. It has advanced considerably further in Fletcher's *The Woman's Prize, or The Tamer Tam'd* (1611), a play written as a sequel to *The Taming of the Shrew*: here Petruchio's second wife, Maria, sets an example to her companions by refusing to sleep with him until he submits himself to her rule. The women sing

> Let this health be a seal,
> For the good of the common-weal
> The woman shall wear the breeches.
>
> (II. vi.)

During the first two decades of the seventeenth century the drama reached a high-water mark in terms of its positive representation of women and women's values, whether humorously, as in *The Woman's Prize*, or more seriously, through memorable heroines such as Isabella in *Measure for Measure* (1604), Marston's *Sophonisba, or The Wonder of Women* (1605), the Lady of Middleton's *Second Maiden's Tragedy* (1611), and Webster's *Duchess of Malfi* (1614), though all can be matched by contrasting representations of women's folly and wickedness.

Representing Themselves

The question of women's moral equality was as keenly debated in the Renaissance as their intellectual equality has been in the twentieth century. Collections of misogynist sayings and tales were countered with lists and lives of virtuous women from the Bible and the classics. By the sixteenth century, defences had come to outnumber attacks, although the majority of the contributors on both sides were men. The debate over women's nature spread into more general discussions of conduct, such as Castiglione's *The Courtier*, and on to the stage. Attacks were mounted in Robert Greene's *A Calling Carde for Philautus and all Fond Lovers* and Thomas Nashe's *Anatomie of Absurditie*. On the opposite side, one Jane Anger published her *Protection for Women* in 1589, a strongly argued defence against the snarling satirists. Most provocative of all was Joseph Swetnam's *An Arraignment of Lewde, idle, froward, and unconstant women* (1615), which rehearsed a series of familiar arguments at tedious length, and prompted at least three vigorous refutations by women during the next two years.

Rachel Speght's *A Muzzle for Melastomus* (i.e. a foulmouth) seems to have been the first of these. Speght was exceptional in writing under her own name; she represented herself as young in years and knowledge, since what knowledge she had was 'the fruit of such vacant hours as I could spare from affairs befitting my sex',[14] although she proved herself more learned than Swetnam, whom she refuted point by point. The second response, *Ester hath hang'd Haman* by 'Ester Sowernam',[15] was written by someone familiar with the earlier contributions to the debate. She identified Swetnam's extensive borrowings, and dismissed his charges, suggesting that his women readers were gratified 'that men have no more able a champion'. She argued that if men were going to lay claim to moral superiority, they would have to make more of an effort to justify themselves in terms of their own behaviour. The third rebuttal, Constantia Munda's *The Worming of a mad Dogge*, took the form of an attack, rather than a defence. Swetnam's pamphlet had been entitled 'An Arraignment', and Ester Sowernam had turned his title against him in order to stage her own 'Arraignment' of him. By 1618 the pamphlet debate had reached the public stage in the form of an engaging comedy, *Swetnam the Woman-hater Arraigned by Women*. Swetnam's trial provides the climax of the sub-plot, while in the main plot the lovers compete in generosity with one another as each attempts to save the other's life by claiming responsibility for their condemned love affair. The play is anonymous, and it would be tempting to suppose its author was a woman, had there been any evidence that women wrote for the public stage before the 1660s.

Constantia Munda had argued that Swetnam stretched the 'antithesis . . . betwixt a warrior and a lover' in order merely 'to show the difference betwixt a man and a woman'.[16] *Swetnam the Woman-hater* seems to pick up her argument, for Swetnam is represented as a fencing-master preoccupied with displaying the virility that he privately doubts, whereas at least two of the women in the play behave with 'masculine' courage. In 1620 a pair of pamphlets took such arguments a step further: *Hic Mulier* ('This he-woman') attacked current fashions for 'mankind' (i.e. mannish) women, who dressed like, or sometimes as, men in doublets and broad-brimmed hats and carried daggers. *Hic Mulier* was answered a week later by *Haec Vir* ('This she-man'), which argued that women had been driven to adopt male dress by men's effeminacy, and their enfeebling preoccupation with love and courtship (supposed to make men weak and womanish), rather than with the traditional male virtues of courage and martial valour, virtues out of fashion at the court of James the Peacemaker. The pamphlet boldly dismisses custom as 'an idiot', proclaiming that women 'are as free-born as men, have as free election and as free spirits'. In practice this was far from the case: some years earlier one real-life cross-dresser, Mary or Moll Frith, had been celebrated in Dekker and Middleton's comedy *The Roaring Girl* (1611). Moll sat on the stage during one of the performances, and afterwards sang a song, as a result of which she was summoned by the ecclesiastical courts for indecent behaviour.

Women's contributions to the controversy over their nature, defending their sex and answering their male critics, reflect a gradual dawning of confidence in their distinctive position, and a desire to articulate it and share it with other women. Their writings in other genres record a similar development: their first attempts were modest and tentative, as often as not couched in the self-effacing mode of translation, but gradually a stronger sense of solidarity and of the particular nature and value of women's social behaviour begins to emerge, speeding up as the seventeenth century progresses. The variety of their experiments cannot be easily summarized, but they displayed a marked interest in dramatic writing, perhaps because it did not require the use of a single authoritative voice, offering instead a variety of positions which gave scope for, but did not need to include, personal feeling. Joanna Lumley, a shining example of the best that humanist education might achieve, wrote mainly in Latin, but she was also the first person (not merely the first woman) to translate a Greek play into English: Euripides's *Iphigeneia in Aulis* told the tale of a young woman who sacrificed herself for the good of her country, and demonstrated the moral strength of the young and vulnerable.

Mary Sidney, Countess of Pembroke, was Philip's sister, to whom he had dedicated his *Arcadia*; she was herself a distinguished poet, and translated Robert Garnier's play *Marc-Antoine* from the French. This is a closet drama, intended for reading or private performance, in which dialogue and choric verse alternate, and the action is reported rather than performed. Though slow-moving by comparison with stage plays, Sidney's *Tragedie of Antonie* (1590) brings out the lovers' inner conflicts and the irresistible nature of their love, within a stoic framework that defines passion as a source of unhappiness and clouded judgement. Sidney also wrote poetry, including elegies for her brother, a pastoral dialogue ('In Praise of Astraea'), and a poem comparing the Queen to David, as the author of the Psalms. She had begun composing metrical versions of the Psalms with her brother Philip, but two-thirds of them were completed after his death, and gradually revised over ten years, a labour of scholarship and piety that also required artistic sensibility. Elizabeth Cary took a step further in writing an original play, *The Tragedie of Mariam* (1604)—its unusual heroine was Herod's second wife whom he had unjustly executed. The play focuses upon the question of women's obedience, as Mariam advances from love and submission to arguing the case for resistance against tyranny. The theme of women's resistance, dramatized by Shakespeare through Cordelia and Paulina, may have been connected with Cary's Catholicism, though earlier in the century it had been more closely associated with Protestant resistance.

Lumley, Sidney, and Cary came from privileged backgrounds and had benefited from humanist education, but the poet Aemilia Lanyer was the daughter of one court musician, and wife to another. In her poem *Salve Deus Rex Judaeorum* (1611) she celebrated feminine companionship and tenderness through the figures of Eve, Pilate's wife, and the Virgin Mary, associating the Women of Jerusalem who tried to save Christ with the great court ladies of her day. Her poem ends with 'The description of Cooke-ham', an elegy for a lost Eden that she had found in the company of the Countess of Cumberland and her daughter, the diarist Anne Clifford, in what may be the earliest example of a country-house poem.

The most versatile and productive of the age's women writers was another court lady, Mary Sidney's niece Mary Wroth, who composed a pastoral play, *Love's Victory*, a sonnet sequence, and a full-scale Arcadian romance, studded with poems: *The Countess of Montgomery's Urania* was published in 1621 but soon afterwards withdrawn, accused of libel. Wroth went on to compose a sequel to the *Urania*, but like her play it remained unpublished. She deliberately reworked the forms made famous by her uncle, Philip Sidney, transforming them into expressions of feminine sensibility and values. Her heroine Pamphilea represents constancy and endurance in love, while Amphilanthus is characterized by his 'pretty humour of changing'. His sister Urania warns Pamphilea that her constancy 'hath limits to hold it in': she should not be wasting her devotion upon the unappreciative and fickle Amphilanthus, but rather turn to the love of God, a progression delicately suggested in the sonnet sequence that rounds off the book. Through the medium of romance, Mary Wroth addressed one of the major fault-lines in contemporary social attitudes, the difference between male and female ways of thinking about sexual behaviour. While there was no pressure on men to avoid promiscuity, women's virtue con-

sisted chiefly in fidelity and constancy. Her romance plays out
the painful effects of this rift on the lives of individuals, assess-
ing its emotional cost from a woman's point of view. While she
could do nothing to alter women's situation, her unflinchingly
feminine view of the battlefield is at once subtle and moving in
itself, as well as being a promise of what later women novelists
would eventually do with such themes.

4

Other Peoples, Other Lands

THOMAS MORE's dialogue *Utopia* (1517) consists of an imaginary
debate between More himself, his friend the Flemish humanist
Peter Giles, and a fictional traveller, Raphael Hythloday, who
has visited Utopia (translatable either as 'no place' or 'good
place'). Hythloday is introduced as a Portuguese, a man who had
accompanied Amerigo Vespucci on one of his famous voyages
to the New World, and had been left behind in Brazil. He has
come across Utopia in his wanderings. The egalitarian and com-
munistic state of Utopia, while providing a commentary on the
practices of Tudor England, also catches up significant aspects of
the voyages of Columbus and his successors. Their encounters
with the peoples of the Americas and with their different languages, cultures, religions, and social organizations, challenged
assumptions—ultimately derived from Aristotle—that human
life everywhere was governed by certain universal laws. In particular, Utopia avoided war and property-holding; it had no
knowledge of the Christian faith and no respect for gold, which
was used only for objects of shame—chamber-pots or prison
fetters. The many literary treatments of the New World that followed constantly returned to a few distinctive features of More's
imaginary country: the possibility of an alternative society; the
absence of God; the presence of gold (which the Utopians
hoarded yet despised). The Americas offered imaginative spaces
on to which Europeans projected the desires that their culture
had aroused yet failed to satisfy: desires for a more just society;
for the proper exercise of authority, whether religious or civil;
but above all, for instant and limitless wealth.

Attitudes to the New World

Far from being a blank space that appeared on European maps, the Americas were inhabited by a variety of peoples, speaking many different languages, and living in many different kinds of community; but the European invaders, trapped within their own limited experience, could only interpret them in the light of inappropriate stereotypes: in appearance, the native Americans reminded them of the traditional 'wild men' of medieval and Renaissance literature, who lived in the woods in 'a state of nature'. Childlike themselves, the Europeans assumed that the peoples they met were childish because they could not speak Spanish, or were interested in objects regarded as toys or trifles by the Europeans (according to Thomas Harriot, they 'do esteem our trifles before things of greater value'). While the native American cultures were complex, varied, and highly organized, the Europeans preferred to regard them as 'primitive', inferior to themselves in terms of civic development and religion (Harriot thought that 'they may in short time be brought to civility, and the embracing of true religion').[1] Thomas Harriot's *Briefe and True Report of the New Found Land in Virginia* (1588), an attempt to encourage prospective settlers from England, was later reprinted with pictures by John White, 'to show how that the inhabitants of the great Brittany have been in times past as savage as those of Virginia'.[2]

Because the concept of historical change itself was often regarded as a process of decay, the native Americans could also be thought of as belonging to a better, because an earlier, social order. The Italian chronicler on Columbus's expedition, Peter Martyr, thought that 'these folks should be the happiest in the world, if only they knew God': 'they seem to live in that golden world of which the old writers speak so much, wherein men lived simply and innocently, without enforcement of laws, without quarrelling, judges, and libels, content only to satisfy nature, without further vexation for knowledge of things to come.'[3] Montaigne also thought of the New World as a golden age, or else at the stage of innocence or infancy: 'If we are right to infer the end of our world . . . this other world will only be coming into the light when ours is leaving it.' He added, with painful foresight, 'I am much afraid that we shall have very greatly hastened the decline and ruin of this New World by our contagion, and that we will have sold it our opinion and our arts very dear' ('Of Coaches', *Essays*, p. 693).

The Spanish invaders had dealt with the peoples of the New World either by treating them as children to be tricked, bullied, or cajoled, or else as rebellious adults to be coerced by captivity, torture, and execution. According to the most reductive view, the 'Indian' (as Columbus had supposed the native Americans) was a ' dumb brute created for our service'. The missionary friars who accompanied the expeditions strongly resisted that position, seeing them rather as 'children of God', potential Christian souls to be saved, and in 1537 their view was officially adopted by the Catholic Church. As long as the labour and co-operation of the native Americans was required to work the silver mines, it was more convenient, as well as more comfortable, for the Europeans to think of them as tractable and capable of learning. If the native Americans could be persuaded to accept the true faith and European rule, as children and peasants had learned to do at home, they might take their proper place in the Christian community; but, like children and peasants, they were in need of firm and confident discipline.

Only a man like Montaigne, capable of thinking himself free of the assumptions of his society, questioned the values thus brutally imposed, and even he believed that cannibalism was practised in Brazil. A detailed account of supposed cannibal practices, derived from conversations with a (possibly imaginary) South American Indian in France, led him to judge their society superior in courage and decency to his own: 'I am not sorry that we notice the barbarous horror of such acts, but I am heartily sorry that, judging their faults rightly, we should be so blind to our own'. He proceeded to denounce the cruelties and tortures inflicted during the Wars of Religion in his own time and country, 'not among ancient enemies but among neighbours and fellow citizens, and what is worse, on the pretext of piety and religion' (*Essays*, p. 155). In this essay, 'Of Cannibals', Montaigne takes up a point first made by the Spanish historian, Bartolomé de Las Casas, who had accompanied Columbus on his first voyage: 'each man calls barbarism whatever is not his own practice; for indeed it seems we have no other test of truth and reason than the example and pattern of the opinions and custom of the country we live in. *There* is always the perfect religion, the perfect government, the perfect and accomplished manners in all things' (*Essays*, p. 152).

In a much later essay, 'Of Coaches', Montaigne denounced the conquest of Mexico by Hernando Cortés (1521) and the overthrow of the Inca kingdom of Peru by Pizarro (1531) far more explicitly, showing how, in both episodes, integrity and good faith on the part of the native Americans had been met not merely with betrayal and treachery, but with gratuitous cruelty and killing on the part of their conquerors. European claims to Christianity and superior civilization collapsed in the face of the atrocities they had committed: 'they not only admit them but boast of them and preach them. Would it be as a testimonial to their justice or their zeal for religion?' (*Essays*, p. 697). In Montaigne's view, the Americans belonged to a younger, better, and more heroic world, characterized by communal ownership, social equality, and harmony with nature. The loss of these virtues was part of the high price to be paid for civilization, which offered more sophisticated technology at the cost of increasing moral corruption. The extent of European degeneration had never and nowhere been so fully displayed as it was in the conquest of the New World: 'Who ever set the utility of commerce and trading at such a price? So many cities razed, so many nations exterminated, so many millions of people put to the sword, and the richest and most beautiful part of the world turned upside down, for the traffic in pearls and pepper!' (*Essays*, p. 695). But Montaigne's rhetoric was exceptional in counting the human cost. For most of Europe, the Spanish empire in Central and South America and the enormous wealth it generated was primarily the source of an envy that was easy to reconcile with moral disapproval.

English Exploration

The English, although geographically and historically a maritime nation, had scarcely involved themselves in the early voyages to the New World, which had been piloted by Italian navigators and financed by Spanish and Portuguese money. Sebastian Cabot, the Bristol-born son of a Venetian pilot, reached the northern shores of the American continent at the end of the fifteenth century, but during the first half of the sixteenth century, when Spain was establishing an empire in Central and South America, English merchants were concentrating upon more local enterprises, such as selling their woollen cloth to Flanders. Yet by the 1570s a belated age of discovery had begun, with English ships searching for new routes to the East, and attacking Spanish treasure ships on the high seas (Spain's New World silver mines had paid for fleets and standing armies). These voyages, like the earliest English plantations in the New World, coincided with the success of the public theatres in the last years of the sixteenth century, inviting comparison between these two commercial ventures, both of which depended upon the exercise of imagination, if in very different ways. Both were fuelled by a sense of growing nationalism, partly defined by religious and political rivalry with Spain; other factors were strong financial incentives, opportunities for exercising talent and acquired skills, and the excitement of exploration. Since then, both the drama and maritime adventure have been regarded as sources of national pride, and this has coloured our view of them.

For the Victorians, the Elizabethan voyagers were their heroic forebears, figuring in a glorious history of the British empire, as represented in Millais's painting of *The Boyhood of Raleigh*, Newbolt's poem on the sinking of the *Revenge*, and the legends of Drake playing bowls and singeing the King of Spain's beard. Yet the earliest and most influential collection of voyage narratives had been assembled to compensate for their slow start: 'I both heard in speech, and read in books other nations miraculously extolled for their discoveries and notable enterprises by sea, but the English of all others for their sluggish security, and continual neglect of the like attempts especially in so long and happy a time of peace, either ignominiously reported, or exceedingly condemned.'[4] In this dedicatory letter, Richard Hakluyt posed the question of whether English exploration genuinely lacked enterprise, or whether it had merely failed to advertise itself sufficiently. Meanwhile he set himself to repair the damage by making the fullest possible compilation of English achievements in the field. The first edition of his *Principal Navigations, Voyages, Traffics and Discoveries of the English Nation* (1589) was a substantial folio volume of more than 800 pages, while the second (1598–1600) ran to three volumes. The historical and patriotic aspects of his undertaking appealed to the Victorian imagination—Hakluyt's aims seemed to provide a programme for their own vast maritime empire. A Hakluyt Society was founded in 1846. Reviewing its earliest publications, the historian James Froude described *Principal Navigations* as 'the great prose epic of the modern English nation', a phrase which tells us more about Victorian narratives of empire than about the book itself.

Hakluyt collected and published the reports of other men. As he liked to remind his readers, he had spent long years of toil and 'travail' in assembling them, though he never actually travelled further than France, and most of his hardships were endured in libraries or suffered by his pocket. He corresponded assiduously with travellers, explorers, and the great map-makers, Mercator and Ortelius, and he collected and collated as many records of newly discovered lands as came his way. He translated Peter Martyr's *De Orbe Novo* from the Spanish, and wrote *A Discourse of Western Planting*, an advertisement on behalf of Sir Walter Raleigh's projected Virginia Plantation. He intended his collection to provide practical information both for seamen in plotting their voyages, and for the London investors who financed them. And he celebrated English virtues—the courage and stoicism evident not only in Drake's circumnavigation of the world, but in the several failures to find the North West passage or to establish viable settlements in Virginia. Ironically,

Hakluyt's own enterprise was far more successful than most of those he recorded, and his project of collecting and issuing reports was successfully carried on by Samuel Purchas in *Hakluytes Posthumus, or Purchas his Pilgrimes* (1625).

The established presence of the Portuguese spice merchants in the East Indies and beyond, and of the Spanish in the West Indies encouraged the earliest English explorers to turn northwards. On contemporary maps it looked possible to reach the East, and particularly Cathay (modern China), by sailing into the Pacific through a North-East or North-West passage, the imaginary equivalents in the northern hemisphere of the passages to the Pacific around the southernmost tips of Africa and South America. Sebastian Cabot's early hopes of English discoveries had focused on these routes. In 1553 three ships set out in search of the North-East passage. Two were trapped in the ice and their crews froze or starved 'for want of experience to have made caves and stoves', in Hakluyt's view, but the third reached Archangel on the White Sea. From there, the survivor, Richard Chancellor, travelled overland by sleigh to Moscow, where he was entertained by Ivan the Terrible. A Muscovy Company was formed, holding joint stock, and made up of nearly 200 shareholders, with the intention of establishing trade with Russia, though the distances involved made it virtually unworkable. English claims to the North-West passage were derived from Cabot's early voyage to Newfoundland: in practice, the passage itself was closed by ice and the explorers discovered little more than the ins and outs of the coastline of Greenland and Hudson's Bay.

On his first voyage in 1576 Martin Frobisher sailed to the north of Hudson's Straits, lost five of his own men, but brought back a kidnapped Inuit (who later died 'of cold which he had taken at sea'), and

a piece of black stone much like to a sea coal in colour which by the weight seemed to be some kind of metal or mineral. This was a thing of no account in the judgement of the captain at the first sight; and yet for novelty it was kept in respect of the place from whence it came. After his arrival in London, being demanded of sundry his friends what thing he had brought them home out of that country, he had nothing left to present them withal but a piece of this black stone.[5]

In true fairy-tale fashion, one of the adventurer's wives happened to throw a piece of this stone on the fire, where, after long heating (and quenching with vinegar), it 'glistered with a bright marquesite of gold'. From that (perhaps mythical) moment, the hunt for gold was on, and Frobisher sailed north-west, representing 'the Cathay Company' in 1577, and again in 1578, returning from his second voyage with 200 tons of the same black stone, and from the third with 1,700 tons of it, when it was finally identified as 'fool's gold' (that is, iron pyrites, whose tiny veins of gold did not justify the cost of extraction). There was no fourth voyage, and Frobisher instead turned his attention to Ireland, a more convenient site for aspiring colonizers.

But the hope of discovering gold was not easily abandoned: Humphrey Gilbert proclaimed Newfoundland an English colony in 1583, and was apparently hoping to establish a Catholic settlement there, although the main town of St John's was already populated by a thriving international fishing community. He too was shown a piece of ore 'seeming rather to be iron than other metal', with the promise that 'if silver were the thing which might satisfy the General and his followers, there it was'. The ore was later lost in a ship that ran aground, and Gilbert's own ship sank in a storm on the return journey. The voyage's narrator, Edward Haye, observed 'it behoveth every man of great calling . . . to examine his own motions: which if the same proceed of ambition or avarice, he may assure himself it cometh not of God, and therefore can not have confidence of God's protection and assistance against the violence (else irresistible) both of sea, and infinite perils upon the land . . .'[6] According to his view of providence, the purity of motive of those who 'go down to the sea in ships' is reflected in the outcome of their voyages, with God judging the heart, and the weather and the waves acting as His executioner.

An easier and more effective method of recovering gold from the New World was to plunder the Spanish treasure ships that carried it: this short-circuited the whole process of locating a mine and extracting its contents, and was the method preferred by Hawkins and Drake. The rivalry between England and Spain lent a patriotic colouring to their activities which otherwise suspiciously resembled piracy and theft, although the government was prepared to acknowledge their legitimacy whenever it was convenient to do so. English intervention in Spanish traffic began with the three voyages of John Hawkins, who transported people as slaves from the coast of Africa for sale in the West Indies, 'being amongst other particulars assured', as Hakluyt brutally put it, 'that Negroes were very good merchandise in Hispaniola, and that store of Negroes might easily be had upon the coast of Guinea'.[7] Only the Portuguese were licensed to conduct the horrific trade of capturing and reselling Africans as slaves to the plantations in the West Indies and Brazil, where the original population had all but died out from European ill-treatment and disease. The Queen wavered, forbidding Hawkins to break Spanish laws and denouncing his trade as 'detestable', while at the same time lending him ships, investing in his ventures, and granting him a coat of arms, bearing as its crest 'a demi-Moor [i.e. African], bound and captive'. On Hawkins's third voyage of 1569 he was sighted and pursued by the Spanish fleet at St Juan de Ulua, off the coast of Mexico. He lost three ships and more than 300 men, a hundred being put ashore for lack of provisions. The captain of the only other ship to escape was his cousin, Francis Drake.

This defeat and others, as well as his first glimpse of the Pacific in 1573, made Drake determined to explore more of South America, with a view to establishing trading posts. His 'famous voyage' around the world was completed in just under three years (1577 to 1580). He sailed round Cape Horn and up towards the Spanish mines in Peru, where he seized a Spanish treasure ship, the *Cacafuego*, taking it north with him up the Californian coast to avoid recapture. His next lap took him across the Pacific via the Moluccas and Java, the legendary spice islands in the East Indies, and he returned via the Indian Ocean and around the Cape of Good Hope. After his return, Drake continued to raid

Spanish settlements and shipping in the New World, and even in the Old World port of Cadiz, where he captured and burnt a section of the Spanish fleet lying at anchor there in 1587. In the following year Spain launched the Armada, the fleet intended to reconquer England for the Pope, and in the sea-battle that followed Drake acted as second-in-command under Admiral Howard, along with Hawkins and Frobisher. After the defeat of the Armada the English continued to harry Spanish shipping, though Drake and Hawkins both died on yet another expedition to the West Indies in 1595. A year later the Earl of Essex organized the 'Island' voyage, an attack upon the Spanish fleet in the Azores. With him went the poet John Donne, whose verse letters 'The Storm' and 'The Calm' give atmospheric accounts of sea-going from a landsman's perspective.

After Humphrey Gilbert's fatal attempt on the North-West passage in 1583, his half-brother Walter Raleigh took over the task of trying to establish an English colony in North America. This project could be justified as offering a safe haven for English privateers harrying the Spanish in the Caribbean, or as a convenient dumping ground for the excess or criminal population of England, or else as a source of crops, gold, or profitable trade with the native Americans (though some accounts of the New World preferred to represent its lands as empty and virginal, awaiting the bridegroom's kiss of possession). A first expedition discovered the island of Roanoke, off the coast of North Carolina, and in 1585 a hundred people attempted to establish a settlement there. Among them were John White and the mathematician and astronomer Thomas Harriot, who sent back a detailed report for Raleigh, its nominal governor, on this 'New found land of Virginia', describing the terrain and its people, whom (as we have seen) he underestimated.

The Algonquians were superior to the settlers in at least one crucial respect: they were self-supporting, something the earliest settlers never managed to become. Francis Bacon suggested that 'the hope of mines is very uncertain, and useth to make the planters lazy in other things' (*Essays*, p. 163). The settlers remained dependent on the Algonquians for food, and in 1586 they returned to England with Drake, when he landed there. Soon afterwards fifteen further colonizers sailed out with Sir Richard Grenville, but they had disappeared by the following year, when John White led a party of over a hundred to resettle Roanoke. White's group also consumed their resources and he returned to England for further supplies, but then found he could not get back again, because of the threat of Spain and the imminent war. When he finally returned in 1590 the 'Lost Colony' had disappeared altogether. Francis Bacon, who had no patience with Raleigh, observed: 'It is the sinfullest thing in the world to forsake or destitute a plantation once in forwardness: for, besides the dishonour, it is the guiltiness of blood of many commiserable persons.' ('Of Plantations', *Essays*, p. 164).

Although Raleigh had raised most of the money for the failed Virginia colony and had heavily invested in it, he never actually visited it, but in 1595 he set out for what promised to be a far more rewarding destination: 'Guiana' (i.e. Columbia), with 'the great and golden city of Manoa (which the Spaniards call El Dorado)'. *The Discovery of Guiana*, Raleigh's account of his expedition inland from the delta of the Orinoco in search of fabulous wealth, is among the most vivid and the most disturbing of Hakluyt's voyages. Riven with inconsistencies, it mingles a factual account of his travels with a fictional discourse of exotic and idealized lands ('I never saw a more beautiful country, nor more lively prospects . . .'[8]), in an attempt to persuade the Queen (who had not forgiven him for marrying without her permission) to invest in further expeditions, or at least to accept its promised wealth on account: he assured her, 'it seemeth to me that this empire is reserved for her Majesty and the English nation'.[9]

Behind Raleigh's search lay the myth of the limitless wealth of the garden of the sun: 'they say, the Incas had a garden of pleasure . . . which had all kinds of garden herbs, flowers and trees of gold and silver, an invention, and magnificence till then never seen'.[10] Raleigh's account also includes several traditional elements of travellers' tales concerning Amazons (mannish women ruling an all-female society), men with heads below their shoulders, and cannibals or anthropophagi. He was sufficiently convinced of the existence of his imaginary city to mount a second expedition in 1617, when under sentence of death for treason. This turned into a complete fiasco: his eldest son, Walter, was killed, and his old and trusted captain Laurence Keymis committed suicide. Raleigh himself got no further than Trinidad, being too ill to oversee the action. He returned to execution, his company having failed to honour his pledge not to fight the Spanish, with whom King James had made peace in 1604.

Though Raleigh's Roanoke colony had failed, it was the first of a series of attempts at establishing settlements on the North American coast. In Massachusetts in 1620 a group of persecuted Dutch and English separatists landed in the *Mayflower*. They were determined to make new lives for themselves, and their settlement at Plymouth became the first self-supporting English plantation on American soil, its early history being recorded in William Bradford's *Of Plymouth Plantation*. Further plantations were set up at Jamestown in Chesapeake Bay, a swampy, malaria-infested area at the mouth of the James River. Here again, either the legends of gold, or attempts to grow tobacco as a cash crop, or the presence of too many gentlemen and skilled craftsmen left the community on the verge of starvation and dependent for food on the native Americans.

The precise details of the history of the Jamestown settlement remain uncertain because their chronicler, Captain John Smith, was himself deeply implicated in the community's power struggles. He famously claimed to have interceded with the Chief Powhatan, whose daughter Pocahontas, according to one of his several accounts, saved his life. Pocahontas herself married another settler, Captain Rolfe, and in 1616 they sailed to England, where she was baptized and then died. Sporadic support for the settlement set out from England: William Strachey was wrecked on the Bermudas on his way to Jamestown in 1609, and his description of the voyage provided Shakespeare with one of the sources for *The Tempest*. Between 1618 and 1621 the Virginia company sent out more than 3,000 social outcasts, vagrants, orphans, and women, many of whom were effectively transported to the new settlement against their will. Living conditions remained difficult for the settlers and a massacre of around 350 settlers in 1622 effectively brought that phase of the plantation to an end.

Representing the Other

Like the community whose fate it dramatized, the tragedy of *The Plantation of Virginia*, performed at the Curtain Theatre in 1623, was lost, but ten years earlier its potential benefits had been dazzlingly enacted in a royal masque: on 16 February 1613 representations of native American priests and princes, and even the figure of 'El Dorado' himself—'his head and beard sprinkled with showers of gold'—arrived at the palace of Whitehall to celebrate the wedding of Princess Elizabeth to Frederick, Elector Palatine. This event, Chapman's *Masque of the Middle Temple and Lincoln's Inn*, focused unashamedly upon the figure of Plutus, the god of wealth, who conducted a torchlight procession down Chancery Lane and along the Strand. He was attended by Virginian priests of the sun, dressed in 'strange hoods of feather' and turbans decorated with butterfly wings, and accompanied by Virginian princes (the lords) in coronets decorated with 'high sprigged feathers', and by masquers dressed in silver and gold, and torch-bearers in blackface, crowned with golden wreaths.[11] Inside the palace, a scene of a rocky landscape opened up to display the setting sun and the twelve aristocratic masquers seated in a mine of gold. After this identification of 'earth's all commanding riches' with James's courtiers, the masque performed another favourite colonial fantasy as the Virginian priests converted from sun-worship to Christianity.

This extravaganza seemed to promise James and his courtiers the wealth of the Americas, but it was actually the Inns of Court who had to foot the enormous bill. Like the Virginia settlement itself, the masque consumed rather than produced the wealth it seemed to offer, multiplying itself only in the form of further representations: in the following year Campion's *Somerset Wedding Masque* included a figure of America ('in a skin coat of the colour of the juice of mulberries'), while Beaumont's *Masque of Flowers* enacted a debate on the relative virtues of wine and tobacco conducted by Silenus and the Indian god Kawasha (who wore a chimney on his head and a skirt cut in the shape of tobacco leaves).[12] Chapman's opulent imagery was itself derived from an earlier Lord Mayor's Show written for the Goldsmiths' Company, Anthony Munday's *Chruso-thriambos: The Triumphs of Gold* (1611), which also featured an Indian king and queen who praised the city and offered up their wealth, as well as a mountain of Indian gold, complete with miners.

Whether they appeared as happy labourers or as royalty, the 'Indians' that figured in the masques and pageants all paid homage to London or the court, and cheerfully surrendered their wealth, and sometimes their religion as well. Shakespeare, however, offered a rather different account of colonial relationships, in representing the first native American on the English public stage: Caliban is described in the cast list as 'a sa[l]vage and deformed slave', characterized by a sense of betrayal, and a baffled and impotent anger: 'You taught me language, and my profit on't | Is, I know how to curse' (I. ii. 363–4). Strictly speaking, *The Tempest* is set on a Mediterranean rather than a Caribbean island, but in writing it Shakespeare drew upon William Strachey's account of being shipwrecked on the Bermudas, and within it Gonzalo quotes verbatim from Montaigne's essay 'Of Cannibals' to describe the kind of ideal commonwealth that was supposed to be found or established in America. But the strongest case for reading the New World into the play lies in the character of Caliban, whose name is an anagram of 'cannibal'. This word is derived from 'caniba, carib', meaning a strong or brave people. It was picked up by Columbus who, in his ignorance, linked it with dog-faced (i.e. canine) men, the people of the Khan or Cham (the ruler of China), and with the 'anthropophagi', mythical man-eaters, supposed to live in distant lands. The very history of the word records the projection of European fears on to the peoples of the New World, whose lives and territories were themselves soon to be 'eaten up' by the invaders.

Caliban is represented in the play as the people of the New World appeared to their European oppressors: to Prospero and Miranda he is a slave, essential to their survival, yet ungrateful, threatening, and sexually rapacious; to Stephano and Trinculo he is a monster, a potential side-show whom people would pay good money to look at, at home. Yet he is also given a voice of his own, in which he denounces the injustice of his enslavement and disinheritance: 'This island's mine by Sycorax my mother, | Which thou tak'st from me' (i. ii. 331–2). Surprisingly, it is Caliban rather than the Europeans who is given a vision of the limitless wealth that regularly inspired colonizing expeditions, but in a form so transcendent, so mystically beautiful, that they would scarcely have recognized their desires within it: 'The clouds methought would open, and show riches | Ready to drop upon me . . .' (iii. ii. 141–2).

Fletcher and Massinger's play *The Sea Voyage* (1622) followed *The Tempest* closely in its opening scenes. It too drew upon Strachey's narrative of shipwreck, and showed something of the grimmer aspects of emigration as the settlers are driven to contemplate eating each other in order to survive—inevitably, it was the starving Europeans, not the native peoples, who resorted to cannibalism. But it also drew upon old fables, as the voyagers discover piles of gold upon the beach and a neighbouring island inhabited by a tribe of Amazons who need men to perpetuate their commonwealth. The Amazons, sometimes located in Africa and sometimes in America, were quite as familiar a feature of travel-writing as men-monsters with their heads beneath their shoulders; they were also famous for resisting foreign, and particularly male, conquest.

Columbus had originally named the islands where he landed off Central America, and the peoples he found there, 'Indies' and 'Indians' in the supposition that he had reached the Indian subcontinent from the other side, and these names were generally adopted. There developed some sense of symmetry between the economic opportunities promised by the East and the West Indies, 'th' Indias of spice and mine' (figured as features of a woman's body in Donne's poem 'The Sun Rising'). The mines were those discovered by the Spanish in South America, while the spices came from India and Indonesia, where Spanish, Portuguese, Dutch, and latterly English merchants were competing for influence. In 1600 the East India Company was granted a charter, and began a series of trading ventures which were potentially highly profitable, though risky for the ships and sailors involved. The Company was supported by the Grocers' Fraternity, who celebrated their connection with it in Thomas Middleton's Lord Mayor's shows for 1613, 1617, and 1622: at these events sugar-loaves, nutmegs, cloves and mace, dates, ginger, and peppers were scattered broadside, islands of spice trees floated on the Thames, and a Moorish King and Indian Queen paid homage to the City and its merchants for converting them to Christianity. The drama of conversion also provided an upbeat ending to Fletcher and Massinger's tragicomedy *The Island Princess* (1621), whose heroine, Quisara, is a pale-skinned princess of Tidore in the Moluccan Islands. Though the English were eventually to build up an extensive empire in the East, in the early stages they found themselves in competition with the Dutch, who in 1623 tried and executed ten English merchants whom they accused of conspiring to seize their fortress at Amboina. The event was celebrated in a ballad, and a play which was suppressed by the Privy Council.

The City's celebration of new markets figured as mines, spice trees, and lavishly costumed foreign princes, drew upon older tastes for the exotic. Wild men and Moors (a term used particularly of Africans, but sometimes for any people of colour) had been traditional figures in court masques and entertainments, often acting as torch-bearers, dancing and making music in 'moriscoes' (Moorish dances, later shortened to 'morris' dances) performed in blackface, or else as Soldans, Saracens, or kings of Egypt in folk-plays and mummings. A Moor riding upon a 'luzern' (lynx) introduces the earliest surviving text of a Lord Mayor's Show, George Peele's *Device of the Pageant* (1585), and he is a precursor of later figures such as that of the Indian boy mounted upon 'an estridge [ostrich] biting a horse-shoe', and carrying a tobacco pipe, who provides the third entry in

Dekker's Lord Mayor's Show of 1629. Both riders represented the value of exotic commodities to the City's economy, although the continents and commodities they represent differ, and the Indian boy himself combines incongruous elements—an African ostrich from the Old World, and a tobacco pipe from the New. He differed from the Moor in Peele's pageant in one crucial respect: the Moor was played by a white man, either wearing a fine cloth mask or else black make-up, while a contemporary illustration to Dekker's pageant suggests that the ostrich-rider was played by a black performer. Later in the seventeenth century black actors increasingly performed (or were exhibited) in city pageants, though in the theatre black roles continued to be taken by white actors.

Africans, Jews, and 'Strangers'

Although the number of people of colour in England was growing during the sixteenth century, they were still unusual enough to be treated as wonders. The Scottish court had a long tradition of employing black entertainers whom they treated as little more than performing animals: at James's marriage to Anne of Denmark, celebrated in Oslo in 1589, four young black men danced naked in the snow in front of the royal carriage, subsequently dying of cold. From the 1570s African slaves were regularly brought to England, where they were set to work as household servants to the fashionable, as prostitutes, or as dancers and musicians in court entertainments. Their numbers are difficult to estimate, but were high enough to arouse official disapproval. In the summer of 1596 the Queen sent out an order with one Edward Banes to transport ten 'blackmoors' ('of which kind of people there are already here too many')[13] out of the realm, and a week later she issued a longer edict to all public officers informing them that a merchant, Casper van Senden, had arranged for the release of eighty-nine English prisoners from Spain and Portugal in return for the right to transport an equivalent number of 'blackamoors' back there in return. She urged her subjects to comply, and behave like good Christians by surrendering their servants, and preferring 'to be served by their own countrymen than with those kind of people'. It is impossible to guess how far her subjects responded, but by 1601 she issued a further statement banishing 'the great number of niggers and blackamoors which (as she is informed) are crept into this realm . . . who are fostered and relieved here to the great annoyance of her own liege people, that want [i.e. lack] the relief which those people consume'. The intolerance of the Queen and her officials is even more distressing in view of the fact that most, if not all, of the Africans in England had been brought over by force rather than choice.

Elizabeth's edicts suggest that her society discriminated against people with different colour skin in the same way that many societies still do today; the point that 'most of them are infidels, having no understanding of Christ or his Gospel', appears as something of an afterthought in the 1601 proclamation. As a colour, blackness was associated with the devil, evildoing, and death, and from the mid-sixteenth century it reflected a new awareness of visible difference by acquiring aesthetic overtones, as the antithesis of 'fair', which had traditionally signified beautiful but now also meant 'desirably pale-skinned', thus beginning the long and insidious association of light skin with sexual attractiveness. This new concept of 'fairness' brought together racial and class prejudices. Pallor had traditionally been more highly valued and more fashionable than dark skin since it was already a measure of status: only the privileged could afford to avoid sunburn and the darkening of the skin that resulted from labour out of doors. But now difference of skin colour was defined in terms that rated pale European skins above darker complexions.

The emphasis on blackness as the antithesis of beauty in the sonnet sequences of the 1580s and '90s finds new ways of defining white skin and light hair colour as preferable, 'better', both aesthetically and morally speaking. Women with dark hair or colouring, like Rosaline in *Love's Labour's Lost*, are only attractive despite their 'blackness', while Shakespeare's sonnets to the Dark Lady play continuously on the paradox that she is sexually arousing despite her unattractive or unfashionable colouring; morally speaking, her character is as 'black' (signifying 'bad') as her looks. Both here and in the language of the comedies, there is a strict hierarchy of colour, in which paleness is always preferable to darkness: in *A Midsummer Night's Dream*, Hermia suddenly appears to her lover Lysander as an 'Ethiop' and a 'tawny Tartar', once he has fallen under Puck's spell (III. ii. 257, 263). Thus a system of visual differences which devalued darker skin at the expense of lighter came to be established within language, laying the foundations for the assumptions of superiority that were to underpin colonial attitudes.

The use of dark skin to offset the privileged European 'fairness' by contrast is evident in a number of Jacobean masques and plays: Jonson's *Masque of Blackness* (1605) is located in Africa, and in it Queen Anne and her ladies appeared as the twelve daughters of the River Niger, searching for a far-off country whose lesser sun (i.e. the King) 'forms all beauty'; in other words, this masque attributes to James the power to perform the proverbially impossible task of 'washing th' Ethiop white'. One courtier was upset at the sight of 'the Queen and some dozen ladies all painted like blackamoors, face and neck bare and for the rest strangely attired in barbaresque mantles to the half leg'.[14] According to Jonson, Queen Anne had herself proposed the subject, and she and her ladies broke with court tradition by 'blacking up', instead of wearing the more traditional black masks. As it turned out, James's wonder-working, his supposed ability to whiten their blackness and transform the alien and (supposedly) ugly into the familiar and beautiful, was postponed until *The Masque of Beauty* was presented, three years later.

On stage, black skin was particularly associated with villainy, so it is probable that Marston's heroic Carthaginian princess, Sophonisba (1605), appeared as white-skinned (while her treacherous maid Zanthia may well have been made up in blackface), and this is likely to have been the case with Shakespeare's Cleopatra, even though she is described as 'tawny' and 'a gypsy' (i.e. Egyptian), and speaks of herself as sunburnt, 'with Phoebus' amorous pinches black . . .' (i. v. 28). In *The White Devil*, Vittoria's maid Zanche (whose name and character recall Zanthia) is seen as the play's black devil, as a foil to her 'white' mistress. Zanche crudely performs the disorderly desires that her mistress is suspected of and punished for, displaying the uncontrolled sexuality widely attributed both to women and to people of different races. In men, blackness was also associated with Machiavellian scheming: the darker the skin, the worse the character. This is the offensive assumption that underlies *The Battle of Alcazar* (1589), dramatized by George Peele from an episode of recent history (1579) in which the Portuguese King Sebastian, the last of his line, was killed in North Africa while defending the claim of the wicked Muly (Ma)Hamet against his 'good' uncle Abdelmelec. Muly Hamet, 'this Negro-Moor', is defined as wicked both by his illegitimacy and by his darker skin.

A more complex treatment of race and colour occurs in another play of the same year, *The Jew of Malta* (1589). Marlowe interrogates racial and religious stereotypes by exaggerating them: the black slave Ithamore is treacherous and double-dealing, having learnt how to survive among white men and Christians, though no more so than his master, the Jew. The play exposes the sordid underside of maritime ventures, the huge sums of money made or lost, and the political compromises they involved, culminating in the Spaniards setting up a slave market on Malta, where 'Every one's price is written on his back' (ii. iii. 3). The capitalist (and Christian) ethic of greed and self-interest that characterizes Maltese society is successfully imitated by the play's outsiders, visibly identified as such by the Jew's huge nose and the Moor's black face. Ithamore's name suggests his nature, but is also a variant of 'Ithamar', a Hebraic name which links him with two later stage Machiavels descended from him, Aaron the Moor in Shakespeare's *Titus Andronicus* (1594) and Eleazer in Dekker's *Lust's Dominion* (1600). In the Book of Exodus, Ithamar and Eleazer are brothers, and sons of Aaron, the brother of Moses (who, according to legend, had married an African wife).

Shakespeare's *Othello* displays some of the qualities attributed to Moors in that he is jealous, superstitious, and vengeful, but the Machiavellianism of Ithamore and his brood is here displaced on to the white Iago who treacherously accuses the white Desdemona of lustfulness in an attempt to 'blacken' her moral and physical purity, while Othello initially repudiates the stage stereotype, conducting himself with dignity and self-control in the play's early scenes. The antithesis of black and fair remains central, but Othello is black without and fair within: Desdemona 'saw Othello's visage in his mind' (I. iii. 252), and the play as a whole invites us to question whether things are really what they seem—Desdemona's behaviour, and sometimes her actual words appear guilty—and also to recognize that outsiders experience insecurities and anxieties that make them feel particularly vulnerable.

Othello, set on the Mediterranean island of Cyprus, begins in its greatest trading centre, Venice, which also provided the setting for Jonson's extravagant satire *Volpone* (1606) and Shakespeare's *Merchant of Venice* (1596), a play that recalls *The Jew of Malta* in its concern with Jewish capital, investment in sea-voyages as a lucrative if risky business, and with racist prejudice in a variety of forms. Africans figure at the extremes of the social scale, as the Prince of Morocco tries to win Portia's hand in marriage (Portia, however, expresses her distaste for his colour at Act II, Scene vii, line 79), while at the other end of the scale is the (offstage) Moor made pregnant by the clown, Lancelot Gobbo (III. v. 37–9). But, as in Marlowe's play, the theme of difference, which includes skin colour, is particularly focused upon difference of religion. Shylock's outlook is based on an Old Testament demand for strict justice rather than the New Testament law of forgiveness, though Portia and the Venetian court, who beg the Jew to show mercy to Shylock, cannot in their hour of victory remember the lesson themselves.

In *The Merchant of Venice* Shakespeare created Shylock as a stereotypical Jew—not the comic and ironic villain of Marlowe, but a miserly patriarch, distrustful and resentful of gentiles in general, and bearing feelings of murderous resentment towards the more generous Antonio, although he conforms to the example of Marlowe's Barabas in one crucial respect: he claims to have learnt his behaviour from gentiles. The play's text makes limited gestures towards exonerating him, but the speech that insists upon his common humanity, 'Hath not a Jew eyes?', goes on to demand 'if you wrong us shall we not revenge?', and concludes 'The villainy you teach me I shall execute and it shall go hard but I will better the instruction' (III. i. 59, 66–7, 71–3). In performance Shylock frequently steals the show, and the audience's sympathy with it. It used to be thought that there were virtually no Jews in late sixteenth-century London, with the exception of the Queen's doctor, Lopez, executed in 1593 for attempting to poison her. In reality, the situation was far more complicated: most of the Jews in London and elsewhere had fled from Spain where they had been forcibly converted to Christianity, so that ostensibly they were no longer Jews, and whatever they practised of their religion tended to be in secret. There may have been as many as 200 Jewish converts in England, working as doctors and in other professional or advisory capacities. Socially and physically they were virtually invisible, and this, along with their (usually) Spanish origins further contributed to the anxiety their presence aroused.

Although Jews and Africans, of whom there may have been a few hundred of each, were unpleasantly represented as stereotypes on the stage, they were far outnumbered by other non-native groups living in London. By the end of the sixteenth century there were almost five thousand 'strangers', that is, aliens, perhaps as much as 5 per cent of the population as a whole. The largest groups were from neighbouring countries, the French, the Dutch, and the Flemish. Huguenots (French Protestants) had fled to London during the Wars of Religion, and particularly in the wake of the St Bartholomew's Day massacre of 1572. The Flemings had constituted a substantial minority since the beginning of the century: the riot of 1517 dramatized in Munday's play *Sir Thomas More* had been directed against them. The Dutch were usually represented on stage as dull and drunk, though Franchescina, Marston's *Dutch Courtesan* (1605), is a woman driven by anger and bitterness. While her thick accent invites laughter, she is painfully doomed by her profession to the neglect and contempt of the man she loves. There were few concessions made to immigrants and, as today, they were often forced to huddle together in overcrowded conditions: 'They swarm in great tenements like flies: six households will live in a garret', wrote Thomas Overbury of the Dutch.[15] There were also substantial Italian, German, and Irish communities living in the City. The strangers often brought with them new technologies, such as iron-smelting, dyeing and starching cloth, or silk-weaving. England was technologically backward compared to the rest of Europe, but their contributions to the economy, if anything, increased the hostility they aroused.

Franchescina's accent points to the way in which the stage quickly came to register difference in terms of regional accents, and class in different forms of speech: Chapman, Jonson, and Marston's *Eastward Ho* (1605) identifies an unnamed gentleman as the King merely by his Scottish accent, while unexpected vowels record the social aspirations of Gertrude, the goldsmith's wife (she seems to have the Jacobean equivalent of a 'posh' accent). Jonson distinguishes some of the large cast of *Bartholomew Fair* (1614) by giving them regional accents: Captain Whit speaks stage Irish, while Nordern and Puppy are given Northern and Western accents. He is following Shakespeare's example in *Henry V* (1599), where the four captains—the English Gower, Welsh Fluellen (i.e. Llewellyn), Scottish Jamy, and Irish MacMorris—are carefully distinguished in terms of their accents, and in Fluellen's case, by the Welsh custom of wearing a leek on St David's Day. Here their companionship seems to make a political point: by fighting together for a common cause, they express an ideal of national unity. But the presence of Irish, Scottish, and Welsh soldiers in an English army was more of a reflection on the poverty of their respective countries than of any common cause or policy.

The Scottish captain, Jamy, shares his name with James VI of Scotland who, when he became King of England, was determined to introduce an Act of Union between the two countries, (his plan was defeated, and the Union took another hundred years to come into being). Henry VIII had tried to bring Ireland and Wales under English rule: Wales, so desperately poor that it had little to lose, accepted the new administrative arrangements, but Henry's assumption of the title 'King of Ireland' in 1541 was somewhat premature and his daughter Elizabeth struggled to impose English rule on Ireland. The fifth-act Chorus of Shakespeare's *Henry V* invites its London audience to imagine the King's triumphant return from France in terms of the Earl of Essex's successful return from Ireland, where he was sent to put down the rebellion of the Earl of Tyrone in the spring of 1599:

> Were now the General of our gracious Empress—
> As in good time he may—from Ireland coming,
> Bringing rebellion broached on his sword,
> How many would the peaceful city quit
> To welcome him.
>
> (v. i. 30–4)

But when it came Essex's return from Ireland brought general disappointment.

Colonizing Ireland

In 1565 Sir Thomas Smith wrote to the Queen's Secretary in support of an imperial project to annex Ireland: 'In my mind it needeth nothing more than to have colonies, to augment our tongue, our laws, and our religion in that isle, which three be the true bands of the commonwealth whereby the Romans conquered and kept long time a great part of the world.'[16] Among those involved in Irish plantation schemes had been speculators like Martin Frobisher, Humphrey Gilbert, and Walter Raleigh, men whose New World schemes had come to nothing. In the event, Ireland was the only country that they actually colonized. Although the Irish were near neighbours, their customs, appearance, speech, and religion made them seem alien, and if they were less mysterious than the New World 'Indians', they were more threatening for being nearer—Ireland had always looked like a possible launching-pad for a Spanish invasion. One popular solution for dealing with nations whose customs the English misread as disorderly was to take over their land, and establish English or Scottish plantations, employing—or rather exploiting—their labour on it. Traditional Irish customs were unacceptable to Tudor officials since they did not easily fit into English systems of government and law, and looked unstable or unpredictable from an English point of view.

Gaelic social structure was tribal, with something like a caste system that included military classes (known as kerns and gallowglasses), bards, and a legal class who administered the 'Brehon' law by imposing various judgements and fines. These orders of professional fighters and farmers had been close enough to the Norman feudal system for earlier English invaders (known as the 'old' English) to have adopted them. Land was not inherited but passed on through 'tanistry', a system of election among a kindred group. Irish farming methods were also unfamiliar, involving the movement of herds to upland pastures during the summer. National dress, a mantle folded and draped around the body rather like a toga, also seemed out-landish. These and other points of difference were misread as signs of savagery. The poet Spenser thought the Irish were descended from the Scythians, an ancient people notorious for 'barbarities' of one kind and another. In *The Faerie Queene* he represented them as cannibals, that recurrent version of the threatening 'other'.

The English attempted to impose their own administrative and legal systems by summoning Irish parliaments at Dublin Castle, within the area of English influence known as 'the Pale' (from which comes the expression 'beyond the pale'), but when these were called, they regularly broke down in disorder since the 'old' English and the 'new' English (i.e. the government offi-cials) were committed to opposing interests. Governor-Generals in Ireland were faced with refusals, rebellions, and shifting loyalties. Sir Henry Sidney (father of the poets Mary and Philip) was succeeded in 1580 by Lord Arthur Grey, whose repressive regime led to his recall two years later. Grey was responsible for massacring a garrison of Spaniards who had landed at Smerwick, but had then surrendered. He also conducted a brutal campaign against the Earl of Desmond in Munster. Spenser went to Ireland as secretary to Lord Arthur Grey, and was one of the beneficiaries of the Earl of Desmond's defeat, acquiring Desmond lands at Kilcolman, where he married and built a house. Book V of *The Faerie Queene* writes Lord Arthur Grey into an exculpating narrative as Artegal, the Knight of Justice, while his brutal military decisions are displaced on to his servant Talus, the iron man. On Grey/Artegal's return, he is attacked by the hags Envy and Detraction, and bitten by the Blatant Beast, another version of ill-fame or misrepresentation.

Fourteen years later Spenser offered his own recommendations for government policy in Ireland in the form of a dialogue, *A View of the Present State of Ireland*, notorious for its cold-blooded account of the starvation of Munster in the wake of the campaign against the Desmonds. Again, the Irish are represented as cannibals, though this time from starvation:

In those late wars in Munster . . . ere one year and a half, they were brought to such wretchedness, as that any stony heart would have rued the same, out of every corner of the woods and glens they came creeping forth upon their hands, for their legs could not bear them. They looked anatomies of death, they spake like ghosts crying out of their graves, they did eat of the dead carrions, happy where they could find them, yea and one another soon after . . .[17]

Despite having seen its horrific results in Munster, Spenser's dialogue recommends further policies of genocide of the type that Grey had tried to put into practice. As it was, the Queen disliked the expense of her Irish wars, and was less eager to enforce Protestant reform than were men like Spenser himself. Her hesitations, and attempts to retain the loyalty of Tyrone, the most powerful of the Irish earls, were thought by some to be delaying the settlement of Ireland under English rule. For Spenser, Ireland was a 'desert', a place of 'grisly famine . . . raging sword . . . nightly bodrags'; yet at the same time it was home in *Colin Clout's Come Home Again*, a pastoral landscape populated by classical river-nymphs. Like many colonists, he suffered from a kind of double vision, loving his adopted country, but preferring to imagine it cleared of its existing occupants.

The Faerie Queene celebrates the beauty of the Munster scenery, culminating in the description of Arlo Hill, close to his home at Kilcolman, in the Mutability Cantos. Elsewhere, the landscape of his epic poem is wild, heavily forested, inhabited sporadically by 'salvages', most of whom are either dumbly benevolent or totally depraved, nightmare figures like the forester who pursues the fleeing Florimel, or the lustful cannibal ogre who imprisons Amoret. The most startling juxtaposition occurs in Book VI, which opposes nature and nurture, the wilderness and the court (it celebrates the virtue of courtesy). A 'salvage man' who dwells shaggily and speechlessly in the depths of the forest rescues Calepine and nurses him and Serena back to health, feeding them and waiting on them like a faithful dog. But soon afterwards Serena falls into the hands of a very different 'salvage nation', who survive by theft and border attacks. Bands of half-starved warriors on a night raid, their knives glittering in the moonlight, must have been the recurrent nightmare of the English settlers. In 1598 a new rising began; Spenser's house at Kilcolman, with those of other planters, was burnt down, and Spenser and his family fled to London, where he died a few months later.

The rising was led by the Earl of Tyrone, and began with a powerful defeat for the English in Ulster. Essex's campaign of 1599, prematurely celebrated by the Chorus in *Henry V*, made no progress and he was replaced by the Earl of Mountjoy. Late in 1601 a small Spanish force landed at Kinsale, west of Cork, and as Tyrone marched south to join them he was unexpectedly and decisively defeated by Mountjoy. In 1603 he surrendered at Dublin Castle, and four years later he and the other great Ulster chieftain, Rory O'Donnell, set sail from Rathmullen in a moment that entered popular mythology as 'the Flight of the Earls'. Their Ulster lands were forfeited to the Crown, and in the years that followed the first successful plantations were established in the North. Soldiers who had fought in Ireland were paid in land, and an Irish Society was formed to sponsor planters emigrating from England and Scotland. In the meantime, growing numbers of Scottish Presbyterians had been crossing the narrow straits to Antrim and County Down, and had begun to settle there. They farmed land taken from the old Irish, but unlike previous invaders they rejected local customs, retaining their self-reliance and the distinctive religion which they had left Scotland to preserve, for, as dissenters, they belonged to a persecuted minority. From the outset their relationship with the old Irish was troubled. Violence broke out between the two communities, and almost 400 years further on they still have not resolved their differences.

The Scottish settlement of Ulster was accepted by the English government because it increased the Protestant vote in the Dublin parliament, called in 1613. Moves towards imposing the Protestant religion were resisted by the old English members, who refused to accept the nomination of a Protestant speaker, and then withdrew altogether, arousing fears of renewed conflict. Meanwhile a group of them went to London to put their case to the King. At court that Christmas Frances Howard's marriage to the Earl of Somerset was celebrated by Jonson with two masques: the second began with an antimasque of four comic Irishmen, supposedly come to England for the wedding. Dressed in their traditional mantles, they addressed the King with comic indecorum in cod-Irish: 'How like tou tish, Yamish?' (l. 144), only to be dismissed by a Gentleman, accompanied by an Irish Bard who announces,

> This is that James of which long since thou sung'st
> Should end our country's most unnatural broils . . .
>
> (ll. 156–7)

Jonson's four Irishmen are also on an embassage to the King: they argue as to who should speak first, and Dennis threatens to withdraw in a comic parody of how the old English members had behaved in parliament in Dublin, but the Gentleman's intervention restores order, and the Bard's music re-establishes harmony. The actors remove their mantles to reveal masquing costumes beneath. *The Irish Masque* dismisses disorder and incivility as belonging to the lower classes, but in Ireland it was the old aristocracy who were refusing to co-operate. One courtier commented, 'the device (which was a mimical imitation of the Irish) was not so pleasing to many, which think it no time (as the case stands) to exasperate that nation by making it ridiculous'.[18] By representing the Irish as stupid but well-intentioned, Jonson sought to reduce the threat that their nobles' independence posed, but in mocking them for their outlandish manners, he consigns them to the obscure and monstrous category of 'the other'.

5

The Natural World

THE Elizabethans inherited the notion that the universe consisted of a complex but ultimately ordered and stable ladder of existence, harmonious and benevolent to human beings, since it had been designed specifically for them. Any shortcomings were due to human, rather than to divine agency. Sir Thomas Elyot's *Boke named the Governour* (1531) makes the case for God's tidiness in its first chapter:

Behold also the order that God hath put generally in all his creatures, beginning at the most inferior or base, and ascending upward . . . so that every kind of trees, herbs, birds, beasts and fishes, beside their diversity of forms, have (as who sayeth) a peculiar disposition appropered unto them by God their creator; so that in everything is order, and without order may be nothing stable or permanent; and it may not be called order, except [unless] it do contain in it degrees, high and base, according to the merit or estimation of the thing that is ordered.

(Book I, ch. i)

Thus a highly hierarchical and graduated society imagined the universe in its own image, and, as Elyot's emphasis on order suggests, the order supposed to be visible in the natural world was then used as an argument to defend the stratified social structure. The elaborate ramifications of the ordered universe might even be used as evidence that the social system, as it had evolved, was essential or even inevitable.

This divinely ordained scheme of things was employed to sanction the claims of authority, and particularly kingship, not only by Elyot but also in the *Homily on Obedience to Ruler and Magistrates* (1547), regularly read from Elizabethan pulpits, and later in Hooker's *Laws of Ecclesiastical Polity* (1594), whose arguments defended the Church settlement established by Elizabeth as governor of the Church. The alternative to order was chaos, as Elyot had warned: 'Moreover take away order from all things, what should then remain? Certes, nothing, finally except . . . Chaos: which of some is expound[ed] a confuse[d] mixture. Also where there is any lack of order, needs must be perpetual conflict . . . whereof ensueth universal dissolution' (Book I, ch. i). Or, as Shakespeare's Ulysses puts it,

> Take but degree away, untune that string,
> And hark what discord follows! Each thing [meets]
> In mere oppugnancy . . .
> 　　　　(*Troilus and Cressida*, I. iii. 109–11)

Ulysses echoes Elyot's warnings, though in context his speech is somewhat ironized by his personality: traditionally, Ulysses had been regarded as the embodiment of wisdom and experience, but in Shakespeare's satirical reduction of the Trojan War he is presented as a political fixer, here attempting to persuade the aggressively individualistic Greeks to observe the basic rules of military discipline if they hope to make any progress with their siege of Troy. The force of his argument is thus modified by the sense that he is deliberately invoking truisms for the purpose of persuasion, as government spokesmen everywhere are inclined to do.

Transience

The optimism of such accounts of universal order was challenged, not merely by their use (or misuse) as propaganda, but by the unpredictable nature of nature itself and the harsh conditions of everyday existence. One modern historian has pointed out that 'Tudor and Stuart Englishmen were, by our standards, exceedingly liable to pain, sickness and premature death . . . those who survived could anticipate a lifetime of intermittent pain . . . There were periodic waves of influenza, typhus, dysentery and, in the seventeenth century, smallpox . . . Most dreaded of all was the bubonic plague.'[1] Perhaps the grim and uncertain circumstances of living encouraged people to cling more tightly to a highly structured view of nature, rather than to question their assumptions. Nevertheless, several of the age's sharpest observers reconsidered conventional or second-hand wisdom in terms of their own experience: Montaigne, in his essay 'That to philosophize is to learn to die', gives his age as 39 and says he hopes to live as long again, but adds that he has already lived longer than most of his friends, and he considers that Jesus's death at 33 more accurately represents contemporary life-expectancy than Methuselah's (*Essays*, p. 58)—and, demographically speaking, he was right. Robert Burton, never an optimist, includes in the first part of *The Anatomy of Melancholy* a memorable subsection devoted to 'Discontents, Cares, Miseries etc.' His discussion moves from a comprehensive account of the troubles that afflict the human race to the dangers of the surrounding world, and then proceeds to describe the difficulties of social life, the master's oppression of the servant, the parents' oppression of the child. He claims that 'for particular professions, I hold as of the rest, there's no content or security in any', concluding with the grim axiom, 'Better never to have been born, and the best next of all, to die quickly' (Part I, section 2, member 3, subsection 10).

Many people did. Infant mortality rates were very high, and death was close in an age when medicine could do little to relieve its patients, and sometimes lowered their resistance by bleeding and purging. The imminence of death had been a favourite subject for medieval writers and artists, and continued to provide a frequent point of reference for sermons, often with a warning to repent while there was still time. Essayists explored the subject as Montaigne does in the essay referred to earlier, and elsewhere; Bacon gives a characteristically bracing account of it, dismissing the night-birds of terror and superstition ('Of Death', *Essays*, pp. 64–6). Tragedy also had much to say about death, both about the spirit in which it should be confronted, and also about the variety of means to achieve it. A splendid apostrophe to all-conquering death concludes Walter Raleigh's

History of the World (1614): 'O eloquent, just and mighty death! ... thou hast drawn together all the far-stretched greatness, all the pride, cruelty and ambition of man, and covered it all over with these two narrow words, *Hic iacet*' (Book V, ch. vi, section 12). John Donne's Holy Sonnet 10, though probably written earlier, might have been written as an answer to Raleigh's claim:

> Death be not proud, though some have called thee
> Mighty and dreadful, for, thou art not so ...

The state exploited the pains of death for its own purposes, staging public executions as dramatic events in which the condemned provided awful warnings to the audience, first by confessing and repenting of their folly and wickedness, and then by their visible sufferings as they were disembowelled and dismembered while still alive.

In an earlier passage of his *History* Raleigh had restated another great commonplace when he contrasted the brevity of man's life with the deathless, cyclical sequences of nature, quoting from a well-known Latin love lyric to make his point. He translated it thus:

> The sun may set and rise,
> But we contrariwise
> Sleep after our short light
> One everlasting night.
>   (Book I, ch. ii, section 5)

The original, Catullus' poem, 'Vivamus, mea Lesbia, atque amemus', had also been translated by Jonson and Campion, and imitated by Marlowe, Marvell, and others. Its warning of the transience of human life amidst the changing but ever-renewed seasons had occurred in medieval literature, but its distinctively hedonist ethic belonged to the Renaissance.

> What is love? 'Tis not hereafter;
> Present mirth hath present laughter
> What's to come is still unsure

sings the Clown in Twelfth Night (II. iii. 47–9), echoing Lorenzo de Medici's 'Song of Bacchus', and long before that, the ending of Horace's ode:

> dum loquimur, fugerit invida
> aetas: carpe diem, quam minimum credula postero.
> (I. xi. 7–8)

(While we're talking, time will have enviously flown by. Enjoy today and don't put any trust at all in tomorrow.)

Elizabethan poets imitated the Roman lyric poets enthusiastically, but tended to bring to them subtle shifts of emphasis. Whereas Horace celebrated spring and young love, mythologizing them as the return of Proserpina and the Graces, the melting snows, blossoming flowers, and weeping springs that he referred to often reappeared as emblems in the work of Renaissance poets:

> The withered primrose by the mourning river,
> The faded summer's sun from weeping fountains,
> The light-blown bubble vanishèd for ever,
> The molten snow upon the naked mountains,
> Are emblems that the treasures we up-lay
> Soon wither, vanish, fade and melt away.
>   (Edmund Bolton: 'A Palinode')

Although London literary life was beginning to evoke nostalgia for the countryside, nature was more often portrayed as reflecting human emotions than as a subject of interest in its own right: the charms of solitary woods echoed the lover's melancholy, the returning spring brought joy and hope, or else misery, if the lover were alone amidst the general rejoicing. Autumn and winter were associated with old age and death, and May was the month for love. Young girls were represented as objects, flowers to be plucked and enjoyed, roses and daffodils, their beauty and sometimes their lives as short as the flowers they were compared to. The poet-suitors urged them to submit to love, alternating blandishments with threats—that they would regret it later if they missed their chance, that in refusing an earthly lover, they consigned themselves to the unlovely embrace of death: 'You grow old while I tell you this', observes one Jonsonian suitor (*The Devil is an Ass*, I. vi. 131). A singer in Spenser's Bower of Bliss urges:

> Gather therefore the rose, whilst yet is prime,
> For soon comes age, that will her pride deflower;
> Gather the rose of love, whilst yet is time,
>   Whilst loving thou may'st loved be with equal crime.
>   (*Faerie Queene*, II. xii. 75)

Arguments based on the transience of women's beauty were sometimes countered by others based on the brevity of love itself. Marlowe's 'Come live with me and be my love' (the first line another Catullan echo) was answered by Walter Raleigh in terms of the turning year, the fading spring, and approaching autumn:

> But could youth last, and love still breed,
> Had joys no date, nor age no need,
> Then these delights my mind might move
> To live with thee and be thy love.

A further harsh irony, that many women died prematurely in or soon after childbirth, was never addressed in lyric poetry at all.

A great many Elizabethan lyrics telescoped human life so that the ageing process paralleled seasonal or diurnal change, but by contrast to self-renewing nature, sunset or winter were final for mortal creatures. In echoing a sense of life's brevity that they found in Latin love poetry, Elizabethan poets had hit upon a theme that corresponded to their own experience. But while Latin verse contrasted human transience to the permanent cycles of nature, Christianity offered an escape from the finality of death through the promise of resurrection. Indeed, the most surprising feature of the Elizabethan lyric is its extensive use of pagan themes and imagery, in a profoundly religious age.

A religious poet might rework the standard emblems of the love-lyric: George Herbert's poem 'Vertue' modulates them into the deliberately familiar imagery of the sermon. Here the transience—and sickliness—of 'sweet day', 'sweet rose', or 'sweet spring' and falling cadences, are dismissed in an energetically earthy conclusion:

> Only a sweet and virtuous soul,
> Like season'd timber, never gives;
> But though the whole world turn to coal,
> Then chiefly lives.

At the end of his elegy 'Lycidas', Milton rearranged the Catullan image of the setting sun to show that Christianity promises rebirth. Mutability (or change) governed the earth, but her powers were ultimately limited, according to a wider or more transcendent view of things. Spenser's *Faerie Queene* (1596) searches for the permanent and eternal amidst the natural world of flux, change, and accident. The last book is unfinished, but in its surviving cantos the titaness Mutability claims to rule over the whole world, only to be overruled by Nature who argues that, since all things change according to a universal law, things may be said to govern change, rather than change governing things. Change is thus a constant, and Mutability, like any contemporary monarch, will have to submit herself to her own laws, and one day undergo the change that will make her unchanging, when the world ends and all time becomes eternity. By a similar logic, man conquers in the very act of submitting to death in Donne's Holy Sonnet, referred to earlier, as well as in Shakespeare's 'Poor soul, the centre of my sinful earth' (Sonnet 146).

Behind Spenser, and Shakespeare's sonnets too, lay the most influential of all accounts of mutability, Ovid's *Metamorphoses* or the Book of Changes (translated by Arthur Golding, 1565). In Book 15 the sage Pythagoras describes the endlessly changing world of nature in which 'the generations of man have passed from the age of gold to that of iron'. Book 1 depicts man living in harmony with nature in a golden age in which labour and social distinctions have no place. Since then the world has degenerated through ages of silver and bronze to the present one of iron, characterized by its warlike savagery. The idea that man once existed in a better, happier, and more peaceful state was common both to pagan and Christian belief. Granted our manifest sickness, misery, and social inequalities, it was not difficult to suppose that humanity had undergone some kind of degeneration from an earlier happiness. Nor was it difficult to equate Ovid's golden age with the Christian view that man had fallen from an ideal existence in the Garden of Eden—both narratives provided explanations for the present 'wearisome condition of humanity'.

Pastoral

Located not in a lost past, but in an idealized countryside, the pastoral convention was concerned with the lives and activities of shepherds. Spenser and Sidney between them effectively introduced pastoral verse and prose into English, through Spenser's *Shepheardes Calender*, his book of twelve verse eclogues, and Sidney's *Arcadia*, a prose romance, interspersed with poems. Pastoral verse can be traced back through Renaissance Italian and Spanish poetry to Vergil's *Eclogues* and the Greek poetry of Theocritus and his disciples. In prose the earliest models were late Greek romances like *Daphnis and Chloë*. Pastoral was enthusiastically imitated by Elizabethan poets, who adopted appropriate names: Sidney called himself Astrophil, Sidrophil, or Philisides (meaning 'Star-lover'), Spenser more prosaically Colin Clout. In the 1590s a host of Coridons and Shepherd Tonys mushroomed overnight. In the anthology *England's Helicon* (1600), poems not originally composed in the pastoral mode were retitled 'The Shepherd's Solace' or 'A pastoral ode to an honourable friend'. George Herbert wrote with conscious irony in 'Jordan I', 'Shepherds are honest people; let them sing'.

However familiar such conventions had become in literary circles, they could still baffle the general public. The playwright John Fletcher was taken aback when the audiences for his pastoral tragicomedy *The Faithful Shepherdess* (1608) apparently expected 'a play of country hired shepherds in grey cloaks, with curtailed dogs in strings, sometimes laughing together and sometimes killing one another; and, missing Whitsun-ales, cream, wassail, and morris dances, [the audience] began to be angry'. He felt obliged to explain the convention he was using in his letter 'To the Reader':

Understand, therefore, a pastoral to be a representation of shepherds and shepherdesses . . . they are not to be adorned with any art, but such improper ones as nature is said to bestow, as singing and poetry; or such as experience may teach them, . . . But you are ever to remember shepherds to be such as all the ancient poets, and modern, of understanding, have received them; that is, the owners of flocks and not hirelings.

Late Elizabethan taste was ripe for the development of pastoral as a literary form. The growth of London as a substantial city, a mercantile and administrative centre increasingly independent of the countryside, created the right conditions for pastoral, an idealized account of the shepherd's life, which is also commonly an exercise in urban nostalgia. The Greek pastoral poet Theocritus had been a citizen of Alexandria, who wrote with nostalgia of the rural Sicilian society he had left behind him. The more individualistic, competitive, and capitalist sixteenth-century men became, under political, economic, and demographic pressures, the more they turned to fantasies of an alternative society based upon contemplation, passivity, and communal values. The more complex grew the rules of society, the more attractive was the idea of a life governed by instinct, rather than one that demanded its suppression. The more old Catholic traditions were officially discouraged, the more they acquired the appeal of the forbidden. So the elaborate rituals of courtly life came to be unfavourably compared in literature with a prettified version of the life of the working man. The traditional antithesis of pastoral was the artifice and hypocrisy of court life.

Book VI of Spenser's *Faerie Queene* is the Book of Courtesy, but the court is remarkable mainly by its absence, while the pastoral society presented is strongly idealized: the shepherds have a wise homespun philosophy that makes them content to exist in a commune whose competitiveness is limited to song contests and games, and whose mutual happiness is expressed in dancing. But Spenser was enough of a realist to perceive how vulnerable such a peaceful and harmonious way of life would actually be. All it required was a band of brigands to smash the idyll to pieces. One day the hero Calidore returns from hunting to find the shepherds' huts empty and sheep and shepherds driven away.

Pastoral offered an imaginative escape from the burdens of responsibility. This motif is poignantly expressed by Shakespeare's Henry VI on the battlefield at Towton:

> O God! methinks it were a happy life
> To be no better than a homely swain . . .
> Gives not the hawthorn bush a sweeter shade
> To shepherds looking on their silly sheep,
> Than doth a rich embroider'd canopy
> To kings that fear their subjects' treachery?
> (*3 Henry VI*, II. v. 21–2, 42–5)

The corruption, pretence, and necessity for diplomatic compromise imposed by court life were contrasted with the honesty, integrity, and simplicity of life in the country. *As You Like It* sets out such a contrast, although the traditional antithesis is complicated and treated ironically. Shakespeare's good Duke has been banished to the wilderness, the Forest of Arden, where songs emphasize 'winter and rough weather', but prefer it to the greater treachery of 'man's ingratitude' (II. v. 8 and vii. 176). There is even a plea such as Montaigne might have made for the rights of the deer, the proper inhabitants of the forest, who are being hunted and eaten (II. i. 60–3). Shakespearean pastoral tends to be 'hard', rather than 'soft', that is, it shows the natural environment as potentially threatening, rather than benevolent. Realistically, his shepherds have greasy hands, 'often tarr'd over with the surgery of our sheep' (*As You Like It*, III. i. 62–3).

If court life looked superfluous when set against the simple necessities of country life, courtly conduct in love seemed artificial and long-drawn-out. Their impulses untrammelled by imposed rules, country couples sported in the hay, and milk-maids were supposed to be less coy than fine ladies, as well as cleaner and more natural:

> I care not for these ladies that must be wooed and prayed;
> Give me kind Amaryllis, the wanton country maid.
> Nature Art disdaineth; her beauty is her own.
> Her when we court and kiss, she cries: forsooth, let go!
> But when we come where comfort is, she never will say no.
>   (Thomas Campion: *Book of Ayres*, i. 3)

The association of unrestricted sexual freedom both with country life and the primal innocence of the golden age were to become favourite themes of seventeenth-century poetry, though such enduring erotic fantasies are unlikely to have had much basis in everyday experience. Country girls normally married much later than court beauties, and like Shakespeare's Audrey, in this respect at least, valued their sexual credit. Jane Smile with her chapped hands, greasy Joan keeling her pot, and Marian whose nose was red and raw are more particularized than the usual stereotypes of country girls, though both women and the lower classes are normally represented as if they have no inner lives.

During the seventeenth century literary representations of town and country life became increasingly polarized, but although their separation had begun, few Elizabethan or Jacobean writers lived exclusively urban lives, so that their pastoral writings are often touched with irony or a sense of the prosaic lurking beneath the convention. Small towns like Shakespeare's Stratford were closely in touch with the rural communities around them. Even Ben Jonson, a Londoner born and bred, and the most urban (and urbane) poet of his age, walked, on one notable occasion, all the way to Scotland. Courtiers expected to spend half the year on their own or other people's estates. Despite its title, Sidney's *Arcadia* is further than Shakespeare's Forest of Arden from being an ideal world. He gives us one glimpse only of Arcadia as it was traditionally imagined, at the moment when his hero Mucedorus first sets eyes upon it:

There were hills which garnished their proud heights with stately trees; humble valleys, whose base estate seemed comforted with refreshing of silver rivers; meadows enamelled with all sorts of eye-pleasing flowers; thickets, which being lined with most pleasant shade, were witnessed so to by the cheerful deposition of many well-tuned birds; each pasture stored with sheep feeding with sober security, while the pretty lambs with bleating oratory craved the dams' comfort; here a shepherd's boy piping as though he should never be old; there a young shepherdess knitting, and withal singing, and it seemed that her voice comforted her hands to work, and her hands kept time to her voice's music.

(The 'New' Arcadia (1590), book I, ch. ii)

It is a moralized landscape: even if pastoral society is egalitarian, the very contours of the land bespeak elevation and baseness, a baseness content with its allotted position. All is order, rhythm, and harmony, an image of musical co-ordination which includes the well-tuned birds, the bleating lambs, the boy piping, and the girl singing and working in time to her song. This is the ordered world picture set out in topographical terms, and is there to satisfy expectation. Nothing else, either in the book itself or in the experience of the age, endorses this as anything but an ideal. Sidney reveals his Arcadians to be as prone to discontents in their wilderness as men are in civilization, as restless, as greedy, and as subject to uncontrollable passions.

Music and Measure

The harmony of Sidney's *Arcadia* is momentary. Although there might be disagreement as to how far human beings and the natural world had fallen from their initial perfection, it was generally accepted that the earth was subject to change and decay and in this respect differed significantly from the heavens, which exhibited order and purpose and, in the regions beyond the moon, were exempt from change. The skies participated in the eternal nature of God, who if He could be supposed to live anywhere, lived in or beyond them. Everything beneath the moon, within the earth's sphere, was subject to change, although certain human activities—those of music and mathematics in particular—were associated with the unchanging movement of the heavens because of their constant proportions, a theme celebrated in Sir John Davies's poem *Orchestra* (1596). Musical harmonies were known to relate to mathematical proportions—double a string, and the note it produces when plucked goes down an octave. Modern physics can explain this in terms of the number of vibrations per second, but the Greek philosopher Pythagoras, the notional founder of mathematical studies, was traditionally credited with the discovery. For Pythagoras (according to Aristotle), numbers were the original building blocks of the universe, and a fundamental aspect of nature. To Pythagoras was attributed the idea that mathematical harmonies governed the movement of the heavenly bodies, and that, in moving across the sky, they produced the ethereal music of the spheres. In the last act of *The Merchant of Venice*, Lorenzo explains to Jessica that

> Such harmony is in immortal souls,
> But whilst this muddy vesture of decay
> Doth grossly close it in, we cannot hear it.
>   (v. i. 63–5)

These inaudible secret harmonies were produced by the planets as they moved within their orbits. The second-century astronomer Ptolemy invented the method regularly used for calculating the movement of the planets up to the sixteenth century. According to his account, the moon, the sun, and the planets circled the earth, their paths inscribed upon a series of crystal spheres, each one inside the next, with the earth at the centre of the whole system. Beyond the paths of the planets lay the region of fixed stars. Like the rest of the sky, the planets moved naturally from east to west, but, as seen from the earth, they also moved backwards (i.e. from west to east) at predictable intervals. There were various ways of describing these small reversed circles within the larger movement of the skies. This 'double motion' of the planets provides a dramatic analogy at the opening of Donne's poem 'Good Friday, 1613, Riding Westward', where the poet's personal desire to face the east, at prayer in church, is contrasted to his imposed task, which carries him westward. Elsewhere, in the *Devotions* (1624), Donne showed his familiarity with the new Copernican accounts of the universe, when he gets up, feeling dizzy, from his bed of sickness: 'I am up, and I seem to stand, and I go round; and I am a new argument of the new philosophy, that the earth moves round' (XXI, Meditation). In his giddiness, the theory of a spinning earth seems to him amusingly plausible. When Marlowe's Faustus demanded that he 'reason of divine astrology', Mephostophilis offered him the standard explanation of planetary movement as currently taught at university, much to Faustus's disgust:

> Hath Mephostophilis no greater skill?
> Who knows not the double motion of the planets . . .
> Tush, these are freshmen's suppositions.
>
> (II. iii. 50–1, 55–6)

Although Marlowe does not refer to it, he could have known of Copernicus's theories of a heliocentric universe, either from an account published in English by Thomas Digges in 1576, or else from the mathematician Thomas Harriot (Raleigh's reporter in Virginia), who also took an informed interest in astronomy. Half a century later another poet, Milton, was still hedging his bets on the issue in *Paradise Lost* (see viii. 66–84); despite having visited Galileo in 1638 and, if we may trust one of the poem's similes, looked at the moon through the 'Tuscan artist's' telescope (i. 288–91).

Poetry aspired to achieve the permanence of music and mathematics, and could be thought of as including elements of both. While verse was often set to music and sung, it also created a verbal music of its own whose rhythms were measured, as the sixteenth-century term 'numbers' and its modern equivalents, 'metre' or 'metrics', suggest. Philip Sidney, defending poetry and linking it with the sacred gift of prophecy, referred to 'that same exquisite observing of number and measure in the words' which 'did seem to have some divine force in it'. Poetry 'considers each word not only . . . by his most forcible quality, but by his best measured quantity, carrying even in themselves a harmony—

without [i.e. unless], perchance, number, measure, order, proportion be in our time grown odious' (*A Defence of Poetry*, pp. 77, 100). The musical and mathematical elements in poetry were connected with its ambitions to achieve permanence, and Renaissance poets liked to imagine poetry as divinely inspired, the result of a poetic frenzy that opened the eyes of the poet to the deep harmonies of the world order.

The belief that the world had been created on mathematical principles and that numbers possessed mystic significance was also reflected in a tradition of numerological interpretation of the Bible (with particular, but not exclusive, reference to the Book of Revelation), as well as one of mystic mathematical thought supposedly descended through Pythagoras and Plato to his followers, the Neoplatonists, who were fascinated by the mystic patterns that could be woven from numbers. Both these traditions encouraged poets to incorporate number patterns into their writings in complex and often secretive ways. A number of medieval poets, including Dante, had established precedents for doing so.

Formal numerological poetry makes significant patterns out of line, syllable, or section numbers. Spenser and Milton were among its foremost exponents, and this may reflect their familiarity with Neoplatonic thinking, as well as the seriousness of their poetic ambitions, and even their strong commitment to the Protestant faith. Numerological investigations were by no means an exclusively Protestant phenomenon, but a significant number of Protestant theologians were engaged in reconstructing biblical chronology, and the significance of numbers was an important assumption in such investigations. The Envoy that concludes Spenser's *Shepheardes Calender* is an example of such number patterning. Its theme is the poet's hope for lasting fame, and Spenser here makes use of the number twelve, associated with constancy. The verse consists of twelve lines, each made up of twelve syllables, a kind of square re-emphasizing the twelve-month cycle that constitutes the *Calender* itself:

> Lo I have made a calendar for every year,
> That steel in strength, and time in durance shall outwear:
> And if I markéd well the stars' revolution,
> It shall continue till the world's dissolution.

Far more complex is Spenser's *Epithalamion*, where the changing ratios of the hours of day and night during a whole year, as well as on one particular day (11 June 1594, then the longest day of the year and the day of his marriage to Elizabeth Boyle) are involved. The numbers used in measuring time (hours of the day, days of the week, month, and year) and those connected with the planets, as well as biblical associations (three as the Trinity, four the gospels, twelve the Apostles, etc.) could all be drawn upon, and as an organizing principle number symbolism was by no means restricted to poetry. Milton's *De Doctrina Christiana* has thirty-three chapters in its first book, corresponding to the years of Christ's life, and seventeen in the second, which emblematically unites the Old and New Testaments, being made up of ten (the number of the commandments) and seven (the gifts of the Holy Ghost, countering the seven deadly sins). Milton was following the example of Augustine, whose *City of God* was composed of twenty-two chapters, corresponding to the letters of the Hebrew alphabet.

Renaissance interest in the harmonies of number and music, and their relationship to the harmonies of the world soul, the individual soul, and the state was largely established by the fifteenth-century Florentine scholar Marsilio Ficino, who revived and reshaped the study of Plato by translating his Greek dialogues into Latin. For Ficino, Plato was one of the transmitters of a repository of secret wisdom, the so-called 'ancient theology', a tradition of mystic, and even magical thought which, Ficino claimed, had been handed down from the Jewish patriarchs through Moses to the Egyptian Hermes Trismegistus, and then through a series of initiates to Pythagoras, who took it to Greece, where Plato became its last great exponent. Especially important for Ficino was a group of writings attributed to the mythical figure of Hermes Trismegistus, and believed to be of great antiquity, though in 1614 the scholar Isaac Casaubon showed that they had been written far later than had previously been supposed: they dated from the early Christian era, when there had been a strong revival of interest in Neoplatonic thought. The Hermetic texts emphasized the power and potential of human beings to do and become whatever they wished, to dominate the natural world through the exercise of will and imagination. At a time of rapid change, such fantasies were particularly appealing. Scholars like Ficino found in them the promise of secret powers that might be gained through self-discipline, and the recovery of that secret knowledge of 'natural magic', which would confer control over the spirits that governed the natural world, and thus of its elements and forces.

Ficino's pupil, Pico della Mirandola, studied the Hermetic texts in association with the mystic Hebrew writings of the Cabbalah, trying to extract from them the principles of natural magic, the art that Prospero appears to practise in *The Tempest*. Such magic was far removed from the charms for toothache or sexual potency, or the techniques for finding lost objects employed by the unlettered wise men or conjurors of the countryside, the witch-doctors of their age. It involved wide scholarship and a lifetime of study, sustained by the promise of some great discovery or power, perhaps that of the philosopher's stone, supposed to turn all metals to gold. For Pico, human beings were the hub or focus of the world, the apex of creation. His *Oration: On the Dignity of Man* (1486) is an optimistic (and aristocratic) assertion of human versatility and capacity, of the protean ability to become whatever one wishes: 'O highest liberality of God the Father, greatest and most wonderful happiness of man, to whom is given whatever he chooses to have, to be what he wills.'[2]

Correspondences

Neoplatonic ideas about the secret harmonies of the universe, and the promise that natural magic would reveal and harness their power, went well beyond standard views of the relationship between heaven and earth, but these also included a number of elements that we would think of as 'magical', or at least unscientific: although the unchanging nature of the heavens contrasted with changing life on earth, the two were elaborately related. The universe was seen as interconnected at every level with human beings, its focal point and purpose, and actions in the heavens produced reactions on earth as surely as the moon governed the tides. These reactions might be felt both in the body politic (the body of the state) and in the body of the individual, which was seen as a 'microcosm' or miniature world, epitomizing the 'macrocosm' or great world. The fate of the individual was thus influenced by the stars, or at any rate foretold by them; more particularly by the movements of the various planets which, at this time, were quite as important for astrological predictions as were the twelve angles of the sky that made up the zodiac. Although the Church officially discouraged 'judicial' astrology (that is, predictions made by casting horoscopes), it was widely practised, sometimes even by clergymen.

Harmony or conflict in society corresponded to events written in the skies by the wanderings of the planets, and in miniature within the psychology of the individual. Within human beings reason was supposed to be king, governing the other emotions and controlling the potentially rebellious passions; its overthrow threatened disaster. Similarly the natural world, divided (according to a tradition going back to Aristotle) into four elements, earth, water, air, and fire, resembled the human body, which in turn was supposed to be made up of four liquids or humours: black bile, phlegm, blood, and choler (or yellow bile), each one corresponding to the four elements in the macrocosm, as well as to the four seasons—autumn, winter, spring, and summer. Ideally these humours were in balance, but in practice one would normally dominate, giving the person a particular temperament or 'complexion' (literally, mixture). Thus 'humour' came to mean a particular type of personality: a predominance of black bile produced depression (i.e. melancholy); too much phlegm made people apathetic (i.e. phlegmatic); too much blood made them

cheerful (i.e. sanguine); and too much choler quick-tempered
(i.e. choleric). More substantial imbalances caused illness and
might require medical intervention. Sometimes elaborate parallels between the world and the human body were developed.
Walter Raleigh suggests in his *History of the World* that flesh
corresponds to earth and rock to bones, while 'blood, which dis-
perseth itself by the branches of veins through all the body, may
be resembled to those waters which are carried by brooks and
rivers over all the earth: his breath to the air; his natural heat to
the enclosed warmth, which the earth hath in itself' (Book I, ch.
ii, section 5).

Aristotle had described the world as an elaborately interlocking mechanism, with everything made up of complex mix-
tures of the four original elements, and classified in a series of
neatly graded ranks, from inert stones, through all vegetable and
animal life, to human beings. The medieval Church had initially
resisted and then embraced his account, and the theologian
Thomas Aquinas had summarized all that was reconcilable with
Christian dogma, extending Aristotle's system so as to take in
the world of the invisible and continue the earthly chain or
ladder of being. Travelling downwards, it now stretched from
God's throne, through the various orders of angels to human
beings, ranked from kings to peasants, and then through the
various forms of animal and vegetable life, to stones again. This
scheme was still prescribed for study at university, although it
had been criticized by various medieval philosophers, and in the
sixteenth century was attacked both by Neoplatonists, who
found it too materialistic, and by humanists, who found it narrow
and pedantic.

By the sixteenth century the number of errors, inconsistencies,
and problems inherent in the old Aristotelian scheme were
increasingly visible, yet the system as a whole withstood individual criticisms, since no one could propose an alternative
world view of comparable scope. Even though several of its
central premises were rejected by philosophers or pioneering
scientists, the general framework survived to the end of the
seventeenth century: Pope's *Essay on Man* (1733) was still

expounding the great chain of being as evidence of the purposive and benevolent nature of creation.

One conspicuous weakness was the system's dependence on observation and common sense to explain the operation of physical phenomena, and its inability to account for such invisible forces as magnetism or gravity, the effects of which were now beginning to be recognized. In 1651 Thomas Hobbes (who had read Galileo's writings on gravity) exposed the circularity of the standard Aristotelian account of the subject:

If you desire to know why some kind of bodies sink naturally downwards toward the earth, and others go naturally from it; the Schools [i.e. universities] will tell you out of Aristotle, that the bodies that sink downwards are heavy; and that this heaviness is it that causes them to descend. But if you ask what they mean by heaviness, they will define it to be an endeavour to go to the centre of the earth. So that the cause why things sink downward, is an endeavour to be below: which is as much as to say, that bodies descend, or ascend, because they do.

(*Leviathan*, part iv, ch. 46)

Comparable difficulties arose when attempts were made to explain the movements of missiles and projectiles. Since military experts, then as now, took a professional interest in ballistics, there was widespread speculation on the subject until Galileo solved various difficulties by proposing the theory of inertial movement (that is, an object naturally continues in movement unless positively interrupted by another force, such as gravity). Here and elsewhere, Aristotle's common-sense view that all movement presupposes a mover was inadequate to account for more complex physical effects.

Discoveries

The most radical attack on the Aristotelian system, with its unchanging heavens and its earth-centred universe, was to come from advances in astronomy. In 1572, the year of the St Bartholomew's Day Massacre in Paris, a substantial nova (i.e. an exploding star) was observed in the constellation of Cassiopeia by Tycho Brahe, and another was observed by Galileo in 1604, thus challenging the idea that the region of fixed stars, beyond the circuits of the planets, was exempt from change. Donne commented on the 1604 nova ('new star') in his epistle 'To the Countess of Huntingdon':

> Who vagrant transitory comets sees
>   Wonders, because they are rare; but a new star
> Whose motion with the firmament agrees,
>   Is miracle; for there no new things are.

Novas were 'miracles', as opposed to comets which were mere 'wonders', since they were much closer to the earth (and therefore much smaller) than novas. Even so, the comets of 1577, 1607, and 1618 appeared to pass straight through the imagined spheres of individual planets. The invention of the telescope, around 1608, enabled its users to observe many stars that had previously been invisible to the naked eye, to chart the irregular surfaces of the moon, and to see sunspots. In 1610 Galileo observed four moons of Jupiter, and noted that the planet Venus had phases, like the moon, thus supplying the first ocular proof that the planets orbited the sun, rather than the earth. He announced his discoveries in *The Starry Messenger*.

A process of deduction had led the Polish cleric Copernicus to describe the planets and the earth as in motion around the sun, and the universe as far larger than had previously been supposed—or at least this is what he proposed in the first book of his *Revolution of the Heavenly Spheres* (1543) (by the third book, this scheme has been modified and complicated beyond recognition). Its outlines were introduced to English readers by Thomas Digges in a relatively popular book of 1576, mainly concerned with astrology. Although the new system was used as a basis for calculations in some Jacobean almanacs, it took many decades to reach widespread acceptance, even though it offered a simpler explanation of planetary movement as seen from the earth than had been possible before.

Aspects of Copernican thought were taken up by the greatest practical astronomer of the day, the Danish aristocrat Tycho

Brahe, who, with state support, had built Uraniborg, an enormous observatory on the island of Hveen. Using specially built instruments, Brahe devoted himself to compiling a series of records of planetary movement, but he did not possess the necessary theoretical skills to interpret them. Near the end of his life he was appointed Imperial Mathematician to the Holy Roman Emperor Rudolf II at Prague, where he met Johannes Kepler, a mathematician and astronomer of genius who would gradually reveal the full significance of Brahe's records. Rudolf was a great patron of the arts, but it was his interest in astrology that brought the greatest practical astronomer of the day and the greatest theoretician to his court, where they were both employed in casting horoscopes for him. The result of their meeting was to be Kepler's discovery of the paths of the planets and the mathematical formulae that govern them.

The modern view that magic and science are fundamental opposites can easily obscure points of continuity between older and more magical ways of thinking about the universe, and what we think of as 'scientific' discoveries. The Elizabethan 'magus', John Dee, another visitor to Rudolf's court, studied mathematics while at the same time exploring astrology and the world of spirits. Kepler, who discovered the laws governing the operation of the solar system, had his own scepticism about the influence of the stars on human activity: he considered traditional methods of casting horoscopes by planetary influence at birth a waste of time. Yet even so he firmly believed in heavenly influences, and devoted many years to trying to analyse their nature: 'That the sky does something to man is obvious enough, but what it does specifically remains hidden.'[3] Both Kepler and his predecessor, Copernicus, were Pythagoreans or perhaps Neoplatonists, in that they believed that the skies moved according to the laws of mathematics and musical harmony. Copernicus, in particular, subscribed to Pythagorean doctrines which regarded the sun as the life-giving force in the universe. His mathematical calculations reinforced his personal convictions when he declared (in Book I): 'in the midst of all dwells the sun . . . Sitting on the royal throne, he rules the family of planets which turn around him . . . We thus find in this arrangement an admirable harmony of the world.'[4]

Kepler used Brahe's records to establish three laws governing planetary movement: that the paths of the planets around the sun run, not in circles (as had always been supposed), but in ellipses; that though planets lose speed as they move away from the sun, an imaginary line joining them to the sun would sweep through equal areas in equal times; finally, that the orbits of any two planets stand in a fixed mathematical ratio to their average distances from the sun. In arriving at his conclusions, Kepler was influenced by an English doctor, William Gilbert, who had studied electricity and magnetism, and argued that the earth was itself a vast magnet, with poles, and that it exerted an attractive force far beyond itself. For Kepler, geometry was the key: it existed before the Creation and was co-eternal with the mind of God himself. Like Copernicus, he believed that the skies revealed significant proportion and mystic harmony. And though some of his ideas led nowhere, his intuitions about the significance of number and measurement, and the presence of gravity as a force determining the movement of the solar system, led him to make great conceptual leaps.

Kepler drew up a set of tables of planetary movement that were used by astronomers and navigators for the next century, and he also wrote an important work on optics explaining the operation of the telescope, and of the human eye in terms of lenses. But unlike Galileo, he made few observations of his own, mainly because he never possessed the necessary instruments. Galileo worked on a range of problems in physics and mechanics. As well as proving the existence of the Copernican system, he investigated movement through the air and along inclined planes, describing the trajectories of objects in motion, recognizing that all objects fall at a constant speed, establishing the principle of the pendulum, and proposing that all sense experience could be described in terms of 'shapes, numbers, sizes, and slow or rapid movements'. His stubborn nature brought the new astronomy into direct conflict with the Catholic Inquisition, and in 1633 he was condemned to life imprisonment, later commuted to house arrest.

Galileo also invented the microscope, although its value in identifying the minute creatures that prey on human beings had yet to be discovered. Virtually nothing was known of the micro-organisms that cause disease in people and animals, while the danger from insects such as the malaria-carrying mosquito, the house fly, and the fleas that carried bubonic plague was not yet fully recognized, though it was clear enough that the plague, like other illnesses, was contagious. Theories of illness were still based upon the old idea of maintaining the balance of liquids (or humours) within the body. Medical treatment normally consisted of attempts to regulate these liquids by bleeding or administering an emetic or purgative (purging upward or downward). Sudden or severe illness, and slow wasting diseases were both puzzling, and sometimes attributed to malignant witchcraft. Herbal remedies were widely used, and in general were safer and probably more effective than the drastic intervention of doctors and might be helpful in easing chronic conditions, but they were useless in cases of serious organic malfunction. Operations to remove growths or gangrened limbs were performed without anaesthetic and with unsterilized instruments. The surgeons who carried these out, like midwives, and in contrast to practising doctors, had not undergone a formal medical training.

Though doctors did not perform operations, they had begun to learn the principles of anatomy from observation. Watching the dissection of human bodies in an anatomy theatre became an important part of medical training, and in 1543 the age's greatest anatomist, Andreas Vesalius, published his lavishly illustrated account of *The Structure of the Human Body* ('*De Fabrica*'). Helkiah Crooke, surgeon to King James, argued that the study of anatomy not only taught self-knowledge but, 'Whosoever doth well know himself, knoweth all things, seeing in himself he hath the resemblances and representations of all things',[5] a variation on the idea that 'the little world of man' epitomized the greater world.

Not everyone shared a sense of nature's benevolence: John Donne, painfully conscious of the frailty of flesh, compared man's diseases and sicknesses to the 'serpents and vipers, malignant and venomous creatures, and worms, and caterpillars, that endeavour to devour that world which produces them'. He concludes triumphantly, 'can the other world name so many venomous, so many consuming, so many monstrous creatures, as we can diseases, of all these kinds? O miserable abundance! O beggarly riches! how much do we lack of having remedies for every disease, when as yet we have not names for them?' (*Devotions*: IV, Meditation). For a few extreme kinds of Neoplatonist all material existence was corrupt and corrupting, but nature was usually thought of as closer to its original state and more innocent than human beings. Nature at least obeyed God's laws unquestioningly, so Raleigh claimed in *The History of the World* (Book II, ch. iv, section 6). Hooker pointed out in his *Laws of Ecclesiastical Polity* what straits human beings would be in if the rest of creation were as disobedient to God as they were: he asks

if the moon should wander from her beaten way, the times and seasons of the year blend themselves by disordered and confused mixture, the winds breathe out their last gasp, the clouds yield no rain, the earth be defeated of heavenly influence, the fruits of the earth pine away as children at the withered breasts of their mother no longer able to yield them relief: what would become of man himself, whom these things now do all serve? See we not plainly that obedience of creatures unto the law of nature is the stay of the whole world?

(Book I, ch. iii, section 2)

According to the Church, human beings misused the reason they had been given to distinguish them from the beasts and raise them above the animals, in order to disobey God, and thus showed themselves unworthy of nature, which had been created for their benefit. Nature is seldom represented as ruthless or destructive. Monsters of the deep might prey on one another but their savagery was the result of appetite untempered by reason. Human beings had no such excuse. The natural order was more often invoked to provide examples of obedience: the social organization of bees exemplifies community spirit in Shakespeare's *Henry V*:

> so work the honey-bees,
> Creatures that by a rule in nature teach
> The act of order to a peopled kingdom.
> (I. ii. 187–9)

All animals had their own peculiar virtues: the strength of the lion and the cunning of the fox were proverbial. In nature, good order was considered the norm; only its breakdowns required explanation.

In England, the chief spokesman for a systematic and methodological investigation of nature was Francis Bacon. After his death he was celebrated as a latter-day Moses who had led the new science into the Promised Land. Yet though Bacon was a sharp analyst of popular misconceptions and outmoded ways of thinking, and though the account of Salomon's House in *The New Atlantis* has sometimes been read as a blueprint for the Royal Society, he was not a forerunner of the scientific revolution in any practical sense: his own experiments were inconsequential, ungoverned by informing theory, and worst of all, he took little interest in mathematics, failing to recognize its centrality at the very moment when it began to emerge as the foundation of other sciences. In this respect, the Neoplatonists and number mystics were nearer the mark.

Bacon contributed significantly to contemporary efforts to cut scientific experiments loose from religious restrictions which were liable to see them as time-wasting or even blasphemous, a dangerous prying into forbidden mysteries—a view suggested in *Dr Faustus* and one that the Catholic Church was to adopt, in the face of Galileo's provocation. In his *Novum Organum* (deliberately named after Aristotle's *Organon*, whose assumptions it set out to question) Bacon proposed that 'the moderns' should 'Give to faith that only which is faith's', and 'should not attempt to found a system of natural philosophy on the first chapter of Genesis, on the book of Job, and other parts of the sacred writings; seeking for the dead among the living'.[6] Bacon was following a tradition, traceable to Thomas Aquinas, that nature can be read as if it were a book; but far from being the devil's showcase, it provided an alternative revelation of God's glory, designed to back up the written revelation of the Bible, God's other text. The opening sections of *The Advancement of Learning* (1605) are similarly concerned to dispose of possible objections to scientific investigation: 'let no man . . . think or maintain, that a man can search too far, or be too well studied in the book of God's word, or in the book of God's works, divinity and philosophy' (Book I, ch. i, section 3). (Philosophy was the current term for scientific study.) It is only 'a little or superficial knowledge of philosophy' that inclines the mind of man to atheism. The popular conception of an atheist was of a man who explained all mysteries exclusively in terms of natural causes and effects. D'Amville, the titular villain of Tourneur's *The Atheist's Tragedy* (1611), is a figure of this sort, with an unhealthy disrespect for thunder. In his preface to *The History of the World*, Raleigh pointed out in so many words that nature could not possibly be regarded as the sole force in the universe ('I do also account it . . . but an impiety monstrous to confound God and Nature . . .'), perhaps remembering that at one time he himself had been under suspicion of atheism.

The conviction that men ought to observe, and even actively investigate, the wonder of God's creation reflected an optimistic view both of the natural world and of man as a reasonable creature, a view that had found expression in Pico's *Oration: On the Dignity of Man*. The classical tag, 'Man is the measure of all things' was often quoted in support of this confident attitude, but such an attitude was also open to question: what in nature justified such egotism? The kind of relativism that makes us interrogate our right to interfere with existing balances in nature or to despoil natural resources had its origin in the sixteenth century. Its great exponent was Montaigne, who refused to take for granted our supposed superiority to the rest of creation, insisting, in his most extended examination of the subject, the 'Apology for Raymond Sebond', that 'Presumption is our natural and original malady' ('Apology', *Essays*, p. 330). The

'Apology' is a defence of Sebond's *Natural Theology*, which Montaigne had translated at the request of his father. Sebond's book had argued along traditional lines that nature was the second revelation of God's creation, and that the elaborate correspondences of the cosmos attested His power. Montaigne gestures towards a defence of Sebond's book and then turns away to reveal far-reaching doubts about its underlying assumptions, and profound scepticism as to whether it is possible to know anything at all. Claims that the universe was designed for 'man', and that the stars direct their influence upon us are dramatically exposed, while aspirations to reason are refuted in terms of our ill-controlled emotions: 'Indeed we have strangely overpaid for this fine reason that we glory in, and this capacity to judge and know, if we have bought it at the price of this infinite number of passions to which we are incessantly a prey' ('Apology', *Essays*, p. 358). Montaigne's vision of human folly and arrogance provides a sharp corrective to the age's dreams of power, knowledge, and reason, echoing in a different key the Church's recognition of the moral and spiritual inadequacy of human beings, their suffering and sin. His question and personal motto, 'Que sais-je?' ('What do I know?': 'Apology', *Essays*, p. 393), echoes that of Erasmus who, in his mock-encomium *In Praise of Folly* (1511), had doubted the possibility of knowing anything other than how little we know.

6

Religion

IF there was a single issue that dominated the half-century from 1580, it was religion; yet, with the exception of the Authorized Version of the Bible, little of the literature still read today reflects this preoccupation. More than half the books published in the reign of Elizabeth concerned religion, but today the many theological tracts, sermons, and books of advice and instruction are hardly ever reread or reprinted. By contrast, the drama, under the surveillance of the Revels Office, was not supposed to present religious issues, or even to refer to God (as opposed to pagan gods), or name Him in the oaths that were a common feature of emphatic language. Even so, the dramatists, like most thoughtful people of the time, were deeply concerned with religion in one way or another: Christopher Marlowe at the time of his death, stood accused of blasphemy and atheism; Ben Jonson, during a prison sentence, became a Catholic convert, and remained so for several years (he has been suspected of involvement in the Gunpowder Plot); John Marston gave up writing plays to become an Anglican priest; Thomas Middleton wrote a version of Ecclesiasticus in verse and a pamphlet on the fulfilment of biblical prophecies—yet their particular beliefs are only intermittently reflected in their plays. Shakespeare's position has prompted the greatest speculation: there is circumstantial evidence that he had a Catholic background and sympathies, though this must have been true of many of his generation. His sonnet 'Poor soul, the centre of my sinful earth' (146) is deeply religious without being visibly sectarian. Religious issues were dangerously contentious in Elizabeth's reign; despite this, or perhaps because of it, the succeeding century was a great age of religious poetry.

The English Reformation

The Protestant Reformation of the English Church has been a subject of great debate among historians: regarded as one of the determining moments in English history, its effects have been considered liberating and democratizing, promoting on the one hand literacy, independence, and self-determination, and on the other an individualism and acquisitiveness that undermined communal values. According to the standard account, the established Church had grown materialistic and corrupt, and by the beginning of the sixteenth century the need for reform was widely recognized. But this narrative suffers from being end-determined: because we know what happened, we may be seeing the process as more inevitable than it actually was. An alternative account sees religious reform as prompted by political greed and opportunism, and imposed by force from above. Historians argue about the extent of popular support for change, and how much impact it had. Some consider its effects have been exaggerated and see the English Reformation as different in kind from the more idealistic European Reformation, though both movements included reactions against the wealth, power, and influence of the Catholic Church.

The German reformer Martin Luther believed that the Church should concern itself with spiritual, rather than actual wealth, and surrender its secular power. Its accumulated funds and lands encouraged greed among the clergy themselves, as well as arousing the envy and resentment of others. As an alternative to the Church's rule, Luther proposed government by a godly prince who would administer the temporal law, leaving the Church to concentrate upon spiritual concerns. His proposal provided Henry VIII with an idealistic charter to dismantle and seize the wealth of the English Church, a programme he proceeded to carry out between 1530 and 1538, when he began to have second thoughts. Protector Somerset and the Earl of

Northumberland, acting on behalf of the boy-king Edward VI (1547–53), revived his policies more energetically. Their Protestant convictions allowed them to continue to redistribute the power, wealth, and authority of the Church, reducing it to a state of financial weakness from which it was never to recover. In 1553 Mary Tudor, daughter of Catharine of Aragon, became queen and for five years reversed these policies and restored Catholicism. Whatever might have happened had she lived longer, the people whom Elizabeth inherited in 1558 were in a state of shock from this series of religious reversals. Mary had staged public burnings of popular Protestant leaders; those who escaped abroad returned inspired by the teachings of radical reformers such as Heinrich Bullinger and John Calvin.

Every individual who lived through these changes experienced them differently. Two accounts from East Anglia, an area strongly influenced by ideas from the Continent, reflect very different responses. Roger Martyn of Long Melford, a prosperous cloth-making village in Suffolk, left an account of 'the state of Melford church and of Our Lady's chapel at the east end, as I, Roger Martyn, did know it'.[1] He recalled the church as it was in his childhood in the 1530s, its great crucifix flanked by life-size statues of the Virgin and St John. The church interior glowed with painting, and the decorated statues of nearly two-dozen saints, specially adorned with jewels and embroidered cloths on high days and holidays, and there were banners, elaborate vestments, an organ, and a choir. Village life was dominated by the sequence of Church festivals that gave symbolic meaning to the turning year. These were celebrated with processions, parades, and communal eating and drinking such as are still to be found in the remoter corners of Southern Europe. The reformers destroyed this thriving community life centred on the church, leaving the very building empty and cold. Martyn kept a few of the now outlawed sacramental objects, a crucifix, the organ, and a bell, willing 'that my heirs, when time serve, shall repair, place there, and maintain all these things again'. According to popular opinion, 'It was a merry world when the service was used in the Latin tongue'; 'It was never so merry in England si[the]nce the scriptures were so commonly preached and talked upon'; 'We shall never have a merry world while the Queen liveth.'[2]

Martyn's lament for a lost world can be contrasted with one of the earliest narratives of conversion, composed by one William Malden, who recalled the first reading of the Bible in English in 1538: 'Immediately after, divers poor men in the town of Chelmsford in the county of Essex, where my father dwelled and I [was] born and with him brought up, the said poor men brought the New Testament of Jesus Christ, and on Sundays did sit reading in [the] lower end of the church, and many would flock about them to hear their reading.' Malden's father, upset at finding his son in this group, called him away and made him say his Latin prayers.

Then I saw I could not be in rest. Then, thought I, I will learn to read English, and then I will have the New Testament and read thereon myself; and then had I learned of an English prymer as far as *Patris sapientia*, and then on Sundays I plied my English prymer. The May-tide following, I and my father's prentice Thomas Jeffrey laid our money together and bought the New Testament in English, and hid it in our bed straw and so exercised it at convenient times.[3]

From reading the New Testament, Malden progressed to reading John Frith's book on the meaning of the mass, which questioned whether Christ was literally present in the communion bread and wine. When he criticized his mother for worshipping the crucifix, his father beat and almost strangled him. Malden's account of his reaction has a twofold significance: for him, the value of reading did not lie in its worldly usefulness—it had become an essential qualification for godliness. For the reformers, the essential Christian experience was no longer the communal singing of the Latin mass but the private reading of the Bible in English. While this changed the nature of faith from within, it also hastened the spread of literacy and the ideas that reading made accessible. Its second significance, though less tangible, was no less crucial: in discovering the Bible for himself, Malden had acquired a degree of spiritual and intellectual independence, a freedom which those in authority might deplore, but could not take away from him.

Traditionally, the Church had subordinated the individual to the community, both socially and spiritually: the clergy and saints interceded on behalf of the community as a whole, as much as on behalf of the individual within it. Protestantism appeared to make individuals responsible for their own salvation, to invite them to discover God within themselves and their own lives, while conferring a dignity on the process of making that discovery. Yet, theologically speaking, this was far from the case. Martin Luther differed from the humanist reformers, particularly Erasmus, in believing that all individual free will had been lost through the fall of Adam, so that salvation was no longer a matter of personal choice, but depended on God's grace. John Calvin took this argument a step further, declaring that the elect, those whom God would save, were already known to Him, having been chosen before the world was made. Despite this knotty paradox at the heart of Protestantism, many believers experienced a new sense of self-determination, such as Malden seems to have felt.

But the cost was high. The old shared values, truths, and certainties had been thrown aside for a thousand private and conflicting convictions; the civil and religious wars that proceeded to tear Europe apart were one immediate result. The reformers' assumption that reading the Bible would lead everyone to recognize the truth of their religion was repeatedly proved to be wrong. The Protestant Church had begun by urging the spiritual nature of its concerns, had argued for universal priesthood and liberty of conscience. But once established as the English state religion in 1559, it too employed the machinery of the state to enforce its cause: people must go to church every Sunday; the clergy must actively preach the word; papists and sectarians must be forcibly deterred from their heresies. The religion of a persecuted minority, as it had once been, has one kind of appeal, but it operates very differently when it becomes the established church. John Foxe warned Elizabeth against persecuting sectarians: 'When men of false doctrine are killed, their error is not killed; nay, it is all the more strengthened, the more constantly they die.'[4]

The worldliness of the Catholic Church and its emphasis on good works had been frequent targets for criticism for at least 200 years. In the fourteenth century John Wyclif and the Lollards had argued for a preaching clergy and an English translation of the Bible (it was then only in Latin, as were church prayers), and had begun work on an illicit translation around 1382. Their contemporaries, the poets Chaucer and Langland, satirized the greed of the lower clergy, and the self-indulgence of some monks and friars. More than a century later, Erasmus (*c.*1469–1536), who, like Luther, had himself been a monk, criticized the monastic orders in his *Praise of Folly* (1511, translated 1549): 'Most of them are a long way removed from religion... they can't even read.'[5] Elsewhere he commented on practices he considered superstitious, ridiculing the worship of particular saints for particular kinds of protection, the buying of pardons and saying of prayers as forms of penance, and the paying of priests to recite masses for the soul as ways of buying salvation. He pointed out that 'St Paul was incessant in his attempts to remove the Jews from their faith in external works. I feel that the vast majority of Christians have sunk once again into this unhealthy situation.'[6] He was particularly horrified by Pope Julius II's military campaigns in northern Italy: in his view, war was the greatest crime against God. Erasmus's views, written in Latin (the language used by educated Europeans) and printed in thousands of copies, reached a wide readership, lending his authority to the demands for change, which quite suddenly passed beyond anything he had ever imagined or intended. He had supposed the Catholic Church to be fundamentally united, and capable of reform from within. But the world around him was changing, and the split (or schism) that followed was more drastic and more permanent than any that had yet occurred in the history of the Western Church.

In the reformers' eyes, the sale of relics and pardons, and the use of signs and prayers as charms to ward off evil all helped to reduce faith to the level of superstition. Educated or semi-educated themselves, they believed that everyone else wanted or was able to cultivate an active spiritual life on the model of their own. Yet up to half the population of sixteenth-century England was living at subsistence level—for them, merely surviving was a struggle. Historians have asked whether the silent majority could be described as Christian at all. How many adults understood the fundamental beliefs of their Church? How many attended church services regularly? Most people believed that good behaviour would be rewarded (or, at any rate, that bad behaviour would be punished), and pictured life as an endless struggle between the powers of good and evil, believing in the notion of lucky and unlucky ('dismal') days, and the influence of the stars on the lives of individuals. White witches, popular healers, or cunning folk were widely consulted, and may even have provided an invisible, unofficial alternative to the clergy.

Between such simple beliefs and the age's theological disputes lay an enormous gap that the parish priest was expected to negotiate, but all too often he was scarcely more knowledgeable than his parishioners. Bishop Hooper's visitation to his Gloucester diocese in 1551 revealed that out of 311 clergymen he examined, 168 could not repeat the ten commandments, thirty-nine did not know where to find the Lord's Prayer in the Bible, thirty-four did not know who had composed it, and ten could not even recite it. The education of the clergy was one area in which both the Protestant Reformation and the Catholic Counter-Reformation made real advances, but this was a more limited (and therefore manageable) goal than educating their parishioners. The reformers were often disappointed by their failure to make their faith understood: a man of 60 who had attended Anglican sermons all his life, both during the week and twice on Sundays, was catechized on his deathbed: 'Being demanded what he thought of God, he answers that he was a good old man; and what of Christ, that he was a towardly young youth; and of his soul, that it was a great bone in his body; and what should become of his soul after he was dead, that if he had done well he should be put into a pleasant green meadow.'[7] The old man's need to visualize and his inability to think in abstract terms suggests that, for people like himself, a religion strong on icons and requiring a regular pattern of works and observances might have been more satisfying than the religion of faith that the reformers sought to impose.

Both Churches were led by intellectuals who did not always grasp the difficulty of the educative tasks before them, if people were to understand the meaning of their religious practices. The reformers, following Martin Luther, aimed to transfer attention from the temporal church, with its thrones, powers, priests, prayers, and good works to the city of God in men's hearts, and the inner life of the believer. The words of St Paul in his Epistle to the Romans 3: 28 ('Therefore we conclude that a man is justified by faith without the deeds of the law') provided one cornerstone of Protestant belief, though they were partially contradicted by the Epistle of James, 2: 17 ('Even so faith, if it hath not works, is dead, being alone'). Luther, hoping to allay the anxiety induced by a religion of works and free will, insisted that faith could be achieved only through God's grace granted to the individual, and not through any act of personal choice or will. Erasmus, and the Catholic Church as a whole, could not accept that the individual had no choice in the matter. For Luther, faith was a comforting trust and confidence that God would save you. His successor, Calvin, also considered the apparently harsh doctrine of predestination (that God had already chosen all those to be saved) as 'full of sweet, pleasant and unspeakable comfort to godly persons', as it is expressed in the *Thirty-nine Articles of the Anglican Church* (1563).

But as one form of religious anxiety was lifted, another replaced it. If Christians were unable to influence God's decision to grant grace, then they might be cast away but could do nothing to save themselves. This was a nightmare that haunted the Protestant imagination, an inescapable theological blind-alley. Fortunately, the majority of Protestants saw themselves as sheep rather than goats, finding in the misery or wickedness around them evidence of their own moral superiority, and thus indirect proof that they were among the elect. Although good works were not of value in themselves, they were evidence of God's grace, so there was still indirect pressure to practice virtuous living and give to the poor.

The Elizabethan Church Settlement was the work of clergy-men, many of whom had spent the five years of Mary Tudor's reign in Geneva or Strasburg, where they had been strongly influenced by Calvin's theology of predestination. Today the idea that a small minority has been specially selected for salvation seems so unfair or so unlikely that we assume it could only have been reached through a counter-intuitive logic, though it has certain affinities with the predetermined nature of a dramatic fiction. In the first scene of Marlowe's tragedy *Dr Faustus*, the hero juxtaposes different biblical quotations to prove that all human beings are condemned to eternal damnation, and that theology itself is a waste of time. His account omits any reference to God's grace or the doctrine that Christ died to redeem His people. Instead, it parodies the systems of sequential logic still taught at university, and the potentially circular theology of Calvin, in which individuals cannot help themselves by an act of will:

> The reward of sin is death. That's hard . . .
> If we say that we have no sin,
> We deceive ourselves, and there's no truth in us.
> Why then belike we must sin
> And so consequently die.
> Ay, we must die an everlasting death.
> What doctrine call you this, *Che sera, sera*,
> What will be, shall be? Divinity, adieu!
>
> (I. i. 41, 44–50)

Ironically, in view of Faustus's dismissal of 'divinity', the whole play can be read as a Calvinist thesis in which the reprobate (i.e. already doomed) scholar cannot humble his heart to repent. But each of the several moments in which he is urged to do so is tense with the possibility that he still might. Calvinists admitted the importance of particular moral decisions, while recognizing God's inescapable foreknowledge of His total scheme, just as the play combines the story of Faustus's inevitable damnation with a series of moments of individual decision.

Sixteenth-century Christians, subject to sudden and inexplicable illness, accident, or death, might, like Faustus, have bought with their souls a guaranteed twenty-four years of life. They recognized the extreme difficulties of understanding God's purposes. Race, class, and gender and innate qualities, both physical and mental, determined one's horizons in early modern society, which officially discouraged social mobility. Predestination provided a rationale for that inner conviction that something beyond the consciously choosing self shapes our actions and our lives. Calvin's doctrines were accepted by many well-informed Elizabethans and defended by many Jacobean Protestants in the face of the arguments for free will advanced by the Dutch theologian Arminius (1560–1609) which, by the late 1620s, were beginning to influence the Anglican Church.

Different social groups and different regions of England responded to the Elizabethan Church Settlement (1559) in significantly different ways. The most remote areas, geographically, were naturally the least accessible and so tended to retain their Catholicism longest. In Scotland, the Highlands were predominantly Catholic while the Lowlands followed John Knox into a more radically Calvinist form of church government. In England, the north and west were the slowest to respond: Lancashire, Cheshire, and Wales remained Catholic strongholds. London and the south-east—the Thames valley, Kent, and East Anglia—traditionally highly populated and exactly those areas where earlier church reform movements had made headway, were most actively Protestant. In the rest of the countryside, much depended on the convictions of the individual parish clergy: a popular reforming minister might lead his congregation towards an active Protestant faith, but it was at the middle levels of society that the new beliefs made their strongest impact. Historians have used the wording of wills as one way of measuring the spread of Protestant beliefs: money left for the saying of prayers, candles, bells, or saints was gradually phased out, but at different rates in different parts of the country. William Malden, the Chelmsford shopkeeper quoted earlier, was typical of the craftsmen, respectable artisans, and merchants who provided its earliest supporters. Protestant belief established itself strongly in towns, where new contacts were made more rapidly and sustained more easily.

It is unlikely that 'the godly' (as they thought of themselves) were ever more than a small, though influential minority, though their adoption of the Protestant 'work ethic', and disapproval of more relaxed and pleasure-loving neighbours helped to create new social divisions. The upper classes displayed a wide range of religious beliefs. The Earls of Pembroke and Leicester and the Sidney family were strongly Protestant, supporting the cause in Europe and promoting Calvinist ministers at home. At the opposite end of the spectrum were a number of great and influential aristocratic families like the Howards and the Petres, who kept their Catholic faith. Although individual courtiers varied greatly in their convictions, the fashionable Protestantism of Elizabeth's reign gradually gave place to a fashionable crypto-Catholicism under the Stuarts which, in Charles I's reign (1625–49), centred upon his wife Henrietta Maria and her French retinue; they contributed substantially to his unpopularity.

The Bible, Foxe, and Providence

The Protestant religion is dominated by the word of God as expressed in the Bible, God's written instructions to his faithful. One of the earliest objectives of the reformers was to make the Bible available in the vernacular, whereas the Catholic liturgy and prayers were still read and said in Latin. An English Bible would be accessible and immediate in a way that the fossilized and learned language of the Vulgate (St Jerome's Latin Bible) could never be; written in the language of everyday life, it would speak directly to the heart, or so thought William Tyndale (1494–1536), who made its translation his life's work in the face of persecution and, ultimately, death. Echoing Erasmus's promise that 'even the lowliest woman' would be able to read the scriptures, he promised the scholars who opposed him that 'he would cause a boy that driveth the plough to know more of the scripture' than they did.[8] In accordance with this commitment, and his sense that English had a sentence-structure closer to Hebrew than to Latin, Tyndale produced a lively, rhythmic, and idiomatic version, full of memorable phrases. Luther, who had translated the Bible into German, had shown how the translator's choice of words could bring Biblical narrative closer to contemporary experience, and also that it could be used either to question or endorse familiar religious practices. Tyndale followed Luther in choosing 'congregation' instead of 'church', 'elder' instead of 'priest', 'knowledge' instead of 'confession', 'love' instead of 'charity', so that the earliest readers found that the words of the Bible as Tyndale had translated them did not necessarily correspond to the Church as they knew it. His translation of the New Testament (1525) and of sections of the Old (1534) were published abroad and denounced as heretical, although they also provided the basis for the several versions that followed.

Another Protestant reformer, Miles Coverdale, completed Tyndale's work, and the resulting Great Bible (it was to be 'of the largest volume') was officially installed in every English church in 1539, though the translation most often used by Shakespeare and his contemporaries was that of the Geneva Bible (1560), made by Protestants in exile on the Continent during the reign of Mary Tudor. This was the first to divide the chapters into verses, and to be printed in Roman, instead of the more familiar Gothic, type (or 'black letter'). Some of its marginal commentaries were too radical for the Elizabethan clergy, who tried to discourage its use by issuing the Bishops' Bible (1568). Early in his reign, King James assembled a committee of forty-seven translators who between them produced the Authorized Version of 1611. Its balanced clauses and graceful, if old-fashioned phrases (it still drew upon Tyndale at many points) contributed enormously and enduringly to English prose. For centuries, its language conferred dignity on ceremonial, lending elegance and formality to English as a whole.

Translation did not remain a Protestant monopoly: in 1582 the Catholic English College at Douai published an English translation of the New Testament, which in its turn contributed particular wording to the Authorized Version. Here, as in other

Catholic developments, there was a tendency to rework Protestant initiatives from a different angle. The Counter-Reformation laid a comparable emphasis on the individual's relation to God, while the Jansenist theology of the seventeenth century, in minimizing the operation of free will, looked back to Calvinist doctrine at a time when Arminian Protestantism had begun to reassert it. For the reformers, the word of God was preferred before all others, so that the singing of psalms came to replace hymns. Godly poets composed metrical versions of the Psalms: Sir Thomas Wyatt wrote a sequence of penitential psalms, and the Earl of Surrey followed his example, while praising Wyatt's versions. Later, Mary and Philip Sidney worked on a set of metrical psalms which Mary completed after her brother's death. John Donne wrote of these that 'They tell us why, and teach us how to sing' ('Upon the translation of the Psalms', l. 22).

The exiles from Geneva brought back Calvin's theories on the nature of salvation, Christian worship, and the government of the Church, and two books with which to establish the new faith in England: the first was the Geneva Bible; the second was a new history of the English Church by John Foxe, *The Acts and Monuments*, better known as 'Foxe's Book of Martyrs' (1563, revised 1570). With the Bible, this was the book most likely to be found in any household until the end of the nineteenth century. Foxe's compilation, greatly expanded in later editions, set out to ensure that its readers remembered the sufferings of those persecuted for their Protestant faith under Henry VIII and his daughter Mary Tudor. His account focused particularly upon the heroism of ordinary women and working people, of little account in their society, who achieved spiritual stature through steadfast resistance in the face of the violence inflicted by Church and State. The drama of their interrogations, in which the simple, scriptural wisdom of the martyrs confutes the clergy's display of learning, is designed to recall the trials of Christ, and the book was illustrated with woodcuts of the tortured and dying, as if to provide the reformers with their own latter-day saints. Foxe saw their suffering as part of a larger pattern that looked forward to the end of the world, casting the community of the reformed as

God's chosen people, who would play a key role in establishing the reign of the blessed on earth and the coming of the New Jerusalem, as promised in the Book of Revelation.

This scheme, and indeed the shape of Foxe's book as a whole, was strongly influenced by his friend John Bale, who had published accounts of the trials of an earlier martyr, Sir John Oldcastle, and of the Henrician victim Anne Askew. He was also the author of *The Image of Both Churches* (*c.*1545), the first full-length Protestant commentary on St John's Book of Revelation (or, in Greek, the Apocalypse). Drawing on earlier traditions, Bale reads it as a symbolic account of Christian history, culminating in a prophecy of the end of the world, with the conversion of the Jews, the thousand-year reign of the saints on earth (the Millennium), and the Second Coming of Christ Himself. The symbolic events witnessed by St John—the sounding of the seven trumpets, the breaking of the seven seals, and so on—are interpreted as particular incidents in the ongoing war between the true Church and the Church of Rome, identified with St John's Scarlet Woman of Babylon on her Great Beast, its seven heads associated with the city's seven hills, while the pope is identified with Antichrist. Although there was no agreed timetable for this sequence of events, between 1550 and 1650 many Protestants believed themselves involved in the beginning of the end of the world, and this gave a special urgency to their demands for change.

The war between the two Churches is illustrated on the title-page of the 1570 edition of *Acts and Monuments*, where 'The Image of the persecuting Church' and 'The Image of the persecuted Church' confront one another, in a reference to Bale's book, which had ended with woodcuts of the two Churches represented as the Scarlet Woman of Babylon and the Woman Clothed with the Sun (another figure from the Book of Revelation, 12:1). Edmund Spenser celebrated the power of the Protestant imagination by giving the apocalyptic history of Bale and Foxe priority in his poem *The Faerie Queene*. Its first book enacts the historical, theological, and psychological struggles of the English nation, personified by St George the Redcross

Knight, against the wiles of Rome, figured as Archimago and
Duessa, the Scarlet Woman of Babylon. With the help of Una,
the true Church and the Woman Clothed with the Sun, he finally
overcomes the dragon and is granted a glimpse of the New
Jerusalem. But not everyone was persuaded by these readings
from the Book of Revelation. Richard Hooker ridiculed the
tendency to identify all older rituals as 'borrowed from the shop
of Antichrist', commenting tartly, 'Nothing more clear unto
their seeming, than that a New Jerusalem being often spoken
of in Scripture, they undoubtedly were themselves that New
Jerusalem, and that the old did by way of a certain figurative
resemblance signify what they should both be and do' (*Of the
Laws of Ecclesiastical Polity*, Preface, ch. viii, section 11). Ben
Jonson also laughed at their pretensions: in a moment of comic
bathos in *The Alchemist*, the puritan deacon Ananias denounces
Surly who has unluckily disguised himself in Spanish costume.
His Spanish 'slops' (or trousers) are

> profane,
> Lewd, superstitious, and idolatrous breeches . . .
> Thou look'st like Antichrist, in that lewd hat.
>   (IV. vii. 48–9, 55)

Spenser's St George reflects a note of chauvinistic pride in
the Anglican Church that emerged during the eighties, which
is also to be heard in Lyly's *Euphues and His England* (1580):
'Oh blessed peace, oh happy prince, oh fortunate people: the
living God is only the English God.'[9] The chauvinistic identification of the true Church with the Church of England represents
a departure from apocalyptic history as written by Bale and
Foxe, for whom the true Church was made up rather of the community of 'the godly', whether in England or Geneva, 'universal
and sparsedly through all countries dilated'.[10] But Foxe believed
that the English Church held a special place in God's scheme,
not merely because of the blood shed by its martyrs, but because
its Church was older and purer than that of Rome. The second-
century King Lucius was traditionally credited with having
brought Christianity to Britain, but Spenser, following Foxe,

claimed that the origin of English Christianity actually pre-dated Lucius:

> Yet true it is, that long before that day
> Hither came Joseph of Arimathy,
> Who brought with him the holy grail, (they say)
> And preached the truth, but since it greatly did decay.
> (*The Faerie Queene*, II. x. 53)

Foxe described how Joseph of Arimathea and the disciples of the Apostle Philip established the true Church in England long before the Roman missionaries, who merely muddied the waters of an earlier and purer faith. According to the 1563 edition of *Acts and Monuments*, the English Church declined under Gregory's mission from Rome, and when the first millennium after Christ's birth ended, in accordance with the numerology of Revelation, Antichrist was once more released on the world, taking Peter's throne at Rome as his own, and driving true faith into the wilderness. In the revision of 1570, however, these events were relocated: the binding of Antichrist was now linked not with the crucifixion, but with the British-born emperor Constantine, and he was loosed again just in time to persecute the Wycliffites. Certain English kings had stood out against the Roman Church, notably Henry II and John (who became an exemplar of the king as reformer, as he had been for Bale—Foxe included a dramatic strip-cartoon of John being poisoned by an evil monk, Simon of Swinstead). The long struggle reached its climax with the deaths of Tyndale, Frith, and the Marian martyrs, who died as witnesses to the truth of the Protestant cause.

For Foxe, and for many of his contemporaries, the mystic truths of Revelation revealed God's intentions for His elect who, like the Israelites of old, could expect to prosper as long as they obeyed His word, for no enemy could overcome those whom God protected. Protestants were inclined to regard the defeat of the Spanish Armada in 1588 and the timely discovery of the Gunpowder Plot to blow up king and parliament in 1605 as clear evidence of God's care for the Anglican Church and its godly prince. The failure of these two major Catholic threats to national security was regarded as providential (i.e. it revealed God's foreknowledge, used on behalf of His people). For many, God's hand was visible wherever one looked, in the patterns of individual lives. Books of God's judgements were popular, one of the most widely read being that of Thomas Beard, later a tutor to the young Oliver Cromwell. His *Theatre of God's Judgements* (1597) described the death of the naughty play-maker and supposed atheist, Christopher Marlowe:

But see what a hook the Lord put in the nostrils of this barking dog: it so fell out, that as he purposed to stab one whom he owed a grudge unto with his dagger, the other party perceiving, so avoided the stroke, that withal catching hold of his wrist, he stabbed his own dagger into his own head, in such sort, that notwithstanding all the means of surgery that could be wrought, he shortly after died thereof: the manner of his death being so terrible (for he even cursed and blasphemed to his last gasp, and together with his breath an oath flew out of his mouth) that it was not only a manifest sign of God's Judgement, but also an horrible and fearful terror to all that beheld him.[11]

Despite Beard's contempt for play-makers and scurrilous poets, he was himself influenced by dramatic structure. In his view, God was the supreme dramatist, neatly fitting the punishment to the crime so that the atheist and blasphemer died, gasping out curses with his final breath. Thirty years earlier, the interlude of *King Cambises* had ended with the King impaled on his own sword, so that he appeared as a living—or rather, dying—emblem of the deadly sin of wrath, traditionally stabbed with his own weapon (as is Beard's Marlowe). In Marlowe's own *Jew of Malta*, the Jew falls into the cauldron of boiling oil he has prepared for his enemies, thus suffering the expected punishment for usurers in hell, and the hand of God is also in evidence at the climax of Tourneur's *Atheist's Tragedy* (1611). The traffic between providential historians and dramatists could be complicated: another popular book of judgements, *The Triumphs of God's Revenge Against The Crying and Execrable Sin of . . . Murder* (1621), written by a puritan merchant of Exeter, John Reynolds, supplied Thomas Middleton with the plot of *The Changeling* (1622).

While godly ballads and plays often portrayed the wicked as fearing and/or incurring God's judgement, both Shakespeare and Marlowe made use of such devices while at the same time exposing the way that they resulted from one particular scheme of interpretation: the enigmatic end of *Tamburlaine, Part II* plays with the idea that Tamburlaine may have been struck down for challenging Mahomet (v. i. 186–201, 217), while in Shakespeare's *King John*, Cardinal Pandulph promises the Dauphin that all kinds of natural effects will be (wrongly) interpreted by popular opinion in his favour, as

> meteors, prodigies and signs,
> Abortives, presages and tongues of heaven,
> Plainly denouncing vengeance upon John.
> (III. iv. 157–9)

If Shakespeare's *King Lear* is read beside the old chronicle play of *King Leir*, it seems especially concerned to expose the emptiness of providential readings, and to baffle expectations of dramatic justice. Such scepticism might have a dangerous edge at a time when one definition of an atheist was someone who believed that all things had a natural cause. When Lear asks 'What is the cause of thunder?' (III. iv. 155), one orthodox reply might have been 'God's anger', as it had been in *King Leir* (e.g. at ll. 1633, 1739), and elsewhere in Renaissance drama.

Dramatists who were themselves engaged in the making of fictions were well placed to see through the process by which fictions of meaning were made. One reaction to a piety which saw God's hand behind all human actions was to find meaning in none, just as one response to the age's multiplying forms of worship was to feel that there was little distinction between them, and, perhaps, less truth in any. In a few hardy individuals, the numerous theological disputes induced scepticism, and possibly atheism, such as Marlowe stood accused of. Shortly before his death in 1593 his former companion, one Richard Baines, denounced him to the Privy Council. Some sentences from his list of Marlowe's supposed opinions may be discounted as the sort of thing that, as an anti-Catholic spy, he might have been required to say in order to test his opponent's views, but there are further scandalous assertions (though the first turns up in several of the Mystery plays):

That Christ was a bastard and his mother dishonest.

That the women of Samaria and her sister were whores and that Christ knew them dishonestly.

That St John the Evangelist was bedfellow to Christ and leaned always in his bosom, that he used him as the sinners of Sodoma.[12]

The document also includes a number of rationalist views that contrast with the orthodoxy of *Dr Faustus*: 'That the Indians and many authors of antiquity have assuredly written of above 16 thousand years agone, whereas Adam is proved to have lived within 6 thousand years. He affirmeth that Moyses was but a juggler and that one Heriots [i.e. Thomas Harriot], being Sir W. Raleigh's man, can do more than he.' A further cynicism originally attributed to Machiavelli, asserts 'That the first beginning of religion was only to keep men in awe'. Finally, like his own Faustus, 'he hath quoted a number of contrarieties out of the scriptures . . .'.

Even if Marlowe believed such things (and it is not at all clear what he did believe), they were certainly not the sort of opinions that it was wise to express. Sir Walter Raleigh himself was suspected of doubting the existence of the soul because, in the course of a dinner-table conversation with the clergyman Ralph Ironside, he pointed out that the standard arguments for it were circular. Though less subversive than Marlowe's views as set out in Baines's deposition, such lines of thought were still considered dangerous. It has been said that it was virtually impossible to be an atheist, as we understand the word, in this intensely religious age, but rapid changes in church policy and fierce arguments on both sides may have contributed to doubt and scepticism among the well-informed.

The Anglican Compomise

Foxe's *Acts and Monuments* had created a sort of instant ancestry and tradition for the new English Church, providing an

answer to those who asked (in Hooker's words), 'where our
Church did lurk, in what cave of the earth it slept for so many
hundreds of years together before the birth of Martin Luther?'
(*Of the Laws of Ecclesiastical Polity*, Book III, ch. i, section 10).
A new respect for history and sources encouraged the search for
origins and precedents, crucial where the Church was concerned,
since its authority still partly depended on being able to claim a
continuity with the missions established by Christ's disciples.

The English Church Settlement of 1559 set up an anomalous
mixture of Calvinist theology and mainly Catholic Church government and liturgy, though the Latin services had been translated into English and adjusted to suit the new beliefs: salvation
by faith alone, the impossibility of free will, and the centrality
of the Bible, rather than the priesthood as the primary source
of religious truth. Committed reformers remained unhappy
with this compromise, seeing the system of church government
through bishops and archbishops (as opposed to that of lay
elders proposed by Calvin, and adopted by the Presbyterian
Church of Scotland), and the use of a modified form of the old
Catholic service as idolatrous or popish relics.

Of the seven original sacraments of the Roman Church,
Martin Luther had accepted only two: baptism and communion.
Baptism at birth was practised in the Anglican Church, and only
questioned by Anabaptists, but the significance and performance
of the communion, as the central ceremony of Christianity
caused endless argument: for Catholics, the bread and wine were
changed into Christ's flesh and blood by the priest before the
altar, which was separated from the body of the church by the
rood-screen and choir. Protestants understood the ceremony
less literally: the bread and wine were to be taken in remembrance of Christ's body and blood, as He had told His disciples
to do at the Last Supper, but details of what the ceremony meant
and how it was to be performed changed considerably, even
between the *First Book of Common Prayer* (1549) and the
Second (1552). The First insists that the host (the bread) shall
not be lifted up, and that it shall be larger than the traditional
wafer. But the Second, the one adopted by Elizabeth's Church,

orders that the communion table stand in the body of the church, covered with a linen cloth, and that 'to take away the superstition, which any person hath, or might have', the bread shall be 'such as is eaten at the table, with other meats' (the Curate might take it home for his supper, if there was any left over).[13] Communicants will kneel, but this is to show gratefulness, not because they believe in 'any real and essential presence' in the bread or wine. Later communicants sometimes preferred to stand or even walk about. In the 1630s William Laud reinstated the communion table in the nave with the traditional altar at the east end, a change that has survived to the present, but which aroused much opposition at the time.

Behind arguments as to how communion should be administered or received lay the larger question of the role of the priest as administrant. The reformers decisively altered the balance of power between the priest and the congregation, demanding greater spiritual involvement from lay people, while reducing the quasi-magical status of the priest: he was now called pastor or minister, rather than priest, his elaborate vestments reduced to a plain surplice, and he was encouraged to marry, and live like everyone else. He no longer performed the transubstantiation of the bread and wine or heard individual confessions, though he did teach children to recite the catechism, an account of their faith which included a renunciation of the world, the flesh, and the devil, and of their duties to God and their neighbours, with the ten commandments and the Lord's Prayer. For Protestants, the minister's main function was to bring people to God by persuasion, to open their hearts to God's word, as the evangelists had done. The good clergyman was thus a preaching clergyman.

Although the reformers were eager to establish an effective clergy, the Church had lost so much of its old endowments, and had undergone so many reverses, that when Elizabeth came to the throne many parishes had no ministers at all, let alone educated ones. New sermons and lectures were set up, and the clergy were to be educated through special discussions, known as conferences and prophesyings. In 1576 these led to a serious quarrel between Elizabeth and her newly appointed Archbishop of Canterbury, Edmund Grindal. The prophesyings were teaching sessions for the clergy at which a sermon was preached and a text expounded, the participants asking questions or raising particular points. Increasingly, lay people had joined in, bringing their Bibles and even their wives and servants, so that they sometimes ended up as large open-air meetings of exactly the sort that the authorities most disliked. Elizabeth, dubious about the doctrines taught and the encouragement to dispute, banned them. Grindal's response was to remind her

that you are a mortal creature. 'Look not only (as was said to Theodosius) upon the purple and princely array, wherewith ye are apparelled, but consider withal what is that that is covered therewith. Is it not flesh and blood? Is it not dust and ashes? Is it not a corruptible body, which must return to his earth again, God knoweth how soon?' ... And although ye are a mighty prince, yet remember that He which dwelleth in heaven is mightier.[14]

The Queen was so offended that she suspended Grindal from office; though never actually deprived of it, he never exercised its functions again. Spenser, an admirer of Grindal, introduced him into *The Shepheardes Calender* (1579) in May and July, thinly disguised as 'Algrin'. Thomalin describes how an eagle (a figure for the Queen) dropped a shellfish on his head, mistaking its baldness for chalk, 'So now astonied with the stroke, | He lies in ling'ring pain' (July, ll. 227–8). Spenser's odd allegory avoids directly blaming the Queen (whose patronage he still hoped for), but cannot pass over the episode without comment. It was symptomatic of the Church's problems that the Queen and her Primate could not agree upon a common policy. From Elizabeth's accession, some of her strongest supporters had been reformers who wanted her to reduce church ritual, support Protestants against Catholics in Europe, and to introduce the Calvinist system of church government in which a committee of lay elders selected and appointed ministers, thus doing away with bishops altogether.

This system, adopted by the Presbyterian Church of Scotland, was seen as a particularly dangerous demand in England. While it increased lay involvement in the Church, it also provided a more democratic model of self-rule than existed in other institutions, and the attack on bishops was interpreted as an attack on hierarchy and order on a wider front. Militant Protestants themselves recognized that the English bishops had given a spiritual lead to the whole movement: bishops like Hooper, Latimer, Ridley, and Cranmer had been enrolled in the list of Marian martyrs, while reforming archbishops like Edmund Grindal reinforced traditional respect for the office. Elizabeth, and later James (who, unlike her, had been brought up a Calvinist), both governed an Anglican Church in which most of the ardent reformers, while actively pressing for change, still hoped that it could be achieved within the Established Church itself. There were bishops like Whitgift and Bancroft who disliked and distrusted their demands, persecuting or preaching against them, but they failed to dislodge them on any significant scale. It was not until William Laud (Bishop of London in 1628, Archbishop of Canterbury in 1633) reversed earlier policies on church ceremony and furniture and Calvinist theology, that an archbishop lost the confidence of committed Protestants finally and completely.

In the last years of Elizabeth's reign her Church was increasingly anxious to maintain the *status quo* in the face of demands for reform, exiling and even executing its critics. Richard Hooker, a clergyman who, early in his career, had found himself competing for the support of a London congregation with a puritan preacher, produced the most powerful and comprehensive defence of the Anglican Church ever written, although at first he could not even find a publisher for it. *Of the Laws of Ecclesiastical Polity* (1593) begins by making the case for the Elizabethan settlement, while carefully pointing out that

He that goeth about to persuade a multitude, that they are not so well governed as they ought to be, shall never want attentive and favourable hearers . . . Whereas on the other side, if we maintain things that are established, we have not only to strive with a number of heavy prejudices deeply rooted in the hearts of men, who think that herein we serve the time, and speak in favour of the present state, because thereby we either hold or seek preferment; but also to bear such exceptions as minds so averted beforehand usually take against that which they are loth should be poured into them.

(Book I, ch. i, section 10)

Hooker constructed an eloquent defence of the Church's position, based on arguments for universal and natural order, and controlled at every level by appeals to historical circumstance, moderation, and common sense. For Hooker, as for many later Anglican apologists, the Church's strength lay precisely in its steering a middle course that could take advantage of the best elements in both the old religion and the new. Though Hooker was tolerant and humane by the standards of the day, much of his argument dismissed as extreme the positions of 'popish persons' (on the one hand) and 'self-conceited brethren' (on the other) in favour of a reasonable compromise, apparent in his discussion of scriptural authority: 'Two opinions therefore there are concerning sufficiency of Holy Scripture, each extremely opposite unto the other, and both repugnant unto truth' (Book II, ch, viii, section 7). Hooker helped to establish the view that a compromise between the Roman and the Reformed Church was not merely legitimate, but made good sense. George Herbert's poem 'The British Church' was to characterize the Church of Rome as wanton and painted, and the Reformed Church as 'so shy | Of dressing that her hair doth lie | About her ears', dismissing them both in favour of a third alternative:

> But dearest Mother, (what those miss)
> The mean thy praise and glory is,
>   And long may be.
> Blessed be God, whose love it was
> To double-moat thee with His grace,
>   And none but thee.

(ll. 25–30)

Separatists and Catholics

A small but significant group of radical Protestants had never accepted Elizabeth's Anglican Church: known as separatists or nonconformists, they included Anabaptists, who insisted on adult baptism and were associated with the notorious Munster episode (see Chapter 2, and Spenser's Anabaptist giant); Familists (members of the Family of Love, inspired by the mystic writings of Henry Niclaes); and a group of English exiles known as the Amsterdam Brethren who fled to the Netherlands in search of religious freedom. The supposedly eccentric practices of these sects made them a favourite target for jokes from both the right and left wings of the Established Church. Active Protestants saw their fanaticism as a threat, liable to bring their own reforming enthusiasms into disrepute by association, rather as some socialists today dislike being thought of as communists.

Jonson satirized the Amsterdam Brethren as 'the exiled saints' in *The Alchemist*, where their deacon Ananias and their pastor Tribulation Wholesome are presented as shameless crooks and hypocrites. Entrusted with goods intended for the benefit of the group's widows and orphans, they embezzle them in the deluded hope that Subtle can convert them not merely into gold, but into Dutch dollars with which to stir up the war against the Spanish in the Netherlands—a topical issue, since a truce had been declared in 1609, shortly before the play was staged in 1610. Mistress Mulligrub, in Marston's *The Dutch Courtesan* (1605) indicates that she is a member of the Family of Love (III. iii. 63–73), a group particularly hard to identify since they conformed outwardly. The standard joke about them was that their prayer meetings were covers for sexual orgies, though given the inward and inspirational nature of their beliefs, they are more likely to have resembled Quaker meetings. Thomas Middleton's early comedy *The Family of Love* (1603) overworks this idea, linking them with the puritans as hypocrites, but they escape the play's final judgement. One recent account[15] argues that the play may itself be subtler than it appears, and Middleton may have known of the existence of an influential cell of Familists who held high office at court.

The separatists were actively persecuted for their beliefs, and escaped only by crossing the Atlantic to find somewhere where they were allowed to live and worship as they chose. William

Bradford's *History of Plymouth Plantation* (written after 1630) recalled their sufferings in the Old World, how 'some were taken and clapped up in prison, others had their houses beset and watched night and day'. On one particularly harrowing occasion, a barge full of women and children going to meet their husbands in order to escape to the Netherlands ran aground. They watched helplessly as a party of soldiers arrived and frightened off the ship with their husbands on board, so that it turned and set sail for the Netherlands without them. They were thus stranded without money or clothes:

But pitiful it was to see the heavy case of these poor women in this distress; what weeping and crying on every side, some for their husbands, that were carried away in the ship as is before related. Others not knowing what should become of them, and their little ones; others again melted in tears, seeing their poor little ones hanging about them, crying for fear and quaking with cold.[16]

Catholics also suffered under the Anglican Church. The unexpected death of Mary Tudor had caught everyone by surprise, and although some Catholic clergy went into exile, others tried to continue their previous practices unobtrusively, or else changed with the times. It took a while before the missionary priests, trained on the Continent, learned to fight Protestantism with its own weapons. Catholicism was practised mainly under the protection of those members of the gentry or aristocracy who maintained large, independent households with strong traditions of internal loyalty, where the old services could still be held in secret, perhaps with a private chaplain to administer them. Elizabeth's formal excommunication by the Pope in 1570 sharply increased official action against them: it implied that the international Catholic powers did not recognize her right to govern, making England a potential target for internal rebellion, and foreign (in practice, Spanish) invasion. Fines for non-attendance at church (i.e. recusancy) were stepped up and further penalties debarred Catholics from taking university degrees or holding state offices. Many of the gentry chose to attend services rather than pay the huge fines, believing that external conformity was insignificant or seeing it as a gesture of loyalty to the Queen, while maintaining their spiritual independence by receiving the old sacraments in private at home.

John Earle's *Microcosmographie* (1628) gives a satirical portrait of 'A Church-Papist' who, when he kneels with the congregation, 'asks God forgiveness for coming thither. If he be forced to stay out a sermon, he pulls his hat over his eyes, and frowns out the hour; and when he comes home, thinks to make amends for this fault by abusing the preacher.' Though Earle leaves his caricature 'hatching plots against the state', the Catholic gentry as a whole remained remarkably loyal to Elizabeth, despite the discrimination against them, and at the end of her reign a group of secular priests made a joint protestation of allegiance to her. Loyalty, or perhaps the fear of a stronger anti-papist backlash, induced a certain quietism, so that when missionary priests began to arrive in England from the late 1570s, eager to spread the word and inspire a less compromising enthusiasm in the faithful, though generally welcomed and concealed, some people feared that their activities would destabilize what until then had been a bearable situation. Though life was far from easy for the Catholics, government policy was mainly one of deterrence, except in Ireland or where the missionary priests from the Continent were concerned.

Among the prominent Catholic clergymen who went into exile at Elizabeth's accession was William Allen, later to be made cardinal. In 1568 he founded a seminary at Douai to train Englishmen as priests so that the old religion might be maintained and even advanced by strengthening Catholics, rather than converting heretics. These priests had to practise the infiltrating and proselytizing techniques that had previously been employed by Protestants. The seminary priests who came to England exploited these methods to powerful effect, preaching, writing and disseminating their beliefs wherever they went. Father Robert Person's 'Book of Resolution' made deathbed converts, according to Robert Greene's pamphlet on his own repentance. Catholic martyrologies recorded the sufferings of women like Margaret Clitherow, executed at York in 1586 for harbouring Jesuit missionaries, or Jane Wiseman, horribly tortured for the same 'crime', as well as that of Thomas More, whose educated and scholarly daughter Margaret Roper helped to maintain the memory of her father's death. Catholic devotional literature was widely read and conversions were made, and not only among those who had long lived abroad, like the poet Henry Constable (1562–1613) or the composer John Dowland (c.1563–c.1626). Ben Jonson was converted in a London prison, and the Protestant clergyman and poet William Alabaster (1567–1630) became a Catholic, although after some difficult years in Rome he reverted to his original faith and ended his days as an Anglican parson: such changes of heart were not always permanent.

If the spiritual work of the missionary priests gave cause for concern, their political activities were even more threatening. They were suspected, sometimes on good grounds, of acting as foreign agents for Spain and the Pope, of stirring up treason, and of plotting the overthrow of Elizabeth and her replacement by a Catholic ruler—either Mary Queen of Scots, or some other claimant. Missionary colleges such as that at Douai or the Jesuit English College at Rome shared with the great Catholic powers the aim of reclaiming England for the Church of Rome by any available means. Jesuits were particularly suspect because of the Spanish origin of their order, and the myth that they were actively promoting a world-wide Catholic conspiracy. The English government responded with a series of vicious persecutions, encouraging their agents to hunt down, entrap, and torture the unfortunate priests, who, if caught, were liable to be publicly disembowelled and hanged. Those who sheltered them were also imprisoned and tortured: John Donne's younger brother died in prison, charged with illegally harbouring a priest. The brutality of such policies reflected fears of Catholic treason, increased by Spanish aggression abroad, and at home by incidents such as the Babington Plot (1586), which attempted to set Mary Stuart on the throne. Philip II launched his Armada, the great fleet sent to invade England, in 1588; the years immediately before this were particularly anxious since he was known to be counting on a massive Catholic uprising, which in the end never took place.

In 1587 Sir William Stanley, an officer in Leicester's army fighting the Spanish in the Netherlands, declared his loyalty to the old faith by handing over the town of Deventer and his own troops (who were mainly Irish) to the Spaniards. This defection of a serving officer was troubling, and Cardinal William Allen's defence of Stanley on the grounds that good Catholics were not obliged to keep faith with a heretic and excommunicate like Elizabeth only made matters worse. The implications of his argument, which could be used by Catholics to break their Oath of Supremacy to the Queen, interested Marlowe, who used it in his next play, *Tamburlaine, Part II*. Baldwin, Lord of Bohemia, persuades the Catholic King Sigismund of Hungary to break the truce he has made with the pagan Orcanes, King of Natolia, on the grounds that

> with such infidels,
> In whom no faith nor true religion rests,
> We are not bound to those accomplishments
> The holy laws of Christendom enjoin . . .
>
> (II. i. 33–6)

The Jew of Malta, extensively concerned with the breaking of oaths, bonds, and obligations in the cause of self-advancement, gives the Jew a further echo of Cardinal Allen's position when he urges his daughter Abigail:

> It's no sin to deceive a Christian,
> For they themselves hold it a principle,
> Faith is not to be held with heretics:
> But all are heretics that are not Jews:
> This follows well, and therefore, daughter, fear not.
>
> (II. iii. 311–15)

Scenes or passages that exploit popular anti-Catholicism occur quite often in Marlowe's plays, for example, the blackly comic murders of Huguenots on stage in *The Massacre at Paris*, or Faustus's fun at the expense of the Pope and his cardinals, or his command to the dragon-shaped Mephostophilis,

> Go, and return an old Franciscan friar;
> That holy shape becomes a devil best.
>
> (i. iii. 26–7)

Marlowe is likely to have known the moralizing ballad of
'Doctor Faustus', entered in the Stationers' Register for 1589,
and though he moved far beyond its range, he retained something of its direct appeal for our sympathy:

> All Christian men, give ear a while to me,
> How I am plung'd in pain but cannot die;
> I liv'd a life the like did none before,
> Forsaking Christ, and I am damn'd therefore.[17]

Most of the popular dramatists—Dekker, Heywood, Munday,
Middleton, and Webster—indulged their London audience's
anti-Catholic sentiments on occasion, though with increasing
subtlety: the Cardinal in *The Duchess of Malfi* is stereotypically
cunning and lecherous. The dumb-show in which he is ritually
armed and then pronounces a sentence of exile on his sister, may
look back to Erasmus's condemnation of Pope Julius II in his
Praise of Folly. Yet the play's attitude to Catholicism as a whole
is less clear-cut. The Duchess wishes to disguise her flight as a
pilgrimage to Loreto, but her maid Cariola begs her to make use
of another, more secular excuse,

> for, if you will believe me,
> I do not like this jesting with religion,
> This feigned pilgrimage.
> DUCHESS: Thou art a superstitious fool—
> Prepare us instantly for our departure . . .
>
> (iii. ii. 316–20)

While the Duchess's reply is quite proper, there is a suggestion
that her cynicism about religion goes too far, as perhaps does
her rhetorical question, after her private betrothal,

> What can the Church force more? . . .
> How can the Church bind faster?
>
> (i. i. 488, 491)

Although a church marriage would have reached the ears of
her evil brothers, her unsanctified union is also problematic, and

turns out to be ill-fated, even in a society in which the corruption of the clergy is so much in evidence. In Ford's play *'Tis Pity She's a Whore* (1632), Friar Bonaventura is represented as generous and sympathetic (perhaps too much so), while the Cardinal and Papal Nuncio misuse their status to lend protection to the known murderer, Grimaldi. Shakespeare's Friar Lawrence in *Romeo and Juliet* is also kind and well-meaning, if disastrously inefficient, and Vincentio's disguise as a monk in *Measure for Measure* confers on him an appropriate spiritual authority; both examples have been used to argue for their author's Catholic sympathies.

Poets and Preachers

The Reformation had suppressed the rich iconographic traditions of Catholicism, closing down the Mystery plays and church pageants which had been such enjoyable and enlivening features of town life. The first generation of reformers attempted to fill the vacuum left by the wholesale destruction of Catholic culture by publishing ballads, metrical psalms, and martyrologies, and even staging Protestant plays and interludes. By about 1580 the early dramatic impulse had given place to opposition to the recently established commercial theatres, and the output of godly ballads began to dry up. But many of them retained their popularity well into the seventeenth century, including those on Anne Askew and the Duchess of Suffolk, as well as ballads of parental wisdom such as 'An hundred godly lessons', 'Solomon's Sentences' (derived from Ecclesiasticus), and religious ABCs. Broadside ballads could be read, sung, or stuck upon the wall. The printing presses also churned out a rising tide of cheap prayer-books, psalters, versified sequences from the Bible, catechisms, sermons, moralizing pamphlets, and guides to godly living.

The ballad of Anne Askew begins 'I am a woman poor and blind', although John Bale and John Foxe had portrayed her as a woman of extraordinary independence and fighting spirit, who was tortured and burnt as a heretic in 1546. A song actually composed by her celebrates faith as the armour of the soul. Thomas Deloney wrote a popular ballad on the sufferings of another popular Protestant heroine, Catherine Brandon, Duchess of Suffolk, who had been driven into exile under Mary Tudor, and in 1624 Thomas Drue wrote a play about her. Many of the early supporters of reform, including Lady Jane Grey and Henry VIII's surviving wife, Katherine Parr, wrote prayers and meditations or translated the Psalms, and their writings were collected and published by Thomas Bentley in *The Monument of Matrones* (1582). Biblical heroines such as Esther, Deborah, Judith, and Susanna were popular subjects for plays and ballads, and their names were sometimes linked with Elizabeth's to illustrate her gifts as a religious leader.

The iconoclasm of the Reformation meant that a great deal of traditionally Christian subject-matter and imagery was, for much of Elizabeth's reign, unavailable to Protestant poets, and was only gradually re-assimilated in the early seventeenth century, although the language and imagery of the Church had been preserved in the English words of the Book of Common Prayer and the various English Bibles. Translations of the Psalms and images from Revelation were acceptable, but many New Testament themes—incidents from the life of Christ, Peter's remorse and Magdalen's tears, and of course the Virgin and the saints, were tainted by association with the old religion, and in Elizabeth's reign were used mainly by Catholic poets such as the Jesuit priest Robert Southwell, executed for treason in 1596 (he may have written his traditional and self-effacing poems in prison). The sonnets that Henry Constable and William Alabaster composed after their conversions, possibly as religious exercises, make use of similar themes, and so does some of the poetry of John Donne, the age's most notable convert to the Established Church, although his imagination retained a Catholic and even Counter-Reformation colouring when evoking Christian images and experiences in poetry.

Donne's family were Catholics, and several had been victims of persecution. His mother was born Anne Heywood, youngest daughter of John Heywood, the playwright and friend of Thomas

More, the memory of whose martyrdom remained as an inspiration to religious fervour within the family. It is not known exactly when Donne conformed to the Anglican Church, though it must have been fairly early in his career. He wrote in the preface to *Pseudo-Martyr* (1610) of his conversion, 'I used no inordinate haste nor precipitation in binding my conscience to any local religion. I had a longer work to do than many other men, for I was first to blot out certain impressions of the Roman religion, and to wrestle both against the examples and the reasons by which some hold was taken . . .' His *Satyre III*, a passionate and moving poem on the choice of religion, strongly opposes the acceptance of 'any local religion' merely because it is imposed by the state. God has not

> Signed kings blank-charters to kill whom they hate,
> Nor are they vicars, but hangmen to Fate.
> Fool and wretch, wilt thou let thy soul be tied
> To man's laws, by which she shall not be tried
> At the last day?
>
> (ll. 91–5)

The poem is filled with bitterness and contempt for sectarian hatred and wars, which perpetuate aggression and provocation, and so further distract attention from the search for truth. A comparable distaste for religious persecution underlies two of Donne's prose polemics—*Pseudo-Martyr*, in which he urges Catholics to take the Oath of Supremacy rather than make martyrs of themselves, and *Ignatius his Conclave* (1611), which attacks the Jesuits for their trouble-making.

In *Satyre III* religious intolerance is compared to the exaggerated behaviour of gallants:

> must every he
> Which cries not, 'Goddess!' to thy mistress, draw,
> Or eat thy poisonous words?
>
> (ll. 26–8)

Holy Sonnet 18, 'Show me dear Christ, thy spouse, so bright and clear', characterizes the two Churches (as Herbert was to do in 'The British Church') as different kinds of women, flaunting or despoiled, following the traditional personification of the Church as the Bride of Christ, but then turns it into a shocking paradox which makes the true Church most 'true and pleasing' to God 'When she is embraced and open to most men'. Donne's sense (which is largely that of his age) of women as objects allows him to represent his own soul as female in its helplessness before the masculine force of God, who is urged to 'Batter my heart . . . ravish me' (Holy Sonnet 14).

Donne's religious poetry moves tormentedly between a Calvinist recognition of his sins ('done before') and desperate pleas for forgiveness, yet his 'impressions of the Roman religion' enabled him to make use of the kinds of figures and analogies that were otherwise mainly absent from sixteenth-century poetry. The seven linked sonnets of *La Corona* outline the main events of Christ's life, while the Trinity, the Virgin, angels, apostles, and so on that make up *A Litany* were also the subjects of Catholic prayer sequences. Donne's eventual status as Anglican Dean of St Pauls may have helped his Protestant disciples to recover the meaning of such images. The imagery of Catholic religious experience used in 'The Canonization', 'The Relic', and 'The Ecstasy', references to pilgrimages and priests, saints and candles, are redeployed as part of a Platonic religion of love, in which the doctrinal debates that had set faith against works, 'remembrance' against 'real presence', and interrogated the relation of body to soul and mind instead provided ways of exploring the interaction of sexual desire and idealizing love. The theological contexts of the love poetry are balanced by the erotic imagery of religious sonnets such as 'What if this present were the world's last night?' (13), which draws a scandalous analogy between Christ's mercy and the sexual generosity of the poet's 'profane mistresses'.

A very different, but equally startling reworking of the theme of womanly pity occurs in Aemilia Lanyer's poem, *Salve Deus Rex Judaeorum* (1611), a Protestant celebration of the piety of a group of noble ladies in the tradition of Bentley's *Monument of Matrones*. This is combined with an account of the passion of Christ, in which He is betrayed both by the Roman authorities

and His own disciples, while the Women of Jerusalem, beginning
with Pontius Pilate's wife (whose warning dream was part of an
apocryphal tradition), attempt in vain to intercede on His behalf.
In a surprising anticipation of modern feminist arguments,
Lanyer presents women as mothers, morally superior in their
tenderness and pity for the weak, and closer in spirit to the suffering Christ. Eve's 'fault was only too much love' (l. 801), while
men 'in malice God's dear son betray' (l. 816):

> Then let us have our liberty again,
> And challenge to yourselves no sov'reignty;
> You came not in the world without our pain,
> Make that a bar against your cruelty.
>
> (ll. 825–8)

Like George Herbert, Donne ended his life as a clergyman,
preaching sermons as well as composing religious poetry. Influenced by Donne's example, both in his life and art, Herbert
described the poems that make up *The Temple* (1633) as giving
'a picture of the many spiritual conflicts that have passed betwixt
God and my soul, before I could subject mine to the will of Jesus
my master'. Herbert's courteous and graceful manner disguises
his exasperation and self-doubt, but Donne's less inhibited sense
of drama and conflict conveys the increasingly dynamic nature
of spiritual life, to which seventeenth-century narratives of conversion, and the developing art of autobiography bear witness.

Once Donne had accepted the necessity of taking orders
(which he did with apparent reluctance), his extraordinary eloquence was quickly recognized and admired, even by the King,
and in 1623 he was appointed Dean of St Paul's. His sermons
reflect his acute sensitivity to language, and the several possible
meanings of words and names (here, his own proper name, and
'More', that of his wife, and possibly his mother's family):

> When thou hast done, thou hast not done,
> For, I have more.
> ('A Hymn to God the Father', ll. 5–6; 11–12)

Puns were thought of, not as accidental or trivial resemblances,
but as indications of hidden affinities or further meanings, as

when Christ promised to found his Church on Peter, whose
name also meant 'rock'. They might be used to reveal mysteries:
Lancelot Andrewes, another great Anglican preacher, did so
when he explored the notion of Christ's infancy, the Word made
flesh, itself literally 'in-fans' (Latin for 'not yet able to speak'):
'What, *Verbum infans*, the Word of an infant? The Word, and not
be able to speak a word? How evil agreeth this! This He put
up.'[18] Clergymen were trained to gloss texts from the Bible, by
explaining and enlarging upon the meaning of particular words,
and both Donne and Andrewes were particularly skilled at
drawing out the relationship of phrases, both in Latin and
English (as in Andrewes' play on the literal meaning of
'infancy'), or the range of meanings contained within particular
words: Donne's 'Hymn to God my God in my Sickness' puns on
the Latin phrase 'per fretum febris', meaning both 'through the
pains of fever' and 'through the tropical straits of Magellan'. His
last sermon, 'Death's Duel', was a bravura performance, deliv-
ered while he was dying: in it, he represented death as a release
from the many lesser deaths we undergo, whereas birth is paradoxically seen as an escape, from the threat of still birth:

But then this *exitus a morte*, is but *introitus in mortem*; this issue, this
deliverance from that death, the death of the womb, is an entrance, a
delivering over to another death, the manifold deaths of this world; we
have a winding-sheet in our mother's womb, which grows with us from
our conception, and we come into the world, wound up in that winding-
sheet, for we come to seek a grave.

('Death's Duel', 1630)

The sermons of Donne and Lancelot Andrewes were
markedly different in form and presentation from the homely
sermons of Hugh Latimer that had inaugurated the Protestant
preaching tradition. They met with disapproval for their displays
of learning, for entertaining rather than plainly expounding
God's word for all to understand. Part of this censure was
directed against the smart London congregations who enjoyed
them. Country parsons like George Herbert were obliged to
adopt a very different style from metropolitan preachers,

although plainness might be adopted anywhere: William Laud, in high favour at court and in all other respects opposed to the reformers, was an unexpected exponent of the plain style of preaching. But Donne's fireworks did not merely reflect his more sophisticated audience; they aimed at a different reaction. Instead of focusing on the power of teaching, he emphasized its limits: for Donne, the mysteries of God could not be understood, nor could the gift of faith be acquired by any individual act of will. Instead, he shared with his congregation his sense of wonder, humility, even inadequacy in the face of God's power. In contemplating God's words and acts, he sought to emphasize human limitation, his own above all.

That sense of inadequacy in speaking of God, who has spoken His own truths in the scriptures, is also present in George Herbert's poetry, though he adopted exactly the opposite solution, substituting for 'sweet phrases, lovely metaphors' a deliberate plainness, 'a bleak paleness', in poems such as 'The Forerunners' and the two 'Jordan' poems. In *A Priest to the Temple*, subtitled the country parson's 'character and rule of holy life', he advised against too close an examination of biblical phraseology:

The parson's method in handling of a text consists of two parts: first, a plain and evident declaration of the meaning of the text; and secondly, some choice observations drawn out of the whole text, as it lies entire and unbroken in the scripture itself. This he thinks natural, and sweet, and grave. Whereas the other way of crumbling a text into small parts, as the person speaking, or spoken to, the subject, and object, and the like, hath neither in it sweetness, nor gravity, nor variety, since the words apart are not scripture, but a dictionary, and may be considered alike in all the scripture.[19]

The energy and fervour invested in religious disputes of all kinds might convert someone to the opposite viewpoint: two brothers who were also well-known Elizabethan theologians, William and John Reynolds (or Rainolds), the first a Catholic and the second a Calvinist theologian, had, according to Anthony Wood, begun as Calvinist and Catholic respectively, each arguing himself into the other's position. John Donne recognized more clearly than most that, while the right choice of religion was the single most vital question in life, every organization from the family unit to the state itself competed to influence that choice and impose a reassuring conformity upon the individual. Disagreement would be resented, might even be punishable with death, yet on the right choice might depend a limitless future existence. Sir Thomas Browne, a physician of strong religious convictions, writing on the eve of the Civil War, took the view that there was some virtue in most forms of Christianity: 'We have reformed from [the Catholics], not against them . . . there is between us one common name and appellation, one faith and necessary body of principles common to us both; and therefore I am not scrupulous to converse and live with them, to enter their churches in defect of ours, and either pray with them, or for them.'[20] Although co-religionists clung together, inevitably people mingled with, met, and sometimes married those who held very different convictions, and one's convictions—as the story of the Reynolds' brothers shows— might change startlingly in the course of a lifetime.

Individuals did not always conform to predictable patterns: for an Elizabethan, royalism and reforming zeal might go hand in hand, as they did for Sidney or Spenser. Sixty years later royalists confronted reformers in the Civil War. A puritan propagandist like John Milton might accept most Calvinist teachings, yet as regards the freedom of the will he followed the doctrine of Arminius, a doctrine whose imposition on the Anglican Church in the late 1620s was partly responsible for driving the reformers from the main body of the Church. Between the Elizabethan poets and Milton lay a not untroubled period in which the Anglican Church, for all its compromises, began to find an identity and justification for itself in terms of a common-sense middle way. Elizabeth had consciously steered her Church between extremes, while James congratulated himself on his role as peacemaker and conciliator. 'To stand in the gap between puritanism and popery, the Scylla and Charybdis of ancient piety', has always been an Anglican ideal. For a short time in the early seventeenth century such a position had seemed tenable, even workable. By 1625 the young King Charles had married a Catholic queen, the intransigent William Laud was already Bishop of St David's, and would later become Archbishop of Canterbury, restoring lost ceremonies and introducing Arminius's doctrine of free will. The old Church settlement was set on a runaway course that would soon shake it to pieces.

Education

'In the end the good or ill bringing-up of children doth as much serve to the good or ill service of God, our prince, and our whole country as any one thing doth beside', wrote Roger Ascham in *The Schoolmaster* (1570),[1] echoing the sentiments of the reformers who saw education as a preparation for a virtuous life. Others saw it as potentially dangerous, producing a class of deracinated and dissatisfied intellectuals, whom it would be difficult to employ. The government was committed to the promotion of reading as part of the Protestant programme, but it took good care to keep strict control over printing presses in England, and made efforts to keep out subversive reading-matter from the Continent. A flood of cheap printing, much of it religious, was directed towards a new generation of readers who still had close links with an active oral culture that had managed many difficult and complex transactions without the skill of reading. As Richard Brathwayte observed, 'Many illiterate [are] of the exactest judgement'.[2] Those who could not read structured their knowledge and experience in very different—sometimes highly creative—ways, as well as participating in print culture at second hand through friends and neighbours who could read. But writing represented power, a power that the illiterate themselves recognized and feared: in Shakespeare's *2 Henry VI*, the rebel Jack Cade has the Clerk of Chatham executed merely because he can read and write: 'Is not this a lamentable thing, that of the skin of an innocent lamb should be made parchment? that parchment, being scribbled o'er, should undo a man? Some say the bee stings, but I say, 'tis the bee's wax; for I did but seal once to a thing, and I was never my own man since' (IV. ii. 78–83).

Protestantism had created a religion of the word, and education reinforced religion at every level: the child's very first reading-matter was his hornbook, a wooden tablet covered with parchment, printed with the alphabet and the Lord's Prayer, and protected by a transparent layer of horn. At the far end of the educational process, after seven years at university and two degrees, the scholar was ready to embark on the crown of his labours, the Doctorate of Divinity, often a matter of a further fourteen years' study. At each stage, religion was a determining influence, extending beyond the content of education to the reasons for acquiring it: demands for an educated clergy and a literate congregation were central to the Protestant Church, and soon became so for the Catholic Church as well, once the Counter-Reformation was launched in the 1560s. The pious hope that all should read their Bibles and understand what they found there helped to extend reading skills. Even a sophisticated literary achievement like Spenser's *Shepheardes Calender* drew on popular forms such as the almanac, addressed to wide audiences. This expansion of education has been seen as 'a quantitative change of such magnitude that it can only be described as a revolution . . .'.[3] Such a description echoes early modern educational propaganda, which is difficult to distinguish from its actual achievements, yet the first twenty years of Elizabeth's reign did see an increase in educational provision in precisely the years that Shakespeare, his literary contemporaries, and his audience were of school age.

John Shakespeare, the playwright's father, left no evidence that he could write his own name, and neither did Shakespeare's daughter Judith, though (as we shall see) this does not mean that they could not read. William, on the other hand, was impressively well-educated, and the range and scope of his knowledge is a tribute to the effectiveness of an Elizabethan grammar-school education. When Jonson referred to Shakespeare's 'small Latin and less Greek', he was making an unfavourable comparison with himself. Despite not knowing

Greek, Shakespeare knew more Latin than most modern readers, and read French and Italian as well, although when he was writing he often worked from contemporary translations such as North's translation of Plutarch's *Lives* (1579). The major texts of classical and modern culture were increasingly being translated into English for comparatively uneducated readers. Philemon Holland, in his introduction to Pliny's *Natural History* (1601), explained that he had framed his pen 'to a mean and popular style', while Florio prefaced his translations from Montaigne (1603) by declaring that 'Learning cannot be too common, and the commoner the better'.

But education cannot be regarded only as a democratizing force in a society where the privileged had the easiest access to it; the growth of middle-class education itself increased the awareness of difference between those who enjoyed its benefits and those who did not. It was greatly sought after, not merely by the godly, but by the middle and upper classes more generally. Both Elizabeth and James were ostentatiously learned, though they showed it in rather different ways. Their patronage of cultural pursuits at court influenced aristocratic views of education, and encouraged the gentry to send their children to schools and universities in greater numbers than before. Yet little of this educational revolution reached the poorest who made up the majority of the population and who could not have spared the child labour nor paid for the various expenses involved: grammar schooling was theoretically free, but the cost of entering, and then of books, paper, and other necessary equipment such as firewood or candles, was normally borne by parents. For those who were struggling to survive, schooling was no more part of their expectations than a regular diet of meat.

The demand for education had a secular as well as a religious aspect: education was seen as refining both society and the individual, and it had helped to bring about the Reformation as well as later gaining from its programme. A substantial number of schools were founded in the fifteenth century, often paid for by guilds, as was the Stratford-upon-Avon grammar school,

established in the 1480s. By the early sixteenth century, Thomas
More estimated that 60 per cent of the London population could
read.[4] While this is probably an exaggeration, his claim suggests
that the reformers underestimated how much had already been
achieved. In the immediate wake of the Reformation the educational system was thrown into confusion, like so much else, but
it was treated as a high priority, reflected in an increase in educational endowments. By 1577 William Harrison could write in
his *Description of England*, 'there are not many corporate towns
now under the Queen's dominion that hath not one grammar
school at the least with a sufficient living for a master and usher
appointed to the same'.[5] Shakespeare's generation, the first to
be born and grow up in the comparative stability of Elizabeth's
reign, was the first to benefit. Although he and several contemporary playwrights were born the sons of artisans or craftsmen,
their range of knowledge and the sophistication of their writing
skills reflect the virtues of a sound humanist education.

Recovering the Classics

It was fifteenth-century Catholic humanists, not the Protestant
reformers, who established the system of Latin education provided in Elizabethan schools. A central feature of the Italian
Renaissance had been the reappraisal of classical literature and
the rediscovery of a number of lost texts, most notably those of
Plato. In Florence, Greek scholars and manuscripts were eagerly
sought for, and intensive study led to more critical and historical readings of ancient literature on every level. One consequence was that Latin was recognized as having altered, and
considerably degenerated, since its use by the politician Cicero
(106–43 BC), whose style was regarded as a model of perfect
prose. The writing of correct (i.e. Ciceronian) Latin soon became
one of the new educational goals, while Cicero himself was
increasingly admired not merely as a stylist but also as a moral-
ist (some purists even connected the two). Cicero had tried to
lead a life of integrity and moral rectitude within a corrupt
society, and the humanists could identify with his difficulties.

Roman and Greek authors began to be quoted as moral authorities, despite the fact that they had not been Christians, and their style and moral lessons were widely taught and imitated.

Close attention to classical authors produced a more thorough and detailed understanding of their society, though judged from a modern point of view Renaissance translations of the classics still blur significant distinctions, so that pagan priests become bishops and Roman cavalry become knights. A unique illustration of a performance of Shakespeare's *Titus Andronicus* shows that on the Elizabethan stage Roman dress included doublet, trunk hose, and farthingale, in addition to the classical helmet and breastplate, yet this was an advance on those medieval manuscripts where Ovid's lovers were dressed entirely in contemporary fashions, in wimples and liripipes. Renaissance Italian painting and sculpture, like Elizabethan book illustrations, reveal a substantial interest in and knowledge of Roman costume and architecture. It would be naïve to judge one society's knowledge of another in terms of how accurately it reproduced its costumes, especially if we recall that Renaissance artists were trained to draw from classical models; yet Shakespeare's Roman plays also reveal a genuine understanding of classical culture and values. Their presentation of Roman attitudes and policies springs from a powerfully well-informed act of historical imagination, and so compelling are their narratives that it is often difficult to set aside their interpretation of events in favour of more modern readings of Roman history.

Closer study of classical authors, together with a greater knowledge of Roman society and its workings, helped to create a sense of the relative, of the difference between one culture and another, providing new social and intellectual frameworks against which contemporary circumstances could be measured. The great sixteenth-century relativists Rabelais and Montaigne were both deeply absorbed in classical culture: Montaigne had Latin and Greek quotations inscribed on the beams of his tower, and his essays everywhere reflect his familiarity with classical authors; he sets their judgements beside his own, treating them as the opinions of old and valued friends. Such intimacy with the classics is a feature of the Renaissance, which arrived in England so late that it is still apparent in the work of Ben Jonson, Robert Burton, John Milton, and Sir Thomas Browne. In northern Europe its greatest exponent had been Erasmus (?1466–1536), who followed the Italian poet Petrarch (1304–74) in laying particular stress on the moral and ethical qualities to be found in the classical authors. He argued that they should be studied on the grounds that, though pagan, they showed how everyday life might be lived with virtue and integrity. He suggested that perhaps their hearts were moved by some divine power, and in his colloquy *Convivium Religiosum* (*The Godly Feast*, 1522), Eusebius admits that he cannot read Cicero 'without sometimes kissing the book and blessing that pure heart, divinely inspired as it was', while another speaker, Nephalius, referring to Socrates' heroic death, admits 'When I read such things of such men, I can hardly help exclaiming, "Saint Socrates, pray for us!" '[6] For Erasmus, Socrates was a secular saint, a man who gave up his life for his principles.

The phrase 'Saint Socrates' was intended to annoy the narrow-minded clerics for whom Socrates, an unbaptized Greek, was condemned to hell. Erasmus thought it no worse than the superstitious prayers to minor saints whom he considered little better than pagan deities. He was sharply critical of ignorance and convinced of the need for a faith and education based on genuine understanding, rather than the automatic recital of rote-learned prayers or grammar rules: such repetition emptied religious services and educational experience of thought or involvement. Criticisms of teaching methods had been made before Erasmus, but never with so much wit and incisiveness, nor did they have the printing press to distribute them. Erasmus supervised the passage of his works through the press, working first with the great Venetian printer Aldus Manutius, and later with Froben at Basle. Educational reform was in the air, and the presses played a crucial part in spreading the views of educationalists and providing the texts required for new programmes of study at great speed and small cost, so that the older process of copying and circulating manuscripts could no longer compete.

A comparison between Chaucer's Clerk of Oxenford, with his twenty expensive volumes of Aristotle, and the sixteenth-century scholar, with a library of a hundred or more books, ranging from large folios to pocket Testaments, all bought comparatively cheaply, reveals what printing contributed to learning, as well as to education more generally.

Self-education now became a practical possibility, arriving in England with the publication of Edmund Coote's *The School-master* (1596), from which a student could learn to read and write, with the aid of graded exercises. Twenty-five editions of it were published within the next thirty years. Although Latin remained the language of grammar-school education, English grammars and dictionaries were also beginning to appear, works such as William Bullokar's *Bref Grammar of English* (1586) or Alexander Gill's more ambitious *Logonomia Anglica* (1619), with examples taken from contemporary poetry, particularly Spenser's, though the earliest dictionaries tended to be little more than lists of difficult words (as John Bullokar's title—*The English Expositor, teaching the interpretation of the hardest words in our language* (1616)—suggests).

The printing-press had made classical and modern texts readily available by a process of mechanical reproduction to an audience which was beginning to acquire a critical awareness of the text itself. Attention to changing word-forms in Latin, one consequence of a developing historical sense, led to more accurate dating of manuscripts and greater sensitivity to textual error, a problem that had affected the whole process of manuscript transmission. Typographical errors occurred quite as often in the printing-house as slips of the pen and misreadings, but they were much easier to identify and correct at every stage. The accumulation of errors from one copied manuscript to the next, and the impossibility in many cases of recovering the earliest version, made it difficult to restore the original text, since each manuscript posed particular problems and inherited particular sets of errors. Newly discovered manuscripts, sometimes Greek originals of works previously known only from inaccurate Latin versions, further encouraged more critical reading, and accuracy began to be valued for its own sake. Scholars set out to establish reliable texts of the main classical authorities.

It was not long before the methods they evolved began to be applied to the Bible, the unchanging word of God, with disturbing results. Having learnt from Italian scholars that the great Latin Bible of St Jerome was obviously corrupt in places, Erasmus set himself the task of retranslating the New Testament from the original Greek, a language that he learned specially for the purpose. His project greatly upset a number of theologians who foresaw that a new version would create unresolvable arguments among the experts about the meaning of particular passages, while increasing the scepticism of the ordinary reader, who would feel that the clergy themselves could not agree as to what was meant by the scriptures. Erasmus had taken only the first step of translating from Greek into Latin, so he was writing primarily for an audience of European scholars. With later translations into English, the power to interpret the Bible began to pass from the clergy to the ordinary reader. In the long run both would gain from the demand that both should be able to read the Bible and understand the main theological issues in dispute, but in the process the authority of the clergy was significantly reduced.

Reading and discussing the meaning of particular passages was one aspect of the Protestant 'priesthood of all believers', an essential part of religious life in the opinion of the reformers, who were inclined to doubt whether 'many . . . shall with God's grace, though they never read word of scripture, come as well to heaven', as More had asserted.[7] Families read the Bible together, and women and servants (less likely to be able to read, statistically speaking) were encouraged to participate. At prophesyings and conferences, public discussions of biblical passages took place. The Catholic priest William Weston watched such a meeting with disapproval while he was imprisoned at Wisbech Castle in 1588:

Each of them had his own Bible, and sedulously turned the pages and looked up the texts cited by the preachers, discussing the passages among themselves to see whether they had quoted them to the point, and accurately, and in harmony with their tenets. Also they would start arguing among themselves about the meaning of passages from the Scriptures—men, women, boys, girls, rustics, labourers and idiots—and more often than not, it was said, it ended in violence and fisticuffs.[8]

Conferences such as Weston witnessed had originally been intended to promote a better understanding of the scriptures among the clergy, but they were also liable to open up grounds for disagreement and sectarian differences. Educational aims were always liable to backfire: once individuals acquired a degree of intellectual independence, they might not use it towards the desired end. Instead of instilling a respect for basic religious and social structures and encouraging conformity, education sometimes produced the reverse effect. And being able to read was no guarantee that the reader would choose to read the Bible: John Bunyan, growing up in the first half of the seventeenth century, recalled

The Scriptures, thought I, what are they? a dead letter, a little ink and paper, of three or four shillings price. Alas, what is the Scripture, give me a ballad, a news-book, *George* on horseback or *Bevis of Southampton*; give me some book that teaches curious arts, that tells of old fables; but for the holy Scriptures I cared not. And as it was with me then, so it is with my brethren now.[9]

Many others must have shared his view. Philip Stubbes's complaint, that 'books and pamphlets of scurrility and bawdry are better esteemed and more vendible than the sagest books that be',[10] can always be heard.

The critical and textual approach to biblical studies, which the humanists and Erasmus had begun, spread quickly. At the outset, Protestants were confident of their powers of persuasion and the appeal of their arguments to the well-informed. They supposed that if only the clergy preached, and the people read their Bibles, society would come to accept a comfortably united Protestant faith. But this did not happen, any more than the moral improvement that the humanists had hoped for from reading good classical authors was the only outcome of a sound humanist education. Making the Bible available to all readers enabled them to take differing views of its message, just as a classical education introduced its beneficiaries to pagan notions of religion, philosophy and politics, as well as a literature written to excite and titillate rather than to edify. One seventeenth-century commentator, Thomas Hobbes, thought classical education was responsible for the radical demands of Charles's parliament. Considering the causes of the Civil War in *Behemoth*, he blamed the universities for spreading politically dangerous lessons:

There were an exceeding great number of men of the better sort, that had been so educated as that in their youth having read the books written by famous men of the ancient Grecian and Roman commonwealths concerning their polity and great actions, in which books the *popular* government was extolled by the glorious name of liberty and monarchy disgraced by the name of tyranny, they became thereby in love with their forms of government. And out of these men were chosen the greatest part of the House of Commons; or, if they were not the greatest part, yet, by advantage of their eloquence, were always able to sway the rest.[11]

Machiavelli grounded his approach to political science in *The Discourses* (composed by 1519, published 1531) in readings from Livy's Roman histories. He had played a leading role in the ill-fated Florentine republic and had strongly republican sympathies, admiring Brutus and condemning Caesar and the later emperors (thus adding to his sinister reputation in a monarchy like England). While it seems unlikely that the seventeenth-century House of Commons was animated by the kind of idealistic republicanism that Hobbes attributed to it (and Machiavelli had subscribed to), classical education certainly introduced students to alternative political systems, and so encouraged them to ask searching questions about their own. The existence of an educated élite would not normally be disruptive, since the individuals belonging to it were likely to be strongly invested in the *status quo*, but in this case it fostered the war of ideas and ideologies that preceded actual warfare. Education enabled individuals to follow political issues through their reading, to discover different views, and arrive at independent opinions. Just as, with the wider dissemination of the Bible, there came a point where control passed from the educator to the educated, so with the reading of the classics, a knowledge of Latin plus cheap printed texts made a much wider range of material available, some of which might have been considered immoral, or else politically or theologically subversive. Far from offering outdated and irrelevant ideas written in a dead language, Latin offered all sorts of new narratives to its readers. In their enthusiasm, the humanists had concealed from themselves how few of these were compatible with traditional Christian beliefs.

Classical texts for use in schools were naturally carefully chosen and often pruned, but the interested student did not have to look far beyond his set authors to find accounts of scandalous pagan practices or erotic encounters that had been omitted from his textbooks. Ovid was a Roman poet whose clear style and syntax ensured that selected extracts from the *Metamorphoses* were read in the upper forms of grammar schools. Montaigne, whose education had begun exceptionally early and was remarkably liberal, recorded that 'the first taste I had for books came to me from my pleasure in the fables of the *Metamorphoses* of Ovid. For at about seven or eight years of age I would steal away from any other pleasure to read them' ('Of the Education of Children', *Essays*, p. 130). The variety of magical and mythical narratives naturally appealed to a child, but an adolescent reader was more likely to respond to the many divine and human rapes and seductions, described in the graphic detail that is Ovid's hallmark as a poet. The account of Philomela's violation and mutilation at the hands of Tereus, for example, has an imaginative power that flows into Shakespeare's *Titus Andronicus*, while his two poems *Venus and Adonis* (1593) and *The Rape of Lucrece* (1594), in their different ways, both reveal the Roman poet's influence.

Ovid's most notoriously erotic poems were the *Ars Amatoria* ('The Art of Love') and his *Amores*, then referred to as the *Elegies*. Christopher Marlowe translated these in the late 1580s, in turn providing a model for John Donne's *Elegies*. Marlowe's poetry reworked classical themes with a self-conscious eroticism present, not only in his version of Ovid's *Elegies*, but in his play derived from Virgil, *Dido, Queen of Carthage* (1586), and in his tantalizingly bisexual treatment of Ovid's most familiar love story, *Hero and Leander*. Like the story of Pyramus and Thisbe, that of Hero and Leander was so well known that any version of it was likely to be mock-heroic—as is Nashe's use of it in *Lenten Stuffe* (*Works*, iii. 195–201), or Ben Jonson's puppet play of it in *Bartholomew Fair* (v. iv. 102–334), where the South Bank and Puddle Dock stand in for Sestos and Abydos, and the lovers have become comically vulgar Cockneys.

Marlowe was fully conscious of the subversive elements in classical education, building them into his tragedy *Dr Faustus*, where the hero's several aims are partly unified by his admiration for the classical world and its values. At the outset, Faustus says of himself,

> This word 'damnation' terrifies not him,
> For he confounds hell in Elysium.
> His ghost [spirit] be with the old philosophers!
> (I. iii. 60–2)

The devil Mephistophilis disagrees. As the traditional language of magic, Latin is used to conjure up the devil, while Faustus's fascination with classical culture is reflected in this reference to Elysium, as well as in his calling up Alexander and his paramour, and in his later worship of Helen of Troy. She appears as a succubus, a demonic spirit who will steal his soul by having intercourse with him, as well as embodying all the enchantment of the ancient world:

> 'Sweet Helen, make me immortal with a kiss.
> Her lips suck forth my soul. See where it flies!'
> (v. i. 93–4)

As time runs out for him, Faustus quotes a line from Ovid's *Elegies* where the poet, in bliss in his mistress's arms, begs Night's galloping horses to slow down: 'O lente, lente, currite noctis equi!' (Run slow, run slow, O horses of the night)' (v. ii. 74). Faustus, in his terror of what is to come, utters the same words. In desperation his mind reverts to those myths of the 'old philosophers' whose lessons had taught him to question the existence of the hell whose reality is about to swallow him up:

> Ah, Pythagoras' *metempsychosis*, were that true,
> This soul should fly from me, and I be changed
> Unto some brutish beast.
> All beasts are happy, for, when they die
> Their souls are soon dissolved in elements;
> But mine must live still to be plagued in hell.
>
> (v. ii. 107–12)

Marlowe's sense of the corruptingly sensual charms of classical literature was shared by other humanist poets, including John Milton.

The ecclesiastical authorities were alerted to the proliferation of erotic poetry and satire in the 1590s—both genres derived their explicitness from classical models. In 1599 copies of the most notorious of these, including John Marston's erotic poem *Pygmalion's Image* (1598), his satirical *The Scourge of Villanie* (1598), and Sir John Davies's *Epigrammes* (1590), were called in and burnt at the Stationers' Hall, on orders from the bishops of London and Canterbury, who laid down that 'no satires or epigrams be printed thereafter'. A quite different set of objections to classical authority came from those who thought its ideas and influence irrelevant to the times, an attitude that was later to develop into the full-scale dispute between 'ancients' and 'moderns'. Spenser's old headmaster, Richard Mulcaster, observed: 'It is no proof because Plato praiseth it, because Aristotle alloweth it, because Cicero commends it, because Quintilian is acquainted with it, or any other else . . . that therefore it is for us to use.'[12]

Education and Society

However valuable it might be to be able to read the Bible or Latin, one primary goal of education was to teach men to govern well. In his *Utopia*, Thomas More had emphasized the need for scholars to steer the ship of state, to participate in government while recognizing that the world of power politics was very far from any ideal. The Tudor monarchs took care to build up efficient administrations. At one time royal advisers had been great aristocrats or powerful churchmen, trained in canon law, who had reached the top of their profession, but now the pattern of government was changing: Henry VIII's break with Rome put an end to the line of great ecclesiastical lawyers (Wolsey was the last and possibly the greatest example); and while noblemen continued to play an important part in the country's government, the Tudors were alert to the danger of any one individual acquiring too much power. They were liable to play their nobles off against one another, or against their own protégés, men like Thomas Cromwell, Francis Walsingham, and William Cecil, of humble or minor gentry origins, who had worked their way up through their own intelligence, energy, and competence. Education had provided the initial openings for such men. Several Elizabethan writers of middling backgrounds pursued careers in government administration. Spenser was the son of a scrivener (a professional scribe): educated at Merchant Taylors School, and graduating from Pembroke Hall, Cambridge, he became secretary first to the Bishop of Rochester and then to Lord Arthur Grey, whose disgrace he survived. John Donne, educated at university and the Inns of Court, was hoping for a career within government circles when he briefly became secretary to Sir Thomas Egerton, Keeper of the Great Seal and subsequently Lord Chancellor.

The gentry were advised to take their sons' education seriously for fear of losing their positions of trust and responsibility to better-informed inferiors. The humanist Richard Pace warned old-fashioned aristocrats that if they continued to see hunting and hawking as more gentlemanly activities than studying, 'Then you and other noble men must be content that your children may wind their horns and keep their hawks, while the children of mean men do manage matters of estate'.[13] Government and politics were no longer in the hands of amateurs.

The upper classes were not slow to respond to demands for better education in administrative circles, or to rising standards at grammar schools and universities, which at one time they had

considered more suitable for clerks and scholars than for gentlemen. Traditionally the gentry had employed private tutors for
their children at home, later sending them to other great households to acquire good manners and courtly accomplishments
such as dancing, sports, and military exercises. Even before
boarding schools existed, the English aristocracy had educated
their children away from home. Later, young men were sent
abroad for two or three years of foreign travel, to 'finish' them.
Under the guidance of a tutor or mentor they would visit France
and Italy (a habit denounced by Roger Ascham, who considered
the Italians capable of any and every vice). Although the older
model continued (William Cecil's household provided formal
schooling for a number of wealthy young aristocrats, many of
whom were also court wards), grammar schools and universities
were now increasingly patronized. Sir Philip Sidney and Fulke
Greville attended the free grammar school at Shrewsbury: it was
the largest of its day and included the teaching of Greek in its
statutes. Like most young gentlemen of their generation they
went on to university, though they did not stay long enough to
graduate. Changing patterns of government produced debate as
to the appropriate education for the ruling classes, and an extensive literature developed around the subject, described in the
next chapter.

It is hard to judge how far the desire for education was connected with social aspiration, partly because the two are so
closely linked in our own society. David Cressy has observed
that 'literacy unlocked a variety of doors but it did not necessarily secure admission'.[14] The dominant ideology held that individuals best served the commonwealth by remaining in the
position allotted them by birth; the gentry must rule and the rest
obey. Social mobility was more often seen as a threat than a
benefit. Lear's Fool warns his master that a madman is 'a
yeoman that has a gentleman to his son; for he's a mad yeoman
that sees his son a gentleman before him' (III. vi. 12–14). The
respect due to parents was only one of a variety of social observances that might be upset by a sudden change of status: by abdi-
cating, Lear provokes an answering degree of insubordination

from his elder daughters. Yet the bourgeois aspirations of the Yellowhammers (in Middleton's *A Chaste Maid in Cheapside*), who are inordinately proud of their son Tim, 'the Cambridge boy', look characteristic of the rising middle classes. It was virtually impossible to achieve high office in central administration without the right family connections or strings to pull; the sudden elevation of lucky or gifted individuals would have acted as an incentive to some, and a source of resentment to others. Under James, money more obviously helped to buy status.

At the lower end of the social scale, the ability to read, write, and keep accounts was a practical help, and could advance professional or vocational standing. Being able to read could save the life of a person found guilty of committing certain felonies (that is, serious crimes), since the ability to read the 'neck verse' (the first verse of the fifty-first Psalm in Latin) enabled the criminal to plead 'benefit of clergy', allowing the death sentence to be commuted. Unless the felon was actually a clergyman (in which case different rules operated), he would be branded on the right thumb, to prevent him from escaping death if he ever committed a second offence. Ben Jonson, found guilty of killing the actor Gabriel Spencer in a fight, pleaded thus and carried the brand mark. Estimates of literacy are controversial, but there was some correlation between being able to read—and much more between being able to write—and one's social status in early modern society: the further people were down the social scale, the less likely they were to be able to read or write. Figures for the seventeenth century show that 11 per cent of women, 15 per cent of labourers, and 21 per cent of smallholders could sign their names. London was exceptional in having a highly literate population, and so did the home counties more generally. In more isolated districts writing skills fell sharply, and remained low among women everywhere. It looks as if at least some poor girls were taught to read, but instead of writing they learned to sew, knit, and spin instead. Only in well-to-do or exceptionally religious or intellectual households was education considered desirable for women.

Until recently, early modern literacy was assessed on the basis of the ability to write one's name, instead of leaving a mark, sign, or pictogram, since it was assumed that reading and writing were learned together, as they are today; but it is now thought that reading skills were taught earlier, and separately from those of writing. Moreover, the ability to read was itself subject to variables: the simplest and cheapest form of print available was 'black letter' or Gothic script, such as was used in broadside ballads, Bibles, and the earliest reading books. Many who read this lettering could not read the Roman typeface we use today (when the opposite is true). And the ability to read type did not necessarily carry with it the ability to read handwriting, which might be written in one of at least three distinct scripts: 'secretary' was the most widely used. Described as a 'Gothic cursive', it is difficult to read. Much easier is the 'italic' (i.e. Italian) hand, which arrived in the mid-sixteenth century and eventually took over altogether; there were also various 'court' and legal scripts used for public record-keeping. Most communities included professional 'scriveners' or semi-professionals (such as schoolmasters or ministers) who could write and read difficult handwriting on behalf of everyone else.

Writing was taught after reading, usually between the seventh and eighth years of age, which was also the point when a child's labour began to be of economic value, so that poor children were less likely to stay at school long enough to learn writing. First or 'petty' schools taught basic literacy, writing, and simple arithmetic, though these were also taught in the preparatory classes of a grammar school, where these existed. Schoolmasters were officially licensed by the Church, but reading could be learned from a variety of unofficial people, including mothers or other women acting in the capacity of child-minders, who taught small groups in the church porch (the informal forerunners of 'dame schools') or visited individual homes.

Schools and Universities

Children learned to read by reciting the vowels and consonants, and then spelling out individual words before they actually tried to read a whole passage, or to write individual letters down. At every level there was a great deal of learning by heart, the purpose of which only became apparent later on. Repetitive exercises were justified as an essential part of memory training, which was highly valued in a society where information was hard to acquire or retrieve. Elaborate techniques were used for training the memory systematically, and various aspects of Elizabethan life reveal the effects of this training, from the extensive literary borrowings of the playwright John Webster to the large number of plays that an acting company could perform in repertory at any one time.

Writing did not merely involve reproducing letters: children had to make their own pen and ink, trimming a suitable quill with a penknife, and making up the ink in a horn bottle from a mixture of soot, water, and gum. Spelling, then known as 'orthography' (i.e. correct writing), was not yet standardized and remained a matter of personal preference, although some scholars thought that spelling should be reformed so as to record the (supposed) origins of particular words. The schoolmaster Holofernes in *Love's Labour's Lost* complains of

such rackers of orthography, as to speak 'dout', fine, when he should say 'doubt'; 'det', when he should pronounce 'debt'—d, e, b, t, not d, e, t: he clepeth a calf, 'cauf'; half, 'hauf'; neighbour vocatur 'nebor'; neigh abbreviated 'ne'. This is abhominable—which he would call 'abominable'.

(v. i. 19–25)

The introduction of an 'h' in 'abominable' was one of a number of additions proposed on the basis of uncertain or even mistaken Latin derivations. This one did not survive, but others did, contributing to a growing gap between writing and pronunciation. Sometimes the new spellings even came to influence traditional pronunciation, as Holofernes apparently thought they should. His spelling (though not his pronunciation) of 'doubt' and 'debt' have survived to the present.

The majority of 'petty' school pupils did not progress beyond basic schooling either to writing or to the study of good Latin that was the main educational objective of the grammar schools—so called because the children began by learning Latin grammar. In *The Merry Wives of Windsor*, William Page recites his Latin lesson to the Welsh schoolmaster Sir Hugh Evans, to the amusement of Mistress Quickly (IV. i. 21–79). If they stayed the course, pupils then progressed to writing Latin compositions. Schoolchildren were customarily whipped or beaten for making mistakes. The jester in Nashe's play *Summer's Last Will and Testament* (1592) declares himself 'an open enemy to ink and paper . . . Nouns and pronouns, I pronounce you as traitors to boys' buttocks. Syntaxis and prosodia, you are tormentors of wit, and good for nothing but to get a schoolmaster twopence a week' (ll. 1474–9; *Works*, iii. 279–80). Better teachers hoped that learning might appeal to the child for its own sake. In the preface to *The Schoolmaster* (1570) Roger Ascham recalls William Cecil telling him that 'divers scholars of Eton be run away from the school for fear of beating'.[15] He was particularly opposed to the cruelty of schoolmasters who beat away the love of learning from children, believing that the young could be taught more effectively by patience and love than by punishment. But such enlightened views were rare, and most schoolmasters continued to whip their pupils.

To provide for different ages and levels of progress, schools were divided into classes, from three to as many as seven, each of which would work on different texts and tasks, though the whole school usually occupied only one or two rooms. A larger school might have an usher as assistant, and older pupils were often expected to help the younger ones. The bottom class studied only grammar, progressing later on to simple Latin texts, specially written colloquies or versions of Aesop's fables or Cato's proverbs. They would then work their way up through texts of increasing difficulty, studying passages from the Roman dramatists Terence and Plautus, speeches from Cicero, and on to the poets Ovid, Horace, and Virgil at the top of the school, when they might also begin Greek. Many school statutes laid down which texts were to be read, though the master might vary these at his own discretion and according to availability. Humanists believed that it was part of a schoolmaster's function to use the set texts to introduce further topics such as ethics, history, geography, or astronomy, as each seemed relevant,—an ideal that few masters would have been capable of achieving.

Children were encouraged to develop their own powers of expression in Latin, and to this end Erasmus recommended that they made collections of notable sayings as they came across them in their reading, grouping them under appropriate headings in a commonplace book. His own collection of adages was a sophisticated example and extension of the same principle. Many Elizabethans made similar compilations in English as well, having been trained to do so at school: Ben Jonson published his under the title of *Timber or Discoveries*, timber being the raw material from which an Elizabethan architect created the framework of a building. The curate, Sir Nathaniel, takes out his table-book to write down the schoolmaster's witty sayings in *Love's Labour's Lost* (v. i. 15), while Hamlet, after speaking to his father's ghost, calls for

> My tables—meet it is I set it down
> That one may smile, and smile, and be a villain!
> (I. v. 107–8)

Note-taking was widely practised, and was speeded up by the various techniques of shorthand (sometimes referred to as 'stenography') currently available. These made it possible to copy down sermons, as well as to pirate plays for unauthorized publication.

Good Latin style was acquired by translating, whether from the pupil's own composition in English or, according to Ascham's double translation method, from a passage already translated into English from a Latin original, so that the pupil's Latin version could then be compared with that of the author being studied. Mastery of Latin led to mastery of rhetoric, the linguistic skill used to win friends, influence people, and generally make a name for oneself in the world. The teaching of rhetoric was broken down into its various technical elements, and schoolchildren practised writing on different topics, sayings, or proverbs, or else constructed arguments for either side of a debatable proposition, such as 'Should Brutus have killed his best friend for the sake of the Roman republic?' Schoolmasters used recitations, debates, and even playlets, to promote rhetorical skills. Shakespeare's mastery of the academic exercise of 'varying'—finding different terms of praise for a particular object—is revealed in the Dauphin's self-conscious celebration of his horse (*Henry V*, III. vii. 11–37). Examples of speeches debating opposite sides of a proposition are frequent in his work, and indeed such formal exercises underpin Renaissance dramatic writing as a whole. In *Richard II*, John of Gaunt urges his exiled son to be patient, since

> All places that the eye of heaven visits
> Are to a wise man ports and happy havens.

while his son replies

> O, who can hold a fire in his hand
> By thinking on the frosty Caucasus?
> (I. iii. 275–6, 294–5)

Very different in tone, but ultimately derived from the same old school exercise, are Leantio's two contrasting speeches on the secret joys and woes of marriage in Middleton's *Women Beware Women* (III. ii. 1–27, 190–214). Dull and harsh though so much schooling was, its emphasis on formal Latin rhetoric was immensely valuable to a generation of dramatists.

The Elizabethan school-day was appallingly long, though it was typical of the much longer working day that was the norm in early modern society. It started at six or seven in the morning, going on until the children went home for lunch at about eleven o'clock. Work began again at one o'clock, and lasted till five or six in the evening, for six days of the week. No wonder boys sometimes played truant instead. Morning and afternoon breaks of fifteen minutes began to be introduced, allowing children to let off high spirits, and providing an alternative to corporal punishment: slow or disobedient children could be kept in instead of being whipped. School holidays were far shorter than today, although there were more single-day holidays. In the

Midlands and the north there were 'barring out' rituals, allowed times when the schoolmaster was locked out of the school by his pupils until he had negotiated their holidays with them.

Despite long hours and a demanding programme of studies, an outstanding schoolmaster could have a lasting influence on his pupils and might even win their affection as well as respect. Richard Mulcaster, high master of Merchant Taylors School for twenty-five years, taught Spenser (who represented him as Wrenock in the December Eclogue of *The Shepheardes Calender*), as well as Thomas Kyd (author of *The Spanish Tragedy*), writer and poet Thomas Lodge, and Bishop Lancelot Andrewes. John Webster also attended the school, though probably after Mulcaster's retirement in 1586. Ben Jonson, taught by William Camden at Westminster School, remained devoted to him, dedicating his 1616 *Works* to

> Camden, most reverend head, to whom I owe
> All that I am in arts, all that I know . . .

From Camden, Jonson acquired scholarly habits of mind, a thorough knowledge of Latin, and good Greek, an unusual accomplishment in a man who had not attended university.

Oxford and Cambridge in the sixteenth century were in transition, as older methods and techniques derived from medieval scholastic theology were gradually abandoned, along with the study of canon (i.e. the Church's) law. Other faculties—civil law, medicine, and divinity—were still taught, but before students could embark on these advanced courses of study they had to obtain the degrees of Bachelor and Master of Arts, a matter of four years' study followed by a further three years. Together these two programmes made up a course of seven years' work, parallel to the seven-year period usually served by apprentices to various trades and skills, the only technical training then available. The Bachelor of Arts degree included the traditional subjects of logic and rhetoric, an introduction to Greek, mathematics (arithmetic, geometry and some optics), music, and a little philosophy. In order to graduate, the student was required to demonstrate his mastery of logic and rhetoric practically, by making speeches and engaging in a public disputation ('wrangling'), defending or attacking a particular position and answering any objections that might be raised against his argument. The degree of Master of Arts involved advanced work in Greek and geometry and introduced the student to astronomy and the three branches of philosophy, natural, moral, and metaphysical.

Oxford and Cambridge were all-male institutions, and although the clergy was now allowed to marry, the two universities retained their old monastic rules of celibacy. Living arrangements within them were gradually changing: students had once lived mainly in halls, but now they were increasingly lodged and taught in colleges (which had previously consisted of small groups of graduates). Undergraduates were usually a year or two younger than today, and sometimes more than that, levels of achievement being less tightly tied to particular age groups. College tutors took on responsibility not only for their students' instruction and behaviour, but sometimes also for the state of their wardrobe and their laundry arrangements as well. They might share rooms with their pupils, visit them in the vacation, and receive fees and allowances directly from their parents. Criticisms of university-based teaching as too narrow encouraged individual tutors to extend the syllabus beyond the statutory requirements, so as to include more modern authors and topics. New university appointments, notably the Savilian professorships of mathematics and astronomy established at Oxford in 1619, introduced students to important recent discoveries such as those of Kepler and Galileo, as well as to John Napier's system of logarithms used for making calculations. But traditional subjects and methods still made up the most part of the four-year Bachelor of Arts degree.

By 1640 as many as two and a half per cent of the total population of 17-year-old boys went on to higher education, although a much smaller number actually graduated. Some failed to complete their studies because they could not afford the fees— this may have happened to Thomas Middleton, who went up to Queen's College, Oxford, but left without graduating. Poor students could work their way through college as 'sizars', servants of the college or of wealthier students, or else take time off to earn the cost of their fees, but only if their families could survive without their earnings. Catholics were unable to graduate since the ceremony required them to subscribe to the Thirty-Nine Articles of the Anglican faith. John Donne, brought up a Catholic, studied at Oxford and probably also at Cambridge for several years and then, like many of the gentry, left without a degree, to round off his general education at the Inns of Court. These offered a professional legal training and were commonly regarded as the third university. Going to law was almost a way of life for a number of Elizabethans who could afford to do so, and fathers were anxious for their sons to pick up at least a smattering of legal terminology so that they would know what to expect when, in due course, they went to law themselves or alternatively administered it, as local Justices of the Peace. Law students, even more than university undergraduates, were famous for their wild behaviour: Shakespeare's Justice Shallow is anxious to maintain his reputation as a tearaway in his youth (*2 Henry IV*, III. ii. 14–34, 194–218).

The growing numbers of gentry attending grammar schools and universities gave rise to complaints that the 'better sort', through misuse of wealth and influence, were preventing the talented and deserving poor from gaining scholarships and fellowships. The early years of Elizabeth's reign were marked by a drive to increase the numbers of poor graduates who would go on to become clergymen, since recruitment had fallen drastically in the years following the Reformation. Endowment of scholarships and the number of places at university grew, and student numbers rose steadily, at least until the crisis years of the 1590s, after which they continued to grow. Historians have argued that one outcome of this expansion was to create more hopeful clergymen than there were adequate livings for them to fill, and that their disappointment and alienation contributed to the disruptions of the 1640s. As Mulcaster had written in *Positions* (1581), 'all may not pass on to learning which throng thitherward, because of the inconveniences which may ensue by want of preferment for such a multitude, and by defeating other trades of their necessary travaillers [workers]'.[16] Bacon echoed this view in his essay 'Of Seditions and Troubles', where he noted the problems of 'an overgrown clergy', and in 1611 he wrote to the King 'Concerning the advancement of learning', to warn him that there were now too many grammar schools, and a corresponding shortage

both of servants for husbandry and apprentices for trade; and on the other side, there being more scholars bred than the state can prefer and employ, and the active part of that life not bearing a proportion to the preparative, it must needs fall out that many persons will be bred unfit for other vocations and unprofitable for that in which they are brought up, which fills the realm full of indigent, idle and wanton people . . .[17]

Alienated Intellectuals

For those who lacked a vocation for the Church and the social contacts necessary to reach even the lower rungs of the administrative ladder, writing pamphlets and plays was one way to support themselves. But the rewards of the literary profession were small and notoriously unreliable: there was no system of royalties, and printers made outright payments for manuscripts (typically around £2), and then sometimes to their current possessors rather than to their actual authors. The habit of circulating work in manuscript, common in élite circles, made it easier to get hold of and publish the work of other writers, so that writing that was admired and imitated did not necessarily benefit its author directly. On the face of it, writing for the theatre looked more promising, but in practice the university-trained writers were often less versatile than full-time hacks such as Heywood, Dekker, or Shakespeare. It was also less profitable to receive an outright payment for a particular play (Henslowe paid a flat £6) than to be a company shareholder, regularly in receipt of a fixed proportion of the takings (as the main actors, including Shakespeare, were) even if one managed to sell the same play twice over, as Greene is supposed to have done.

Christopher Marlowe's career exposes the difficulties of a young man whose education left him in a social no-man's-land. His father was a Canterbury shoemaker, an artisan comparable in status to that of the glove-maker and tanner who was Shakespeare's father. Both playwrights were born in 1564. Marlowe won a scholarship to King's School, Canterbury, and then a further scholarship, intended to help poor scholars study at Cambridge in order to take holy orders. It had been endowed by Matthew Parker, Elizabeth's first Archbishop of Canterbury, as part of a drive to create more and better clergymen. Marlowe completed his BA and proceeded to the MA, which he took in 1587. By this time he seems to have begun working as an anti-Catholic spy, and his first stage success, *Tamburlaine*, was performed that year by the Admiral's Men. Marlowe was not temperamentally suited to the monotonous, demanding, and badly paid life of the average country parson, and he lacked the patience and discretion required in the corridors of power, at least from underlings. The government was only prepared to employ him in an irregular and underhand capacity.

Marlowe's education entitled him to call himself a gentleman and a master of arts, but it did not give him the wherewithal to maintain such a position. He was not trained to follow his father's trade; he could not accept the Church, and the administrative system would not accept him. This problem affected a number of young men of his generation, educated far above their parents' social level. Some drifted, as Marlowe had done, into working as spies for Sir Francis Walsingham. The literary figure of the malcontent, commonly a melancholy, disaffected intellectual, was often seen as the product of disappointed hopes. Bosola in Webster's *The Duchess of Malfi* is driven by poverty first to spying, and then to murder. Delio recalls him in early days:

I knew him in Padua—a fantastical scholar, like such who study to know how many knots was in Hercules' club, of what colour Achilles' beard was, or whether Hector were not troubled with the toothache; he hath studied himself half blear-eyed, to know the true symmetry of Caesar's

nose by a shoeing-horn; and this he did to gain the name of a specula-
tive man.

(III. iii. 41–7)

The first and second parts of *The Return from Parnassus*, performed at Cambridge between 1598 and 1602, dramatized the
problems that confronted a group of university graduates in
search of jobs. In the first part, Ingenioso (who may represent
Nashe) talks of putting his wit out to interest to 'make it return
two pamphlets a week' (i. i. 206–7), but his patron dismisses him
with two groats (i. i. 312). In Part Two, the tough publisher
Danter is only interested in offers of libellous satires (such as
might land their author in gaol), and the actors Burbage and
Kempe regard the graduates' talents as uncommercial: 'Few of
the university [men] pen plays well . . . Why, here's our fellow
Shakespeare puts them all down, aye, and Ben Jonson too' (IV.
iii. 1766, 1770). They are reduced to such degrading tasks as
whipping dogs out of church and administering enemas. These
plays help to explain the vogue for satire and social criticism in
the 1590s.

The 'university wits' (as they have been called) who attempted
to make a living from writing in the 1590s found it difficult to
do so. Little is known about Marlowe's financial situation, but
the fact that he was arrested in the Netherlands in 1592, implicated in an attempt to forge English coins, suggests he was in
difficulties. Greene, on his own admission a drunkard and a
spendthrift, apparently died in misery and want, while Nashe
confessed that when 'the bottom of my purse is turned downward, and my conduit of ink will no longer flow for want of
reparations . . . I prostitute my pen in hope of gain' (*Have with
you to Saffron-Walden*, *Works*, iii. 30–1). Several writers turned
to the comparative security of the Church, as did the dramatist
John Marston and his fellow-satirist Joseph Hall (later to
become Bishop of Exeter). John Donne and George Herbert
also turned to the Church after the failure of more worldly
careers; such moves were not necessarily cynical.

Education equipped these authors to write, but financial security was only achieved by those who were exceptionally lucky or

talented. Yet though the predicament of the 'university wits' is painfully vivid, it was probably the grammar schools, rather than the universities, that made the biggest impact on the social system, and particularly on the urban bourgeoisie, from whose ranks nearly all the great dramatists were drawn—Marlowe, Shakespeare, Jonson, Marston, Middleton, and Webster, as well as the major poets Spenser and Milton, and such versatile writers as Nashe, Greene, and Lodge. Education did not satisfy worldly needs or bring wealth or status, yet it was the only high road to 'Parnassus', the prerequisite for the creativity that was regarded by the humanists as the most divine of human gifts, conferring a freedom and mastery far above the daily round. Elizabethan writers hovered uneasily between a value system in which literary inspiration was the highest good, and the actual economic system into which they had been born, and in which they often had to struggle to make a living.

The Court and its Arts

'THE most striking feature of the great nation states of the sixteenth and seventeenth centuries was the enormous expansion of the court and the central administration', according to Lawrence Stone.[1] This was reflected in the development of a primitive civil service, the increasing concentration of wealth and aristocracy at court, and the self-conscious cultivation of an extravagantly 'courtly' way of life, intended to impress foreign statesmen and the lower orders. The court represented itself as an object of national pride, its activities of increasing interest to outsiders, and not only from a political standpoint: like a Hollywood film-star, Queen Elizabeth figured in men's unconscious fantasies, if the secret diaries of the astrologer Simon Forman are anything to go by:[2] his dream of arguing with her, kissing her, and lifting her skirt is a 'low' version of Prince Arthur's Platonic dream of Gloriana (*The Faerie Queene*, I. ix. 13–15). Much literature was written for or about the court, which not only supplied a cultural focus but also offered potential sources of financial support for the aspiring writer. Images of courtliness and court life embody either a unique refinement of manners and morals, or alternatively an unacceptable level of corrupt privilege and vice.

Courts had always provided, and would continue to provide a system of support for favoured writers such as Chaucer and Gower at the court of Richard II or Dryden at the court of Charles II, but Elizabethan culture was particularly focused upon the court, and London was closely linked with, interested in, and resentful of this grossly overgrown household in its midst.

Great aristocrats were actively discouraged from setting up rival establishments: Elizabeth preferred to have her nobles about her and to know exactly what they were up to. If she thought herself neglected, she was liable to insist on their prompt attendance. It was, moreover, in their own best interests to remain close to the throne as the chief source of whatever glittering prizes were going. The monarch had three main forms of reward to hand out—honours, privileges, and offices. Honours were given in return for support, and included knighthoods, and even peerages, though Elizabeth was notoriously mean with these compared to James I: while Sir Walter Raleigh received no more than a knighthood, James's two great favourites became Earl of Somerset and Duke of Buckingham—the latter caused deep resentment since it gave automatic precedence over all the inherited titles of the kingdom. Privileges conferred financial benefits, in a variety of forms, ranging from government annuities or pensions through the leasing or buying of royal lands on generous terms, to more complex and often dubious privileges: the right to collect customs fees on particular goods, exemption from certain export regulations, monopolies to make and distribute particular commodities, and patents or licences to develop new products. Most of these rights might be resold at a profit. New projects and patents that might corner the market were popular, though the absurdity of many of these schemes is parodied in Jonson's *The Devil is an Ass* (1616), where the projector Meercraft proposes to make wine out of raisins, take out a patent on toothpicks, and drain the Fens, making the gull Fitzdotterel 'the Duke of Drowned Lands' (II. i. 97; IV. ii. 39; II. iv. 97). According to Jonson, this joke turned out to be so close to reality that 'the King desired him to conceal it'.[3] The most dubious of the royal handouts were the guardianship of wards, the rights to collect fines from Catholics (honourably turned down by Sir Philip Sidney), or to follow up unpaid state rents or debts. With no formal system of tax collection, monarchs handed over the rights to collect bad debts as a form of reward.

The rewards of office were political power (such as privy councillors enjoyed), status (as Justices of the Peace, or county sheriffs), influence gained from distributing court favour, and the profits to be made from possessing influence. Court positions were either inadequately paid or not paid at all, but it was accepted that those in positions of influence accepted a variety of fees or gratuities in lieu, so that their incomes came from their clients rather than from their employer. When Francis Bacon, as Lord Chancellor, was impeached for accepting bribes in 1621 he made no attempt to deny the charge, but argued that he had never allowed them to influence his judgements. Competition for office was part of an extensive system of patronage, in which powerful aristocrats each sought to strengthen their position by establishing their supporters in particular offices: these might give access to the monarch (such as Groom of the Privy Chamber), or to the court (like the Provisorship of the Horse, given to Bosola in *The Duchess of Malfi*). They might include places on the judicial bench or the Council of the North; secretaryships or captaincies of garrisons (like Leantio in *Women Beware Women*); or at a more everyday level, clerical livings, college fellowships, or jobs as clerks or royal park-keepers. The client, bound by gratitude or obligation, did what he could when he could to advance his patron's interests or prestige. Often, like Bosola, he would be required to provide 'intelligence', that is, inside information. There existed a wide range of offices, from the most influential to the most menial; some were farmed out or sublet for a profit, a fixed proportion of their income returning as rent to the formal office-holder, though, as we have seen, few positions carried proper salaries. The patronage system extended throughout society: even noblemen tended to form into factions, 'packs and sects of great ones', the lesser seeking out the protection of the greater (those without wealth or connections sought it most eagerly).

While there were pickings to be had at court, it was something of a lottery, with the high costs of attendance often outweighing the benefits. The court provided luxurious meals and sometimes lavish entertainment, but in return courtiers had to maintain themselves in a style appropriate to the setting, in expensive clothes, with liveried servants and a coach and horses. The grandest nobles were required to entertain the Queen and her entourage on her annual progresses, and finance diplomatic missions or even military expeditions, all of which could prove cripplingly expensive; any official payment was unlikely to cover the actual costs. Despite the various gifts to come their way, many of the greatest nobles died desperately in debt: Elizabeth's favourite, the Earl of Leicester, owed more than £35,000 (several million pounds, in today's terms) to the Crown alone, while Essex was in similar difficulties when he lost the Queen's favour; his rebellion in 1601 was the gesture of a man with nothing more to lose. At times, the Queen used debts as a way of enforcing her nobles' dependence. The burden of debt fell not only on the noblemen themselves, but on their small tradesmen and suppliers who had little hope of being repaid; aristocratic privilege protected peers from being sent to debtors' prisons, but not their unpaid grocers or bootmakers. Shakespeare's *Timon of Athens* provides a graphic account of extravagance and generosity suddenly turning into poverty and bad debts, and in this respect, Timon seems more of an Elizabethan than an Athenian aristocrat. Yet whatever the gains or losses, the court remained a source of wealth, status, and influence, and only there could Hobbes's 'perpetual and restless desire of power after power' find fulfilment.[4]

The Courtier's Skills

The development of centralized power and national self-consciousness, and the recognition of the court's influence on the evolving state encouraged humanist thinkers to theorize as to how such influence might best be employed. The earliest writings on the subject were addressed either to princes or to the ruling classes in general, to the courtier and the governor (whether prince or magistrate), but these gradually extended down the social scale to *The Compleat Gentleman* (the title of Henry Peacham's guide of 1622). Handbooks on statecraft could even overlap with advice on etiquette, since rules for political and social conduct were not as distinct as they are today, and political attitudes were reflected in terms of ceremonial, or its absence: Antony whipping Caesar's messenger, Thidias (*Antony and Cleopatra*, III. xiii. 93), or Cornwall stocking Lear's servant, the disguised Kent (*King Lear*, II. ii. 125) carried sharper implications when the treatment of messengers or servants was a measure of the respect accorded to their masters. Different social gradations were reflected in various gestures of deference—bowing or curtseying, standing bareheaded, or kneeling in the presence of a superior. The monarch, as well as a host of other offices, were distinguished by special modes of address—'your majesty', 'your highness', 'your honour', 'your grace', and so on, while superiors in general were 'sir' or 'madam'. Apart from God Himself, only one's nearest and dearest, lovers, children, or obvious social inferiors were addressed with the old-fashioned singular 'thou'. Kent's use of that singular to King Lear, and later to Oswald, was a deliberate attack on court protocol, an impertinence sufficient to justify Lear's fury and, perhaps, Cornwall's punishment (I. i. 146–52; II. ii. 64).

Handbooks for princes normally presupposed some form of monarchy, and followed Plato in assuming that a better society would be achieved through wiser rule, ideally that of a philosopher king, but otherwise of philosophical counsellors. The first book of Thomas More's *Utopia* (1516), written in the Platonic form of a dialogue, discusses the need for wise men to involve themselves in politics. In the same year, More's friend Erasmus composed *Institutio Christiani Principis* ('The Education of a Christian Prince') which recommends a humanist education, with an emphasis on the individual's obligation to the state, as described in Cicero's *De Officiis*. According to Erasmus, the prince's primary aim should be to act as a Christian, and a good Christian was also a pacifist: 'If you cannot defend your kingdom without violating justice, shedding much blood and injuring the cause of religion, give up your crown and yield to the necessities of the times . . . prefer rather to be a just man than an unjust prince.'[5]

Shakespeare's Henry VI recalls Erasmus's gentle, passive and unworldly ruler. Three years earlier Machiavelli's *The Prince* (written 1513, published 1536) had considered the ruler's obligations to his people from the standpoint of a tough, competitive power politics: it frightened its readers by ignoring Christian ethics altogether, and instead offering practical advice as to how a ruler could achieve strength and stability within the state in the face of unscrupulous rivals. Machiavelli believed that princes needed at times to make use of force and fraud in order to rule effectively, and he permitted his prince to lie, dissemble, and break his word as 'reasons of state', that is, the state's best interests, required. Although he was caricatured on the English stage as a monster of cynicism and atheism, it was obvious that politicians were 'much beholden to Machiavel[li] and others, that write what men do and not what they ought to do', as Bacon put it in *The Advancement of Learning* (Book II, ch. xxi, section 9). *The Prince* reflected a growing interest in power politics as a practice in the sixteenth century. Although no English translation was published until 1640, it was widely read in Italian, French, and in the several manuscript translations. Its assumption that states need effective leadership underpins the historical dramas of Shakespeare, Marlowe, and Jonson.

Different again from Erasmus's Christian or Machiavelli's pragmatist prince was Castiglione's *The Courtyer* (*Il Libro del Cortegiano*, completed in 1518, published 1528, and translated by Sir Thomas Hoby, 1561). Castiglione concerns himself less with the prince's moral or political dilemmas, and more with the courtier as a social being, and this is reflected in its structure—four dialogues between a group of courtiers at Urbino in which they attempt to define their ideal. While traditional morality is upheld, Castiglione's emphasis falls on personal accomplishments, both indoors and out. In addition to the key ability to speak well, displayed in the dialogue itself, the courtier should be able to write gracefully in prose and verse, draw and paint, play music, sing, and dance. This scheme was so influential that more than a century later Molière's *Bourgeois Gentilhomme* was still attempting to master these arts in his erratic progress towards gentility. Handbooks for courtiers or gentlemen were especially valued by the socially aspiring, and the growth of a new urban gentry contributed to their popularity.

Sir Thomas Elyot's *The Boke named the Governour* (1531) reflects Castiglione's influence: it recommends similar lists of accomplishments, while addressing a more suspicious and less cultivated audience. Elyot has to persuade them of the value of humanist educational ideals in the first place. He does so partly by using the traditional argument that without it their talents are threatened by more bourgeois, clerkly competitors, but then he changes tack, reassuring his readers that practising the arts to beguile leisure hours is fundamentally different from practising them as a craftsman would, to earn his daily bread: 'I intend not . . . to make of a prince or nobleman's son a common painter or carver, which shall present himself openly stained or imbrued with sundry colours' (Book I, ch. viii).

Sixteenth-century painters were in fact a highly professional group, close knit through intermarriage, and holding the status of artisans rather than artists. Their work records English isolation from Continental developments: the painters of Elizabeth's court were either miniaturists like Nicholas Hilliard, or painted elaborate portraits focused on emblematic costume and accessories, the badges and rewards of office. Though the details of an embroidered dress, a jewelled ring, or a patterned carpet are brilliantly registered, they imprison their subjects in official trappings, transforming them into icons in a style that looks primitive beside much contemporary Dutch or Italian painting. Neoclassical influences on painting, sculpture, and architecture began to appear in James's reign, under a more outward-looking regime.

Elyot's distinction between living to play and playing to live remained a crucial one, reflected in various ways, for example, in the upper-class reluctance to publish. Manuscript circulation remained the normal mode of distribution for the Elizabethan gentleman. Courtiers composed poems to be sung at court, passing them on to professional musicians to provide musical settings for them. Later, these lyrics often appeared anonymously in songbooks published under the composer's name.

John Dowland's collections contain poems by leading courtiers of the day, including the ill-fated Earl of Essex; Sir Edward Dyer; Fulke Greville; William Herbert, third Earl of Pembroke; George Clifford, Earl of Cumberland, and Sir Henry Lee. Although the songbook lyrics are often very beautiful, it is difficult to identify the authors of many of the items that appear in them, or in the many contemporary commonplace books that include scraps of verse. Prose also circulated in manuscript, as Sidney's *Arcadia* had done before its publication in 1590.

The performance aspect of music also worried Sir Thomas Elyot since 'a gentleman playing or singing in a common audience impaireth his estimation'(Book I, ch. vii). He felt on safer ground in recommending more traditional courtly pastimes, such as riding, hunting, and other outdoor sports. Dancing, in particular, occupies four chapters of Book I (xix–xxii), being delightful in itself, and a symbol of universal harmony. Unlike the great chain of being, the dance provided an image of active participation in the social order that implied the conscious acceptance of an allotted role. The only alternative was to break time and measure, disrupting the efforts of one's fellow-dancers. The dance figures repeatedly in Renaissance literature, bringing comedies to a formal end (as in *Much Ado about Nothing*), uniting the courtly performers with their audience in a masque, and providing a theme for cosmic rhapsodies in Sir John Davies's poem *Orchestra* (1596). In associating the creative efforts of the individual with the divinely ordered creations of God, *Orchestra* resembles the sequence in *The Faerie Queene* where Calidore stumbles upon the dance of the Graces on Mount Acidale (VI. x. 10–17). The dance was a pastime that appealed to all classes, from country-folk trotting through their traditional rounds to the Queen stepping out in a galliard; moreover, according to Elyot, Plato's disciples had interpreted the movements of the heavens as a form of 'dancing or saltation'. In Jonson's masque *Pleasure Reconciled to Virtue* (1618), the archetypal creator, Daedalus, praises the power of dancing to display the skill of the participants and instruct the onlookers:

> For dancing is an exercise
>   Not only shows the mover's wit,
> But maketh the beholder wise,
>   As he hath power to rise to it.
>   (ll. 269–72)

If dancing signified the right ordering of society and nature, riding, another courtly accomplishment, could figure the triumph of reason or intellect over rebellious animal passions and, by extension, benevolent mastery over the more violent aspects of the natural world. Stephen Orgel has observed that 'To bring the destructive energies of nature under control, both within and without, was the end of Renaissance education and science'.[6]

While Elyot addressed the improvement of society as a whole, Castiglione focused upon personal goals of self-improvement (or 'self-fashioning', as Stephen Greenblatt terms it). In his view, courtly skills should be displayed with an easy negligence, *sprezzatura* or *grazia*, which makes them more pleasing than if they look studied or the outcome of conscious effort. His definition of this desirable 'simplicity or recklessness' (in Hoby's translation) nevertheless suggests an art concealing art, pretending to a spontaneity it does not possess, and so suggests that self-consciousness, insincerity, and even dissimulation may be part of the courtier's skills. Yet an ideal of self-forgetfulness, of absorption into something beyond the self, is also powerful within *The Courtyer*. It is most forcefully conveyed in the discourse on divine love at the end of Book IV, where Pietro Bembo performs the self-forgetfulness he recommends. Castiglione justified the cultivation of courtly skills as a way of gaining the prince's favour and thus of influencing him to rule virtuously, but all practical purposes fall out of sight in the final pages, which culminate in a rapt exposition of Neoplatonic love doctrine.

Bembo challenged the conventional view of physical beauty as a sensual snare, insisting that all expressions of beauty in the world, including physical beauty, result from the presence of spiritual or heavenly influences; such beauty, rightly understood, leads not to sensual indulgence, but to a rational or intellectual love focused upon the heavenly elements within earthly beauty. The lover then ceases to desire sexual fulfilment, or even the physical presence of the beloved, ascending the stairway of love, as Socrates had described it in Plato's *Symposium*, to the contemplation of all beauty and goodness wherever they may be found on earth, and finally to beauty or virtue as ideals in themselves, in their most transcendent forms. Such a contemplation might carry one out of the body and up to heaven, as in an ecstasy: even as Bembo is speaking, he is '(as it were) ravished and beside himself ... without once moving, holding his eyes toward heaven as astoni[sh]ed'.[7] When Emilia Pia touches his robe, he comes to himself, scarcely knowing what has happened to him.

The Neoplatonic assumption that there were heavenly elements present in all earthly beauty became a commonplace of Renaissance love poetry, recurring, in one form or another, in much of the love poetry of the age. It often acts as a point of departure in Sidney's sonnet sequence *Astrophil and Stella*: Sonnet 5 recognizes that

> true beauty virtue is indeed,
> Whereof this beauty can be but a shade,
> Which elements with mortal mixture breed ...
> (ll. 9–11)

while Sonnet 25 invokes Plato's authority for the view

> That virtue, if it once met with our eyes,
> Strange flames of love it in our souls would raise ...
> (ll. 3–4)

an image which Bembo had also borrowed: 'What happy wonder, what blessed abashment may we reckon that to be, that taketh the souls which come to have a sight of the heavenly beauty? What sweet flame?'[8] Donne was another poet who drew upon Neoplatonic ideas and imagery, further complicating them with jokes, twists, and paradoxes of his own. While some of his lyrics distinguish between sensual lust and the spiritual love that survives sexual satisfaction and absence, his poem 'The Ecstasy' begins with an experience of spiritual love, but ends with a plea

for sexual expression, thus reversing the usual progress of Neoplatonic love. Like Bembo, Donne glimpsed 'the true image of
angelic beauty' within the loved one. Michael Drayton entitled
his sonnet sequence *Idea* (1593), and in varying ways, Sidney,
Spenser, and Donne were all influenced by these theories of
ideal love, or divine aspiration, which saw the soul as imprisoned
in the decaying body and longing for escape. The way in which
Neoplatonic love was eagerly adopted as a way of courtly
writing and loving also suggests a desire to transcend the material world of wealth, show, and faction, expensive clothes, and
rich, indigestible food.

Thomas Campion's love lyric composed in classical metrics
combines images of musical harmony and heavenly influence:

> Rose-cheeked Laura, come
> Sing thou smoothly with thy beauty's
> Silent music, either other
> Sweetly gracing.
>
> Lovely forms do flow
> From consent divinely fram'd;
> Heav'n is music, and thy beauty's
> Birth is heavenly.[9]

Campion, like Donne, Herbert, and a number of others, developed his metrical skills by composing Latin verses; following
Sidney's example, he experimented with writing English verse
in classical metres, forcing the irregular and heavily stressed
rhythms of English into the quantitative system of Latin verse.
Rhyme had been unknown to the Greeks or the classical Roman
poets; it was a late invention, associated with medieval Latin
verse. Sidney, followed by Campion (in his *Observations in the
Art of English Poesie*, 1602), attempted to restore the purity of
unrhymed metre in English, and though their attempts were
generally unconvincing, their success with rhymed verse derived
from an exceptional sensitivity to rhythm, which must have been
further developed by exercises such as 'Rose-cheeked Laura'.

Sidney's experiments in classical metre were part of a concern

with 'imitation' common to all serious writers. The critical
practice of the day required a poet to copy his predecessors—
whether in subject-matter, form, style, or treatment—while
creating new variations upon them. Originality was less highly
valued than a fresh interpretation of some recognized and
familiar element. In being a great imitator, Sidney was also a
great innovator, in that he introduced many European verse
forms into English poetry. The eclogues of the *Old Arcadia* provided a showcase of examples for later English poets to imitate
in their turn: they include the first formal epithalamium (i.e. marriage poem) in English, the first formal pastoral elegy (unless
Spenser's November Eclogue precedes it), the first 'crown' poem
(in which the last line of one stanza becomes the first of the
next), and the first sestina. This was a Provençal form in which
the six final words of a six-line stanza appeared in a different
order; Sidney composed a traditional sestina, a rhymed version,
and, in an extraordinary display of virtuosity, a double version.
There are nine different types of sonnets alone, and the metrical variety is dazzling. The experiments in classical metres are
spoken by the disguised princes, and include elegiacs, sapphics,
and asclepiadics. An example of the last is Dorus's song,

> Ō sweēt wo͞ods, thĕ dĕlīght ōf sŏlĭtārĭnĕss
> Ō hōw mūch Ĭ dŏ līke yo͞ur sŏlĭtārĭnĕss.

Pleasing though these lines sound, the long and short syllables
of the Latin metre are virtually impossible to identify in English,
unless they are marked in. Differences between them depend
partly on spoken emphases, although Sidney and his disciples
tried to establish a system for deciding the length of particular
syllables in English words. Many words of more than one syllable have a natural rhythm (e.g. 'dĕlīght', or 'sŏlĭtārĭnĕss'), but
monosyllables vary according to sense and emphasis, which
makes them conveniently versatile, but unhelpful where a particular sequence is required. Sidney and Campion wrote delightful poems in classical metre, but unless a reader is thoroughly
familiar with their Latin models, their rhythms are only audible
when they are set to an accompanying tune that imposes the

right length on each note (as, for example, does Campion's hymn 'Come, let us sound with melody, the praises', in his first *Book of Ayres*).

Campion was a composer as well as a poet. Music (like literature but unlike painting) seemed to borrow whatever it needed from Continental models in order to strike out in a new direction, and the great age of English music lasted from the sixteenth to the end of the seventeenth century. In 1588 Nicholas Younge published *Musica Transalpina*, a set of Italian madrigals, substituting English words for the Italian texts, and within a few years English music had recapitulated all the major developments that had taken place in Italian music over the previous century. Most secular music was written for court performance, but music, like dancing, was enjoyed at every social level: peddlers like Autolycus sold new ballads to be sung, while the popularity of the court composer John Dowland extended well beyond the court, if dramatic allusions are anything to go by. His mournful pavane 'Lachrymae' was a particular favourite: the grocer's wife in Beaumont's *Knight of the Burning Pestle* (Act II, interlude ii, line 9) specially requests it be played, and there are many other stage references to it and musical arrangements of it. Dowland was versatile, but his special gift was for melancholy music.

Printing had contributed substantially to music-making, particularly new music: ballads were often written to be sung to particular tunes, which were either named (e.g. 'To the tune of "Fortune my foe" '), or the tune might be printed with the words. Part-songs could have their music printed in four blocks, forming an outward-facing square, so that four participants could sit or stand round a small table and each read the music in front of them, printed the right way up. Four-part music was particularly adaptable since the parts—soprano, alto, tenor, and bass—might be sung, or else played on consorts of recorders (woodwind) or viols (strings).

Elizabethan songs may be divided into airs and madrigals, although the terms were not always used very precisely: the air is a song for a single voice or part, accompanied by a lute or a keyboard instrument, sometimes with several verses, but all to the same tune. The madrigal is a part-song written for four, or even six parts, and strongly influenced by Italian examples. Madrigal composers rapidly developed complex rhythms and harmonies, and a variety of decoration and invention—Byrd, Morley, and above all Weelkes were masters of the form. Using several voices, with little singing in unison, the madrigal usually consisted of a single stanza, often with varied line-lengths, expressing strong, simple emotions in repeatable phrases, as in the following (anonymous) example, from Thomas Morley's *Canzonets To Five And Six Voices* (1597):

> O grief! e'en on the bud that fairly flowered
>   The sun hath lowered.
> And, ah, that breast which Love durst never venture,
>   Bold Death did enter.
> Pity, O heavens, that have my love in keeping,
>   My cries and weeping.[10]

One convention of song-writing was that the music should emphasize the meaning of the words by imitation. Thomas Morley advised the composer to 'dispose your music according to the nature of the words which you are therein to express, as whatsoever matter it be which you have in hand, such a kind of music must you frame to it'.[11] Thus sad words must be matched with minor keys, cheerful words with quick music and short notes, while 'when your matter signifieth ascending, high heaven and suchlike, you make your music ascend; and by contrary where your ditty speaketh of descending lowness, depth, hell and others such, you must make your music descend'. While it was possible to achieve such effects in the madrigal, where short phrases were repeated by different singers, it was more difficult with the air, in which several stanzas were sung to the same tune, and close verbal parallels between verses had to be maintained, both in terms of the rhythms and the meanings of words, so that the same tune would fit each stanza. The greatest exponent of this art was Thomas Campion, who wrote the music for his own lyrics, though it is not known which came first. He had a fine ear for the rhythms of words and could make the different verses of a song correspond perfectly with one another: 'Shall I come, sweet love, to thee', from his *Third Book of Ayres* (1617), is an excellent example. Writing words for airs in which several verses were sung to one tune necessitated close attention to word-rhythms (and so did the practice of writing words to fit existing tunes, as Nicholas Younge had done in *Musica Transalpina*). Poets also wrote words for songs to fit pre-existing tunes, as Sidney had done in *Certain Sonnets*, and John Donne in *Songs and Sonnets*. Close attention to the rhythms of accompanying music contributed to the remarkable aural appeal of the age's lyric poetry.

Sidney's skill as a versifier was only one among many moral and intellectual qualities that encouraged his contemporaries to see him as Castiglione's ideal courtier, and he displayed the care-lessness or *sprezzatura* required for that role: in *A Defence of Poetry* he observed, 'as I never desired the title [of poet], so have I neglected the means to come by it. Only, overmastered by some thoughts, I yielded an inky tribute unto them' (p. 111), and his sonnet sequence *Astrophil and Stella* similarly disclaims poetic ambition:

> In truth I swear, I wish not there should be
> Graved in mine epitaph a poet's name . . .
> (Sonnet 90, ll. 7–8)

Such careless grace was combined with great moral earnestness, and a humanist (and Protestant) conviction that to teach was even more important than to entertain. In his *Defence of Poetry* Sidney insisted that the poet's first responsibility was to instruct, to set before his reader the finest models that might be: 'so true a lover as Theagenes, so constant a friend as Pylades, so valiant a man as Orlando, so right a prince as Xenophon's Cyrus, so excellent a man every way as Virgil's Aeneas' (p. 79). Epic or 'heroical poetry', as Sidney calls it, is the 'best and most accom-plished kind', since it 'inflameth the mind with desire to be worthy, and informs with counsel how to be worthy. Only let Aeneas be worn in the tablet of your memory . . .' (p. 98).

Spenser, in dedicating *The Faerie Queene* to Walter Raleigh, endorsed this view, declaring that his 'general end' had been 'to fashion a gentleman or noble person in virtuous and gentle discipline', and pointing out how 'much more profitable and gracious is doctrine by example than by rule'. Sidney himself attempted the heroic or epic style, though not in verse—indeed he did not consider verse an essential attribute of poetry (or 'making') at all: 'it is not rhyming and versing that maketh a poet . . . But it is that feigning notable images of virtues, vices, or what else, with that delightful teaching, which must be the right describing note to know a poet by' (pp. 81–2).

Sidney's pastoral romance, the *Old Arcadia*, was dedicated to his sister Mary, Countess of Pembroke. It is a tragicomedy, set out in five acts, its characters few in number, its action often farcical, its outcome a comic reversal of fortune. The heroes, Pyrocles and Musidorus, overmastered by passionate love, can no longer distinguish the sensual from the spiritual so that the force of their feelings drives them first to irrational, then to shameful behaviour. Pyrocles seduces the innocent Philoclea, while Musidorus's rape of Pamela is only prevented by the timely arrival of a band of rebels, who personify his rebellious desires. Sidney seems to have agreed with Castiglione's Master Bernard when he said: 'Truly, the passions of love bring with them a great excuse of every fault, yet judge I (for my part) that a gentleman that is in love, ought as well in this point as in all other things, to be void of dissimulation, and of upright meaning.'[12]

Sidney later rewrote the *Arcadia* in the heroic mode, articulating the moral lessons appropriate to that genre. The three books of the unfinished *New Arcadia* are much darker in tone, so that when, after Sidney's death, the last two books of the *Old Arcadia* were tacked on to them, they did not fit too well. The revised text is structurally far more complex, introducing many new strands of plot and digressions, and its heroes acquire a moral integrity that makes them better examples, at the cost of some interest. Attention is now transferred to Amphialus, whose unrestrained passions make him the guilty victim of evil fortune. The *New Arcadia* has widened its horizons, dealing more explicitly than before with international conflict and political action and reaction, in ways that directly reflect its author's hopes and concerns. Sidney was a nephew of the Earl of Leicester, and passionately committed to the Protestant cause in Europe. He died in 1586, fighting for his religion against the Spanish in the Netherlands, exceptional among Elizabethan noblemen in being killed in battle.

Images of Elizabeth

Much of Elizabeth's support came from active Protestants, who saw her as the biblical Deborah, leading God's people against their enemies (Judges, 4: 5), or as the Emperor Constantine establishing the true Christian faith; yet she was a reluctant champion, forced into a more militant stance by her excommunication (in 1570) and the threat of Spain, rather than her own instincts. By nature she was cautious, conservative, and careful of expense, and though she was herself educated and cultivated, knew Greek, Latin, and Italian, translated and wrote verses, she generally left literary patronage to her great noblemen, Leicester and Burghley, or to lesser figures such as Sidney or Walter Raleigh. From 1583 she patronized an acting troupe, but it is not known whether they actually received regular wages, or simply performed at court on commission. She created among her courtiers an atmosphere of rivalry for favours that required them to compete in their celebrations of her, while she was well aware of the value of good propaganda: in London she moved from palace to palace by road or river, attended by showy processions of guards and the courtiers of her own household, and sometimes by the city's liveried companies as well. During the summer months the court went on a progress through the countryside, stopping at towns and the houses of the great, where she was greeted with speeches, pageants, and country-house entertainments, such as Mary Sidney's *Dialogue between two shepherds, Thenot and Piers*, written to welcome her to Wilton, or her brother Philip's *Lady of May*, a dialogue performed for her in the gardens of Leicester's house at Wanstead. She encouraged her courtiers to foot the bill, whenever she could gracefully do so.

Elizabeth celebrated her accession day, 17 November, as a public holiday, the first truly Protestant (and therefore secular) holiday. The old popish festival of St Hugh gave place to Elizabeth's day, marked all over the country by sermons and thanksgiving services, as well as feasting, bell-ringing, bonfires, and cannonades. Later in her reign, her birthday (7 September) and Armada Day (19 November) were also celebrated, and at court, accession days became the occasion for pseudo-medieval tournaments, conducted in fancy-dress. While these involved some initial expenditure, the greater part of the cost fell on the contestants who were required to provide their own elaborate costumes, horse, armour, and whatever else might be required in the way of chariots, musicians, or speakers to make an impressive entrance—part of the fun was to see what roles individual challengers would adopt.

Sidney himself took part in the accession day tilts: in his sonnet sequence *Astrophil and Stella*, Astrophil carries off the prize on one occasion (Sonnet 41), though he also makes himself a laughing-stock by looking at Stella instead of riding to meet his opponent at the barriers (Sonnet 53). All three books of the *New Arcadia* include tilting episodes: in the first, there is a pageant followed by formal jousting in which Phalantus defends the beauty of his love Artesia; in Book II a full-scale tournament celebrates the wedding anniversary of the Iberian queen, and in Book III Amphialus wages war on Arcadia in a series of single combats. On each occasion Sidney describes in detail the elaborate fancy-dress armour worn by the participants, and the *impresa* or device painted on his shield, which combined with the knight's outfit to convey the symbolic role he had adopted. In the Iberian tournament of Book II, the shepherd knight Philisides (Sidney himself), dressed in a conspicuously extravagant imitation of rustic garb, rides against Lelius, a name elsewhere used for Sir Henry Lee, Queen Elizabeth's Champion at Tilt until 1590, and the chief organizer of the accession-day tournaments. Surviving records show that in 1581 and 1584 Sidney and Lee were matched against each other in the tilts, and on the second occasion opened the proceedings, so that the Iberian tournament may have fictionalized a real event in which Sidney had taken part. Other poets also drew on these romantic festivities in celebrating the Queen.

George Peele's verses commemorated the tournaments in 1590 ('Polyhymnia') and 1595 ('Anglorum Feriae'), while Spenser may have had the accession-day celebrations in mind when he described the general structure of his epic in the dedicatory letter to Raleigh: 'The Faerie Queene kept her annual feast xii days, upon which xii several days, the occasions of the xii several adventures happened.' A manuscript found at Ditchley, and probably written by Sir Henry Lee, contains speeches for a 'damsel of the Queen of the Fairies', a clownish knight, and a hermit, apparently intended for presentation at an accession-day tilt, though when or if they were actually used is not known. Spenser's scheme in his letter to Raleigh also included a 'tall clownish young man', later revealed as Redcross, the knight of holiness, and a hermit or palmer who would accompany Sir Guyon on the adventures of the second day. Gloriana's annual feast was itself modelled on King Arthur's feast of the Round Table at Pentecost, and clownish knights and hermits, as well as fairy damsels, were among the stock properties of romance. Yet Spenser himself identified Gloriana with the Queen, and Elizabethan courtiers and their clients excelled at transposing actual events into imaginative compliments. As it turned out, the scheme of *The Faerie Queene* as described in the letter to Raleigh was not fulfilled in the poem itself, though what we have may be incomplete.

The strongest link between Spenser's poem and the tournaments staged for Elizabeth's accession day lies less in specific references than in a general nostalgia for the world of medieval romance, and the artificial resurrection of knightly chivalry as an ideal for courtly conduct. Roy Strong sees this as 'one of the great paradoxes of the Elizabethan world . . . that an age of social, political and religious revolution should cling to and deliberately erect a façade of the trappings of feudalism'.[13] Formal jousting may have been one way of disguising the sordid reality of contemporary warfare, deprived of its heroic potential by the use of gunpowder and the sacrifice of 'cannon fodder'. There is certainly a stark contrast in the *New Arcadia* between heroic single combat and the mangled corpses of a full-scale battle that 'uglily displayed their trailing guts'.[14] Sidney himself did not actually die on the battlefield, as Fulke Greville's story of his giving his water-bottle to a dying man suggests; in fact, his death occurred some days later, when his gunshot wound became infected.

Medieval chivalric traditions were linked with romance ideals of integrity and loyalty, simpler and more familiar version of Castiglione's courtly ideals; but they also worked to endorse Elizabeth's claims to allegiance as the descendant of English kings, and particularly through her grandfather, Henry VII, from a line of Welsh princes descended from the legendary King Arthur. In Spenser's *Faerie Queene* the champion of virtue is Prince Arthur, an allusion to Elizabeth's supposed forebears. Sometimes Elizabeth's descent was traced even further back, to Brut, the mythical Trojan founder of Britain, from whom 'Brutain' was believed to have taken its name. By extension, London might become 'Troynovant', or New Troy. A madrigal by Thomas Watson, performed for the Queen at Elvetham in 1591, prays

> O beauteous Queen of second Troy,
> Accept of our unfeigned joy!

Elizabeth's virginity had once been a source of anxiety for those concerned with the succession, but as she outlived the time for child-bearing it became part of her mystique. She spoke of being 'wedded to her people', combining the role of wife and mother of her country with the chastity of the moon goddess Diana, or Tuccia, the vestal virgin who miraculously carried water in a sieve. The sieve, like the spotless ermine and the single self-renewing phoenix, were favourite emblems, employed in royal portraits. Shakespeare referred to this aspect of her image in *A Midsummer Night's Dream*, when Oberon describes how Cupid loosed his arrow in vain

> At a fair vestal throned by [the] west, . . .
> But I might see young Cupid's fiery shaft

> Quench'd in the chaste beams of the wat'ry moon,
> And the imperial vot'ress passed on,
> In maiden meditation, fancy-free.
>
> (II. i. 158, 161–4)

The cult of the Virgin Queen was sometimes seen as an alternative to the officially outlawed worship of the Virgin Mary, whose combination of chastity and motherhood Elizabeth took up. A lyric in Dowland's *Second Book of Songs* (1600), usually attributed to Sir Henry Lee, proposes the singing of a 'Vivat Eliza for an Ave Mari!' Portraits of Elizabeth as Astraea show her crowned with stars, as the Virgin sometimes was, while memorial poems described her ascent to heaven and coronation there.

Such an attitude of worship, part-playful, part-serious, is evoked in the prologue to Thomas Dekker's play *Old Fortunatus* (1599), spoken by two old men:

1. Are you then travelling to the temple of Eliza?
2. Even to her temple are my feeble limbs travelling. Some call her Pandora; some Gloriana; some Cynthia; some Belphoebe; some Astraea; all by several names to express several loves. Yet all these names make but one celestial body, as all those loves meet to create one soul.
1. I am of her country, and we adore her by the name of Eliza.

The alternative names suggest classical goddesses, often worshipped under different titles in different cities, and they indicate the range of literary homage she received. 'Pandora', meaning 'all gifts', referred to the benefits she conferred on her happy people. Gloriana and Belphoebe were her names in *The Faerie Queene*, as Spenser had explained in his letter to Raleigh. Cynthia was the Greek name for Diana, 'Queen and huntress chaste and fair', the goddess of the moon, ruler of the waters, perhaps with a glancing reference to her defeat of the Spanish Armada. Elizabeth had appeared as Cynthia in Lyly's play *Endymion* (1588), as well as in Raleigh's long, unfinished love-poem, 'The Ocean to Cynthia'. Raleigh, whose first name Walter was pronounced 'water', punningly becomes the Ocean, and it was as the Shepherd of the Ocean that he appeared in Spenser's *Colin Clout's Come Home Againe* (1595), where the Queen was still referred to as Cynthia, as she was in Jonson's play, *Cynthia's Revels* (1600).

Astraea was the goddess of Justice who had left the earth long ago; her return, prophesied by Virgil, would restore the golden age, as Elizabeth had done. She figured as Astraea in George Peele's pageant *Descensus Astraeae* (1591), in Mary Sidney's *Dialogue between Thenot and Piers*, in the complimentary masque that ends John Marston's play *Histriomastix* (1599), and as the subject of Sir John Davies's *Hymns to Astraea* (1599), a series of twenty-six poems based on the acrostic 'Eliza-betha Regina'. As plain Eliza, she was 'Queen of shepherds all' in the April Eclogue of Spenser's *Shepheardes Calender*, as well as in many of the pastoral poems collected in the anthology *England's Helicon* (1600). As Zabeta she received Paris's apple, awarded to the fairest in Peele's *Arraignment of Paris* (1581) (as she does in Hans Eworth's painting at Hampton Court), while Sidney's *Lady of May* invited her to choose between rival suitors, a shepherd and a forester, for the Lady's hand.

As time wore on, the flattering addresses grew less and less appropriate. The Duke of Guise in Chapman's play *Bussy D'Ambois* (1604) complains of the English

> making semi-gods
> Of their great nobles; and of their old Queen
> An ever-young and most immortal goddess.
>
> (I. ii. 11–13)

The necessity of complimenting the ageing Queen stimulated poetic imaginations, producing flights of fantasy that left the sad reality far behind. Elizabeth herself had participated actively in her own myth-making, and the power of that propaganda can be felt even today, when her reign is still pictured as one of peace and plenty, the moment of 'merry England'. While the rest of Europe was at war, the English, were 'neither to be molested with broils in their own bosoms, nor threatened with blasts of other borderers; but always, though not laughing, yet looking as through an emerald at others' jars', according to Lyly's *Euphues and his England* (1580).[15] This idealized view of her reign increased, rather than diminished, with her death.

Although 1588 saw the miraculous victory over the Spanish Armada, the 1590s were years of plague, dearth, and civil unrest, culminating in the disaster of Essex's rebellion in 1601. The Earl had been a former favourite of the Queen, and like Sidney, subscribed to a code of military honour; he had starred in accession-day tilts as well as on real battlefields: he had fought beside Sidney at Zutphen, and had led a successful expedition against Cadiz in 1596. In 1599 he had set off for Ireland to put down the Tyrone rebellion, but returned in disgrace. More and more isolated, and heavily in debt to the Queen, he attempted with a number of other nobles to start a rebellion in London in 1601, but found no support at all. One Londoner remarked disapprovingly that 'he marvelled that they could come in that sort [i.e. brandishing swords and pistols] in a civil government, and on a Sunday'.[16] He was tried, and executed for treason, though like the Queen herself, and Sir Walter Raleigh, he was later remembered as a champion of England against Spain and Catholicism.

Morley's collection of madrigals *The Triumphs of Oriana*, presented to the Queen in the year of Essex's rising, were not happily named, for all their allusion to Spenser's Gloriana. Oriana means 'rising'; in fact, Elizabeth was sinking, growing old and increasingly bad-tempered and tight-fisted. For Shakespeare's generation, born close to her accession, she must have seemed to have reigned forever, and the shadow of that old, impatient ruler who had governed time out of mind falls across *King Lear*. Behind the joyful celebrations of her visits, for example, to Ditchley in 1592,

> Happy hour, happy day
> That Eliza came this way

can be glimpsed Sir Henry Lee, her former Champion at Tilt, prophesying his own ruin on hearing that 'Her Majesty threatens a progress and her coming to my houses'.[17]

Disillusion

If there was a gulf between the welcome publicly given and the financial panic it caused behind the scenes, there was a similar gap between the projected images of noble patrons, praised by their clients as protectors of the faith or benefactors of the arts, and the methods of money-making they were required to practise in order to maintain their status and influence. Great men scrambled for ignoble offices: the Earl of Leicester acquired the rights to customs dues on a variety of Mediterranean imports, as well as reclaiming, with some harshness, lapsed royal rights in the Forest of Snowdon, while the third Earl of Pembroke bought one of the great sinecure offices in the Court of Common Pleas. The old ideals of generous and open housekeeping, so carefully celebrated in Jonson's poem 'To Penshurst', could not be sustained without recourse to whatever dubious financial enterprises were available.

Great aristocrats may have lacked resources, but lesser men could not obtain positions at all: from the 1590s the number of those seeking court positions far outstripped the supply. Now criticism of the court came from those who could not get in, as well as those who had got in and found the atmosphere of competition, self-display, suspicion, and betrayal more than they could bear. It was Walter Raleigh, a man who had built his career as a court favourite, who wrote in 'The Lie',

> Say to the court it glows
> And shines, like rotten wood.
> (ll. 7–8)

Francis Bacon, who held a range of court offices, ultimately becoming Lord Chancellor, was also disarmingly frank in his essays—in particular 'Of Great Place', but also 'Of Empire', 'Of the True Greatness of Kingdoms and Estates', and 'Of Faction'— as to how monarchs and their followers behaved. The sharpest criticism came not from any oppositional country party nor from London puritans, but from the courtiers themselves, or their clients and dependants. For many, the antagonism between court and country (or pastoral) values had been internalized: the majority of courtiers came from the landed gentry, but had been brought up to regard the court as a focus of power, culture, and sophistication.

Literature, in particular, needed its patrons, and not merely for poetry: histories, sermons, translations, and learned discourses were hawked about in search of patrons to finance their publication, and attitudes hardened in the face of frequent requests. When Richard Robinson presented Sir Thomas Egerton with his translation of a learned theological tract, the great man asked 'What have we here? Begging letters?'[18] In creating so many new readers and writers, the printing press had broken down an older system of noble patronage of individual authors, yet an author's receipts were often inadequate, and some had to pay to have their books printed at all. Large numbers of writers now expected rewards both from readers and patrons, and were regularly disappointed. By the end of the sixteenth century fulsome dedications were being urged on reluctant patrons, expecting some financial return (about £2 was average) or perhaps a more lasting reward, for example, a place in a household as tutor, clerk, or secretary. In *Pierce Penniless* (1592), Thomas Nashe warned his friends to be more circumspect: 'Alas, it is easy for a goodly tall fellow that shineth in his silks, to come and outface a poor simple pedant in a threadbare cloak, and tell him his book is pretty, but at this time he is not provided for him' (*Works*, i. 241). Though Nashe's sympathy is with the poor pedant, unsolicited dedications could be a nuisance, especially when accompanied by a demand for prompt repayment. If Thomas Dekker is to be believed, there were rogues who printed pamphlets with elaborate dedicatory epistles into which they inserted, by hand-printing, the names of several different noblemen, in the hopes of being rewarded by as many of them as possible. Dekker describes this trick in *Lanthorne and Candle-light* (1608), calling it 'falconry'.

Some writers found the system of flattering dedications so repellent that they made fun of the whole thing, as did the satirist John Marston. His first book, *The Metamorphosis of Pygmalion's Image* (1598), was dedicated 'To the world's Mighty Monarch,

Good Opinion', his volume of satires 'To his most esteemed and best beloved self', while his play *Antonio and Mellida* was published in 1602 with a full-blown dedication 'To the only rewarder and most just poiser of virtuous merits, the most honorably renowned Nobody, bounteous Maecenas of poetry and lord protector of oppressed innocence'. Under such circumstances, the only way to avoid insincerity was to dedicate a text to a colleague or friend from whom no reward could be expected, so in 1604 Marston dedicated his best play, *The Malcontent*, to his friend Ben Jonson. Francis Bacon dismissed the whole convention: 'Neither is the modern dedication of books and writings, as to patrons, to be commended: for that books (such as are worthy of the name of books) ought to have no patrons but truth and reason' (*The Advancement of Learning*, Book I, ch. iii, section 9); he could afford to do so more easily than many of his contemporaries.

Although Shakespeare and a handful of other popular playwrights supported themselves comfortably on their stage earnings, the coterie dramatists had a more difficult time. Lyly wrote a desperate letter to the Queen at the end of his life, apparently in great financial straits. Jonson, who depended on court commissions, also seems to have found himself in difficulties, to judge by 'The Humble Petition of Poor Ben' and several other elegantly begging verses. In addition to his royal pension of 100 marks (about £33 per annum, but worth perhaps a hundred times as much today), Jonson was also granted a pension of £25 a year for books by the Earl of Pembroke. The poets Michael Drayton and Samuel Daniel depended on private patronage for most of their lives, while John Donne, in his years of unemployment at Mitcham, was glad of the patronage of Sir Robert Drury, whose daughter's early death he celebrated so extravagantly in *The First Anniversary* (1611). Spenser was awarded a royal pension of £50 a year on the strength of *The Faerie Queene*. Earlier he had obtained the position of secretary to Lord Arthur Grey, probably through the good offices of Leicester or Sidney. The habit of courtly compliment was so deeply ingrained in Spenser that he published *The Faerie Queene* with sixteen

dedicatory sonnets addressed to different courtiers, and even
this looks restrained beside the ninety-three different dedications of Geoffrey Whitney's *The Choice of Emblems* (1586).
Spenser had few illusions about the operation of the patronage
system. *Mother Hubberd's Tale* vividly evokes the frustration of
needy talent compelled to wait upon the whims of privilege:

> Full little knowest thou, that hast not tried
> What hell it is, in suing long to bide:
> To lose good days that might be better spent;
> To waste long nights in pensive discontent;
> To speed to-day, to be put back tomorrow;
> To feed on hope, to pine with fear and sorrow;
> To have thy Prince's grace, yet want her peers';
> To have thy asking, yet wait many years;
> To fret thy soul with crosses and with cares;
> To eat thy heart through comfortless despairs;
> To fawn, to crouch, to wait, to ride, to run,
> To spend, to give, to want, to be undone.
> Unhappy wight, born to disastrous end,
> That doth his life in so long tendance spend.
>
> (ll. 895–908)

In the October Eclogue of *The Shepheardes Calender*,
Spenser's persona Colin Clout had lamented that the days of
patronage were over: 'Maecenas is yclad in clay.' *Colin Clout's
Come Home Againe* portrayed the court as corrupt, even if the
Queen and her ladies were honourable exceptions. Although
Gloriana signified Elizabeth, and *The Faerie Queene* was dedicated to her, within the poem she appears only as an unattainable ideal, and even her fairy knights are carefully distinguished
from human knights, and have their own separate genealogy
(consulted by Guyon in Memory's chamber, Book II, canto x,
line 716). Book V, the most topical and political, begins by pointing out the injustice of the present times, and here the Queen is
figured as Mercilla, reluctantly accepting the necessity of executing Duessa/Mary Queen of Scots, driven by grim necessity,
rather than rejoicing in the freedom of her other persona, the
huntress Belphoebe. For Spenser, human courts were sad places.

His courtly knight, Calidore, inspired by Philip Sidney, escapes into the green world. Sidney himself had composed a pastoral 'Dispraise of a Courtly Life' which preferred the shepherd's simplicity to the insincerity and dissimulation of the court. The Faerie Queen's court at Cleopolis is a golden-age dream, as beautiful as it is impossible.

The material nature of courtly rewards and shows led to a misplaced emphasis on appearance: as Spenser had complained in *Colin Clout's Come Home Againe*, 'each man's worth is measured by his weed [clothes]' (l. 711). Elizabeth herself set the tone by dressing magnificently. She could hardly have been pleased when, early in her reign, Thomas Drant preached to her of Adam and Eve's nakedness; later, her godson Sir John Harington recorded her irritation when the Bishop of London 'seemed to touch on the vanity of decking the body too finely . . . perchance the bishop hath never sought [gone to] Her Highness' wardrobe, or he would have chosen another text'.[19]

The court laid itself more open to criticism because it had to fulfil several very different functions simultaneously: it was the seat of government and justice for the nation as a whole, but also the site of an ongoing upper-class house-party: the monarch's wisest councillors might turn from high-level decision-making to put on masquing robes or tournament armour and transform themselves into courtiers. As the source of government, it was responsible for setting moral and cultural standards for the rest of the country, leading by its good example. Wicked courtiers, according to Castiglione, 'do infect with deadly poison not one vessel, whereof one man alone drinketh, but the common fountain that all the people resorteth to'.[20] The image was a powerful one, for the health of the community as a whole depended on the water supply, in the form of a fountain or spring, remaining clean and untainted. The image of the court as a fountain became a commonplace, used by Jonson in the dedication of *Cynthia's Revels*, where he slips easily from compliment to scolding:

To the special fountain of manners: the Court. Thou art a bountiful and brave spring: and waterest all the noble plants of this island. In thee, the whole kingdom dresseth itself, and is ambitious to use thee as her glass. Beware, then, thou render men's figures truly . . . It is not powdering, perfuming, and every day smelling of the tailor, that converteth to a beautiful object: but a mind, shining through any suit, which needs no false light, either of riches, or honours to help it.

It recurs in the opening scene of *The Duchess of Malfi*, where Webster, echoing Castiglione and Thomas Elyot's *Image of Governance* (1541), refers to the fountain's capacity to pollute the whole of society:

> a prince's court
> Is like a common fountain, whence should flow
> Pure silver drops in general: but if't chance
> Some curs'd example poison't near the head,
> *Death, and diseases through the whole land spread.*
>
> (I. i. 11–15)

Nor was this merely a figure of speech. Webster's contemporaries believed that God rewarded or punished a whole nation according to whether He was pleased or displeased, not merely with their behaviour, but with that of their rulers, so that bad times, evil enough in themselves, might further point to something wrong at the top. The wickedness of princes and their tendency to corrupt the rest of society was a favourite theme of Jacobean tragedy.

Castiglione had avoided the problems posed by evil princes by concentrating upon the courtier's potential to influence the prince to act virtuously, but what if the prince's vices corrupted the courtier? In More's *Utopia* Raphael Hythloday argues, 'At court there is no room for dissembling, nor may one shut one's eyes to things. One must openly approve the worst counsels and subscribe to the most ruinous decrees. He would be counted a spy and almost a traitor, who gives only faint praise to evil counsels.'[21] A later handbook for courtiers, Lorenzo Ducci's *Ars Aulica* (1601, translated by Edward Blount, 1607), written to help the courtier win his prince's favour, openly recommended the use of 'praise and flattery'. The courtier may achieve a position of special trust by satisfying the prince's desires, 'As of *ambition* in procuring some high degree of honour: or of *covetousness*, gaping after gain, or of *wrath*, thirsting for immoderate revenge, or of *love*, longing impatiently for the fruition thereof'.[22] Here Castiglione's self-consciously spontaneous courtier gives place to a Machiavellian dissembler, and moral scruples must be sacrificed to the great art of getting on. Possibly such instructions were intended to be ironic, but the Italian art of the courtier was suspect; according to Nashe, it made a man 'a curious carpet knight: which is, by interpretation, a fine close lecher, a glorious hypocrite' (*The Unfortunate Traveller*, *Works*, ii. 301).

The treachery and uncertainty of court life were topics familiar from Latin literature. In *Pierce Penniless*, Nashe had quoted 'Fraus sublimi regnat in aula' (treachery reigns in the lofty palace) from Seneca's *Hippolytus* (ll. 982), translating it as ' 'tis rare to find a true friend in kings' palaces' (*Works*, i. 186). The second chorus of Seneca's *Thyestes* expresses a preference for private life, led far away from the court, where death is peaceful, unlike that of the courtier who dies 'known . . . too much to other men . . . yet unto himself unknown' (ll. 391–403). Seneca's tragedies and essays appealed strongly to those Tudor nobles who read his teachings of stoic indifference to misfortune as the product of a stormy career under difficult Roman emperors (Seneca had served the state, and was eventually sentenced to death for conspiracy). His relationship with his pupil, the emperor Nero, as well as his enforced suicide were analysed by the historian Tacitus in his account of the Roman Empire. The writings of Seneca and Tacitus were central to the work of Justus Lipsius, who rewrote their philosophies for his own times, discussing how civil war and tyranny might be endured in *Constancy* (1584) and how the state should conduct its affairs in his *Six Books of Politics* (1589).

For Elizabethan courtiers, the world of political machinations that Tacitus described was both recognizable and informative, but its message, that power corrupts, was bleak and short on conventional morality. His histories were widely read and admired in the Earl of Essex's circle, and his teachings were sometimes held responsible for the Earl's disastrous conspiracy, though it was just as possible to interpret Essex's fall as that of an ambitious favourite who went too far, as had Sejanus, discussed by Tacitus and dramatized by Ben Jonson in 1603. When James came to the throne, former Essex supporters like Francis Bacon, Fulke Greville, and Tacitus's translator Henry Savile were rewarded with knighthoods, and they re-gathered around his son Prince Henry, who favoured more active intervention on behalf of Protestants in Europe. His followers were seen as troublemakers, 'the moths and mice of court at that time . . . maligners of true virtue and only friends to their own ambitions and desires'.[23] When Prince Henry died in 1612, some saw parallels with Tacitus' account of the poisoning of Germanicus.

The Court of King James

Sir John Harington left a scandalous report of Cecil's entertainment for King James and his brother-in-law, the King of Denmark, at Theobald's in 1606. A masque had been planned representing 'Solomon his Temple and the coming of the Queen of Sheba', but when the latter arrived, she tripped over the steps to the throne, and emptied her tray of wine, cream, jellies, and sweetmeats into the Danish king's lap. Among the other speakers 'Charity' was the only one sober enough to recite her lines, but she soon rejoined 'Hope and Faith, who were both sick and spewing in the lower hall'. 'Victory' had to be put to bed, while Peace, 'much contrary to her semblance, most rudely made war with her olive branch'. Harington concludes: 'I ne'er did see such lack of good order, discretion, and sobriety as I have now done.'[24]

Harington's account is an early example of a new genre that was to become a feature of James's reign: the gossipy newsletters written from the court complaining of its scandals and excesses. Comparisons between the courts of James and Elizabeth are difficult to make since nostalgia for her reign, characterized as militantly anti-Catholic, set in so quickly, but in general, Elizabeth was a firm disciplinarian who kept a tight hold on the purse-strings and was grudging with her favours and gifts, whereas James was lax, extravagant, and generous to a fault. Exasperated by endless requests, he was once driven to exclaim: 'You will never let me alone. I would to God you had first my doublet and then my shirt, and when I were naked I think you would give me leave to be quiet.'[25]

Like Elizabeth, James had received a sound humanist education—in his case, under the Protestant tuition of George Buchanan—and he himself wrote poems and tracts and liked to think of himself as a scholar, though his attacks on witches and tobacco reflect anxieties and prejudices. If Elizabeth was cast as the Virgin Queen, James's chosen persona was Solomon (as the fiasco at Theobald's recalls), learned, wise, just, and peaceful: he had made peace with Spain in 1604, and hoped to establish himself as a negotiator, rather than as an actor, in Europe's religious conflicts. James was a more active and generous patron than the old Queen, staging court masques that introduced the designs of Inigo Jones. Jones brought the neoclassical architecture of Palladio to Britain, building the Queen's House at Greenwich, the Banqueting House at Whitehall, and designing the piazza at Covent Garden. James enjoyed theology, lending his patronage to John Donne and Lancelot Andrewes; he also adopted Shakespeare's company, turning them from the Lord Chamberlain's Men to the King's Men, and making them Grooms of the Royal Chamber. They performed plays by Thomas Middleton, Ben Jonson, Beaumont and Fletcher, and of course Shakespeare himself: *Macbeth* (1606) showed the line of Stuart kings that included James and his family as descending from Banquo and stretching out to the crack of doom.

James's accession brought a substantial change in the running of the royal residence at Whitehall (Westminster Palace now housed parliament, the lawcourts, and the Exchequer). Henry VIII had laid out Whitehall, like other palaces of the time, as a suite of rooms of increasing privacy. The royal household consisted of the kitchens and the great hall, and was run by the Lord

Steward; the royal chambers, the guard and presence chambers were the responsibility of the Lord Chamberlain. These were the monarch's rooms for public entertainments. Further back lay a sequence of more private chambers for which the Groom of the Stool was responsible, and these were closed to all but members of the Privy Council or other privy officers. In 1603 the boundary between public access and private household retreated a stage further as the privy chamber passed into the hands of the Chamberlain, and James's private household held office as Gentlemen or Grooms of the Royal Bedchamber. James's favourites were quickly elected to posts in his inner circle.

The gentlemen of the inner household came into close contact with the King, and under Henry VIII they held positions of power, eagerly sought after. Elizabeth's private entourage consisted of her waiting-women, who could play no part in political decision-making, though they could exercise a little discreet patronage. If they kept to the rules, and did not marry or otherwise annoy her, they remained in office indefinitely, and her attendants changed little during her reign. Elizabeth's ladies distanced her from her (male) courtiers, who could not enter her rooms without specific invitation. Instead, she worked closely and trustingly with her secretary William Cecil, Lord Burghley, the single most powerful man in the country. When he died in 1598 he passed what he could of his duties on to his younger son Robert, later Earl of Salisbury.

James's position was very different: as King of Scotland he already had his own household, though it was smaller and less formal. James brought his closest companions south with him, and tried to divide up the available positions as Gentlemen of the Bedchamber and Privy Councillors equally between the English and the Scots, though the Scottish gentlemen were resented, and there were tensions between them and the English nobles. And he also had a family: his Queen, Anne of Denmark, had her own independent household, and among those close to her were Lucy, Countess of Bedford, patroness of Donne and Jonson and herself an occasional poet, and Penelope Rich (Sidney's 'Stella'), both of whom belonged to the group formerly associated with the Earl of Essex. John Florio and Samuel Daniel were attached to the Queen's household, and her Lord Chamberlain was Sidney's brother Robert, whose daughter Mary Wroth wrote sonnets, a play, and the romance *Urania* (1621).

James's eldest son, Prince Henry, also had his own household, first at Oatlands and later at St James's Palace. The heir to the throne was famous for his love of learning and his skill in martial arts. His excellence at tilting and fighting with the pike made him an appealing alternative to his father's studious pacifism, and the prince's court attracted those who wanted England to support the Protestant cause more actively on the international scene. Prince Henry's household was well regulated and organized, and he acted as patron for a number of ambitious works of national scope, including Michael Drayton's 'chorographic' poem, *Poly-Olbion* (part 1, 1612), celebrating English history in terms of geography or topography, Walter Raleigh's *History of the World*, and George Chapman's translation of Homer's *Iliad* (completed, 1611). Jonson's masques for Prince Henry (discussed below) linked him with the old chivalric traditions, with Sidney and Elizabeth's accession-day tilts, King Arthur and Spenser's *Faerie Queene*. His acting company, the Prince's Servants, were based at the Fortune Theatre, and Chapman's tragedy *Bussy D'Ambois* (1604) may have been intended to catch his attention: it portrays the fall of a true nobleman, a man of simplicity and honour out of step with 'the Courtiers schoolery', the world of politicians and time-servers who now dominated the French court. Bussy is

> A man so good, that only would uphold
> Man in his native noblesse, from whose fall
> All our dissensions rise . . .   (III. ii. 90–2)

Henry's death in November 1612 was widely mourned. Thomas Campion's 'Elegie upon the untimely death of Prince Henry' spoke for many:

> O Spirit full of hope, why art thou fled
> From deeds of honour? Why's that virtue dead
> Which dwelt so well in thee?   (ll. 57–9)

James's indulgence of his favourites, and the power he conferred on them, created envy and resentments which contributed to their downfall, and in the case of Robert Carr, helped to blacken the reputation of the court as a whole. Carr was a young Scotsman who fell in love with Frances Howard, the heiress of the Howard family. She had been married very young to the son of the Earl of Essex, who had rebelled against Elizabeth in 1601. In order for her to be able to marry Carr, her first marriage had to be dissolved on grounds of non-consummation. James set up a panel of bishops that included the Archbishop of Canterbury, George Abbot, and Lancelot Andrewes, which declared her a virgin (though not unanimously), and she remarried Carr, now Earl of Somerset, at court on 26 December 1613. The marriage was celebrated with masques by Campion, Jonson, Middleton, and the anonymous 'Masque of Flowers' (paid for by Francis Bacon), while Jonson, Chapman, and William Alabaster contributed poems.

Within two years the Countess of Somerset was on trial for the murder of her husband's confidant and secretary, Sir Thomas Overbury, supposed to have opposed their marriage. Overbury had been imprisoned in the Tower in April 1613, where he had died under mysterious circumstances in September, and it was now thought that he had been poisoned, though suspicion had not been aroused until the summer of 1615. The murder trials began with cases brought against the lesser people supposed to have acted as accessories: first Richard Weston, appointed by the Countess as Overbury's keeper, then her waiting-woman Anne Turner, and Sir Gervase Elwes, appointed governor of the Tower in May 1613. All were found guilty and died on the scaffold, Sir Gervase Elwes recalling how his father had 'charged him on his blessing that he should not follow the court nor live about London',[26] while Mrs Turner exclaimed: 'O the Court, the Court! God bless the King and send him better servants about him, for there is no religion in most of them but malice, pride, whoredom, swearing and rejoicing in the fall of others. It is so wicked a place as I wonder the earth did not open and swallow it up. Mr Sheriff, put none of your children thither.'[27]

The Countess of Somerset, implicated by their evidence, made her own confession which fully exonerated her husband, but both of them were found guilty. They were reprieved on grounds of rank (i.e. theirs was significantly higher than Overbury's), imprisoned for a while, and permanently exiled from the court. If they were actually responsible for Overbury's murder and employed their servants to carry it out, there was little justice in their escape, but it is possible that Overbury died of natural causes, that undue pressure was put on the witnesses, and that the trial reflected the growing resentment of Carr's power, disapproval of Frances Howard's divorce (she was constantly represented as an adulteress, and referred to as a 'whore'), and a more general paranoia about poisoning triggered by deaths for which there was no known medical explanation (such as that of Prince Henry in 1612). The whole episode is suspiciously reminiscent of revenge tragedy, with its go-betweens and tool villains.

Late in 1614, a few months before Carr's enemies began investigating Overbury's death, George Villiers had been introduced at court as a possible rival for the King's favours. James fell deeply in love with him, appointing him first cupbearer, then Knight and Gentleman of the Bed Chamber (1615), Earl of Buckingham (1617), and Duke in 1623, the first appointed since 1572, so that he took precedence over all but the King's immediate family. At every stage Buckingham used his power to secure his position, planting his own family in key court offices, and rapidly becoming the most powerful (and the most unpopular) man in the kingdom. As the King aged, Buckingham built a close and trusting relationship with his son Charles, who valued him as a counsellor and companion as highly as his father had done. Buckingham took little or no interest in literature, but he built up a great collection of European painting and sculpture, including major works by Titian, Tintoretto, and Veronese, and he met and formed a friendship with Rubens, who came to England and painted a number of portraits and the magnificent 'Allegory of War and Peace' for the ceiling of Inigo Jones's neoclassical Banqueting Hall. In 1627 Buckingham bought Rubens's personal collection of paintings and antique sculpture, and encouraged Charles to patronize his pupil Van Dyck. His activities as a collector had a substantial influence on English art and architecture, but in the country at large Buckingham was widely seen as an evil influence on James and Charles, and he was the subject of a variety of libellous or lampooning verses, which increasingly represented him as an enemy of the people. Two months before his own death at the hands of the assassin John Felton in 1628, the Duke's astrologer John Lambe was stoned to death by a London mob, who caught sight of him at the Fortune Theatre and attacked him as he left. This couplet ran through the city streets:

> Let Charles and George do what they can
> Yet George shall die like Doctor Lambe.[28]

The Court Performed

Criticism of courtiers and the court is to be found in popular ballads and verse libels, in satirical poetry and reforming tracts, in sermons and the news-letters sent from the court to the countryside. It was also performed in the public theatres, though less directly expressed here since the Master of the Revels read and licensed each new play text before it was performed. The courts shown were therefore mainly those of France or Italy, Denmark, Spain, or perhaps England at some remote date. The scandals enacted partly reflected an English view of abroad, especially Italy, as a paradise for poisoners and sexual perverts (recent Italian history lent some support to this view). Yet the flattery, spying, whispering, plotting, bribery, abuse of status and privilege, and general depravity were also aspects of English court life, and were recognizable as such. At times, political events seemed almost to imitate dramatic art, as in the Essex rising or the trials for the murder of Sir Thomas Overbury.

Stage courtiers conformed to a limited number of stereotypes: they were absurdly affected, like Le Beau in *As You Like It*, or Hotspur's 'certain lord, neat, and trimly dress'd' in *1 Henry IV*

(I. iii. 33), Osric or Oswald, or else old foxes like Polonius. John Marston, a professional satirist, was preoccupied with the excessive flattery that typified court manners: *Antonio and Mellida* includes a caricature of this type, called Castilio Balthazar (Baldassare Castiglione's name reversed). When Rossaline spits at him, he hastens to assure her, 'By my wealthiest thought, you grace my shoe with an unmeasured honour; I will preserve the sole of it as a most sacred relic, for this service' (II. i. 101–4). Later he pretends to have a love-letter from her, but it turns out to be a tailor's bill for taffeta to cover his old canvas doublet (III. ii. 93–105), a further image of ostentatious display concealing poverty. Marston's plays are full of images of courtly glitter concealing the corruption beneath.

Marston, Webster, and Middleton were all much more obviously preoccupied with courtly vices than Shakespeare. *Hamlet* (1601) is Shakespeare's most vivid re-creation of an atmosphere of court corruption. Perhaps as chief dramatist to the King's Men, he felt such criticism to be inappropriate (though royal patronage did not inhibit other dramatists writing for the company). *Timon of Athens* focuses upon flattery, but not in a court context. *King Lear* contrasts the bleak truth-speaking of Kent and Cordelia with the pleasing flattery, the 'court holy-water', of her sisters, in a way that suggests that court ceremonial and polite lying are linked at some level, and being present at the one may let you in for the other. Cordelia's insistence on stating things as they are breaks up the proceedings in a 'most admir'd disorder', but the play is more widely concerned with the nature of authority and loyalty than with court manners and morals.

There was a strong tradition that one of the functions of tragedy was to act as a mirror for princes, warning great men to perform their duties justly and conscientiously, and listen to their wisest counsellors by representing before them the vices of tyrants and the corruption of courts. Middleton's tragedies speak eloquently of the moral dangers incurred at court: *The Revenger's Tragedy* (1606) emphasizes the sexual rapacity of the courtiers and the defencelessness of their victims, both in speech and action. Vindice, making a trial of his sister's virtue, urges the attractions of high life:

> O, think upon the pleasure of the palace;
> Secured ease and state; the stirring meats,
> Ready to move out of the dishes, that
> E'en now quicken when they're eaten;
> Banquets abroad by torch-light, music, sports . . .
> Nine coaches waiting,—hurry, hurry, hurry.
> (II. i. 199–203, 206)

Similar accounts of court life occur in Middleton's *Second Maiden's Tragedy* (1611) and *Women Beware Women* (1621), as well as in plays by Marston and Chapman. Antonio's last words in Webster's *The Duchess of Malfi* urge 'Let my son fly the courts of princes' (v. iv. 72), while Vittoria in *The White Devil* dies declaring

> O happy they that never saw the court,
> Nor ever knew great men but by report.
> (v. vi. 261–2)

Such lessons were sometimes echoed by those about to die on the public scaffold, a moment that called for repentance for a misspent life, and acceptance or even justification of state punishment. The accessories to the Overbury murder, Mrs Turner and Gervase Elwes, had denounced the court in their final speeches, and so did Sir Walter Raleigh, who declared: 'I have been a soldier, a sailor and a courtier; which are courses of wickedness and vice.'[29]

Women Beware Women, a play which dramatizes the power of wealth and status to corrupt, ends with a court masque, seized by most of the central characters as an opportunity for murder. In it, they perform roles that are the opposite of what they really are: thus the marriage-destroying Livia plays Juno the marriage goddess, murdering her priestess, while being poisoned in turn by the smoke of the young woman's offering. The vicious Hippolito and Guardiano play shepherds, archetypal innocents, bringing about one another's deaths. Here the masque projects moral virtues the court conspicuously lacks, while the play exposes the masque as a false representation. In Beaumont and Fletcher's *The Maid's Tragedy* (1610), Strato dismisses masques on the grounds that they 'must commend their king, and speak in praise of the assembly, bless the bride and bridegroom in the person of some god: they're tied to the rules of flattery' (I. i. 8–10).

Whereas entertainments for Elizabeth were often put on at country houses where she stopped in the course of a progress, James and his Queen staged masques at court for special occasions such as weddings, and ambassadorial visits, and regularly on Twelfth Night and Shrove Tuesday. This change of practice reflects the greater isolation and self-absorption of the Jacobean court. Though masques, like tragedies and the best of praise-poems, were expected to include constructive criticism or instruction, in practice court arts tended to lose their moral content, rather as the virtuous courtier of Castiglione and Elyot gave place to the politician or time-server of Machiavelli or Lorenzo Ducci.

James and Anne of Denmark had acquired a taste for complex, emblematic pageants at the Scottish court, which was strongly influenced by the French court. The traditional structure of court masques (or mummings) had been based on the arrival of guests whose identity was somehow mysterious or disguised. Grand entries, often accompanied by speeches or songs, had long been popular at court and in great men's houses. Shakespeare depicted such an occasion in *Henry VIII*, where the King and certain courtiers arrive at Wolsey's palace masked and 'habited like shepherds', and the King, still incognito, leads Anne Boleyn into a dance (I. iv. 63–76). But the Jacobean court masque passed far beyond such simple prototypes: employing the most elaborate spectacle and the finest music, poetry, and dancing of the day, it embodied courtly magnificence at its most expansive—and expensive.

While the costumes, sets, and machinery of the masque all spoke of conspicuous consumption, these 'worldly toys' regularly drew on the highly unworldly philosophy of Plato and his Renaissance disciples: the power of imagination to transform the world by projecting its images on to actuality, a power attributed to Renaissance artists and natural magicians, also belonged to the masque. Such power was the spiritual counterpart of the King's actual power, and all three roles combine in Shakespeare's Prospero: as mage, he can control the disruptive elements and spirits of the natural world; as king, he can restore and redeem corrupt society through his authority; and as artist, he creates a masque intended to work on his auditors, leading them delightfully towards personal virtue and self-control.

Notions of Plato's philosopher king and Renaissance accounts of the court as a storehouse of virtue and taste were presented to a courtly audience both as an imaginative exemplification of themselves as they were, and as an ideal of what they might become, 'a kind of mimetic magic on a sophisticated level, the attempt to secure social health and tranquillity for the realm by miming it in front of its chief figure', as one critic has expressed it.[30] Celebration and moral education were supposed to combine within the form, as Sidney thought they ought to in epic or heroic poetry, and as Spenser had combined them in *The Faerie Queene*. The excitement, splendour, and action present in the accession-day tilts were fused with a poetry that mingled epic, dramatic, and lyric elements into a new form. It was the ideal mode for princely instruction, Sidney's 'delightful teaching', blending usefulness and pleasure. Ben Jonson, its most ambitious librettist, defined the paradoxical nature of the masque in his preface to *Hymenaei* (1606), where he pointed out that whatever was subject to the understanding outlived whatever was subject to the senses, as the soul outlived the body:

This it is hath made the most royal Princes and greatest persons (who are commonly the personators of these actions) not only studious of riches and magnificence in the outward celebration or show (which rightly becomes them), but curious after the most high and hearty inventions to furnish the inward parts (and those grounded upon antiquity and solid learnings); which, though their voice be taught to sound to present occasions, their sense or [either] doth or should always lay hold on more remov'd mysteries.

(ll. 10–19)

Reading the texts of Jonson's masques, we are in danger of overlooking 'the glory of all these solemnities' that 'like a blaze' has 'gone out in the beholders' eyes': the dancing, the singers, and the music, the brilliant costumes of the actors, the masquers, and the courtiers who danced with them, the elaborate triumphal cars drawn on to the dancing floor, and the entrancing transformation scenes designed by Inigo Jones. An elegant proscenium arch (then unknown in the theatre) enclosed an idealized scene, with a deep perspective (also unknown in the theatre), which slid apart or suddenly became transparent to reveal a further interior, a temple or a garden beyond. These inner depths were the visual equivalent of Jonson's 'removed mysteries', emblems framed within an opening book. Machines swung the set round or opened it up to reveal the courtly masquers within. Previously, masques had often been staged at several different points within the hall. Now Inigo Jones tucked his stage effects behind the proscenium arch, with the perspective correctly aligned to the King's chair of state, a focus of attention quite as important as the stage itself. This was the first modern stage in England, and the first stage sets to use theatrical illusion. They were not used for play performances until the 1630s, and until then stage plays operated with a minimum of scenery, on platforms thrust out into the audience.

Ben Jonson's earliest masques were written for Queen Anne, beginning with *The Masque of Blackness* (1605), discussed in Chapter 4. *The Masque of Queens* (1609) was the first to make use of an antimasque, a dance of grotesques dismissed or driven away by the central figures of the main masque. According to Jonson's preface, the suggestion for this 'foil or false masque' came from the Queen herself, who is here praised as Bel-Anna, Queen of the Ocean. The antimasque created a situation of conflict, as well as an occasion for the kind of comic or indecorous effects that amused the King. It was often used to represent the chaos of nature or the material world, before its redemption by the spiritual powers invested in the main deities or heroes. Those roles were taken by courtiers, who had elegant speeches to deliver but were not required to act indecorously. The anti-masque and any other unsuitable parts were performed by professional actors, usually from Shakespeare's company.

In 1610 Jonson wrote *The Speeches at Prince Henry's Barriers* for the 15-year-old Prince of Wales, representing him as the heir to older traditions of chivalry, long since fallen into decay. Chivalry is sunk in sloth in her cave, until the Lady of the Lake, King Arthur, and Merlin summon the young prince, at whose name Chivalry re-awakes. This masque did not culminate in a dance, but in an indoor tournament at barriers, designed to show off the young prince's prowess. The following year Arthurian and Spenserian imagery was developed in the masque of *Oberon*, in which Henry was presented in a triumph as King Arthur's heir, subduing a band of wild satyrs.

At the centre of the two masques written for Prince Henry lay the concept of transformation, for Jonson, the heart of the genre. A basic assumption of Neoplatonism had been man's ability to transform both himself and his world, and such transformations were embodied in the plots as the drowsy figure of Chivalry awoke or the wild satyrs were tamed to the Prince's service. The playwright's faith in the potential of his myth to educate and thus to change the court is visible both in the situations depicted and in the act of depicting them. His intention was to present philosophical truths delightfully—Sidney's old ideal, later echoed by John Milton in *Comus*, his masque of 1634. Jonson never forgot that it was primarily the poet's task to lead men to reformation, but even the humble engineer participated in the process, since it was his *machina versatilis*, his sliding flats and panels, that created the most literal transformations. Above all, the masque celebrated the power of the king to change society, restore ancient virtues and lost integrity, reconcile pleasure and virtue, change winter to summer, or night to day, as in *The Vision of Delight* (1617), where Wonder asks

> What better change appears?
> Whence is it that the air so sudden clears,
> And all things in a moment turn so mild?

And Phant'sy replies

> Behold a king
> Whose presence maketh this perpetual spring,
> The glories of which spring grow in that bower,
> And are the marks and beauties of his power.
>
> (ll. 173–5, 201–4)

Such myths of absolute power, far from inducing royal virtue, might have a dangerous effect on an imaginative man. Prince Henry's younger brother Charles seems at times to have succumbed to his own propaganda. In his years of rule without parliament, the court masques in which he played variants on the philosopher king grew more lavish and elaborate. Their astonishingly high costs either demonstrated the noble virtue of magnificence or else appalled his courtiers with their wastefulness.

Others dramatists—Beaumont, Chapman, and Middleton—and the poets Thomas Campion and Samuel Daniel all wrote court masques with some success (Daniel resented Jonson's claims for the coherence and complexity of his myths), but it was Jonson who brought the full weight of his inventive genius to bear on this slight form, turning out surprising and ingenious antimasques and wonderfully memorable songs year after year. Perhaps his most extraordinary achievement was *The Gypsies Metamorphosed*, written for Buckingham when he entertained the King at his country house at Burley-on-the-Hill in 1621. Here spectacle was kept to a minimum, the real spectacle being provided by Buckingham and his family, dressed up as a troupe of gypsies who proceed to tell the fortunes of the royal guest and his retinue in the canting language familiar from cony-catching pamphlets. Buckingham himself played the chief gipsy or 'jackman', and the masque broke all rules of decorum in presenting him and his family as a close-knit band of rogues and tricksters, especially as there were those at court who regarded them as just that. James was so amused by it that he asked for it to be performed on two further occasions, as we know from further adjustments made to the text.

Although the daring of this piece was unparalleled, Jonson never ceased to take risks. In 1623 Prince Charles determined to marry the Infanta of Spain, and he and Buckingham cut through court protocol by travelling to Spain incognito— James had long had hopes of balancing his daughter Elizabeth's marriage to the Protestant Elector Palatine by having Charles marry into a Catholic royal family. It had been a reckless and deeply unpopular move, and when negotiations finally broke down and the Prince had returned safely, the failure of his mission was openly celebrated in the London streets. For Twelfth Night 1624 Jonson wrote *Neptune's Triumph for the Return of Albion*, which, although rehearsed and ready for performance, was cancelled at the last minute on the grounds that the King was ill, although court gossip suggested that either the Spanish or the French ambassador would have been offended by it. As relations between Spain and England deteriorated, James could scarcely have invited the Spanish ambassador to a masque whose final tableau discovered the fleet, poised to set sail against Spain. In such an atmosphere, even the choice of Neptune to figure James's maritime power might have looked tactless.

The opening of Jonson's masque was particularly audacious: it begins in the empty banqueting hall itself, where the poet is waiting to distribute leaflets describing the masque's action. He is interrupted and cross-questioned by the cook as to the principles of his art, and then ticked off for failing to supply an antimasque. The cook remedies this by producing a giant cauldron full of dancing vegetables. The masque then moves into the magical depths of Neptune's palace (whereas earlier masques had begun in wild or desolate settings, later ones often began in or around Whitehall, moving from the familiar to the ideal world). Jonson's cook asks the poet why he has taken so long to celebrate Albion/Charles's return: 'But, why not this till now?' The poet replies

—It was not time
To mix this music with the vulgar's chime.
Stay, till th'abortive and extemporal din

> Of balladry were understood a sin,
> Minerva cried . . .
>
> (ll. 159, 161–5)

The popular acclaim for the failure of the mission is described in the masque in terms of 'all the country, and the city wit, | Of bells, and bonfires, and good cheer' (ll. 168–9). If Jonson had overstepped the mark as far as James was concerned, another dramatist, Thomas Middleton, went very much further. His satirical play *A Game at Chess* was performed six months later, in August 1624. The most successful play of its age, it ran for nine consecutive days to packed audiences (estimated at more than 3,000 on each occasion), after which the Privy Council closed the theatre and issued a warrant for Middleton's arrest. It must either have bypassed the Master of the Revels altogether, or been mounted with his connivance.

This play presented the events of the previous year in the form of an allegory, culminating in Charles's mission to Spain, and making particular fun of the unpopular Spanish ambassador Gondomar, whom James trusted and who had been chiefly responsible for the initial negotiations. He suffered from an anal fistula and had to be carried about London in a litter specially equipped with a 'chair of ease'. On one occasion rude apprentices had shouted after him, 'There goes the devil in a dung cart'. A fight ensued, and Gondomar had insisted upon the culprits being punished. One of them had died as a result of the whipping he received. Now this hated figure had been put on the London stage, with all his tricks of speech and manner, carried in the very same litter, which the actors had managed to obtain or copy. The effect was sensational.

Faced with the problems similar to those that confronted Jonson—how to present the royal family without criticizing their policies—Middleton distanced his narrative, giving it an allegorical outline by presenting it in terms of a chess game, in which the English, naturally, are the white pieces, and the Spaniards the black ones. Just as Jonson had done, Middleton represents Charles (the White Knight) and Buckingham (the White Duke, since 'Duke' was a name for the rook or castle) as heroes, and there is no reference to their intention of negotiating a Spanish marriage (nor had there been in Jonson's masque). Instead, they enter the black house (i.e. Madrid) solely in order to expose its plots, which Gondomar (the Black Knight) is tricked into revealing, resulting in the gambit 'checkmate by discovery'. Middleton, who was also experienced in writing pageants and masques, here evokes something of the formality of such entertainments, avoiding the psychological inwardness he normally used to show that the rules governing international politics were quite as arbitrary as those of the chessboard. In representing the court, dramatists like Jonson and Middleton intended to intervene and influence élite or popular opinion, the sites of ongoing struggles between contesting factions. When the court was represented, it was always in terms of how it figured within particular debates, rather than as a straightforward celebration of monarchic authority.

The theatre's fascination with the court and the court's fascination with theatricals suggest their shared concern with the nature of self-representation and self-display, activities that aroused distrust and sometimes alarm in society at large: James disliked being on display far more than Elizabeth, who cheerfully joined in her own celebrations. Courtiers such as Philip Sidney, Walter Raleigh, and Francis Bacon were sharply aware 'Of Simulation and Dissimulation', and often used metaphors of the world as stage, as did the playwrights (some of whom were also actors). That theatrical prince, Hamlet, is the perfect epitome of the courtier who watches himself perform in the theatre of the court and the theatre of the mind, uncertain as to whether he is the playwright, the actor or merely the audience.

The Theatre

OF the age's many forms of representation, drama was the most vital, fully responsive both to general human emotions and experiences and to the particular pressures, ideas, philosophies, and attitudes of the day. Though audiences, as well as their language, culture, and religion, have altered substantially, Renaissance plays are still performed and enjoyed today. Their vigour was largely due to their commercial character: the need to please London audiences allowed the drama to reflect contemporary problems and behaviour with few constraints, and freed it from voicing establishment views (unlike the literature that sought for court patronage), so that it could respond to wider and, on occasion, more critical or subversive social forces. There was a price to be paid for such freedom: the Lord Chamberlain, through the Revels Office, imposed censorship on plays, and this might range from the excision of a few words to cutting passages and scenes, and sometimes to the suppression of an entire play, as seems to have happened in the case of *Sir Thomas More* (1595), where the 'Evil May Day' riot of apprentices against aliens was too topical to be acceptable to the Master of the Revels. In general, censorship operated along fairly rigid and predictable lines, and several plays that are profoundly subversive in some respects (for example, *Measure for Measure* or *Bartholomew Fair*) seem to have been performed unchallenged. The drama developed into an exact and sensitive register of the age's central issues: the relative nature of moral judgement, the unstable nature of language and character, and the individual's changing position in relation to the universe, and to society, the state and the family, and the growing awareness of their conflicting claims.

Until the middle years of the century drama was performed in halls and inn yards by companies of travelling actors. The earliest custom-built theatres for the performance of plays were ambiguously and precariously placed, both metaphorically and literally, and this contributed to their flexibility and versatility. The Red Lion, built at Stepney in 1567, and James Burbage's Theatre, built at Shoreditch in 1576, were probably the first commercial theatres in England. They were a new phenomenon, both architecturally and economically speaking, and many of their features were anomalous, including their location: they were put up outside London's city walls in the so-called 'liberties' of Shoreditch (in the county of Middlesex) or on the South Bank (in the county of Surrey), part of the rapidly expanding city yet separated from it by suburbs, fields, or the river, and outside the immediate control of the city authorities, although they could and did have them closed on occasion. Then the mixed audiences of the public theatres represented an exceptional blend of the nobility and gentry, respectable middle-class merchants, artisans, and 'mere riff-raff', a social range that took in ambassadors and apprentices, peers, pickpockets, and prostitutes. The varied clientele paid different prices to sit in the galleries or stand in the yard. The theatres themselves were simultaneously under cover yet out of doors, the playing area and galleries being roofed, while the yard below the stage was open to the elements.

The actors' status, too, was uncertain: according to the 1572 'Act for the Punishment of Vagabonds', 'common players in interludes' might be liable for punishment as 'rogues, vagabonds and sturdy beggars' unless they belonged to 'any baron of this realm or towards any other honourable personage of greater degree'.[1] Thereafter actors formed themselves into professional companies, as part of the household of their patron. Shakespeare joined the Lord Chamberlain's Men as a shareholder in 1594, and after 1603 they became the King's Men, and thus members of the royal household. The greatest actor of the 1580s and '90s,

Edward Alleyn, retired, having acquired wealth and social status: he held office as Master of the Royal Game, Squire of Dulwich Manor, and founder of the charitable institution of Dulwich College. When his first wife died he married a daughter of the then Dean of St Paul's, John Donne.

There were numerous other anomalies associated with the playhouses: women's roles were always taken by boys (though this did not happen on the Continent), and the plays performed had developed from a rich and strange mixture of sources, from the native, mainly biblical plays performed on pageant wagons, to Greek and Roman drama. The classical rules of structure and genre described by Aristotle in his *Poetics* and approved by Italian Renaissance critics, never operated on the English stage (although Shakespearean heroes are sometimes analysed by later critics in terms of a 'tragic flaw', Aristotle's *hamartia*). Instead, English dramatists 'thrust in the clowns by head and shoulders to play a part in majestical matters, with neither decency nor discretion', as Sidney complained in *A Defence of Poetry* (p. 114). In his Prologue to *Midas*, John Lyly described it as 'a gallimaufry. If we present a mingle-mangle, our fault is to be excused, because the whole world is become an hodge-podge.' Laughter was liable to erupt in the middle of tragedy, for this was an art as irregular and unclassical as it was coarse and energetic.

It is the nature of drama to represent a variety, as well as a conflict of viewpoints. Playwrights seized the opportunities it offered to pose complex and difficult moral problems, involving the audience in trying to resolve them. Though sometimes constrained by censorship, the drama concerned itself with current issues, presenting them with an open-mindedness that its later critics have sometimes lacked. The readiness to debate moral issues at length, and the conviction that such debate would hold an audience's attention, are closely related to the central position occupied by the art of rhetoric in the humanist tradition. A classical education trained its pupils to debate moral and political issues, to structure evidence in a telling argument, and finally to speak their views so as to persuade their audience. It produced the lawyers and politicians required by an expanding bureaucracy, and was ultimately derived from Cicero. Rhetorical training included the art of delivery as well as of composition, so students practised formal speech-making both at school and university, where plays, usually in Latin, were performed as exercises in memory, correct pronunciation, and the effective matching of gestures to words, an element in speech-making as well as an essential dramatic skill. Some of the most powerful scenes in Shakespearean drama had their roots in school rhetoric exercises: the contrasting speeches of Brutus and Antony in the forum, in Shakespeare's *Julius Caesar*, rework the kind of school exercise in which pupils were required to attack or defend Brutus's murder of Caesar.

Familiarity with a range of different philosophies or outlooks, and the differences between pre-Christian, classical and Christian attitudes, enabled the dramatists to present particular issues or situations from inconsistent, or even opposing angles. In *Hamlet*, for example, suicide is at first seen as 'self-slaughter', a sin forbidden by God and traditionally excluding the victim from burial in consecrated ground; at the end, when Horatio proposes suicide, it is seen as an act of stoic fortitude, as it had been at the end of *Julius Caesar*. Revenge, at the centre of a whole genre of tragedies, can be seen as an act of justice required by society to right a secret wrong, as an obligation to a murdered kinsman, or as explicitly forbidden by God: 'Vengeance is mine; I will repay, saith the Lord' (Romans 12: 19), while the first half of this sentence (in Latin, '*vindicta mihi*') took on a quite different meaning in the mouth of the revenger, where it became an assertion of the right to take revenge, privileged above other claims. Contemporary laws punished premeditated murder more harshly than killings on the spur of the moment, yet this does not seem to have affected revenge plays, which assume that the audience will understand and even partly identify with the revenger.

Perhaps the very nature of dramatic experience is anomalous, for the performance requires the audience to believe and disbelieve simultaneously, yielding themselves up to it selfforgetfully, while letting the play work upon them, involve them, possibly even change them. It requires an immediate and unthinking response, yet pausing to consider the nature of the theatrical illusion makes its paradoxes of appearance and reality difficult to define. They certainly worried a number of Shakespeare's contemporaries, who saw the stage as an industry for the deliberate manufacture of lies, tricks, and falsehoods. While they overestimated the deceptive intention of the medium, Dr Johnson's claim that 'It is false, that any representation is mistaken for reality' seems, in its turn, to understate it.[2] By offering a complex experience and demanding a complex response, the drama could express provisional or relative ways of thinking and feeling, and represent a new consciousness of simulation and dissimulation, both within the self and in others. At the same time, so much that was anomalous, marginal, and/or difficult to categorize aroused suspicion, as did the very novelty of its premises, both literal and metaphorical. Some suspicions were justified, for the dramatists found ways of saying what they wanted without arousing official censure, and from the outset they were fascinated by ethical dilemmas and extreme forms of behaviour; their expanding moral horizons contributed to the distrust and disapproval they aroused. When the public theatres closed in 1642, a powerful but unpredictable influence on London's public opinion had gone for good.

A Commercial Theatre

The development of the commercial theatre in London was disturbing to many, and not merely to puritans, because it was so wholly unprecedented. While the value of entertainment for its own sake had long been accepted in courtly circles, and defenders of poetry invoked doctrines of teaching through pleasing, the right of working people to enjoy themselves was less firmly established. Popular pastimes had more opponents than supporters, and were widely under attack throughout Europe: it was not only in Protestant countries that acting, dancing, and a host of other traditional pastimes were being actively suppressed.

There had been no need to justify earlier popular drama, since its moral and religious elements had been apparent, while secular acting and mumming had been sufficiently occasional not to provoke any serious opposition. Medieval drama had begun under the protection of the Church, had been staged by town guilds, had made no profits, and had been performed for the glory of God. Its purpose was to teach, and while rude jokes sometimes interrupted, the moral message was clear: good triumphed and evil was overthrown. Drama's potential as a medium for instruction had impressed the early reformers, men like John Bale or James I's tutor, George Buchanan, who saw in its popular appeal opportunities for propaganda. Scholars might also have quoted Aristotle's claims for drama's seriousness and value, yet neither of these arguments could have been advanced on behalf of the first commercial theatres, since their main aims were neither moral or artistic, but rather to attract a paying audience.

The earliest recorded theatre was the Red Lion, built to the east of the city by a grocer, John Brayne: plans for it survive, specifying a stage with a trap-door, built five feet above ground level, backed by a thirty-foot tower. Little more is known about it, but in 1576 Brayne joined forces with his brother-in-law James Burbage, an actor with the Earl of Leicester's Men, in building the Theatre at Shoreditch, north-east of the city. A year later it was joined by the little Curtain, on the opposite side of the road, but the next group of playhouses were put up on the other side of the city, south of the river on Bankside, among the brothels and the bull- and bear-baiting yards. Here stood the Rose (1587), managed by Philip Henslowe whose surviving account-books provide our main source of information on the day-to-day organization of the theatres. The Lord Admiral's Men, whose star was Edward Alleyn (married to Henslowe's stepdaughter), played at the Rose. It was followed by the Swan (1595), famous for its elegant furnishings, and in 1599 by the Globe, rebuilt from the timbers of Burbage's old Theatre at Shoreditch, which was pulled down and reconstructed on its new site after a disagreement with the original landowner. James Burbage's son Richard was the star of Shakespeare's company, the Lord Chamberlain's Men, who were the resident company, first at the Theatre and later at the Globe; Shakespeare's great tragic roles were written for him. Two more open-air theatres were built, the Fortune (1600) at Finsbury, north of the city, and the Red Bull (1606) in the suburb of Clerkenwell, notorious for its rowdy audiences.

All these theatres looked roughly circular from the outside, though recent excavation of the Rose's foundations has shown that it was constructed as an irregular polygon, with as many as fourteen sides. Along one section stood an elevated stage or scaffold (trestles supporting a floor), sheltered by a canopy which protected the actors' costly and elaborate costumes,— these were often bought second-hand from courtiers. Behind the stage, and concealed by a wall or curtain, was the 'tiring house' (i.e. dressing room), and above it was a tower containing a gallery used to represent castle walls or for overhearing scenes, and sometimes occupied by members of the audience, who might also sit on the stage. Higher still was another room used by the musicians, the trumpeter whose fanfare announced that the play was to start, and also for the tackle for making descents from on high. The open yard below the stage was occupied by the groundlings who stood or sat on hired stools, those 'under-standers' who, the dramatists complained, lacked understanding. The open yard at the Rose seems to have sloped downwards, though this feature is not recorded elsewhere. It was surrounded by a roughly circular polygonal building consisting of roofed galleries, reached by stairs, with wooden seats and a number of private rooms like theatre boxes, hired out to wealthier or more fastidious patrons. The whole structure was generally larger than most modern theatres, and held more spectators: at capacity, a smaller theatre such as the Rose held up to 2,000, while the Globe could hold 3,000 or more.

Costs for entry were comparatively low: in 1599 it cost a penny to stand in the yard, another to sit in the sheltered galleries, and a third 'to sit in the most comfortable seats which are cushioned, where he not only sees everything well, but can also be seen'.[3] Such sums would have been well within the range of a London merchant. Even day-labourers, when working, received three or four pence a day (though few were employed on a regular basis). Costs rose in the new century, and by 1614 Jonson's induction to *Bartholomew Fair* (performed at Henslowe's latest investment, the Hope Theatre) refers to seats costing sixpence, a shilling, and even half-a-crown (two shillings and sixpence); on less grand occasions, a shilling marked the upper limit.

London's growing population supported several public theatres and their resident companies who competed against one another. The companies were made up of, perhaps, eight to twelve actors who invested jointly in a stock of costumes, properties, and playbooks. They paid the owner of the theatre an agreed proportion of the takings from each performance, and in addition paid musicians, tire-men (who looked after the costumes), stage-keepers (stage managers and cleaners), scriveners (scribes or professional copyists), book-keepers (prompters), gatherers (who collected the money), and extra hired men and boys, when they were required, though speaking parts were regularly doubled.

Some actors belonged to professional guilds, such as grocers, goldsmiths, or even bricklayers (there was no actors' guild), and these were entitled to take on apprentices, ostensibly to their particular craft, but in fact as boy actors to play women's parts. Some of these like Richard Robinson who played the lead in Middleton's *Second Maiden's Tragedy* or Richard Sharpe, the first Duchess of Malfi, grew up to become shareholders and to play 'juvenile leads' or other standard male roles in their turn (Robinson later played the Cardinal in *The Duchess of Malfi*). The shareholders of a successful company made substantial profits, but they worked tremendously hard for them, daily performing old plays and learning new ones, which were acted with a minimum of rehearsal time and no designated director. Shakespeare made his money as a company shareholder rather than as a playwright, although the King's Men's partly owed their success to his contributions as resident dramatist.

Many plays were written in collaboration. The playwright(s) would be paid a flat fee (about £5 in the 1590s) for the script, all rights to which then passed into the company's hands. At least two fair copies would be made from the dramatist's script (known as 'foul papers'): one was cut up into the different 'parts', and each actor's speeches would be stuck together to form a continuous scroll, with brief cues and stage directions added in, so that the actor playing the lead had the longest scroll. Actors were expected to learn and look after their 'parts', but they were technically the property of the company, and reckoned among its assets. A second fair copy of the whole text was sent to the Master of the Revels to be licensed (with a fee). On the manuscript of Middleton's *Second Maiden's Tragedy*, the Master of the Revels marked a number of oaths, hostile references to the court and topical allusions for deletion, and licensed it for performance, with his amendments. This particular manuscript was then returned to the playhouse, where five new passages by the playwright were pinned in, further changes and many more cuts were made, and the book-keeper wrote in several stage directions for trumpet calls, offstage knocking, and singing. The corrected script now became the prompt copy. Companies kept their plays carefully, but hard-up dramatists might resell their plays for publication as quartos (i.e. small books; shareholders like Thomas Heywood thought this dishonest). Pirated copies of plays, made by shorthand or with the help of some of the actors, also crept into print, and sometimes playwrights published their own plays merely to expose and correct pirated versions. With so many plays circulating, lines from one often strayed into another, sometimes as deliberate parody, but quite as often by accident.

The companies had an astonishingly large repertoire of plays, a different one being performed each day, according to Philip Henslowe's accounts which record the takings at every performance for several months at a time: for example, in a ten-week period in 1595 the Admiral's Men gave nearly sixty performances of twenty different plays, four of them new. A synopsis or 'plot' was pinned up backstage, to remind actors which part they were playing, listing their entrances and the properties required for each scene. Higher admission rates seem to have been charged for new plays, and takings went up on public holidays, and perhaps prices too. Sunday had traditionally been the day for presenting plays, and Elizabeth could still command a court performance then, but efforts were made to ban public playing on that day. Complaints about Sunday acting and some rather inconclusive evidence from Henslowe's accounts suggest that the ban, like so much Elizabethan legislation, was not always effective.

Certain plays became well-established favourites such as *Dr Faustus* and *Hamlet*, and, according to the induction of *Bartholomew Fair*, *The Spanish Tragedy* and *Titus Andronicus*, but there was also a tremendous demand for new plays—the majority of those known to have been performed from records such as Henslowe's have not survived. Those that have survived have done so only by chance, often in single printed copies, for the products of the commercial theatres were mainly valued by their actors before the mid-seventeenth century. 'Closet drama', that is, plays written to be read or performed in private, were respected on the grounds that they were exercises in art rather than commerce, the work of aristocrats such as Elizabeth Cary, Fulke Greville, Sir William Alexander, Mary Sidney, Countess of Pembroke, and her niece Mary Wroth. The professional playwrights, on the other hand, belonged to the sordid world of business transactions; they were regarded as hacks and their writings considered of little or no value. Sir Thomas Bodley, collecting books for his great new library at Oxford in 1612, instructed his agent to leave out such 'idle books and riff-raffs' as 'almanacs, plays and an infinite number, that are daily printed', in case his collection might be thought to lack discrimination: 'Haply some plays may be worth the keeping, but hardly one in forty . . . the more I think upon it, the more it doth distaste me that such kind of books should be vouchsafed a room in so noble a library.'[4]

When Ben Jonson published sixteen plays in a folio volume of his collected *Works* in 1616, his arrogant gesture was regarded with a mixture of admiration and disapproval. Until then plays had only been published in small quarto editions, retailing at sixpence and resembling cony-catching pamphlets, accounts of contemporary scandals, and similar writings. Thus *Dr Faustus*, *Hamlet*, *King Lear*, even Jonson's *Volpone* and most of the other plays of the period first appeared in quarto editions. The Folio collection of Shakespeare's plays published in 1623 was inspired by Jonson's example, and was only the second such volume to appear in the large and imposing format used for works such as the Bible, Foxe's *Acts and Monuments*, sermons, or classical texts. These two folios, and the *Comedies and Tragedies of Beaumont and Fletcher* (1647), contributed to the reassessment of the drama and its authors that took place in the second half of the seventeenth century.

The commercial success of the theatre brought financial rewards to its most successful actors, and with these, social status, but it was not so much the success or respectability of particular individuals as a gradual differentiation among the audiences, and an increasing refinement of taste that improved its standing. By the early seventeenth century forward-looking companies were beginning to perform in the private, indoor theatres originally used by choirboys and the boys' companies (Hamlet's 'little eyases'), whose smaller voices could not carry across the arenas of the outdoor playhouses, traditionally the haunt of criminals, tobacco-smoking 'stinkards', and loud-mouthed watermen (the sixteenth-century equivalent of taxi-drivers). Particular theatres such as the Fortune and the Red Bull acquired reputations for catering to vulgar or old-fashioned tastes, but both outdoor and indoor theatres provided accommodation at different prices, for different classes, though with this difference, that the best seats in the public playhouses were those in the galleries furthest from the stage, whereas the best seats in the indoor theatres (where everyone was seated) were those in the pit, closest to the stage (the cheapest position in the public theatres).

The indoor theatres—the Blackfriars (used by the King's Men after 1608), the Phoenix, and the Salisbury Court—were smaller (the second Blackfriars theatre took up to 500), more expensive, and more select. At first they charged sixpence for admission, but as public theatre prices rose, entrance costs increased to a shilling, and even half-a-crown for the special lords' rooms on either side of the stage. There were windows, but the stage was candle-lit for the performance. Singing and music were an important part of the entertainment, and music was played in the intervals, while the stage candles were trimmed.

The boys' companies had their own particular repertoire, and a number of plays were specially written to take advantage of the opportunities for spectacle provided by the private theatres, where limited lighting effects could also be used; but when the King's Men were performing at the Globe for the four summer months and at Blackfriars for the rest of the year, they often performed the same plays at both, as well as at court; to some extent, the repertoires of indoor and outdoor playhouses overlapped, though different companies increasingly performed plays designed to appeal to their own particular clientele. Court patronage of actors further raised their status, and the Lord Chamberlain's obligation to provide entertainment for the monarch and the court was one justification for the companies' existence. London's several theatres also contributed substantially to the city's attractions, and made a deep impression on foreign visitors who recorded their admiration for the size and beauty of London's theatres, as well as for the rich clothes, both of actors and audience (in the public theatres, both actors and audience were lit by daylight). Thomas Heywood made the point in his *Actor's Apology* (1612): 'playing is an ornament to the city, which strangers of all nations, repairing hither, report of in their countries, beholding them here with some admiration.'[5] English dramatic skills were also in demand on the Continent, and English acting companies toured Europe, as well as England, in the early seventeenth century, performing their repertoire in English.

Foreign visitors also commented on the presence of well-dressed women in the audience, and the dramatists addressed them: epilogues to *2 Henry IV*, *As You Like It*, and *Henry VIII* appeal specifically to 'the merciful construction of good women' in the audience (Epilogue to *Henry VIII*, l. 10) , assuming that if the women applauded, then the men in the audience would

follow their example; their taste strongly influenced the otherwise almost exclusively male companies (there were female
managers and shareholders, from time to time, but usually
through marriage or inheritance). Their increasing influence on
the drama is reflected in the development from *The Taming of
the Shrew* (1592) to Fletcher's *The Woman's Prize, or the Tamer
Tamed* (1611), where Petruchio's second wife more than pays
back the wrongs done to the first, as well as in the strong
heroines of Shakespeare, Middleton (*The Roaring Girl*; the Lady
in *The Second Maiden's Tragedy*, both 1611), and Webster.

Opposition

Despite or perhaps because of its improving status, the theatre
had many critics. The public playhouses had been built outside
the city's boundaries in order to avoid the city authorities, who
were its most consistent opponents, and had tried unsuccessfully
to close the theatres down at least once in each of the three final
decades of Elizabeth's reign. They succeeded in closing them
temporarily when plague casualties rose above a particular level
(when deaths rose above thirty a week, in James's reign). The
city fathers regarded the playhouses as potent sources of moral
and physical infection: in addition to spreading illness, they
encouraged criticism of the government or undermined personal
morality since the actions presented were 'nothing else but
unchaste fables, lascivious devices, shifts of cozenage and
matters of like sort', as successive Lord Mayors complained to
the Privy Council, adding that they drew the audience 'into
example of imitation and not of avoiding the said lewd
offences'.[6]

Play-going caused idleness and time-wasting, especially
among the young who had to learn to work hard and save their
pennies. Apprentices who slipped away to visit plays in working
hours were particularly resented since it cost their masters
money and time. Economic and religious motives mingle uncomfortably in the complaint that plays 'draw apprentices and other
servants from their ordinary works and all sorts of people from

the resort unto sermons and other Christian exercises, to the great hindrance of trades and profanation of religion'.[7] Thomas Nashe provided the most intelligent and penetrating defence of the theatre in a few paragraphs from *Pierce Penniless* (1592), in the course of a discussion of Sloth, where he points out that the actors themselves did not want audiences of apprentices since, like modern football hooligans, they were inclined to vandalism (*Works*, i. 214). The two main apprentice holidays, Shrove Tuesday and May Day, often became occasions for destructive rampages.

Built in the sleazier areas of the city, the theatres provided a natural focus for criminals: thieves, pickpockets, and prostitutes operated among the crowds, aided by their permanently diverted attention, and the large crowds assembled seemed threatening in themselves: 3,000 people deliberately aroused to fever pitch embodied the very worst fears of the authorities. A public theatre might provide an ideal platform for preaching sedition, as the specially commissioned performance of *Richard II* at the Globe on the eve of the Essex Rebellion suggests. As Henry Crosse (in *Vertues Commonwealth*, 1603) demanded:

what more fitter occasion to summon all the discontented people together than plays? To attempt some execrable actions, commotions, mutinies, rebellions, as it happened at Windham in Norf[olk] in the time if Ed[ward] the 6 where at a stage play (according to a drunken custom there used) the horrible rebellion of Ket and his accomplices, by a watch-word given, broke out, to the trouble of the whole kingdom.[8]

This was the threat that made the Revels Office's censorship so vital: the state had to know exactly what would be said on the stage in advance, and if necessary remove any dangerous or subversive passages. Granted such fears, it was pointless to argue that plays more often advanced moral than immoral sentiments, more often reinforced state authority than undermined it. The Church also regarded the playhouses as a threat, drawing their audiences away from church at evensong or on holidays. In practice, playwrights tended to endorse the moral lessons of the clergy, as they sometimes pointed out, but arguments of that kind only gave further offence. I.G. in *A Refutation of the Apology for Actors* (1615) asserted that: 'God requireth no such thing at their hands, that they should take it upon them . . . God gave authority to instruct and preach, to correct and anathematize, only to the Apostles and to their successors, and not to players; for it is unlawful to cast pearls before swine.'[9] Although critics might challenge or reject the drama's claims to instruct, the age's religious teachings were often vividly enacted upon the stage. By showing the bad ends to which bad rulers or bad men might come, drama reflected the Church's preoccupation with self-indulgence, sexual licence, irresponsibility, extravagance, and hypocrisy. Tragedy often rehearsed precisely those lessons that Protestant preachers were so eager to point out, sometimes in books whose titles reflected the theatrical nature of God's punishments.

There was antagonism between those Protestants who disapproved of entertainment and similar frivolous distractions, and the theatre which responded by caricaturing the puritans as killjoys and hypocrites, yet both dramatists and patrons might themselves be 'puritans' in the sense of 'strong Protestants', and the type of stage puritans most commonly held up to ridicule were the separatists, disliked and disapproved of by almost everybody else. As Margot Heinemann has argued, Thomas Middleton's writings and his association with the City Fathers, for whom he wrote pageants and Lord Mayor's Shows, suggest strong Protestant sympathies. Several of the great Protestant patrons also took an active interest in the theatre: the Earl of Leicester had his own company of actors, while William Herbert, third Earl of Pembroke, paid Ben Jonson a pension, and Shakespeare's First Folio was jointly dedicated to him and his brother Philip. In the 1630s a number of important parliamentarians patronized the theatre, including John Milton, whose poetry reflects his admiration of Jonson and Shakespeare. Milton's country-house masque *Comus* (1634) draws on Jonson's *Pleasure Reconciled with Virtue* (1618). In practice, the Lord Mayors opposed the companies, while their aristocratic patrons, often represented by the Privy Council, fought to protect them.

In addition to the objections of the City Fathers and the Church, there were other complaints against the theatres derived from a general unease about their role within the social structure, and what happened in them. One particular source of offence was the boys' playing of female parts, which was seen as promoting effeminacy, both among actors and audience; in any case, transvestism had been specifically forbidden in the Old Testament (Deuteronomy 22: 5). Cross-dressing was a convention to which the dramatists themselves drew their audience's attention, in various suggestive ways: Lyly's *Gallathea* (1585), written for choirboys, includes two heroines who fall in love; Shakespeare's heroines Julia, Portia, Rosalind, Viola, and Imogen all dress as boys, while Jonson's comedy *Epicoene* (1609) turns on a boy player pretending to be a woman, and in Act V, Scene v of *Bartholomew Fair* a rabbi and a puppet conduct a debate on the subject. On stage the boy dressed as a girl provided an ambiguous object of male desire, as he performed femininity. While in practice men's love for men was quietly accepted, particular sexual acts were condemned by Church and law. Theatrical travesty (or transvestism) was seen by critics of the theatre as a threat to social order, confusing gender roles and encouraging members of the audience to feel desire for the boy actors. The Continental alternative of actresses was sometimes regarded as an even greater threat: Thomas Nashe argued that the English convention was preferable to having 'whores and common courtesans to play women's parts' (*Pierce Penniless*; *Works*, i. 215).

Another frequent objection was to the kind of economic exchange that the theatres seemed to offer. In them, good money earned by the citizens was not ploughed back into trade for the general benefit, but came to rest in the undeserving pockets of the players. Nashe made a tart reply: 'As for the hindrance of trades and traders of the city by them, that is an article foistered in by the vintners, alewives, and victuallers, who surmise, if there were no plays, they should have all the company that resort to them lie boozing and beer-bathing in their houses every afternoon. Nor so, nor so, good brother bottle-ale . . .' (*Works*, i. 214).

It was hard to see what the actors gave of measurable value in return for all those pennies they took. Far from providing goods in exchange, the boards gave opportunities to any young upstart who fancied himself better than he was to take up showing-off as a profession, swaggering about in the clothes of his betters, a potential threat to the settled order and fabric of society:

We are commanded by God to abide in the same calling wherein we were called, which is our ordinary vocation in a commonweal. . . . So in a commonweal, if private men be suffered to forsake their calling because they desire to walk gentleman-like in satin and velvet, with a buckler at their heels, proportion is so broken, unity dissolved, harmony confounded, that the whole body must be dismembered and the prince or the head cannot choose but sicken . . .

argued Stephen Gosson in *Plays Confuted in Five Actions* (1582).[10] In the eyes of its critics, drama was based upon the principles of lying, pretence, and deception, and, which was worse, it elevated these sins into a commercially rewarding practice. Elizabethan defenders of the form, with the exception of Thomas Nashe, were ill-equipped to deny such charges, partly because they themselves were confused as to how commercial drama fitted into existing social and economic structures. Its only predecessors had been the bands of travelling players and minstrels, who had played to small audiences and needed civic permission to perform, and so had not constituted a serious threat.

Anxiety about the status of 'playing' seems to have affected the dramatists and seeped into their plays. Revenge tragedy, in particular, developed a range of imagery which, though chiefly directed against the illusion and artifice of court life, also functioned to question the nature of the theatrical experience itself. Pretence and hypocrisy stand condemned: 'Seems, madam? nay, it is, I know not "seems"' (*Hamlet*, i. ii. 76). Affected courtiers like Osric or Marston's Castilio Balthazar were ridiculed, and face-painting, common to actors and courtiers, was satirized: 'I have heard of your paintings, well enough. God hath given you one face and you make yourselves another' (*Hamlet*, iii. i.

142–4). Disguise and role-playing are often forced on the hero by his situation, but they are also a burden, a source of inner confusion and self-doubt, for the line between necessary or 'politic' dissimulation, and treacherous or Machiavellian simulation (as drawn by Francis Bacon in his essay on them, pp.76–8) was a particularly fine one. The very word 'hypocrite' had originally meant 'actor' in Greek. The perception of hypocrisy was particularly acute at this period. In a famous sermon of 1612, Thomas Adams denounced 'the White Devil' of hypocrisy that had eaten through the whole of Jacobean society—he seems to have borrowed the title of Webster's latest play to do so.

Plays-within-plays usually fulfilled a sinister purpose, providing occasions for murders which an on-stage audience of actors watched as impassively as their actual, off-stage counterparts; actors and audience conspired to take mutual pleasure in a fiction, to reject the truth of experience for a glitteringly dangerous invention. Comedy too criticized its audiences for being unable to distinguish between truth and illusion: Jonson's work is full of confidence-tricksters, versatile performers whose easy manipulation of their victims parallels the players' deception of their audience, eagerly paying to be imposed upon for three hours, and perhaps, like the on-stage fools, to have their pockets picked and their purses cut into the bargain.

Both Jonson and Shakespeare at times expressed revulsion from their chosen medium, indirectly through the symbolism and action of particular plays, or through the more personal voice of poetry:

> O, for my sake do you with Fortune chide . . .
> That did not better for my life provide
> Than public means which public manners breeds.
> Thence comes it that my name receives a brand,
> And almost thence my nature is subdued
> To what it works in, like the dyer's hand.
>
> (Sonnet 111)

It is difficult to imagine that Shakespeare ever felt ashamed of his profession, as this sonnet implies. Jonson's ode 'Come, leave the loathed stage' is more obviously bad-tempered. It is impossible to tell whether it was the artificial nature of the medium, with its adoption of alien clothes and roles, the fact that playwriting was undertaken for pay rather than for its own sake, or the low esteem in which the profession was generally held, that caused such reactions; but it is striking that the age's two major professional playwrights at times echoed the discourse of their detractors.

Theatrical Illusion

While the distinction between truth and illusion was felt to be one of great importance, in practice it was extraordinarily difficult to define. Sidney's *Defence of Poetry* confidently dismissed accusations of theatrical lying by insisting that the difference between the real and the make-believe was obvious: 'What child is there, that, coming to a play, and seeing *Thebes* written in great letters upon an old door, doth believe that it is Thebes?' (p. 103). Thomas Heywood, the most prolific dramatist of the day (fifty-six plays have been identified, though he claimed to have 'had a main finger in' 220), took rather a different line: His *Apology for Actors* (1612) blurs Sidney's simple distinction by suggesting that the actor's power to convince an audience of the reality of the dramatic experience might prove useful in the right circumstances, and he provides several examples. For Heywood, Hamlet's belief

> That guilty creatures sitting at a play
> Have by the very cunning of the scene
> Been strook so to the soul, that presently
> They have proclaim'd their malefactions . . .
>
> (II. ii. 589–92)

is an item of faith. He reports two episodes involving women who had secretly murdered their husbands (a paranoiac anxiety characteristic of the age), and who gave themselves away publicly by crying out in the middle of a theatrical performance. A play in which a murderess is haunted by her husband's ghost made one guilty woman believe she had seen a real ghost, since her own murdered husband's 'fearful image personated itself in the shape of that ghost'.[11] As well as confusing real and simulated experience, Heywood's narrative suggests that the presentation of the supernatural on stage still had a peculiar power. Devils were a special threat, since even their pretended presence was in danger of summoning the real thing. Modern stage superstitions about *Macbeth* (referred to only as 'the Scottish play') dimly echo this attitude. The conjuring scenes in Marlowe's *Faustus* were a particular source of anxiety. One performance at Exeter triggered off a full-scale panic among nervous actors and audience:

as a certain number of devils kept every one his circle there, and as Faustus was busy in his magical invocations, on a sudden they were all dashed, every one harkening other in the ear, for they were all persuaded there was one devil too many amongst them, and so after a little pause desired the people to pardon them, they could go no further with this matter; the people also understanding the thing as it was, every man hastened to be first out of doors.[12]

Another incident reported by Heywood involved a further confusion of play-acting with reality, when a band of Spaniards landed at Cornwall 'with intent to take in the town, spoil and burn it'. At the same time, a company of actors was presenting a battle on stage nearby, and 'struck up a loud alarm, which the enemy hearing, and fearing they were discovered, amazedly retired, made some few idle shots in a bravado, and so in a hurly-burly fled disorderly to their boats'. This incident seems to have justified Heywood in crediting the actors with the conduct of a successful (if entirely accidental) military operation. Heywood's critical thinking was more naïve than his dramatic practice, but it reflects commonly held positions: comedy encourages self-examination, since the clown's 'slovenly and unhandsome behaviour' makes men 'reform that simplicity in themselves, which others make their sport'.[13] The astrologer Simon Forman seems to have taken a similar approach. After watching a performance of *The Winter's Tale* in 1611, he reminded himself (apropos of Autolycus, presumably) to 'Beware of trusting feigned beggars or fawning fellows',[14] a lesson he might have learned from any cony-catching pamphlet.

Despite confusion as to the precise nature, workings, and morality of dramatic illusion, in practice the dramatists employed a wide range of techniques that openly acknowledged or even emphasized the mechanics of stage illusion, including prologues and other framing devices, asides, soliloquies, and plays-within-plays, moving confidently and skilfully within an old and well-established tradition of give-and-take with an audience. Indeed, from its beginnings medieval drama had blended theatrical illusion with reality, reminding the audience that they were watching a play, and generally employing 'alienation' techniques in which the permanent and ancient truths of the Bible were redirected to the particular here-and-now of the audience's conscience. Mystery plays had moved freely between local references and the biblical settings of their stories, identifying Christ's inquisitors with unpopular clerical types, sometimes even bishops, and making Herod threaten the mothers with young children in the audience. Since the universal truths of Christian history were constantly being acted out in the lives of every individual, the biblical narratives could be updated and 'given a local habitation and a name'.

Audiences had thus accepted theatrical illusion, and recognized it as such from an early stage. Henry Medwall's humanist play *Fulgens and Lucrece*, written at the end of the fifteenth century, has for its main presenters two young men known only as A and B who seem at first to be members of the audience, chatting as they wait for the play to begin. A asks B whether he is one of the actors, which B denies. They then decide to take part in the play's action as servants to the main characters, keeping up a commentary on events as they unfold, rather as the character of the Vice did in interludes, moving backwards and forwards between the action and the audience. More than a hundred years later, Jonson's induction to *Bartholomew Fair* (1614) begins with a comparable simulation of reality as the stage-keeper, broom in hand, chats familiarly to the audience, warning them that the play they are about to watch is a waste of time, since the dramatist knows nothing about his subject: 'He has not hit the humours, he does not know 'em' (ll. 10–11). Framing devices such as these negotiated the gap between the audience settling in their seats and cracking their hazel-nuts (the Elizabethan equivalent of rustling sweet-papers), and the illusion to follow. For pageant wagons, as for the Globe theatre, there were no house lights to be dipped, so the opening scene had to establish the right atmosphere immediately. Many plays start straight into the action—the platform at Elsinore at midnight, or the fight between Subtle and Face that opens Jonson's *Alchemist*: Face menaces Subtle with his dagger: 'Believe't, I will.' Subtle sneers, 'Thy worst. I fart at thee.'

Plays open in a variety of ways: with expository dialogue, as in *King Lear* or *Othello*; with long, informative soliloquies, as in *Richard III*, *Volpone*, and *The Revenger's Tragedy*; or with a chorus or a narrator as in *Henry V*, *Pericles*, or Middleton's *Hengist, King of Kent*. In addition to actors pretending to be themselves or members of the audience, as in *Fulgens and Lucrece* or Beaumont's *Knight of the Burning Pestle*, a prologue might involve a distinct set of characters who were neither audience nor characters in the main action, as in the 'Christopher Sly' episode that opens *The Taming of the Shrew*, or in Kyd's *The Spanish Tragedy* (1587), where the ghost of Don Andrea and Revenge have come to witness the drama, and remain on stage throughout. They are awaiting revenge for Don Andrea's untimely death, but at first they are disappointed. This play employs a series of dramatic tricks designed to draw attention to the theatrical nature of the action. The standard forms of address to the audience were the soliloquy, a speech addressed to them directly by an actor alone on stage, confiding his or her private thoughts or plans, and the aside, an (often sarcastic or ironic) comment on the action made by an actor on stage which only the audience is supposed to hear. As these dramatic conventions indicate, the actors acknowledge the audience's presence, entrusting them with secret or confidential information. The audience often discovers a character's motives, plans, or attitudes before they are revealed to the rest of the characters on stage.

In addition to direct addresses to the audience in the form of soliloquy or asides, *The Spanish Tragedy* includes an overhearing scene in which the villains eavesdrop on the lovers as they make an assignation, adding threatening comments which the lovers cannot hear. As the villains repeat the lovers' language, their words blend into a single poetic effect, rather like that of an operatic quartet in which the principles sing together of their different intentions:

BELIMPERIA: Why stands Horatio speechless all this while?
HORATIO: The less I speak, the more I meditate.
BELIMPERIA: But whereon dost thou chiefly meditate?
HORATIO: On dangers past, and pleasures to ensue.
BALTHAZAR [*hidden above*]: On pleasures past, and dangers to ensue.
BELIMPERIA: What dangers and what pleasures dost thou mean?
HORATIO: Dangers of war, and pleasures of our love.
LORENZO [*similarly concealed*]: Dangers of death, but pleasures none
    at all.
BELIMPERIA: Let dangers go, thy war shall be with me,
    But such a war as breaks no bond of peace.

(II. ii. 24–33)

In this scene, the audience watch Revenge and Andrea's ghost (Horatio's reference to the 'dangers of war' reminds us that Andrea was killed in battle) watching Lorenzo and Balthazar (on the gallery above the stage) watching Horatio and Belimperia. An even more complex effect is produced when Hieronymo performs his play of 'Soliman and Perseda' before the court, in which the murders are not simply acted but actually carried out, so that the play-within-a-play provides a cloak for the killing of the villains, Lorenzo and Balthazar.

The use of plays-within-plays (Hamlet's 'Mousetrap' is the classic example) continued to be a popular device in revenge tragedy, a genre committed to exploring the relations between appearance and reality. Once masques became the favourite form of court entertainment, these were often introduced instead: wedding masques are staged in Beaumont and

Fletcher's *The Maid's Tragedy* (1610) and in Middleton's *Women Beware Women* (1621) and Ford's *'Tis Pity She's a Whore* (1632), where they provide opportunities for murder, as Hieronymo's play had done in *The Spanish Tragedy*. Murders carried out during elaborate court ceremonials such as masques or banquets have seemed artificial to later critics, but their popularity as a device suggests that, for the original audiences, the inevitable and uninterruptable sequence of a state ritual added to the tension (perhaps as music does in the cinema). The powerful demands of court ritual are reflected in Ford's *The Broken Heart* (1630), where Calantha receives a series of heart-breaking messages during a dance, but refuses to break step, declaring

> 'tis, methinks, a rare presumption
> In any, who prefers our lawful pleasures
> Before their own sour censure, to interrupt
> The custom of this ceremony bluntly.
>
> (v. ii. 24–7)

Calantha exemplifies a stoic, perhaps an aristocratic refusal to give way beneath fortune's blows.

The play-within-a-play was as much a feature of comedy as tragedy, as can be illustrated from Shakespeare's *A Midsummer Night's Dream* and *Love's Labour's Lost*, or Middleton's *A Mad World, My Masters*, where it is used as a cover, not for murder but robbery. Jonson's comedies abound in play-acting of various kinds: *Bartholomew Fair* includes a puppet show, while Volpone's household act out little dialogues for him. Overhearing scenes such as that in *The Spanish Tragedy* could also be turned to comic effect, as in *Much Ado about Nothing* or *Twelfth Night*. As much as tragedy, comedy had numerous ways of reminding its audiences of their status as onlookers.

Earlier sixteenth-century drama had addressed its audience directly, and manipulated their reactions uninhibitedly. The figure usually employed for this purpose was the Vice, a comic character who acted as both presenter and participant, but unlike A and B in *Fulgens and Lucrece*, he also tempted the other characters to sin. Ambidexter in Thomas Preston's *Cambises*

(1561) is a typical Vice, chatting up the audience and asking a girl in the front row, 'How say you, maid? to marry me will ye be glad?' (l. 953). At the same time he deceives the tyrant Cambises into thinking that his brother plans to overthrow him, and so must be killed first. He also takes part in the comic sub-plot, getting into fights with Meretrix and Marion May-Be-Good, and he takes the audience into his confidence as the action unfolds. After one of several brutal murders, he pulls them up sharply by jumping from noisy grief to coarse jesting:

> A, a, a, a! I cannot choose but weep for the queen!
> Nothing but mourning now at the court there is seen.
> Oh, oh! my heart, my heart! O, my bum will break!
>
> (ll. 1133–5)

Abrupt shifts from tears to harsh laughter remained characteristic of the drama's powerful 'hodge-podge' of tragedy and comedy. Much of Marlowe's work was written in this tradition of rapidly contrasting and sometimes overlapping moods, which reached its height in *King Lear*. The difference between Shakespeare and Thomas Preston (whom Shakespeare parodied in *1 Henry IV*, ii. iv. 387–94) lies less in the techniques they employed than in their command of those techniques. And even when plays created a uniformly sober atmosphere, as *Julius Caesar* does, they might be followed by a jig in the form of a dance, or even a comic song-and-dance routine performed by the clown.

The patently non-realistic tradition within which the Vice had operated was gradually abandoned. Earlier sixteenth-century drama had mingled personified abstractions with individualized characters. Marlowe and Kyd's more psychological dramas still sometimes included allegorical figures such as Revenge in *The Spanish Tragedy*, the old man who stands for conscience in *Dr Faustus*, the poor men who speak for the common people at the outset of *Edward II*, and the Death-like mower who betrays the King's whereabouts. In Shakespeare's plays, the most marginal figures are given individualizing touches: the prisoner Barnardine in *Measure for Measure*, whose cut-off head must be substituted for Claudio's (and is, in Shakespeare's source), refuses to co-operate with the plot: 'I swear I will not die to-day for any man's persuasion' (IV. iii. 59–60). Although Elizabethan dramatists were not interested in realism, and did not envisage character in terms of consistent behaviour patterns, as Victorian novelists did, they were interested in unfolding complex stories in carefully orchestrated detail, so that there was no room for a character like the Vice, whose essence was his disruptiveness.

The Vice's role had been largely functional, his purpose being to hold the audience's attention: his cheerful mischief-making kept them amused and helped to break up the action into manageable units, adapted to the audience's limited concentration spans. London theatre audiences came to accept far more demanding forms of entertainment, in terms of expression and ideas, and learned to give their sustained attention to complex sequences of events. Elizabethan drama includes many references to the figure of the Vice but there were comparatively few attempts to revive the looser and more open structure within which he had operated. Other characters were developed who might stand outside and inside the action simultaneously, in order to control or comment on it, figures like Vincentio (in *Measure for Measure*) or Prospero (in *The Tempest*), Marston's Malcontent or Middleton's Revenger, Vindice. But these never possessed the Vice's comic unpredictability, nor did they exercise the compère's role as fully and freely as he had done.

While Elizabethan drama grew less episodic, acquiring greater coherence and intensity, these were never achieved at the expense of variety. Clear linear development, that unity of action recommended by Aristotle, could scarcely have been further from English dramatic construction. Shakespeare's late play *The Tempest*, located on a single island and acted continuously, is unusual in observing the unities of place and time, but its diversity of action prevents it from conforming to the three unities required of neoclassical drama, and for all Jonson's commitment to classical ideals, none of his major plays possesses a simple outline. The taste for variety ran deep, and though audiences learned to follow complicated stories with different groups of characters interacting, sustained over two or three hours, playwrights were still liable to abrupt changes of mood or atmosphere, as when the succubus precipitates Sir Penitent's repentance in Act IV of *A Mad World, My Masters*. The subplot of *The Changeling* (like that of *Hengist, King of Kent*) is so different in tone from the main plot that until William Empson's appreciation (in *Some Versions of Pastoral*), it was dismissed out of hand, as the work of Middleton's collaborator, Rowley.

Developments in narrative and psychological complexity went hand-in-hand with an easy acceptance of the artificial nature of the medium, and no obvious desire to heighten the element of illusion. Only the indoor theatres made use of stage lighting at all, and even then it could not be adjusted. Performances in the public playhouses began at 2.00 p.m. (an hour or two later at the indoor playhouses), so night had to be represented by the carrying of burning torches, making the stage brighter, rather than darker. Little is known about the hangings that screened the tiring house, though they seem to have been black for tragedies, and painted for other occasions. A 'discovery space' could be revealed behind the curtains, but the rapid, continuous action of the plays made intricate scene-changes impractical. Settings were more often suggested by props, pushed forward on to the stage—a bower for the lovers' assignation in *The Spanish Tragedy*, a bed for Duke Humphrey or Desdemona to die on, a tomb for Juliet, a bank of flowers for Titania, as well as shops, chariots, and hell-mouths. Perspective scenery, with backcloth and wings, was first used by Inigo Jones for his masques, and did not reach the public theatres until much later in the century.

Costumes, on the other hand, were expensive and elaborate, as well as important in defining the gender, profession, or class of a character for the audience. Two people wearing the same costume were identical twins, and could not be distinguished from one another. A girl dressed as a boy was perceived as a boy by those on stage until she resumed her 'women's weeds'. Some kinds of dressing or undressing were regularly performed on stage, particularly donning armour or unpinning hair before going to bed. Some kinds of undress, such as untied points or loose hair, indicated mental disorder. Various conventions of dress and gesture simplified communication between actors and audience, and the actors employed facial expressions, words, and movements that were larger than life. Sword-fights, a great feature of Elizabethan drama, were probably alarmingly realistic, their realism enhanced by bladders of pig's blood. Costumes were acquired second-hand from courtiers, and so, occasionally, were props such as the Spanish ambassador Gondomar's special litter, featured in Middleton's *A Game at Chess*.

By contrast with nineteenth-century dramatic tradition, Elizabethan drama made no attempt to conceal the medium in which it operated. More often playwrights deliberately exaggerated its artificial qualities, as they did when writing for the children's companies, whose charm lay in the piquant contrast between what they were and what they played. In the earliest phase of the boy actors' popularity, during the 1580s, John Lyly had written formal, elegant comedies for them, often on classical themes, with witty dialogue and plenty of songs to show off their choirboy voices. The songs were full of sexual innuendo, and the boys were credited with a sexual sophistication which we find troubling, but which the dramatists exploited. By the end of the sixteenth century plays for the children's companies increasingly focused on adult passions. Most of John Marston's plays were written for the boy companies, and they are full of exaggerated language and emotion, as well as lines that deliberately undermine the theatrical illusion, as when the courtier Balurdo in *Antonio's Revenge* (1600) comes on with his beard half-off, complaining 'the tiring-man hath not glued on my beard half fast enough. God's bores, it will not stick to fall off' (II. i. 32–4).

Its predecessor, *Antonio and Mellida* (1599), includes an induction in which the boys, wearing cloaks thrown over their costumes, discuss each others' roles, arguing and scrapping among themselves—a device reworked by Jonson in *Cynthia's Revels* (1600). It is difficult to decide how Marston's many references to the illusory character of the stage were intended to affect his audience: perhaps they were an assertion of the author's confidence in the power of the boy actors to carry them off, acts of bravado comparable to Shakespeare's in *Antony and Cleopatra*; here (the boy playing) Cleopatra, fearing capture by the Romans, warns

> The quick comedians
> Extemporally will stage us . . . I shall see
> Some squeaking Cleopatra boy my greatness
> I' th' posture of a whore.
>   (v. ii. 216–17, 219–21)

In *Antonio's Revenge*, the elderly stoic Pandulpho breaks down on hearing of his son's murder, comparing his vain attempt to master his feelings with that of a child actor struggling to maintain a heroic posture:

> Man will break out, despite philosophy.
> Why, all this while I ha' but play'd a part,
> Like to some boy that acts a tragedy,
> Speaks burly words and raves out passion;
> But when he thinks upon his infant weakness,
> He droops his eye.
>   (IV. ii. 69–74)

The role-playing and self-deception of daily life are here compared to the child's performance in the theatre. But where Cleopatra's lines work to reinforce the theatrical illusion, Pandulpho's speech seeks to undermine it.

In twentieth-century theatre and cinema, frame-breaking is acceptable in comedy, but seldom occurs in a serious context: Groucho, gagging a train driver in *The Marx Brothers Go West*, adds 'This is the best gag in the whole picture', while Fabian in *Twelfth Night* observes in an aside, 'If this were play'd upon a stage now, I could condemn it as an improbable fiction' (III. iv. 127–8). In its own way, Renaissance tragedy also draws attention to its ironic, bizarre, or theatrical elements as openly as comedy does: we are invited to relish the element of the grotesque when Lavinia in *Titus Andronicus*, whose tongue and hands have been hacked off, picks up her father's severed hand between her teeth, while he picks up one of the two severed heads of his sons in his remaining hand, saying to Marcus:

> Come, brother, take a head,
> And in this hand the other will I bear;
> And, Lavinia, thou shalt be employ'd;
> Bear thou my hand, sweet wench, between thy teeth.

(III. i. 279–82)

Comedy

Though Elizabethan critics referred to tragedy and comedy as separate categories, the forms had much in common with one another, and were not regarded as mutually exclusive until neo-classical rules were more generally adopted in the second half of the seventeenth century. Distinctions between tragedy and comedy often look arbitrary when, in addition to the catch-all chronicles and histories, and 'mongrel tragi-comedy', some plays are described as both at once: Preston's *Cambises*, referred to earlier, relates the fall of a tyrant—a tragic event, as commonly defined—and is described on the title page as a 'lamentable tragedy', but the presence of the Vice Ambidexter and the elements of knockabout farce in the sub-plot justify its description as a comedy in the running-head, as well as its alternative title of 'Huff, Snuff and Ruff'. Nor is it only early plays like *Cambises* that suffer from uncertainty as to their status: Shakespeare's *Troilus and Cressida* poses similar problems. Hector's death suggests a tragic ending, and the First Folio editors originally intended it to stand among the tragedies, but some accident during printing finally placed it between the tragedies and the histories. The 1609 quarto of the play describes it as a history on the title-page, but advises the reader that it is 'passing full of the palm comical', and praises Shakespeare's achievements in that kind.

One explanation for this overlap is that in England tragedy developed out of comedy and did not entirely outgrow its parent, so that English tragedy continued to mingle kings and

clowns, and match funerals with hornpipes until the closing of
the theatres in 1642. Comedy, the earlier form of drama, derived
its structure from the Mystery cycles which took as their overall
framework the divine comedy in which the tragic falls of Lucifer
and Adam had provided the occasion for God's incarnation as
Christ, redeeming mankind. These plays included moments of
intense grief and horror, as Christ was scourged and crucified,
and Mary mourned her son's death, but they were followed by
the joy of the Resurrection and the wild farce of the Harrowing
of Hell, played for laughs with the devils beating each other and
letting off fireworks. Many other biblical episodes were treated
comically, and even threatening figures such as Cain, Herod, or
Christ's persecutors were exaggerated, so that absurdity light-
ened their terror. Morality plays also introduced extra comic
stuffing while reminding their audience of God's goodness to
man. The meaning of the Christian message and the natural
tendency of popular entertainment to invite laughter combined
to make comedy the dramatic prototype.

Elizabethan critics like Puttenham and Webbe recognized
this, but re-described the development of English drama in
terms of the development of classical Greek drama: English
traditions, such as the acting of plays on pageant-wagons pulled
about the streets, were attributed to ancient Greece. Tragedy was
recognized as a later form, while Webbe saw it as evolving from
a type of drama closely resembling that of the morality play,
though the example he gives of this style of drama is
Aristophanes:

Comedies took their name . . . to go a feasting, because they used to go
in procession with their sport about the cities and villages . . . But not
long after (as one delight draweth another) they began to invent new
persons and new matters for their comedies, such as the devisers
thought meetest to please the people's vein: and from these they began
to present in shapes of men the nature of virtues and vices, and affec-
tions and qualities incident to men as Justice, Temperance, Poverty,
Wrath, Vengeance, Sloth, Valiantness and such like, as may appear by
the ancient works of Aristophanes. There grew at last to be a greater
diversity between tragedy writers and comedy writers . . .[15]

Though inaccurate as an account of the development of Greek drama, this throws some light on how the history of six-teenth-century drama looked to late Elizabethans: tragedy con-sisted of a particular type of plot, rather than a distinctive set of dramatic conventions such as Aristotle had described in his *Poetics*. This accorded with the medieval conception of tragedy as a particular sequence of events, the fall of a great man from prosperity into misery. No single literary genre had been con-sidered more appropriate than another for such a plot. Before the 1580s tragedy usually took the form of verse narrative, as it does in Chaucer's *Troilus and Criseyde* (1382), Lydgate's *Falls of Princes* (1494), or Sackville and Buckhurst's *Mirror for Magistrates* (1559).

Since tragedy had no peculiar techniques of its own, drama-tists fell back on the devices of comedy, padding out their tragic structures with comic episodes that offended later critics, accus-tomed to 'purer' tragic forms. Even in the work of a great tragic writer like Shakespeare, the primacy of comedy is still evident. *The Comedy of Errors* is more obviously characteristic of his developing art, anticipating the patterns of loss and restoration apparent in such late plays as *Pericles* and *The Winter's Tale*. The skills evident in the early comedies are nowhere equalled by the early tragedies. Despite its power and originality, *Titus Andron-icus* owes more to Marlowe than *The Comedy of Errors* does to Plautus. A second early tragedy, *Romeo and Juliet*, draws exten-sively on Shakespeare's own Italianate comedy, and its most memorable figures are comic. Between them, Shakespeare, Kyd, and Marlowe established the tragic genre that blossomed so sud-denly and so fully under James. As Nicholas Brooke noticed: 'There was no English tragedy before Kyd and Marlowe outside the Inns of Court, where it was amateur, private and incredibly dull.'[16]

Though comedy, unlike tragedy, belonged to a well-established tradition, the earliest comedies can seem naïve and unsophisticated. This has less to do with their structure than with the type of humour they employed, which was vulgar, and often focused upon the control (or lack of it) of bodily functions, though early twentieth-century editors sometimes attempted to disguise this aspect. J. Q. Adams omitted from his text of *Mankind* all but the opening lines of the rude song which the audience is tricked into joining in. In this type of knockabout comedy, the ultimate joke is the devil who frightens the simple peasant into fouling his breeches, a joke popular from *Mankind* (1465–70) to Ulpian Fulwell's *Like Will to Like* (1568) and the more sophisticated *Gammer Gurton's Needle* (1552), whose plot derives from Plautus. Even George Gascoigne, translating the Italian comedy *Supposes* for an audience at Gray's Inn in 1566, could not resist a quibble on 'supposes' and 'suppositories' in the last speech. If laughter reveals a society's inner tensions, Tudor audiences must have been childishly preoccupied with bodily control (though they have been defended on the grounds that lack of sphincter control functioned as a metaphor for the failure of moral control in the presence of supernatural temptation).

With the establishment of the professional theatres, taste changed rapidly. Nervous incontinence was no longer considered amusing, and though the clowns might be allowed the occasional low joke (Launce's dog in *Two Gentlemen of Verona* farts at a banquet, and urinates against a lady's farthingale), excremental humour was replaced by a much wider range of laughing matter. Some jokes involved subtle social distinctions; others reflected a growing taste for word-play and for sexual innuendo. By the early seventeenth century, dramatists like Middleton, Marston, Webster, and Tourneur devoted speeches and sometimes whole scenes to *double entendres*: an example from Tourneur's *The Atheist's Tragedy* moves from the embroidery of plants (medlars, poppering pears, and bachelor's buttons) to music: 'Dost not see *mi* between the two crotchets? Strike me full there. So—forward.—This is a sweet strain, and thou finger'st it beastly. *Mi* is a large there, and the prick that stands before *mi*, a long . . . Here's a sweet close—strike it full; it sets off your music delicately' (IV. i. 49–53, 55–6).

Such changes in taste reflected differences between London society and the provincial audiences for whom earlier comedies had been performed. From the first, professional dramatists introduced elements of romance as well as laughter into comedy. Medwall's *Fulgens and Lucrece*, in so many respects ahead of its time, included it, and so did Italian comedies like George Gascoigne's *Supposes*, ultimately derived from Roman New Comedy, with its plots of divided lovers. Morality plays and interludes had seldom included lovers, and one dramatist, Ben Jonson, found himself in sympathy with their exclusion. The comedies of the 1580s often combined romance with legendary material from classical literature, from contemporary fantasy (as did Greene's *Orlando Furioso*), or from native English fairy-tales (as did Peele's *The Old Wives' Tale*, with its three sisters, oracular heads in the well, and its dead travelling companion). Folk-tale elements remained popular: Robin Goodfellow materialized in a wood near Athens, while fairies and Herne the Hunter haunt Windsor Forest.

The originality and inventiveness of Shakespearean comedy dominated the 1590s, preferring exotic settings to the rural English locations of Wakefield or Fressingfield, favoured by Greene. The exception is *The Merry Wives of Windsor*, linked through its setting to the ceremony of the Order of the Garter, and through Falstaff to the London tavern scenes of the *Henry IV* history cycle: here, rather than in his comedies, Shakespeare presented the world of tapsters and hostesses, of bar-room heroics and tipsy practical jokes that had long been popular in interludes. After the turn of the century comedy abandoned Arden and Athens, country villages and romantic forest wastes, in favour of the familiar rough-and-tumble of Cheapside, Smithfield, and Finsbury. London and familiar London types—courtezans, rogues, ambitious merchants, pleasure-hating puritans, swaggering gallants—dominated the Jacobean stage, characters who brought with them local and political satire, and a range of topical reference that would have been out of place in more romantic comedy.

Marston, Jonson, and Middleton held up a looking-glass to London, analysing its citizens within dramatic structures notable for their complexity and cohesiveness. Their audience's knowledge of London life challenged the dramatists to synthesize it into freshly observed and ever more pointed inventions. The lasting success of citizen comedy, which presented the audience with theatrical versions of themselves, is reflected in the fact that though Restoration comedy was more obviously stylized and upper-class, it was essentially an extension or continuation of that tradition. The direct presentation of London life not only appealed to those in the know, it also fitted the traditional justification of comedy as a mirror of society, 'an imitation of the common errors of our life, which [the dramatist] representeth in the most ridiculous and scornful sort that may be, so as it is impossible that any beholder can be content to be such a one', as Sidney put it in *The Defence of Poetry* (pp. 95–6).

Tragedy

Though much Jonsonian comedy is in verse, comedy after the turn of the century was increasingly written in prose. Tragedy, on the other hand, expressed its intensest moments in self-consciously patterned language—the stronger the emotion, the more highly wrought was its form of expression. Hieronymo's lament over his murdered son in *The Spanish Tragedy* uses a rhetoric as elaborate as that of a Petrarchan sonnet:

> O eyes, no eyes, but fountains fraught with tears;
> O life, no life, but lively form of death;
> O world, no world, but mass of public wrongs,
> Confus'd and fill'd with murder and misdeeds . . .
>
> (III. ii. 1–4)

It was in fact inspired by the fourth line of Petrarch's exclamatory Sonnet 161, 'oi occhi miei (occhi non gia, ma fonti)' ('O my eyes, not eyes, but fountains').

Shakespeare's early work represented intense feeling in elaborate repetitive structures. In *Richard III*, Queen Margaret urges the other queens,

> Tell over your woes again by viewing mine:
> I had an Edward, till a Richard kill'd him;
> I had a Harry, till a Richard kill'd him;

Thou hadst an Edward, till a Richard kill'd him;
Thou hadst a Richard, till a Richard killed him.

(IV. iv. 39–43)

As the taste for such formal repetition declined, Shakespeare devised a different kind of rhetoric in which to express intense feeling, creating a complex but dynamic syntax using thickly laden imagery that felt closer to 'the quick forge and working-house of thought', though it was still highly wrought and very far from normal speech patterns. Antony laments the loss of his fortune and his followers after Actium:

> The hearts
> That span[i]ell'd me at heels, to whom I gave
> Their wishes, do discandy, melt their sweets
> On blossoming Caesar; and this pine is bark'd
> That overtopp'd them all.

(*Antony and Cleopatra*, IV. xii. 20–4)

Shakespeare's mature work employed a variety of methods to convey intense emotion. It could be deflected into indirect expression, as when Desdemona voices her distress and her continuing love for Othello through the willow song. Sometimes it is very simply expressed, as at the climax of *King Lear*, whose heroine, Cordelia, has already confessed that she 'cannot heave | My heart into my mouth':

LEAR: If you have poison for me, I will drink it.
   I know you do not love me, for your sisters
   Have (as I do remember) done me wrong:
   You have some cause, they have not.
CORDELIA: No cause, no cause.

(IV. vii. 71–4)

In Cordelia's mumbled response, psychological truth and dramatic convention interact. The difficulty of speaking coherently, even of speaking at all, at moments of intense feeling was part of a dramatic tradition derived from Seneca that 'light griefs speak, but heavy ones are silent' ('Curae leves loquuntur, ingentes stupent', *Hippolytus*, l. 607), an insight that also governs the climax of *Titus Andronicus* where the hero, after receiving a series of harrowing messages, breaks a long-held pause by bursting into hysterical laughter (III. ii. 263–4).

Serious writing was expected to justify itself by teaching a lesson, and this applied as much to tragedy as it did to comedy, epic, and romance: Nashe defended chronicle plays such as Shakespeare's *Henry VI* cycle on the grounds that they immortalized the heroic achievements of the past and stirred young minds to virtuous imitation (*Pierce Penniless*; *Works*, i. 212). The lessons that tragedy taught were at once obvious, and yet lacking in moral content—that evil would be punished, that the whirligig of time brought in its revenges, or that Fortune's wheel, which carried the Scythian shepherd Tamburlaine to world conquest and the tyrant Cambises to destruction, turned inexorably:

> Base Fortune, now I see, that in thy wheel
> There is a point to which, when men aspire,
> They tumble headlong down.
> (*Edward II*, v. vi. 58–60)

Mortimer uses the concept of Fortune's wheel to warn great men how far they have to fall.

Tragedy particularly addressed itself to great men—tyrants and oppressors—and offered warnings to corrupt princes and magistrates. This narrowly directed teaching function is referred to by several commentators: for Sidney, it is 'the high and excellent tragedy, that openeth the greatest wounds, and showeth forth the ulcers that are covered with tissue; that maketh kings fear to be tyrants, and tyrants manifest their tyrannical humours' (*A Defence of Poetry*, p. 96; here, 'tissue' has its earlier meaning of cloth of gold, rather than layers of flesh). His friend Fulke Greville asserted that the function of tragedy was 'to trace out the high ways of ambitious governors, and to show in the practice, that the more audacity, advantage, and good success such sovereignties have, the more they hasten to their own desolation and ruin',[17] while Sir John Harington saw tragedy as 'representing only the cruel and lawless proceedings of Princes, moving nothing but pity or detestation'.[18]

The fifteenth chapter of George Puttenham's *Arte of English Poesie* (1589) is entitled 'In what form of poesy the evil and outrageous behaviours of princes were reprehended'. It describes how, when society began, men were 'in a manner popularly equal', but after a time certain individuals acquired power over others, and 'having learned them all manner of lusts and licentiousness', fell into evil. While alive, tyrants could command through fear, but,

> after their deaths, when the posterity stood no more in dread of them, their infamous life and tyrannies were laid open to all the world, their wickedness reproached, their follies and extreme insolencies derided, and their miserable ends painted out in plays and pageants, to show the mutability of fortune, and the just punishment of God in revenge of a vicious and evil life.[19]

Such latter-day revenges afforded cold comfort to an age in which royal authority had been consolidated to an unprecedented extent. With the loss of the Church's temporal powers, the prince's position was greatly strengthened and his wealth increased. If the prince failed in his duties to his people, it was read as God's punishment inflicted on a sinful nation, since God had allowed his rule, had implanted him in his mother's womb and allowed him to grow to manhood. Tyranny must be suffered patiently, with tears and prayers; God would intervene in His own way and time. But the prince's increased power also entailed increased responsibility. He might now be held accountable, as the Church had once been, for the state of his people's souls as much as for their bodies, especially if he led them into an unjust war: the point is discussed in Shakespeare's *Henry V* (IV. i. 132–58).

Evil princes and their depraved courts were favourite subjects for Jacobean tragedy, while classical discussions of depravity in high places, such as those occurring in Seneca's tragedies (translated by Jasper Heywood and others in the 1560s), gained immediacy from their topical nature. All subjects owed allegiance to the monarch and the state, so that for their audiences the drama's warnings to tyrants could only provide imaginary satisfactions. The murder of Julius Caesar on stage must have enacted a revenge on privilege and prerogative which gratified at least a few members of the audience.

In the *Poetics*, Aristotle had laid it down that tragedy should present the lives of the great, but the professional dramatists were well aware of citizen interest in their own lives as reflected in ballads and news pamphlets. Heywood, Middleton, and Dekker, in particular, specialized in drawing bourgeois or provincial protagonists, though they did so more often in comedies or tragicomedies. The plots of 'domestic tragedy' were taken from contemporary fiction or from much-publicized cases of domestic violence, such as Alice Arden's murder of her husband in 1551 (dramatized in *Arden of Faversham*, 1591), or Walter Calverley's murder of his wife and children in 1605 (shown in *A Yorkshire Tragedy*, 1606), narratives that reflected widespread fear of wives' infidelity (leading to adultery and murder), or the dangers of excessive parental authority (Calverley had apparently been forced into marrying against his will). The subject-matter and attitudes of domestic tragedy were particularly close to those of popular contemporary literature.

The varied and complex development of tragedy suggests that certain topical feelings and concerns had found a form well-adapted to express them. Its rapid development may be compared with that of the novel in the eighteenth century. The elements of debate or conflict within dramatic form allowed playwrights to present increasingly contested values and standards in terms of urgently opposed individual convictions, for the essence of drama is conflict, and conflicting positions are more lastingly interesting than any mere disagreement. Even in an early and in some respects schematic play like *Tamburlaine*, which rehearses opposing viewpoints rather than dramatizing conflict, a variety of responses are provoked. In becoming a world conqueror, the shepherd Tamburlaine breaks all accepted doctrines of hierarchy, yet his success seems to be sanctioned by supernatural forces. He believes that he has mastered Fortune (as Machiavelli recommended), or else that he is God's scourge, punishing the puny tyrants he overthrows. In Act II, Scene vi (of

Part I) his true nature is discussed—is he really human? In the following scene, Tamburlaine insists that all men are driven by ambition (which leaves the question of his singularity unresolved), but the empire he rules so effectively grows steadily more cruel and oppressive. Agydas and the King of Arabia find a way out through death, the traditional escape-route from tyranny for the stoic. There are no simple answers to the problems posed by Tamburlaine's relentless ambition, and the play demands the continuous exercise of judgement and sympathy. While it lacks the enlivening detail and psychological inwardness of later and greater tragedies, *Tamburlaine* was a significant landmark in the development of the drama.

In comparison with later tragic heroes, Tamburlaine himself is short on inner life: indeed, he appears to have no personality, as distinct from his unremitting self-confidence. The audience is invited to examine, and perhaps in the Second Part to feel compassion for a character of whom they cannot approve. The playing off of audience sympathy against moral judgement became a feature of tragedy, allowing it to explore the hearts and minds of a ruthless usurper and tyrant in *Macbeth*, a murderous serving-man and a fickle young woman in Middleton's *Changeling*, an incestuous brother and sister in Ford's *'Tis Pity She's a Whore*, and many other characters trapped by their passions. Insight into their lives and desires created sympathy and understanding for them, while in no way exonerating them. Elizabethan drama was not immoral, yet those critics who insisted on the immorality of the medium must have recognized that an audience's sympathy and interest go out to the most dynamic characters on stage, those who do or suffer most, irrespective of their moral qualities. This factor, already suggested by the popularity of the old Vice, was further exploited through manic figures such as the Jew of Malta or Richard III; virtue, as exemplified in the Jew's daughter Abigail, risked appearing comically ineffectual.

Both tragedy and comedy tested inner convictions against the assumptions of the day, sometimes arriving at potentially subversive conclusions. In arranging marriages, parents or relatives were more interested in pursuing financial advantage than in promoting true love, as Middleton's *Chaste Maid in Cheapside* and Webster's *The Duchess of Malfi* reveal, in very different ways. On the other hand, young women often found it difficult to distinguish genuine love from passing fancy, and their lack of foresight might lay them open to the fatal moral lapses dramatized in Middleton's *The Changeling* and *Women Beware Women*. One of the most consistent themes of tragedy was the depravity that accompanied power and privilege, the dangers of attendance at court with its servitude to ephemeral pleasure rather than eternal joy.

In exploring different moral positions and relating them to the self-interest of their speakers, Jacobean tragedy voiced an ultimate scepticism, a doubt that recalls Erasmus or Montaigne as to whether there can be any impartial judgement or certain knowledge in this world. Yet just as scepticism had accompanied firm religious convictions in both these philosophers, so most plays, however radical their implications, came to rest in the traditional wisdom that God was not mocked and sin brought punishment in its train: thus the Cardinal at the end of *Women Beware Women* warns 'Sin, what thou art these ruins show too piteously' (v. ii. 222), and *The White Devil* concludes

> Let guilty men remember their black deeds
> Do lean on crutches, made of slender reeds.
>
> (v. vi. 300–1)

In the process, tragedy reconsidered a number of received opinions which would never look quite the same again. Vindice in *The Revenger's Tragedy* gazes at the skull of his lover, remembering the fatal desire she had aroused in the Duke, and seeing the whole world, on-stage and off, in the grip of some collective mania. His vision has its roots in medieval condemnations of worldly pleasure, but its direct and horrified expression is peculiarly Jacobean:

> Surely we are all mad people, and they
> Whom we think are, are not; we mistake those:

'Tis we are mad in sense, they but in clothes.
(III. v. 80–2)

In drama, the most exploratory form of that exploratory age, there were few assumptions so basic that they were not open to question.

Conclusion

The Music of Division

> What is our life? A play of passion,
> Our mirth the music of division;
> Our mothers' wombs the tiring houses be,
> Where we are dressed for this short comedy;
> Heaven the judicious sharp spectator is
> That sits and marks still who doth act amiss;
> Our graves that hide us from the searching sun
> Are like drawn curtains when the play is done.
> Thus march we playing to our latest rest,
> Only we die in earnest, that's no jest.

SIR Walter Raleigh's epigram on life as theatre combines grace-ful accomplishment (Castiglione's *sprezzatura* or *grazia*) with a sense that, in life's comedy, it is the actors who are deceived by the play: as in *The Spanish Tragedy* or *Women Beware Women*, they are the ones who will 'die in earnest'. The tone is at once wry and amused, yet also saddened at life's brevity, its known and predetermined boundaries. Such metaphors were suffi-ciently common, both on- and off-stage to constitute something of a cliché. In a stoic passage from the Preface to his *History of the World*, Raleigh refers to God not as 'the judicious sharp spec-tator' of a short comedy, but rather as 'the author of all our tragedies', who 'hath written out for us, and appointed us all the parts we are to play . . . Certainly there is no other account to be made of this ridiculous world than to resolve that the change of fortune on the great theatre is but as the change of garments on the less.'

Changing costumes, changing roles—such images express a sense of alienation, of watching the self from a distance which a man of Raleigh's searching and introspective habits of mind must often have experienced within the highly structured routines of military or diplomatic missions, and the equally demanding formality of court life. Raleigh had his allotted part to play within the established patterns of court ceremonial, as well as within the more difficult (because less clearly formulated) games of compliment and flirtation addressed to the Queen. His frequent use of images of life as theatre, no less than his secret marriage to Elizabeth Throckmorton, suggest that he could not subscribe wholeheartedly to his court role as Cynthia's Knight of the Ocean.

In *Renaissance Self-Fashioning*, Stephen Greenblatt pointed out that 'Theatricality, in the sense of both disguise and histrionic self-presentation, arose from conditions common to almost all Renaissance courts... The manuals of court behaviour which became popular in the sixteenth century are essentially handbooks for actors, practical guides for a society whose members were nearly always on stage.'[1] Though Raleigh was gifted with qualities of mind, body, and personality far above average, he shared his sense of acting a part with many of his contemporaries. Actors and playwrights were particularly fond of theatrical metaphors, using them to express a more general unease at the widening gap between public performance and private reservation. This might be voiced in terms of deluded vanity:

> like a strutting player, whose conceit
> Lies in his hamstring, and doth think it rich
> To hear the wooden dialogue and sound
> 'Twixt his stretch'd footing and the scaffol[d]age...
>   (*Troilus and Cressida*, I. iii. 153–6)

or of total despair:

> Life's but a walking shadow, a poor player,
> That struts and frets his hour upon the stage,
> And then is heard no more.
>   (*Macbeth*, V. v. 24–6)

or of an intense anxiety that all action is merely acting:

> What's Hecuba to him, or he to Hecuba,
> That he should weep for her? What would he do
> Had he the motive and the cue for passion
> That I have?
>
> (*Hamlet*, II. ii. 559–62)

Anne Righter, analysing Shakespeare's use of theatrical metaphors, noticed 'A sense of futility, of the vanity or folly of human ambition . . . characteristic of all meditative Elizabethan comparisons of the world to a stage. Even at their most cheerful, such descriptions manage to mock the seriousness of man's pursuits, to point out the somehow ludicrous nature of his perpetual activity.'[2] Her perception links this metaphor to displays of scepticism, disaffection, or alienation in contemporary satire, and to the closely related figure of the stage malcontent, the age's cults of melancholy, and of withdrawal from *negotium* to *otium*, from state business to leisure, from the world of public concerns to privacy and retirement. In Sonnet 30 of Sidney's *Astrophil and Stella* the poet backs away from a sequence of urgent political questions, confessing to Stella:

> I cumbered with good manners, answer do,
> But know not how, for still I think of you.

Duke Basilius enacts a more substantial withdrawal into retirement in Sidney's *Arcadia*. Conflict between an imposed public role, and older or more private loyalties was widespread. The need to justify, defend, and validate the inner life and its convictions was played out in the public events of European cultural, social, and religious history as clearly as it was within the lives of individuals.

Until the sixteenth century, society had expressed itself and its values in terms of symbols, externalizing its beliefs in the form of the many rituals that pervaded life in virtually every area of experience: religion, literature, social structure from the family to the state, were expressed as a series of finely graduated privileges and obligations, providing a stable framework in which the individual sought satisfaction in the fulfilment of allotted tasks, and those tasks defined individuals so closely that they were scarcely distinguishable from their roles. But now structural, economic, and demographic changes were dividing society along new and unfamiliar lines, so that it was increasingly being differentiated in terms of what had once been the common interests or the shared values of particular groups. While these were breaking down, religious and cultural movements developed which challenged the whole symbolic system as artificial and deceitful, a series of images valued for themselves rather than what they stood for. In future truth would be 'felt along the heart', not embodied or figured as pictures or statues, or as words or rituals that could be memorized and repeated mechanically, without the active participation that gave them meaning.

Substantial changes in how a society sees and expresses itself take place over generations rather than decades, and in this case they were accompanied by eager and sometimes frantic efforts to shore up existing systems and beliefs, creating little eddies or counter-currents against the long withdrawing tide of symbolic and sacramental modes of thought. That tide expressed itself in its most characteristic form in the Protestant Reformation, which challenged the Church's hierarchies of human power, as well as its images, its shared and routine practices, its material exchanges symbolizing spiritual acts. It replaced them with a trust in inner conviction which, in its extreme forms, rejected a great many existing authorities: the reduction of the priest's powers, Calvin's scheme of Church government by elected elders, the Quaker hope of overthrowing social distinctions by treating everyone as equals (and reviving the old-fashioned second-person pronoun 'thou')—all pointed in the same direction. Yet the Reformation itself was only one element in a wider reaction: before Luther, the Catholic reformer Erasmus had criticized the mechanical aspects of prayer and observation, without any intention of dismantling the Church's secular wing or splitting it from itself. Peter Burke has observed movements to suppress traditional rites and rituals, against popular religious drama, holiday festivities, May games, and carnivals taking place right across Europe, involving both Catholic and Protestant regimes, and perhaps the Eastern Church as well. One effect of both Reformation and Counter-Reformation in the long run was to isolate the priesthood (and, to some extent, the judiciary), in a rather different way from before, from the life-style of their parishioners.

The court was another area where hierarchy and its expression in ceremonial came under criticism. In general, the courts of Europe strengthened and consolidated themselves in the sixteenth century, and so were in better shape to cultivate courtly manners and to demonstrate their standing in displays of extravagance and magnificence, at a time when the whole concept of display was beginning to cause unease (and for the English court, some financial stress). The more splendid the court's self-presentation, the more its critics railed against privileged wealth, pride, and vanity. An uncompromising rejection of anything that could be seen as performance or pretence fuelled puritan and anti-theatrical propaganda throughout this period, inspiring the Presbyterian 'Martin Marprelate' tracts of 1588–9, with their scandalous personal attacks on the bishops for failing to be what they seemed or set up to be. The Mass was regarded as a particularly blasphemous form of 'playing to the gallery', its actors being 'these *Mar-Martins*, these stage-players, these prelates'.[3] By focusing on the gap between formal or official self-presentation and the sadder reality, the Marprelate tracts established a strategy for much of the prose satire and some of the verse that was to follow. The difference between how people like to be seen and how they are produces a rich comedy of exposure, and many would have agreed with King Lear's complaint, that 'A dog's obey'd in office' (IV. vi. 159), though the play balances this recognition against its opposite as Kent observes in Lear's countenance, 'that . . . which I would fain call master':

LEAR: What's that?
KENT: Authority.
        (I. iv. 27–30)

Shakespeare's Roman plays, in particular, explore the ways in which traditional aristocratic virtues such as martial honour, nobility, and magnificence (in the sense of conspicuous generosity or display) seemed increasingly irrelevant to a younger and more practical generation, typified by the thrifty Octavius. Yet less than a decade earlier, Spenser had celebrated those virtues, making them central to the action of his *Faerie Queene*, which dresses its Protestant sentiments in the garb of medieval romance, making it the last great poem to be written in the symbolic mode. It was left to Milton to adopt a more classical style with which to express the new inwardness. Since literature is itself a highly structured and artificial mode of representation, the full impact of the social and cultural critique of symbolism, ritual, and display could not be fully absorbed and articulated through the medium of literature itself, though a number of poems of self-questioning—Herbert's 'Jordan' poems or Marvell's 'The Coronet', for instance—reveal their authors as fully aware of the issues involved. Perhaps it is in the great puritan autobiographies, works such as Bunyan's *Grace Abounding* (1666), that this opposition between false fiction and the heart's truth is felt at its most intense.

Inevitably, there was a reactionary tendency to shore up older values and systems of belief, or to promote alternative emblematic systems, such as classical iconography or schemes of mystic Hermetic correspondences that conflicted less directly with current forms of iconoclasm. Drama, which opened with a fanfare and concluded with a jig, and which had originated in ritual exchanges between choir and congregation in church and still included many traditional routines, was very much the product of a symbolic and ritualized way of thinking. Yet the variety of devices it employed to remind its audience of its artifice was designed to draw attention to, and thus perhaps to neutralize or draw the fire of its critics, while the communal rituals so often enacted in revenge tragedy in the form of masques, plays, banquets, or duels, are often interrupted by private acts of self-authentication, denunciations of 'court holy-water', of lying words and empty gestures. Such interventions, sometimes in the form of murders, were at once directed against the particular rite being performed, and the more

general hypocrisy of the decadent state that concealed its corruption beneath the golden tissue of ceremonial. The need to
discover or recover the self or the inner life beneath the desen-
sitizing habits of convention is everywhere in evidence, from
Martin Luther's announcement to the Diet of Worms, 'Here I
stand; I cannot do otherwise', through Montaigne's insistence on
his own inconsistency ('Of Repentance', *Essays*, p. 611), to the
Shakespearean hero's search for himself: 'Who is it that can tell
me who I am?' (*King Lear*, I. iv. 230). There are many similar
gestures in contemporary writing: Sidney's deliberate rejection
of fashionable poetics in his *Astrophil and Stella* is caught up
by Shakespeare and Donne, becoming a familiar feature of
seventeenth-century verse. Here certain expectations are
aroused, only to be baffled as the poet slips into some more
personal and individual variation on a theme.

In Sidney's sonnets, conventional tropes of idealization are
interrupted by the crude force of physical passion:

> So while thy beauty draws the heart to love,
> As fast thy virtue bends that love to good:
> 'But ah,' Desire still cries, 'give me some food.'
>
> (Sonnet 71)

Shakespeare's sonnets take divided feelings a stage further,
occasionally using their final couplets to offer a verbal resolution that merely exposes the inadequacy of language to resolve
human suffering:

> But here's the joy, my friend and I are one;
> Sweet flattery! then she loves but me alone.
>
> (Sonnet 42)

or

> Therefore I lie with her, and she with me,
> And in our faults by lies we flattered be.
>
> (Sonnet 138)

The couplets' failure to resolve the problems posed by the rest
of these two sonnets transforms them into silent cries of anguish.
In both, the reference to flattery, associated with self-deception,

leaves the poet (and consequently the reader) painfully unde-
ceived. The tidy conclusion tacked on to the end draws attention
to the absence of inner concord, as it must often have done for
queasy consciences, reacting against one or other of the public
ceremonies of the age.

Critics, recognizing these depths of expression and feeling, and
the contesting kinds of consciousness embedded in the single
unit of the couplet, sought explanations for their fullness of
meaning. In 1921 T. S. Eliot proposed that a 'dissociation of sensibility' occurring in the seventeenth century had broken up previously syncretic habits of mind.[4] While his account has been
repudiated often and in detail, there is a sense in which Renaissance English literature articulated ideas and experience with a
fullness and intensity that is neither the encyclopaedic or comprehensive fullness of medieval literature, nor the relaxed and
felicitous treatment of *concordia discors*, the harmonious confusion, to be found in Augustan literature,

> Where order in variety we see,
> And where, though all things differ, all agree.
> (Pope, *Windsor-Forest*, ll. 15–16)

Opposing visions are inextricably intertwined: for Sidney,
sexual desire is ultimately inseparable from Neoplatonic admiration, just as Othello's high-minded idealism is implicated in his
worst suspicions, and Hamlet's sense of something rotten in the
state is scarcely distinguishable from his own self-doubt. Jonson
never entirely separated his classical and ethical concerns from
a sharp-eyed observation of what went on in London's booths
and alley-ways, and Donne could not isolate the insubstantiality
of love from his recognition of its self-interest, its source in the
body's involuntary demands (extending Sidney's debate). The
ability to retain opposing points of view in a volatile synthesis,
the refusal to ignore contrary evidence or to reject refutations
of their strongest convictions, is a source of great power for all
these writers. Perhaps habits of intellectual analysis are fostered
by the experience of growing up in a society whose deepest
values and ways of understanding have been called in question:

the result is a literature that offers exceptional insights into the conflicted and provisional nature of human life and culture:

> but man, proud man,
> Dress'd in a little brief authority,
> Most ignorant of what he's most assur'd
> (His glassy essence), like an angry ape
> Plays such fantastic tricks before high heaven
> As make makes the angels weep . . .
>
>   (*Measure for Measure*, II. ii. 118–23)

Chronology

Normally, dates given for books are those of first publication and for plays, those of first performances and so are often approximate.

1509	Accession of Henry VIII.
1515	Erasmus, *In Praise of Folly*.
1516	Sir Thomas More, *Utopia*.
1517–21	Lutheran Reformation begins in Germany.
1525	Tyndale translates the *New Testament*.
1531	Elyot, *The Boke named the Governour*.
1532	Henry VIII divorces Catherine of Aragon.
1533	Henry VIII excommunicated, marries Anne Boleyn; birth of Elizabeth I.
1534	Acts of Succession and Supremacy mark formal breach between England and Rome; Anabaptists take control of Munster.
1535	Execution of More and Fisher.
1536	Calvin's *Institutes* (first Latin version).
1536–9	Dissolution of monasteries.
1542–7	Henry VIII dissipates wealth taken from the Church on campaigns in Scotland and France.
1543	Publication of Copernicus's *De Revolutionibus Orbium Coelestium*.
1545	Council of Trent begins reform of Roman Catholic Church (till 1563). John Bale, *The Image of Both Churches*.
1547	Death of Henry VIII; accession of Edward VI. Period of radical Protestantism begins in English Church.
1549	First Protestant Prayer Book (mainly by Cranmer).
1552	Second Prayer Book. Birth of Spenser.
1553	Death of Edward VI; accession of Mary Tudor. Catholicism re-established in England; Protestants flee to Geneva and Zurich. Stevenson (?), *Gammer Gurton's Needle*. Hakluyt born.
1554	Mary marries Philip of Spain. Births of Lyly, Hooker, Raleigh, and Sidney.
1555	Burning of Latimer and Ridley. Peace of Augsburg accepts

Protestant domination of Germany by allowing individual rulers self-determination.

1556   Burning of Cranmer.

1557   *Tottel's Miscellany* (reprinted poems by Wyatt and Surrey).

1558   Death of Mary; accession of Elizabeth I.

1559   Acts of Uniformity and Supremacy (Elizabethan Church settlement). Book of Common Prayer.

1560   Geneva Bible.

1561   Preston, *Cambises*. Awdeley, *Fraternity of Vagabonds*; Castiglione, *The Courtyer* (trans. Sir Thomas Hoby); Francis Bacon born.

1562   French Wars of Religion begin; English troops sent to help Protestants, but withdrawn the following year. Hawkins begins slave trade.

1563   Thirty-Nine Articles of Anglican church. Foxe, *Acts and Monuments* ('Book of Martyrs'). John Bale dies.

1564   Birth of Shakespeare and Marlowe.

1566   Gascoigne, *Supposes*.

1567   First revolt of the Netherlands, suppressed by Spanish troops under Duke of Alva. English (Catholic) College founded at Douai. Red Lion playhouse built. Harman, *Caveat for Common Cursetors*. Birth of Thomas Nashe, Thomas Campion.

1568   The Bishops' Bible. Mary Queen of Scots flees to England. Fulwell, *Like Will to Like*. Roger Ascham dies.

1569   Revolt of northern Earls suppressed.

1570   The Pope excommunicates Elizabeth, freeing her subjects from allegiance. Ascham, *The Schoolmaster* (posthumous). Birth of Thomas Middleton, Thomas Dekker.

1571   Birth of Johannes Kepler.

1572   St Bartholomew's Eve massacre of leading French Protestants in Paris. Dutch revolt begins when Sea Beggars seize Brill and Flushing. Statute for Punishment of Vagrants and Relief of Poor. Births of Donne and Jonson.

1576   Sack of Antwerp by unpaid Spanish troops, followed by collapse of Spanish control throughout Netherlands. Statute provides 'outdoor relief' (work) for poor. Missionary priests from Douai arrive in England. Frobisher's first voyage. Burbage's Theatre built.

1577   Drake begins voyage around world (till 1580). The Curtain

Theatre built. Holinshed's *Chronicles* (including Harrison's *Description of England*).

1578   Sidney, *The Lady of May*; Lyly, *Euphues: the Anatomy of Wit.*

1579   Prince of Parma begins reconquest of southern Netherlands for Spain. Jesuit mission to England begins. Spenser, *Shepheardes Calender*; North's translation of Plutarch's *Lives.*

1580   Spenser goes to Ireland as secretary to Lord Arthur Grey; Smerwick Massacre. Lyly, *Euphues and his England*; Montaigne, *Essais*, vols. i–ii.

1581   Recusancy laws against Catholic laity reinforced. Execution of Edmund Campion. Peele, *The Arraignment of Paris*; Mulcaster, *Positions.*

1582   Lord Arthur Grey returns in disgrace. All seminarists and Jesuits declared to be traitors. Raleigh becomes favourite of Elizabeth I. Thomas Bentley (ed.), *The Monument of Matrones*; Lyly, *Campaspe* and *Sappho and Phao*; Sidney writing *Defence of Poetry* and *Astrophil and Stella.*

1583   The Queen's Men established. Gilbert's last voyage.

1584   Assassination of William of Orange. Spanish ambassador Mendoza expelled from England. Puritan campaign for further reform of Church reaches its peak, but is frustrated by Elizabeth's opposition.

1585   Leicester's expedition to the Netherlands inaugurates state of undeclared war with Spain. First Roanoke plantation. Lyly, *Gallathea.*

1586   Babington Plot; trial of Mary Queen of Scots. Sidney killed fighting Spanish at Zutphen. Webbe, *Discourse of English Poetrie.*

1587   Pope proclaims crusade against England. Drake's attack on Cadiz. Execution of Mary Queen of Scots. Raleigh's (second) Roanoke plantation. Rose Theatre built. Kyd, *The Spanish Tragedy*; Marlowe, *1 Tamburlaine.*

1588   Defeat of Spanish Armada. First Marprelate Tracts. Lyly, *Endymion*; Marlowe, *2 Tamburlaine*; Younge, *Musica Transalpina*; Montaigne, *Essais*, vol. iii.

1589   Catholic League takes over much of France; King Henri III assassinated; Henri of Navarre becomes Henri IV, and Elizabeth supports his efforts to reconquer France. Raleigh visits Spenser in Ireland and returns with him to court. Greene, *Friar Bacon and Friar Bungay*; Marlowe, *The Jew of*

Malta; Peele, *The Battle of Alcazar*; main Marprelate Tracts; Hakluyt, *Principal Navigations*; Puttenham, *The Arte of English Poesie*.

1590   Campaign against leading puritan ministers, under direction of Whitgift and Bancroft. Greene, *George a Greene, the Pinner of Wakefield*; Peele, *The Old Wives' Tale*; Shakespeare, *1* and *2 Henry VI*; Mary Herbert, *The Tragedie of Antonie*; Sidney, *Arcadia* (published posthumously); Spenser, *Faerie Queene*, Books I–III; Watson, *First Sett of Italian Madrigalls Englished*.

1591   Anon., *Arden of Faversham*; Peele, *Descensus Astraea*; Shakespeare, *3 Henry VI*, *King John*; Sir Henry Savile's translation of Tacitus' *Histories*; Sidney, *Astrophil and Stella*; Spenser, *Complaints*. Entertainment for Elizabeth at Elvetham.

1592   Plague in London; playhouses closed for two years. Raleigh's secret marriage to Elizabeth Throckmorton leads to his disgrace. Mary Herbert, *In Praise of Astraea*; Marlowe, *Dr Faustus*, *Edward II*; Shakespeare, *The Comedy of Errors*, *Richard III*, *The Taming of the Shrew*; Nashe, *Summer's Last Will and Testament*, *Pierce Penniless*. Henslowe's account book begins. Montaigne dies. Greene dies.

1593   Plague continues. Shakespeare, *Two Gentlemen of Verona*, *Venus and Adonis*; Hooker, *Laws of Ecclesiastical Polity*, I–IV; Nashe, *Christ's Tears over Jerusalem*. Death of Marlowe.

1594   First of four successive years of bad harvests. Henri IV crowned in Paris. Spenser marries Elizabeth Boyle. Shakespeare, *Titus Andronicus*, *The Rape of Lucrece*; Nashe, *The Unfortunate Traveller*.

1595   Rising of the Earl of Tyrone. Execution of Robert Southwell. Raleigh's first voyage to Guyana. Swan built. Shakespeare, *Love's Labour's Lost, Richard II*; Munday, *et al. Sir Thomas More*; Sidney, *Defence of Poetry*; Spenser, *Amoretti, Epithalamion, Colin Clout's Come Home Againe*. Kyd dies.

1596   Worst harvest of century. Shakespeare, *A Midsummer Night's Dream, Romeo and Juliet*, and *The Merchant of Venice*; Sir John Davies, *Orchestra*; Spenser, *The Faerie Queene*, I–VI, *Prothalamion, Fowre Hymns*; Raleigh, *Discovery of Guyana*.

1597   Statutes for the relief of the poor and the punishment of vagrants. Shakespeare, *1* and *2 Henry IV*, *The Merry Wives of Windsor*. Nashe imprisoned for *The Isle of Dogs*. Bacon, *Essays*; Dowland, *First Book of Songs*. Peele dies.

1598   Edict of Nantes ends Wars of Religion in France, with partial toleration guaranteed to Protestants. Death of Burghley. Rising in Munster; Spenser flees to London. Shakespeare, *Much Ado About Nothing*; Jonson, *Every Man In His Humour*; Chapman's translation of Homer's *Iliad*; Marlowe's *Hero and Leander* (completed by Chapman); Marston, *The Metamorphosis of Pygmalion's Image, with Certain Satires* and *The Scourge of Villainie* (also verse satires by Guilpin and Hall).

1599   Essex, in command in Ireland, makes truce with Tyrone. Episcopal action against satire and erotic verse. Globe Theatre opens. Shakespeare, *As You Like It*, *Henry V*, *Julius Caesar*; Dekker, *The Shoemaker's Holiday* and *Old Fortunatus*; Jonson, *Every Man Out of His Humour*; Marston, *Histriomastix* and *Antonio and Mellida*. Death of Spenser.

1600   Mountjoy sent to Ireland. East India Company founded. Fortune Theatre built. Jonson, *Cynthia's Revels*; Marston, *Antonio's Revenge*; Anon., *The Return from Parnassus*; *England's Helicon*; Dowland, *Second Book of Songs*. Death of Hooker.

1601   Rebellion and execution of Earl of Essex. Mountjoy defeats the Irish at Kinsale. Statute consolidates Elizabethan Poor Law. Donne, secretly married, loses his position. Shakespeare, *Hamlet*, *Twelfth Night*; Morley, *The Triumphs of Oriana*. Nashe dies.

1602   Shakespeare, *Troilus and Cressida*; Campion, *The Art of English Poesie*.

1603   Death of Elizabeth; accession of James I. Surrender of Tyrone. Raleigh found guilty of high treason and imprisoned in Tower. Shakespeare, *All's Well That Ends Well*; Middleton, *The Family of Love*; Jonson, *Sejanus*; Heywood, *A Woman Killed with Kindness*; Dekker, *The Wonderful Year*; Dowland, *Third Book of Songs*; Montaigne, *Essays* (trans. Florio).

1604   Peace with Spain. Hampton Court Conference fails to satisfy puritan demands, but James adopts a moderate policy in ecclesiastical appointments. Elizabeth Cary, *The Tragedie of Mariam*; Shakespeare, *Measure for Measure* and *Othello*; Chapman, *Bussy D'Ambois*; Marston, *The Malcontent*.

1605   Discovery of the Gunpowder Plot. Jonson, *The Masque of Blackness*; co-author, with Chapman and Marston, of *Eastward Ho!*; Shakespeare, *King Lear*; Marston, *The Dutch Courtezan, Sophonisba*; Bacon, *The Advancement of Learning*.

1606   Jonson, *Hymenaei* and *Volpone*; Shakespeare, *Macbeth*; Middleton, *A Mad World, My Masters*; *Michaelmas Term*; *The Revenger's Tragedy*, and (?) *A Yorkshire Tragedy*.

1607   The flight of the Earls of Tyrone and Tyrconnell. First settlement at Jamestown, Virginia. Shakespeare, *Antony and Cleopatra* and *Timon of Athens*; Beaumont and Fletcher, *The Knight of the Burning Pestle*.

1608   The plantation of Ulster begins. The telescope is invented. Shakespeare, *Coriolanus* and *Pericles*; Fletcher, *The Faithful Shepherdess*; Dekker, *Lanthorne and Candle-light*. Birth of Milton.

1609   Twelve-year truce between Spain and the Netherlands. Jonson, *The Masque of Queens* and *Epicoene*; Shakespeare, *Cymbeline* and *The Sonnets*.

1610   Parliament and King fail to agree on Salisbury's 'Great Contract' (his plan for financial reform). Henry IV assassinated. Jonson, *Prince Henry's Barriers* and *The Alchemist*; Shakespeare, *The Winter's Tale*; Beaumont and Fletcher, *The Maid's Tragedy*; Campion, *Two Bookes of Ayres*; Donne, *Pseudo-Martyr*.

1611   Authorized Version of the Bible. Jonson, *Oberon, the Fairy Prince* and *Catiline his Conspiracy*; Shakespeare, *The Tempest*; Middleton, *The Second Maiden's Tragedy*, and, with Dekker, *The Roaring Girl*; Tourneur, *The Atheist's Tragedy*; Aemilia Lanyer, *Salve Deus Rex Judaeorum*; Donne, *Anatomy of the World* (The First Anniversary).

1612   Death of Prince Henry. Webster, *The White Devil*; Heywood, *Apology for Actors*; Campion, *Third and Fourth Booke of Ayres*; Donne, *Second Anniversary*.

1613   Princess Elizabeth marries Frederick, Elector Palatine. Countess of Essex obtains divorce and marries James's favourite, the Earl of Somerset. Sir Thomas Overbury dies in the Tower. Globe Theatre burns down. Jonson, *The Irish Masque*; Chapman, *Masque of the Middle Temple and Lincoln's Inn*; Shakespeare and Fletcher, *Two Noble Kinsmen*, *Henry VIII*; Middleton, *A Chaste Maid in Cheapside.*

1614   Jonson, *Bartholomew Fair*; Webster, *The Duchess of Malfi*; Chapman's translation of Homer's *Odyssey*; Raleigh, *History of the World.*

1615   Overbury murder scandal: trial of lesser figures. Donne ordained. Jonson, *The Golden Age Restored*; Swetnam, *The Arraignement of Lewd, Idle, Froward . . . Women.*

1616   Trial and conviction of Earl and Countess of Somerset. Advancement of George Villiers (later Duke of Buckingham). Jonson, *The Devil is an Ass*; publishes his *Works* in folio. Deaths of Shakespeare, Beaumont, Hakluyt.

1617   Raleigh sails on last voyage to Guyana. Jonson, *Lovers Made Men* and *The Vision of Delight*; Esther Sowernam, *Esther hath hanged Haman*; Constantia Munda, *The Worming of a mad Dog.*

1618   Bohemian Revolt begins Thirty Years War. Synod of Dort (apparent success for strict Calvinists against Arminians in the Netherlands). Execution of Raleigh. Bacon becomes Lord Chancellor. Jonson, *Pleasure Reconciled to Virtue*; visits William Drummond in Scotland; Middleton, *Hengist, King of Kent*; Anon., *Swetnam the Woman-Hater Arraigned by Women.*

1619   The Elector Palatine (Frederick, son-in-law of James) accepts the crown of Bohemia. Harvey discovers the circulation of blood.

1620   Battle of the White Mountain; the Elector loses the Palatinate and is driven from Bohemia. Voyage of *The Mayflower* to New England. Serious trade depression over whole decade causes much unemployment and misery, mainly among cloth-workers. Bacon, *Novum Organum*. Death of Thomas Campion.

1621   Parliament meets to debate international crisis and attacks monopolies, impeaching Sir Giles Mompesson; also Francis Bacon, for taking bribes. Donne becomes Dean of St Paul's. Jonson, *The Gypsies Metamorphosed*; Fletcher, *The Island*

Princess; Middleton, *Women Beware Women*; Lady Mary
Wroth, *The Countess of Montgomery's Urania*; Robert
Burton, *The Anatomy of Melancholy*.

1622   King James negotiates with Spain for marriage between
Prince Charles and the Infanta, with the return of the Palati-
nate to Frederick. Fletcher and Massinger, *The Sea Voyage*;
Middleton and Rowley, *The Changeling*.

1623   Abortive expedition to Madrid by Charles and Buckingham;
marriage negotiations with Spain abandoned. Massacre of
English merchants at Amboina. Shakespeare, First Folio.

1624   Charles and Buckingham lead war party against Spain.
Jonson, *Neptune's Triumph for the Return of Albion*; Middle-
ton, *A Game at Chess*; Donne, *Devotions upon Emergent
Occasions*.

1625   Death of James I; accession of Charles I, who marries
Henrietta Maria, sister of Louis XIII of France. War with
Spain. Plague in London. Massinger, *A New Way to Pay Old
Debts*. Deaths of Fletcher, Webster.

1626   Buckingham impeached. Jonson, *The Staple of News*. Death
of Bacon.

1627   Buckingham fails to intervene on behalf of Huguenots at La
Rochelle. Death of Middleton.

1628   Assassination of Buckingham. Surrender of La Rochelle to
Louis XIII. Parliament passes Petition of Right. Laud
becomes Bishop of London. Earle, *Microcosmographie*.
Fulke Greville murdered.

1629   Parliament dissolved; Sir John Eliot and other leaders imprisoned. Personal rule of Charles I begins. Peace with France.
Jonson, *The New Inn*.

1630   Peace with Spain. Ford, *The Broken Heart*. Kepler dies.

1631   Death of Donne.

1632   Ford, *'Tis Pity She's a Whore*.

1633   Laud becomes Archbishop of Canterbury. Donne, *Poems*
(posthumous); Herbert, *The Temple*. Death of Herbert.

1634   Milton, *Comus*.

1637   Trials of John Hampden for non-payment of Ship Money and
Prynne for criticism of Laud. Death of Jonson.

1638   Milton, *Lycidas*.

1639   War with Scots (First Bishops' War).

1640   Short Parliament. Scots defeat royal forces (Second Bishops' War). Long Parliament meets.

1642   Charles and his family flee from London, and Civil War begins. Closing of the theatres. Death of Galileo. Birth of Newton.

References

In general, I have tried to keep references short and on the page where they appear. Information about the sources of ideas or arguments is provided in the section on 'Further Reading' below. All quotations given in the text have been modernized, and I have tried to locate them by providing line or section references: this is comparatively straightforward in the case of poetry, where line numbering seldom varies from one edition to another, but more complicated in the case of plays, especially if they include prose sequences, and most complicated of all in the case of prose. I have therefore identified dramatic quotations by act, scene, and line references in the text, and have listed below the editions of plays that I have cited. Where dates for the performance of plays are provided in the text (often approximate), they have been taken from Alfred Harbage's *Annals of English Drama, 975–1700*, third edition, revised by S. S. Wagonheim (Routledge, 1989).

The list of dramatic texts that I have cited is followed by a further alphabetical list of prose writers, giving details of the texts cited in this book. Finally, a substantial number of quotations remain which have not been taken from any of the texts listed here, and therefore have no source indication on the page: these are listed beneath the list of editions of drama and prose texts used, under their chapter and page numbers.

DRAMATIC TEXTS

William Shakespeare
The Riverside Shakespeare, ed. G. Blakemore Evans (Houghton Mifflin: Boston, 1974).

Ben Jonson
References to plays are from G. A. Wilkes's *Complete Plays* in 4 vols. (Oxford University Press, 1981); for the masques, I have used vol. 7 of Herford and Simpson's *Ben Jonson* (Oxford University Press, 1941).

John Marston
The Selected Plays of John Marston, eds. MacD. P. Jackson and Michael Neill (Cambridge University Press, 1986).

Anonymous
Pilgrimage to Parnassus: The Three Parnassus Plays, ed. J. B. Leishmann (Nicholson and Watson, 1949).

In the case of plays listed below, I have used the Revels editions, currently published by Manchester University Press, where these exist:

Francis Beaumont
The Maid's Tragedy, with John Fletcher, ed. T. W. Craik (1988); *The Knight of the Burning Pestle*, ed. Sheldon P. Zitner (1984).

George Chapman
Bussy D'Ambois, ed. Nicholas Brooke (1964).

John Ford
The Broken Heart, ed. T. J. B. Spencer (1980).

Thomas Kyd
The Spanish Tragedy, ed. Philip Edwards (1959).

Christopher Marlowe
Tamburlaine the Great, ed. J. S. Cunningham (1981); *The Jew of Malta*, ed. N. W. Bawcutt (1978); *Doctor Faustus*, eds. David Bevington and Eric Rasmussen (1993); *Edward II*, ed. Charles R. Forker (1994).

Thomas Middleton
The Revenger's Tragedy (as by Tourneur), ed. R. A. Foakes (1966); *The Changeling*, with William Rowley, ed. N. W. Bawcutt (1979); *Women Beware Women*, ed. J. R. Mulryne (1975); *Michaelmas Term*, ed. Richard Levin (Regents Renaissance: University of Nebraska Press, 1966).

Cyril Tourneur
The Atheist's Tragedy, ed. Irving Ribner (1964).

John Webster
The White Devil, ed. John Russell Brown (1960); *The Duchess of Malfi*, ed. John Russell Brown (1964).

PROSE TEXTS

Frances Bacon
The Essays, ed. John Pitcher (Penguin Books, 1985).

Michel de Montaigne
The Complete Essays of Montaigne, trans. Donald M. Frame (Stanford University Press, 1943, 1958).

Thomas Nashe
The Works of Thomas Nashe, ed. R. B. McKerrow (Basil Blackwell, Oxford, 1966).

Philip Sidney
A Defence of Poetry, reprinted in *Miscellaneous Prose of Sir Philip Sidney*, ed. Katherine Duncan-Jones and Jan van Dorsten (Oxford University Press, 1973).

FURTHER REFERENCES

Preface
1. Michael Baxendall, 'Art and Society and the Bouger Principle', *Representations*, 12 (1985), 40–1, cited by Stephen Greenblatt, 'Towards a Poetics of Culture', *Learning to Curse: Essays in Early Modern Culture* (Routledge, 1990), p. 158.
2. Full details of these books are given in Further Reading.
3. W. H. Auden, 'In Memory of W. B. Yeats'.
4. Mervyn James, 'At a Crossroads of the Political Culture: The Essex Revolt, 1601', in *Society, Politics and Culture: Studies in Early Modern England* (Cambridge University Press, 1986), 453 (also cited in ch. 8).
5. Stephen Greenblatt, 'Invisible Bullets', *Shakespearean Negotiations: The Circulation of Social Energy in Renaissance England* (University of California Press, 1988), 65.
6. Louis Montrose, *The Purpose of Playing: Shakespeare and the Cultural Politics of the Elizabethan Theatre* (University of Chicago Press, 1996), 5.
7. Pierre Bourdieu, *In Other Words: Essays Towards a Reflexive Sociology*, trans. Matthew Adamson (Cambridge: Polity Press, 1990), 147 (cited by Randal Johnson in his introduction to Bourdieu, *The*

Field of Cultural Production: Essays on Art and Literature (Oxford: Polity Press, 1993), 9.

Chapter 1

1. Dedicatory letter to *Lanthorne and Candle-light* (1608), reprinted in A. V. Judges, *The Elizabethan Underworld: A Collection of Tudor and Early Stuart Tracts and Ballads* (Routledge, 1930), 313–14.

Chapter 2

1. 'A Most Horrible and Detestable Murder, Committed by a Bloody Minded man upon His Own Wife' (London, 1595), cited by Peter Lake, 'Deeds against Nature: Cheap Print, Protestantism and Murder in Early Seventeenth-Century England', in Kevin Sharpe and Peter Lake (eds.), *Culture and Politics in Early Stuart England* (Macmillan, 1994), 263.
2. Lambarde's charge at the commission for almshouses, 17 Jan. 1594, C. Read (ed.), *William Lambarde and Local Government* (Folger Shakespeare Library, Ithaca, 1962), 182.
3. *The Wonderful Year*, reprinted in F. P. Wilson (ed.), *Dekker's Plague Pamphlets* (Oxford University Press, 1925), 28.
4. Bastard's epigram on enclosure (Book III, 22), repr. in R. H. Tawney and Eileen Power (eds.), *Tudor Economic Documents* (Longmans Green, 1924), iii. 80.
5. James Spedding (ed.), *The Letters and the Life of Francis Bacon* (Longmans Green, 1890), ii. 82.
6. 'A Most Horrible and Detestable Murder . . .', 267–8.
7. William Harrison, *The Description of England, 1587*, ed. F. J. Furnivall (The New Shakespeare Society: N. Trübner, 1877), Part 1. The Second Book, ch. x, p. 213.
8. Edward Hext's letter, *Tudor Economic Documents*, ii. 341.
9. *The Defence of Cony-Catching*, reprinted in Gamini Salgado (ed.), *Cony-Catchers and Bawdy Baskets* (Penguin Books, 1972), 342–3.
10. Ibid. 361.

Chapter 3

1. James I's first speech to Parliament, C. H. McIlwain (ed.), *The Political Works of James I* (Harvard University Press, 1918), 272.
2. Sir Robert Filmer, *Patriarcha and other Political Works*, ed. Peter Laslett (Basil Blackwell, Oxford, 1949), 57, cited by S. D. Amussen, 'Gender, Family and the Social Order, 1560–1725', in Anthony

Fletcher and John Stevenson (eds.), *Order and Disorder in Early Modern England* (Cambridge University Press, 1985), 197.

3. William Camden, *The History of the Most Renowned and Victorious Princess Elizabeth Late Queen of England*, ed. Wallace T. Mac-Caffrey (University of Chicago Press, 1970), 29.

4. William Gouge, *Domesticall Duties* (1622), 224; William Whateley, *A Bride Bush* (1623), 25, both cited by Anthony Fletcher, 'The Protestant Idea of Marriage in Early Modern England', in Anthony Fletcher and Peter Roberts (eds.), *Religion, Culture and Society in Early Modern Britain* (Cambridge University Press, 1994), 178.

5. Preface to Gouge, *Domesticall Duties*, cited by Anthony Fletcher, ibid. 167.

6. T. E., *The Lawes Resolutions of Womens Rights* (1632), 126.

7. Cited by Roy Strong, *The Elizabethan Image: Painting in England 1540–1620* (The Tate Gallery, 1969), 24 (though the picture referred to is misidentified).

8. L. Bradner and C. A. Lynch, *The Latin Epigrams of Sir Thomas More* (University of Chicago Press, 1953), cited by Lawrence Stone, *The Family, Sex and Marriage in England 1500–1800* (Weidenfeld & Nicolson, 1977), 167.

9. Roger Ascham, *The Schoolmaster*, ed. L. V. Ryan (Folger Shakespeare Library: Cornell University Press, 1967), 36.

10. The question famously asked by Joan Kelly in an essay with this title, reprinted in her *Women, History and Theory* (University of Chicago Press, 1984).

11. Erasmus, *The Institution of Christian Marriage* (1526), cited by Constance Jordan, *Renaissance Feminism* (Cornell University Press, 1990), 62 (see also p. 121 for Luther reference).

12. From Edward Gosynhyll, *The School House of Women* (1560) (Sig. Bii), cited by Linda Woodbridge, *Women and the English Renaissance* (Harvester, Sussex, 1984), 27.

13. Sir Anthony Fitzherbert, *Boke of Husbandry* (1523), cited by Alice Clark, *Working Life of Women in the Seventeenth Century* (Routledge, 1919), 49.

14. Rachel Speght, *A Muzzle for Melastomus*, reprinted in Simon Shepherd (ed.), *The Women's Sharp Revenge* (Fourth Estate, 1985), 74.

15. Ester Sowernam, *Ester hath hang'd Haman*, ibid. 112.

16. Constantia Munda, *The Worming of a Mad Dog*, ibid. 146–7.

Chapter 4

1. Thomas Harriot's *A Briefe and True Report*, reprinted in Richard Hakluyt, *The Principal Navigations, Voyages, Traffics and Discoveries of the English Nation* (1600, reprinted Glasgow, James Maclehose, 1904), viii. 375, 376.

2. From De Bry's 1590 edition of Harriot's *Briefe and True Report*, cited by Stephen Greenblatt in a footnote to 'Invisible Bullets', *Shakespearean Negotiations* (Oxford University Press, 1988), 170, n. 19.

3. Peter Martyr, *De novo Orbe, or The Historie of the West Indies*, trans. Richard Eden and Michael Lok (London, 1612), 15ʳ, quote by Harry Levin, *The Myth of the Golden Age* (Oxford University Press, 1969), 61–2.

4. Richard Hakluyt's dedicatory letter to Walsingham, *Principle Navigations*, vol. i, p. xviii.

5. George Best's Discourse, ibid. vii. 282–3.

6. Edward Haye's account of Gilbert's Voyage (1583), ibid. viii. 60, 36.

7. Hakluyt's account of John Hawkins's first voyage to the West Indies (1562), ibid. x. 7.

8. *The Discovery of Guiana*, ibid. x. 404.

9. Ibid. x. 362.

10. Ibid. x. 357.

11. Chapman's 'Masque of the Middle Temple and Lincoln's Inn', in *The Plays of George Chapman: The Comedies*, ed. T. M. Parrott (Russell and Russell, 1961), 439.

12. Campion's 'Somerset Wedding Masque', in *The Works of Thomas Campion*, ed. Walter R. Davis (Faber & Faber, 1969), 272. Beaumont's 'Masque of Flowers', ed. E. A. J. Honigmann, in Sybil Rosenfeld (ed.), *A Book of Masques* (Cambridge University Press, 1967), 164.

13. Proclamations of 1596 and 1601, cited by Peter Fryer, *Staying Power: The History of Black People in Britain* (Pluto Press, 1984), 10–12.

14. Vincent to Benson, 10 Jan. 1605, C. H. Herford and P. and E. Simpson (eds.), *Ben Jonson* (Oxford University Press, 1950), x. 449; cited by Kim F. Hall, *Things of Darkness: Economies of Race and Gender in Early Modern England* (Cornell University Press, 1995), 129.

15. Sir Thomas Overbury, *New and Choice Characters* (1615), reprinted

in Lawrence Manley (ed.), *London in the Age of Shakepeare: An Anthology* (Croom Helm, 1986), 321.

16. Smith to Cecil, 1565, in Mary Dewar, *Sir Thomas Smith: A Tudor Intellectual in Office* (Athlone Press, 1964), 157, quoted by Joyce Youings, *Sixteenth-Century England* (Penguin Books, 1984), 246.

17. Edmund Spenser, *A View of the Present State of Ireland*, ed. W. L. Renwick (Eric Partridge, Scholartis Press, 1934), 135.

18. Chamberlain to Dudley Carleton, 5 Jan. 1614, *Ben Jonson*, x. 541, cited by David Lindley, 'Embarrassing Ben: the Masques for Frances Howard', in A. F. Kinney and D. S. Collins (eds.), *Renaissance Historicism: Selections from English Literary Renaissance* (University of Massachusetts Press, 1987), 260.

Chapter 5

1. Keith Thomas, *Religion and the Decline of Magic* (1971; Penguin Books, 1973), 6–8.

2. Pico della Mirandola's *Oration* is reprinted in Stevie Davies (ed.), *Renaissance Views of Man* (Manchester University Press, 1978), 67.

3. Quoted by Arthur Koestler, *The Sleepwalkers: A History of Man's Changing Vision of the Universe* (Hutchinson, 1959), 243.

4. Ibid. 193.

5. Quoted by Jonathan Sawday, 'The Fate of Marsyas: Dissecting the Renaissance Body', in Lucy Gent and Nigel Llewellyn (eds.), *Renaissance Bodies* (Reaktion Books, 1990), 129.

6. The 65th aphorism of first book of the *Novum Organum*, Arthur Johnston (ed.), *Francis Bacon* (Batsford, 1965), 95–6.

Chapter 6

1. 'The Religious World of Roger Martyn', Christopher Haigh, *English Reformations* (Oxford University Press, 1993), 1.

2. Ibid. 2; Barry Reay, 'Popular Religion' in Reay (ed.), *Popular Culture in Seventeenth-Century England* (1985; Routledge, 1988), 110.

3. A. G. Dickens, *The English Reformation* (Batsford, 1964), 190.

4. J. F. Mozley, *John Foxe and His Books* (Macmillan, 1940), 87, cited by Richard Helgerson, *Forms of Nationhood* (University of Chicago Press, 1992), 344, n. 16.

5. Ch. 54 of *Praise of Folly*, trans. Betty Radice (Penguin, 1971), 164.

6. The Fifth Rule at the end of the *Encheiridion* ('The Handbook of

the Militant Christian'), *The Essential Erasmus*, trans. John P. Dolan (New American Library, 1964), 68. The colloquy 'Concerning the Eating of Fish', also in this volume, includes criticism of superstition; on Pope Julius II, see ch. 59 of *Praise of Folly* (ibid.), p. 178.

7. This, and the details of Bishop Hooper's visitation, are cited by Keith Thomas, *Religion and the Decline of Magic*, 194.

8. Tyndale's words quoted by Foxe, *Acts and Monuments*, ed. Josiah Pratt, 8 vols. (George Seely, 1870), v. 117; Erasmus's words occur in the *Paraclesis*, his preface to his translation of the New Testament; both are cited by Stephen Greenblatt, *Renaissance Self-Fashioning from More to Shakespeare* (University of Chicago Press, 1980), 106.

9. *Euphues and his England* in *The Complete Works of John Lyly*, ed. R. Warwick Bond (Oxford University Press, 1902, 1973), ii. 210.

10. Foxe's *Acts and Monuments*, i. 5, cited by Helgerson, *Forms of Nationhood*, 263, n. 6.

11. *Theatre of God's Judgements* (London, 1597), ch. 23, p. 149, reprinted in Judith O'Neill (ed.), *Critics on Marlowe* (George Allen & Unwin, 1969), 11–12.

12. 'The Baines Note' appears as an appendix to J. B. Steane, *Marlowe: A Critical Study* (Cambridge University Press, 1970), 363–4.

13. *The First and Second Prayer-Books of King Edward the Sixth*, ed. Edgar C. S. Gloucester (J. M. Dent, 1910), 223, 230 (the First); 377, 392–3 (the Second).

14. Grindal to the Queen, Dec. 1576, *The Remains of Edmund Grindal*, ed. W. Nicholson (Parker Society, 1843), 376–90, quoted in Joel Hurstfield and Alan G. R. Smith (eds.), *Elizabethan People* (Edward Arnold, 1972), 127.

15. Christopher W. Marsh: *The Family of Love in English Society, 1550–1630* (Cambridge University Press, 1994), 205–12.

16. Bradford's 'History of Plymouth Plantation' in Perry Miller and Thomas H. Johnson (eds.), *The Puritans* (1938, revised edn., Harper Torchbooks, 1963), i. 92, 94.

17. Quoted by Tessa Watt, *Cheap Print and Popular Piety, 1560–1640* (Cambridge University Press, 1991), 123.

18. Lancelot Andrewes, *Works*, eds. J. P. Wilson and J. Bliss, 11 vols. (Oxford University Press, 1851–4), i. 204.

19. *The Works of George Herbert*, ed. F. E. Hutchinson (Oxford University Press, 1941, 1970), 234–5.

20. *Religio Medici*, Part 1, section 3, in *Sir Thomas Browne, The Major Works*, ed. C. A. Patrides (Penguin, 1977), 62.

Chapter 7

1. *The Schoolmaster*, ed. L. V. Ryan (see Ch. 3, above), 20.

2. Richard Brathwayt, *The Scholler Medley* (1614), p. 32, cited by Sir Keith Thomas in 'The Meaning of Literacy in Early Modern England', in Gerd Baumann (ed.), *The Written Word: Literacy in Transition* (Oxford University Press, 1986), 106.

3. Lawrence Stone, 'The Educational Revolution in England, 1540–1640', *Past and Present*, 28 (July 1964), 68.

4. In *The Apologye* (1533), p. 20–20ᵛ, cited by David Cressy, *Literacy and the Social Order* (Cambridge University Press, 1980), 44.

5. *The Description of England*, ed. F. J. Furnivall (1877), Second Book, ch. iii, p. 83.

6. 'The Godly Feast', *The Colloquies of Erasmus*, translated by Craig R. Thompson (University of Chicago Press, 1965), 65, 68.

7. *The Apologye*, quoted by David Cressy, *Literacy and the Social Order*, 2.

8. Weston, *The Autobiography of an Elizabethan*, trans. P. Caraman (London, 1955), 164–5, cited by Margaret Spufford, *Contrasting Communities* (Cambridge University Press, 1974), 263.

9. Bunyan, *Sighs from Hell* (2nd edn., London, 1666?), 147–8, cited by Spufford, ibid. 210.

10. Stubbes, *Anatomy of Abuses* (1583), ed. F. J. Furnivall (1877), 184–5; quoted by David Cressy, *Literacy and the Social Order*, 8.

11. Hobbes, *Behemoth or The Long Parliament*, ed. F. Tönnies (Simpkin, Marshall, 1889), repr. and introduced by Stephen Holmes (University of Chicago Press, 1990), 3.

12. Richard Mulcaster, *Positions* (Thomas Vautrollier, 1581), intro. R. H. Quick (Longmans Green, 1888), 11, cited Joan Simon, *Education and Society in Tudor England* (Cambridge University Press, 1966), 353.

13. William Camden's account of Richard Pace's preface to *De Fructu*, in *Remaines . . . Concerning Britain* (London, 1605), 220, cited by Fritz Caspari, *Humanism and the Social Order in Tudor England* (University of Chicago Press, 1954), 137.

14. Cressy, *Literacy and the Social Order*, 189.

15. *The Schoolmaster*, 6.

16. Mulcaster, *Positions*, 142.

17. Spedding (ed.), *The Letters and Life of Francis Bacon*, iv. 252–3.

Chapter 8

1. Lawrence Stone, *The Crisis of the Aristocracy, 1558–1641* (Oxford University Press, 1965), 385.

2. A. L. Rowse, *The Casebooks of Simon Forman: Sex and Society in Shakespeare's Age* (Weidenfeld, 1974), 31.

3. Conversations with Drummond of Hawthornden, in Herford and Simpson (eds.), *Ben Jonson*, i. 144.

4. *Leviathan*, ed. Michael Oakeshott (Oxford: Basil Blackwell, n.d.), 64.

5. Quoted by Margaret Mann Phillips, *Erasmus and the Northern Renaissance* (Hodder & Stoughton, 1949), 131.

6. Stephen Orgel, *The Illusion of Power: Political Theater in the English Renaissance* (University of California Press, 1975), 77.

7. Castiglione, *The Book of the Courtier*, trans. Thomas Hoby (J. M. Dent, 1928, 1974), 322.

8. Ibid. 320.

9. 'Rose-cheeked Laura' appears as an example of trochaic verse in *Observations in the Art of English Poesie* (1602), reprinted in *The Works of Thomas Campion*, ed. Walter R. Davis (Faber & Faber, 1969), 310.

10. E. H. Fellowes, *English Madrigal Verse 1588–1632*, rev. F. W. Sternfeld and D. Greer (Oxford University Press, 1967), 154–5.

11. Thomas Morley, *A Plain and Easy Introduction to Practical Music* (1597), cited by Wilfred Mellers, 'Words and Music in Elizabethan England', in Boris Ford (ed.), *The Age of Shakespeare* (Penguin Books, 1955), 391.

12. *The Book of the Courtier*, Book II, pp. 179–80.

13. Roy Strong, *The Cult of Elizabeth* (Thames & Hudson, 1977), 161–2.

14. *Arcadia*, ed. Maurice Evans (Penguin Books, 1977), Book III, 469.

15. *The Complete Works of John Lyly*, ed. R. Warwick Bond (Oxford University Press, 1902, 1973), ii. 210.

16. Cited by Mervyn James, 'At a Crossroads of the Political Culture: The Essex Revolt, 1601', in *Society, Politics and Culture: Studies in Early Modern England* (Cambridge University Press, 1986), 453.

17. 'The Song at their departure', Jean Wilson, ed., *Entertainments for Elizabeth I* (D. S. Brewer: Rowman & Littlefield, 1980), 135; Lawrence Stone, *The Crisis of the Aristocracy*, 454.

18. E. H. Miller, *The Professional Writer in Elizabethan England* (Harvard University Press, 1959), 98.

19. Sir John Harington, *Nugae Antiquae* (London, 1804), 170–1.

20. *The Book of the Courtier*, Book IV, p. 266.

21. *Utopia*, trans. Edward Surtz, SJ (Yale University Press, 1964), 51–2.

22. *Ars aulica, or the courtiers arte*, trans. Edward Blount (London, Melch. Bradwood, 1607), 172.

23. Sir Charles Cornwallis, 'A Discourse of the Most Illustrious Prince Henry, late Prince of Wales', cited by J. H. M. Salmon, 'Seneca and Tacitus in Jacobean England', in Linda Levy Peck (ed.), *The Mental World of the Jacobean Court* (Cambridge University Press, 1991).

24. Harington, *Nugae Antiquae*, i. 349–52.

25. Stone, *The Crisis of the Aristocracy*, 478.

26. A. Amos, *The Great Oyer of Poisoning* (1846), cited by Stone, ibid. 394.

27. Ibid.

28. Quoted by Alastair Bellany, ' "Raylinge Rymes and Vaunting Verse": Libellous Politics in Early Stuart England, 1603–1628' in Kevin Sharpe and Peter Lake (eds.), *Culture and Politics in Early Stuart England* (Macmillan, 1994), 288.

29. T. Birch (ed.), *The Works of Sir Walter Raleigh* (1751), vol. i, p. lxxxiv, cited by Stone, *The Crisis of the Aristocracy*, 394.

30. Jonas Barish, *Ben Jonson and the Language of Prose Comedy* (Harvard University Press, 1960), 244.

Chapter 9

1. Quoted by Andrew Gurr, *The Shakespearean Stage, 1574–1642*, 2nd edn. (Cambridge University Press, 1980), 28.

2. *Preface to Shakespeare* (1765), in *Dr Johnson on Shakespeare*, ed. W. K. Wimsatt (1960; Penguin Books, 1969), 70.

3. Thomas Platter, of a performance at the Curtain in 1599, quoted by Gurr, *The Shakespearean Stage*, 197.

4. Sir Thomas Bodley, *Reliquiae Bodleianae* (1703), 277–8, quoted by Phoebe Sheavyn, *The Literary Profession in the Elizabethan Age*, 2nd ed., rev. by J. W. Saunders (Manchester University Press, 1967), 157.

5. Reprinted in G. E. Bentley (ed.), *The Seventeenth-Century Stage: A Collection of Critical Essays* (University of Chicago Press, 1968), 15.

6. The Lord Mayor to the Lord High Treasurer, 3 Nov. 1594, in A. M.

Nagler (ed.), *A Source Book in Theatrical History* (1952; New York: Dover Publications, 1959), 114.

7. Lord Mayor to the Privy Council, 1597, ibid. 115.

8. Cited by Alfred Harbage, *Shakespeare's Audience* (Columbia University Press, 1941), 15.

9. *A Refutation* (1615), 57–8, cited in M. C. Bradbrook, *The Rise of the Common Player: A Study of Actor and Society in Shakespeare's England* (Cambridge University Press, 1962), 93.

10. *Plays Confuted* (1582), G6ᵛ, G7ʳ, ibid. 73.

11. *Apology for Actors*, in Bentley, *The Seventeenth-Century Stage*, 19.

12. E. K. Chambers, *The Elizabethan Stage* (Oxford University Press, 1923), iii. 424.

13. *Apology for Actors*, 19; 17.

14. Rowse (ed.), *The Case Books of Simon Forman* (see Ch. 8, above), 311.

15. Webbe, *A Discourse of English Poetry* (1586), in G. Gregory Smith (ed.), *Elizabethan Critical Essays* (Oxford University Press, 1904), i. 248–9.

16. Nicholas Brooke, 'Marlowe the Dramatist', John Russell Brown and Bernard Harris (eds.), *Elizabethan Theatre: Stratford-upon-Avon Studies 9* (Edward Arnold, 1966), 94.

17. Fulke Greville's *Life of Sidney*, 221, quoted by J. W. Lever, *The Tragedy of State* (Methuen, 1971), 7.

18. Preface to the translation of *Orlando Furioso*, *Elizabethan Critical Essays*, ii. 209.

19. George Puttenham, *Art of English Poesie*, ibid. ii. 35.

Conclusion

1. Stephen Greenblatt, *Renaissance Self-Fashioning: From More to Shakespeare* (University of Chicago Press, 1980), 162.

2. Anne Righter, *Shakespeare and the Idea of a Play* (Chatto & Windus, 1962), 148.

3. William Pierce, ed., *The Marprelate Tracts 1588–1589* (London, 1911), 328, quoted by Jonas Barish, *The Anti-theatrical Prejudice* (University of California Press, 1981), 162.

4. T. S. Eliot, 'The Metaphysical Poets' (1921), *Selected Essays* (Faber & Faber, 1932; 1951), 288.

Further Reading

Chapter 1

The Shepheardes Calender is discussed in ch. 3 of David Norbrook's *Poetry and Politics in the English Renaissance* (Routledge & Kegan Paul, 1984). Ch. 11 of Isabel Rivers's *Classical and Christian Ideas in English Renaissance Poetry* (George Allen & Unwin, 1979) considers theories of poetry in particular; the book as a whole illustrates the age's poetic forebears, as does Robin Sowerby's *The Classical Legacy in Renaissance Poetry* (Longman, 1994). Peter Burke's *The Renaissance* (Longmans, 1964) is an enjoyable introduction; in a later book, *The Renaissance: Studies in European History* (Macmillan, 1987), he examines the myth of the Italian Renaissance and its impact on other cultures. Bacon's attitude to English law is discussed in ch. 2 of Richard Helgerson's *Forms of Nationhood: The Elizabethan Writing of England* (University of Chicago Press, 1992).

AUTHORITIES

The lost wisdom of the ancients is the subject of D. P. Walker's *The Ancient Theology: Studies in Christian Platonism from the Fifteenth to the Eighteenth Century* (Duckworth, 1972). For political philosophy, see Quentin Skinner's *The Foundations of Modern Political Thought*, 2 vols. (Cambridge University Press, 1978); Richard Tuck's *Philosophy and Government, 1572–1651* (Cambridge University Press, 1993).

WRITERS AND THE AGE

Two excellent overviews are Penry Williams's in *The Later Tudors, England 1547–1603* (Oxford University Press, 1995) and Robert Ashton's *Reformation and Revolution, 1558–1660* (1984; Paladin, 1985). On censorship, see Janet Clare, *'Art made tongue-tied by authority': Elizabethan and Jacobean Dramatic Censorship* (Manchester University Press, 1990); Annabel Patterson, *Censorship and Interpretation* (University of Wisconsin Press, 1984).

POPULAR LITERATURE

'Popular literature' is discussed by Bernard Capp in Barry Reay's collection of essays, *Popular Culture in Seventeenth-Century England*

(1985; Routledge, 1988), and by Tessa Watt in *Cheap Print and Popular Piety, 1550–1640* (Cambridge University Press, 1991), and the interface between drama and popular culture is examined by Frances E. Dolan in *Dangerous Familiars: Representations of Domestic Crime in England, 1550–1700* (Cornell University Press, 1994). John N. King's *English Reformation Literature: The Tudor Origins of the Protestant Tradition* (Princeton University Press, 1982) outlines the popular alternatives to the traditions of high culture, and the connections between Spenser's *Shepheardes Calender* and popular culture are examined by Annabel Patterson in *Pastoral and Ideology: Virgil to Valèry* (Oxford University Press, 1988) and by Robert Lane in *Shepheards Devises: Edmund Spenser's 'Shepheardes Calender' and the Institutions of Elizabethan Society* (University of Georgia Press, 1993).

Chapter 2

Spenser's Anabaptist giant is discussed in Christopher Hill's essay, 'The Many-headed Monster', reprinted in his *Change and Continuity in Seventeenth-Century England* (Weidenfeld, 1974). Keith Wrightson's *English Society, 1580–1680* (Hutchinson, 1982) is an excellent introduction to the social history of the period, as is Penry Williams's detailed and very readable account in *The Tudor Regime* (Oxford University Press, 1979).

THREATS TO STABILITY

Ian Archer discusses *The Pursuit of Stability: Social Relations in Elizabethan London* (Cambridge University Press, 1991), and the debate is extended in Paul Griffiths, Adam Fox, and Steve Hindle (eds.), *The Experience of Authority in Early Modern England* (Macmillan, 1996). On Munster, see Euan Cameron, *The European Reformation* (Oxford University Press, 1991).

CHANGES IN LANDHOLDING

On demography, J. D. Chambers, *Population, Economy and Society in Pre-Industrial England* (Oxford University Press, 1972) provides a useful introduction; E. A. Wrigley and R. S. Schofield's *The Population History of England, 1541–1871* (Edward Arnold, 1981) is the authoritative account. The growth of towns in general is described in Peter Clark and Paul Slack (eds.), *English Towns in Transition, 1500–1700* (Oxford University Press, 1976), and of London in particular by Ian Archer (listed above), and in A. L. Beier and Roger Finlay (eds.), *London, 1500–1700* (Longman, 1986).

Barry Coward's *Social Change and Continuity in Modern England, 1550–1750* (Longman, 1988) and Paul Slack's chapter in Christopher Haigh (ed.), *The Reign of Elizabeth* (Macmillan, 1984) summarize material explored more fully by Paul Slack in *Poverty and Policy in Tudor and Stuart England* (Longman, 1988) and by A. L. Beier in *Masterless Men, 1560–1640* (Methuen, 1985). Margaret Spufford examines three *Contrasting Communities: English Villagers in the Sixteenth and Seventeenth Centuries* (Cambridge University Press, 1974).

CONY-CATCHING PAMPHLETS AND CITY COMEDY

Gamini Salgado, *The Elizabethan Underworld* (1977; Alan Sutton, 1984) and Sandra Clark, *The Elizabethan Pamphleteers: Popular Moralistic Pamphlets, 1580–1640* (Athlone Press, 1983) discuss cony-catching pamphlets, and there are several collections—by A. V. Judges, *The Elizabethan Underworld* (Routledge, 1930); J. A. McPeek, *The Black Book of Knaves and Unthrifts* (University of Connecticut, 1969); Gamini Salgado, *Cony-Catchers and Bawdy Baskets* (Penguin Books, 1972); and Arthur Kinney, *Rogues, Vagabonds and Sturdy Beggars* (Imprint Society: Barre, Massachusetts, 1973).

The pioneering account of Jacobean comedy as a social phenomenon was that of L. C. Knights, *Drama and Society in the Age of Shakespeare* (Chatto & Windus, 1937), succeeded by Brian Gibbons, *Jacobean City Comedy* (1968; Methuen, 1980); Alexander Leggatt, *Citizen Comedy in the Age of Shakespeare* (University of Toronto Press, 1973) and Theodore B. Leinwand, *The City Staged: Jacobean Comedy 1603–13* (University of Wisconsin Press, 1986). Margot Heinemann discussed *A New Way to Pay Old Debts* in her last essay, 'Drama and Opinion in the 1620s', in J. R. Mulryne and Margaret Shewring (eds.), *Theatre and Government under the Early Stuarts* (Cambridge University Press, 1993).

Chapter 3

Much of the material in this chapter is drawn from Susan Dwyer Amussen's *An Ordered Society: Gender and Class in Early Modern England* (Basil Blackwell, 1988) and Amy Louise Erickson's *Women and Property in Early Modern England* (Routledge, 1993), two highly informative overviews. Anthony Fletcher's *Gender, Sex and Subordination in England 1500–1800* (Yale University Press, 1995) takes in a wide range of material. Gordon Scochet discusses *Patriarchalism in Political Thought* (Basic Books, New York, 1975).

WOMEN AND MARRIAGE

Anthony Fletcher's article 'The Protestant Idea of Marriage in Early Modern England', in Anthony Fletcher and Peter Roberts (eds.), *Religion, Culture and Society in Early Modern Britain* (Cambridge University Press, 1994) makes a recent contribution to the long debate on Protestant marriage guidance—see also Kathleen M. Davies's 'Continuity and Change in Literary Advice on Marriage', in R. B. Outhwaite's *Marriage and Society* (Europa Publications, 1981). Evidence about the nature of marriage is explored by Martin Ingram in *Church Courts, Sex and Marriage in England, 1570–1640* (Cambridge University Press, 1987) and courtship patterns are investigated in Anne Jennalie Cook's *Making a Match: Courtship in Shakespeare and his Society* (Princeton University Press, 1991). See also Anne Barton's essay ' "Wrying but a little": Marriage, Law and Sexuality in the Plays of Shakespeare', ch. 1, in *Essays, Mainly Shakespearean* (Cambridge University Press, 1994).

THE HOUSEHOLD

Lawrence Stone's *The Family, Sex and Marriage, 1500–1800* (Weidenfeld, 1977) is a wonderful source of information, though its thesis, that early modern parents did not invest great emotion in their children, has been widely questioned, notably by Linda Pollock in *Forgotten Children: Parent–Child Relations from 1500 to 1900* (Cambridge University Press, 1983); Keith Wrightson's *English Society 1580–1680* (see Ch. 2, above) gives a more balanced account. Current historical debates on the early modern family are reviewed by Patrick Collinson in the third chapter of *The Birthpangs of Protestant England: Religious and Cultural Change in the Sixteenth and Seventeenth Centuries* (Macmillan, 1988); and Paul Griffith has analysed *Youth and Authority: Formative Experiences in England 1560–1640* (Oxford University Press, 1996).

'DID WOMEN HAVE A RENAISSANCE?'

Patricia Crawford discusses 'Public Duty, Conscience, and Women in Early Modern England', in John Morrill, Paul Slack, and Daniel Woolf (eds.), *Public Duty and Private Conscience in Seventeenth-Century*

England (Oxford University Press, 1993), and more generally, in *Women and Religion in England 1500–1720* (Routledge, 1993). Lynda Boose discusses 'Scolding Brides and Bridling Scolds' in *Shakespeare Quarterly*, 42 (Summer 1991).

Witchcraft has been extensively discussed, most notably by Sir Keith Thomas in *Religion and the Decline of Magic* (Weidenfeld, 1971), by Alan Macfarlane in *Witchcraft in Tudor and Stuart England, 1560–1680* (Routledge, 1970), and most recently by J. A. Sharpe in *Instrument of Darkness: Witchcraft in England 1550–1700* (Hamish Hamilton, 1996). Diane Purkiss's *The Witch In History* (Routledge, 1996) offers a feminist rereading of some early modern representations of witches.

THREATENING SEXUALITY

David Underdown has asked whether there was 'a crisis in gender relations in the years around 1600' in 'The Taming of the Scold', in *Order and Disorder in Early Modern England* (Cambridge University Press, 1985). Popular attitudes to marriage are examined in J. A. Sharpe's 'Plebeian Marriage in Stuart England', in *Transactions of the Royal Historical Society*, 5th ser., 36 (London, 1986), and two articles by Martin Ingram, 'Sex and Marriage' and 'Ridings, Rough Music and Mocking Rhymes', in Barry Reay's *Popular Culture in Seventeenth-Century England* (see Ch. 1, above). Disturbing attitudes to women's sexuality are recorded in Laura Gowing, *Domestic Dangers: Women, Words, and Sex in Early Modern London* (Oxford University Press, 1996), and in Miranda Chaytor's 'Husband(ry)', *Gender and History*, 7: 3 (Nov. 1995). Sir Keith Thomas considered 'The Place of Laughter in Tudor and Stuart England' in the *Times Literary Supplement*, 3906 (21 Jan. 1977).

Thomas Laqueur's *Making Sex: Body and Gender from the Greeks to Freud* (Harvard University Press, 1990) examines how women's sexual anatomy was interpreted, as does Ian Maclean's *The Renaissance Notion of Women* (Cambridge University Press, 1980). Popular representations of women are discussed in Catherine Belsey's *The Subject of Tragedy: Identity and Difference in Renaissance Drama* (Methuen, 1985), Peter Lake's essay in his and Kevin Sharpe's *Culture and Politics in Early Stuart England* (Macmillan, 1994), and Frances Dolan's *Dangerous Familiars* (See Ch. 1, above).

REPRESENTING THEMSELVES

Linda Woodbridge, *Women and the English Renaissance: Literature and the Nature of Womankind 1540–1620* (Harvester, Sussex, 1984) traces the controversy over women, and several of the pamphlets are reprinted in Simon Shepherd's anthology *The Women's Sharp Revenge* (Fourth Estate, 1985) and K. U. Henderson and B. F. McManus (eds.), *Half Humankind: Contexts and Texts of the Controversy about Women in England, 1540–1640* (University of Illinois Press, 1985). Jean Howard writes on cross-dressing in ch. 5 of *The Stage and Social Struggle in Early Modern England* (Routledge, 1994), as does Stephen Orgel in *Impersonations: The Performance of Gender in Shakespeare's England* (Cambridge University Press, 1996).

Elaine Beilin's *Redeeming Eve: Women Writers of the English Renaissance* (Princeton University Press, 1987) and Barbara Lewalski's *Writing Women in Jacobean England* (Harvard University Press, 1994) are excellent introductions to women's writing; some examples are given by Betty Travitsky (ed.), *The Paradise of Women* (Columbia University Press, 1989) and S. P. Cerasano and Marion Wynne-Davies (eds.), *Renaissance Drama by Women* (Routledge, 1996). Book I of Mary Wroth's *Urania* is reprinted in Paul Salzman's *Anthology of Seventeenth-Century Fiction* (Oxford University Press, 1991).

Chapter 4

ATTITUDES TO THE NEW WORLD

Jeffrey Knapp, *An Empire Nowhere: England, America and Literature from 'Utopia' to 'The Tempest'* (University of California Press, 1992) examines the expectations and reality of the New World, as does Stephen Greenblatt in *Marvelous Possessions: The Wonder of the New World* (Oxford University Press, 1991), the title essay of his *Learning to Curse* (Routledge, 1990), and two further essays, 'Invisible Bullets' and 'Martial Law in the Land of Cockayne', both in *Shakespearean Negotiations* (Oxford University Press, 1988). European perceptions of native Americans are discussed by Anthony Pagden in *The Fall of Natural Man: The American Indian and the Origins of Comparative Ethnology* (Cambridge University Press, 1982). Anthony Grafton's *New Worlds, Ancient Texts: The Power of Tradition and the Shock of Discovery* (Belknap Press of Harvard University Press, 1992) offers a wonderfully illustrated overview.

ENGLISH EXPLORATION

Mary C. Fuller's *Voyages in Print: English Travel to America, 1570–1624* (Cambridge University Press, 1995) examines the writing of exploration of the New World, and Robin Blackburn surveys *The Making of New World Slavery: From the Baroque to the Modern, 1492–1800* (Verso, 1997). The tenth chapter of Joyce Youings's *Sixteenth-Century England* (Penguin Books, 1984) is concerned with voyages and their financiers (as well as with aliens), and Kenneth R. Andrews gives a more detailed account in *Trade, Plunder and Settlement, 1480–1630* (Cambridge University Press, 1984). Laura Stevenson explores *Praise and Paradox: Merchants and Craftsman in Elizabethan Popular Literature* (Cambridge University Press, 1984), and ch. 14 of Louis B. Wright's *Middle-Class Culture in Elizabethan England* (University of North Carolina Press, 1935) looks at popular travel writing.

Hakluyt's *Principal Navigations* is a central text but there is no convenient modern edition—Jack Beeching's *Voyages and Discoveries* (Penguin Books, 1972) is inevitably heavily abridged, and more of *The Discovery of Guiana* can be found in *Sir Walter Raleigh: Selected Writings*, ed. Gerald Hammond (1984; Penguin Books, 1986). A complete edition of Hakluyt in 8 volumes introduced by John Masefield, was published (1907–1962) by Everyman. Ch. 4 of Richard Helgerson's *Forms of Nationhood* (see Ch. 1, above) focuses upon Hakluyt, and D. B. Quinn discusses his posthumous reputation in *The Hakluyt Handbook* (Hakluyt Society, 1974). *The Puritans*, ed. Perry Miller and Thomas H. Johnson (Harper Torchbooks, 1938, 1963), reprints writings of the earliest settlers, including William Bradford and extracts from John Smith.

REPRESENTING THE OTHER

The early chapters of Peter Fryer's *Staying Power: The History of Black People in Britain* (Pluto Press, 1984) estimate numbers of Africans in London and look at their representation in city pageants. Peter Hulme's *Colonial Encounters* (Methuen, 1986) discusses the origins of the word (and concept) 'cannibal'. Stephen Orgel's edition of *The Tempest* (Oxford University Press, 1994) reprints extracts from William Strachey's letter (originally published in *Purchas his Pilgrimes*).

AFRICANS, JEWS, AND 'STRANGERS'

On the representation of Africans and other people of colour on stage, the pioneering account is Eldred Jones, *Othello's Countrymen: The African in English Renaissance Drama* (Oxford University Press, 1965): see also Ruth Cowhig's essay 'Blacks in English Renaissance Drama', in David Dabydeen's *The Black Presence in English Literature*

(Manchester University Press, 1985), Ania Loomba's important *Gender, Race, Renaissance Drama* (Manchester University Press, 1989), and Jack D'Amico's *The Moor in English Renaissance Drama* (University of South Florida Press, 1991). Kim F. Hall's *Things of Darkness: Economies of Race and Gender in Early Modern England* (Cornell University Press, 1995) explores the antithesis of 'black' and 'fair' in the sonnet tradition, in Jonson's *Masque of Blackness*, and elsewhere in Renaissance literature. James Shapiro's *Shakespeare and the Jews* (Columbia University Press, 1996) uses Shylock as the starting-point for a discussion of English perceptions of Jews before Cromwell, and Laura Hunt Yungblut has written on the *'Strangers Settled Here Amongst Us: Policies, Perceptions and the Presence of Aliens in Elizabethan England'* (Routledge, 1996).

COLONIZING IRELAND

On Ireland, see Cyril Falls's *Elizabethan Irish Wars* (Constable, 1950, repr. 1996). D. B. Quinn's *The Elizabethans and the Irish* (Cornell University Press, 1966) and Roy Foster's *Modern Ireland, 1600–1972* (Penguin, 1989). Some literary representations of Irish politics are discussed in Patricia Coughlan (ed.), *Spenser and Ireland: An Interdisciplinary Perspective* (Cork University Press, 1989). David Lindley analyses *The Irish Masque* in his essay 'Embarrassing Ben', reprinted in A. F. Kinney and D. S. Collins (eds.), *Renaissance Historicism: Selections from 'English Literary Renaissance'* (University of Massachusetts Press, 1987).

Chapter 5

The 'Homily on Obedience' is reprinted in A. F. Kinney (ed.), *Elizabethan Backgrounds: Historical Documents of the Age of Elizabeth I* (Archon Books, 1975). Two collections of essays particularly relevant to this chapter are S. Pumfrey, P. L. Rossi, and M. Slawinski (eds.), *Science, Culture and Popular Belief in Renaissance Europe* (Manchester University Press, 1991) and C. B. Schmitt and Q. Skinner (eds.), *The Cambridge History of Renaissance Philosophy* (Cambridge University Press, 1988).

TRANSIENCE

The prologue to Sir Keith Thomas's *Religion and the Decline of Magic* (see Ch. 3, above) on 'The Environment' gives a vivid account of living conditions in early modern England; Isabel Rivers discusses *Classical and Christian Ideas in English Renaissance Poetry* (see Ch. 1, above).

PASTORAL

On pastoral, see the second half of Helen Cooper's *Pastoral: Medieval into Renaissance* (Ipswich; D. S. Brewer, 1977) and Annabel Patterson's *Pastoral and Ideology* (cited Ch. 1, above).

MUSIC AND MEASURE

Robin Headlam Wells's *Elizabethan Mythologies: Studies in Poetry, Drama and Music* (Cambridge University Press, 1994) explores relationships between music, cosmology, and inherited ideas. A more technical account of musical theory is offered in Claude Palisca's essay 'The Science of Sound and Musical Practice', in J. W. Shirley and D. F. Hoeniger (eds.), *Science and the Arts in the Renaissance* (Washington: Folger Shakespeare Library, 1985). Christopher Butler's *Number Symbolism* (Routledge & Kegan Paul, 1970) is a general introduction to poetic numerology; for more detail, Alastair Fowler's *Triumphal Forms: Structural Patterns in Elizabethan Poetry* (Cambridge University Press, 1970) and A. Kent Hieatt's *Short Time's Endless Monument: The Symbolism of the Numbers in Edmund Spenser's Epithalamion* (New York: Columbia University Press, 1960).

On Renaissance Neoplatonism, see Frances Yates, *Giordano Bruno and the Hermetic Tradition* (Routledge & Kegan Paul, 1964) and D. P. Walker, *The Ancient Theology* (see Ch. 1, above); Yates's thesis is questioned by R. S. Westman and J. E. McGuire, *Hermeticism and the Scientific Revolution* (Los Angeles: Clark Memorial Library, 1977); also Rossi's essay in *Science, Culture and Popular Belief* (listed above). Stevie Davies (ed.), *Renaissance Views of Man* (Manchester University Press, 1978) reprints passages from Ficino's commentaries on Plato and Pico's *Oration*.

CORRESPONDENCES

Arthur O. Lovejoy's *The Great Chain of Being* (Harvard University Press, 1936) describes the system of correspondences more tendentiously outlined by E. M. W. Tillyard in *The Elizabethan World Picture* (Chatto, 1943), as does Leonard Barkan, *Nature's Work of Art: The Human Body as Image of the World* (1975; Yale University Press, 1977).

DISCOVERIES

Thomas S. Kuhn gives a lucid account of *The Copernican Revolution* (Harvard University Press, 1957). Peter Dear describes Galileo's confrontation with the Church in 'The Church and the New Philosophy', in *Science, Culture and Popular Belief* (listed above). James Ackerman examines 'The Involvement of Artists in Renaissance Science' in *Science and the Arts in the Renaissance* (above), and on the developing study of anatomy, see Jonathan Sawday, *The Body Emblazoned: Dissection and the Human Body in Renaissance Culture* (Routledge, 1995).

On Bacon, see Paolo Rossi, *Francis Bacon: From Magic to Science* (Routledge, 1968), Lisa Jardine, *Francis Bacon: Discovery and the Art of Discourse* (Cambridge University Press, 1974)—the opening chapter examines the use of dialectic in the sixteenth century—and more recently, Julian Martin, *Francis Bacon, the State, and the Reform of Natural Philosophy* (Cambridge University Press, 1992).

Chapter 6

John Bossy's *Christianity in the West 1400–1700* (Oxford University Press, 1985) gives a wide overview of Christianity before the Reformation. Ch. 8 of Joyce Youings's *Sixteenth-Century England* (Penguin, 1984) outlines the immediate effects of the Reformation in England, while Euan Cameron's *The European Reformation* (Oxford University Press, 1991) summarizes its main agents and ideas abroad.

THE ENGLISH REFORMATION

A. G. Dickens, *The English Reformation* (Batsford, 1964) and Christopher Haigh, *English Reformations* (Oxford University Press, 1993) describe the Reformation from Protestant and Catholic points of view, respectively. Passages from Erasmus and Luther's debate on free will are included in Stevie Davies (ed.), *Renaissance Views of Man* (see Ch. 5, above). Sir Keith Thomas's *Religion and the Decline of Magic* (see Ch. 3, above) gives a wonderfully readable account of popular beliefs, including ideas of providence; see also Barry Reay's essay on, 'Popular Religion' in his *Popular Culture in Seventeenth-Century England* (see Ch. 1, above) and Margaret Spufford in *Contrasting Communities* (see Ch. 2, above). On the Reformation in Scotland, see Jenny Wormald's *Court, Kirk and Community, Scotland, 1470–1625* (Edward Arnold, 1981).

Peter G. Lake writes on 'Calvinism and the English Church,

1570–1635', in *Past and Present*, 114 (1987), 32–76 and in *Anglicans and Puritans? Presbyterianism and English Conformist Thought from Whitgift to Hooker* (Unwin Hyman, 1988). On Arminianism, see Nicolas Tyacke's 'Puritanism, Arminianism and Counter-Revolution, in Conrad Russell (ed.), *The Origins of the English Civil War* (Macmillan, 1973), and Tyacke's *Anti-Calvinists: The Rise of English Arminianism* (Oxford University Press, 1987).

THE BIBLE, FOXE, AND PROVIDENCE

Tyndale is discussed by Stephen Greenblatt in *Renaissance Self-Fashioning* (University of Chicago Press, 1980), and John Bale by John King in *English Reformation Literature* (see Ch. 1, above); in the final chapter of *Forms of Nationhood* (see Ch. 1, above), Richard Helgerson contrasts the achievements of Foxe and Hooker. For apocalyptic ideas, see Katharine R. Firth, *The Apocalyptic Tradition in Reformation Britain, 1530–1645* (Oxford University Press, 1979) and C. A. Patrides and Joseph Wittreich (eds.), *The Apocalypse in English Renaissance Thought and Literature* (Manchester University Press, 1984).

SEPARATISTS AND CATHOLICS

On Protestantism, see Patrick Collinson, *The Religion of Protestants: The Church in English Society, 1559–1625* (Oxford University Press, 1982), and on Familists, Christopher Marsh, *The Family of Love in English Society, 1550–1630* (Cambridge University Press, 1994). On Catholicism, John Bossy's 'The Character of English Catholicism' in Trevor Aston (ed.), *Crisis in Europe, 1550–1660* (Routledge & Kegan Paul, 1965) and *The English Catholic Community, 1570–1850* (Darton, Longman, and Todd, 1975), and for William Stanley and the Deventer incident, Simon Adams, 'A Patriot for Whom: Stanley, York and Elizabeth's Catholics', *History Today*, 37 (July 1987), 46–50. See also Patricia Crawford, *Women and Religion in England, 1500–1720* (Routledge, 1993).

POETS AND PREACHERS

Popular Protestant literature is discussed by Collinson in ch. 4 of *The Birthpangs of Protestant England* (see Ch. 3, above), by Tessa Watt in *Cheap Print and Popular Piety* (see Ch. 1, above), and by Bernard Capp in 'Popular Literature', in Reay's *Popular Culture in Seventeenth-Century England* (see Ch. 1, above).

Debora K. Shuger examines sermons and theological writing in *Habits of Thought in the English Renaissance* (University of California Press, 1990), and Stanley Fish analyses 'Death's Duel' in *Self-Consuming Artefacts* (University of California Press, 1972). There are selections of sermons by John Chandos, *In God's Name* (Hutchinson, 1971) and by Martin Seymour-Smith, *The English Sermon, 1550–1650*, vol. 1 (Carcanet, 1976). The last chapter of Graham Parry's *The Golden Age Restor'd: The Culture of the Stuart Court, 1603–42* (Manchester University Press, 1981) examines 'The Religious Arts under James and Charles'.

Chapter 7

Kenneth Charlton's *Education in Renaissance England* (Routledge & Kegan Paul, 1965), gives a helpful overview. Lawrence Stone's article 'The Educational Revolution in England, 1540–1640', *Past and Present*, 28 (July 1964), 41–80, makes important, if controversial claims.

REREADING THE CLASSICS

R. R. Bolgar examined *The Classical Heritage and its Beneficiaries* (Cambridge University Press, 1954, repr. 1973), and edited *Classical Influences on European Culture, A.D. 1500–1700* (Cambridge University Press, 1976). On the humanist movement, see Anthony Grafton and Lisa Jardine, *From Humanism to the Humanities: Education and the Liberal Arts in Fifteenth and Sixteenth Century Europe* (Duckworth, 1986), Jill Kraye (ed.), *The Cambridge Companion to Humanism* (Cambridge University Press, 1996), and Markku Peltonen's more specialized *Classical Humanism and Republicanism in English Political Thought 1570–1640* (Cambridge University Press, 1995).

Useful selections of texts are provided by Joanna Martindale (ed.), *English Humanism: Wyatt to Cowley* (Croom Helm, 1985); K. W. Gransden (ed.), *Tudor Verse Satire* (Athlone Press, 1970), and Sandra Clark (ed.), *Amorous Rites: Elizabethan Erotic Verse* (J. M. Dent, 1994); see also Stephen Orgel's edition of Marlowe's *Complete Poems and Translations* (Penguin, 1971).

EDUCATION AND SOCIETY

Joan Simon's *Education and Society in Tudor England* (Cambridge University Press, 1966; 1979) is clear and informative. On reading, see David Cressy, *Literacy and the Social Order: Reading and Writing in Early*

Modern England (Cambridge University Press, 1980), and Sir Keith Thomas, 'The Meaning of Literacy in Early Modern England', in Gerd Baumann (ed.), *The Written Word: Literacy in Transition* (Oxford University Press, 1986). Thomas also discusses 'Numeracy in Early Modern England' in *Transactions of the Royal Historical Society*, 5th ser., 37 (1987), 103–32. See also essays by Cressy, Eisenstein, and Spufford in Harvey J. Graff (ed.), *Literacy and Social Development in the West: A Reader* (Cambridge University Press, 1981). Margaret Spufford examines popular reading in *Small Books and Pleasant Histories: Popular Fiction and its Readership in Seventeenth-Century England* (Cambridge University Press, 1981), as does Bernard Capp in 'Popular Literature' in Barry Reay's *Popular Culture in Seventeenth-Century England* (see Ch. 1).

SCHOOLS AND UNIVERSITIES

David Cressy's collection of documents, *Education in Tudor and Stuart England* (Edward Arnold, 1975), reprints a number of school statutes. On universities, see Mark Curtis, *Oxford and Cambridge in Transition, 1558–1642* (Oxford University Press, 1959); H. F. Kearney, *Scholars and Gentlemen: Universities and Society in Pre-Industrial Britain* (Faber, 1970).

ALIENATED INTELLECTUALS

Mark Curtis is the author of a classic, though widely disputed, account of 'The Alienated Intellectuals of Early Stuart England', reprinted in Aston, *Crisis in Europe* (see Ch. 6). David Aers and Gunther Kress consider John Donne's poetry from this standpoint in D. Aers, B. Hodge, and G. Kress (eds.), *Literature, Language and Society in England 1580–1680* (Gill and Macmillan, 1981).

Chapter 8

Lawrence Stone's *The Crisis of the Aristocracy, 1558–1641* (Oxford University Press, 1965) gives a wonderful overview of upper-class conduct, full of fascinating detail. W. T. McCaffrey's 'Place and Patronage in Tudor Politics', in S. T. Bindoff, J. Hurstfield, and C. H. Williams (eds.), *Elizabethan Government and Society: Essays presented to Sir John Neale* (Athlone Press, 1961) can be supplemented with the same author's 'Patronage and Politics under the Tudors', in Linda Levy Peck (ed.), *The Mental World of the Jacobean Court* (Cambridge University

Press, 1991), and Peck's own essay, 'Court Patronage and Government Policy: The Jacobean Dilemma', in Guy F. Lytle and Stephen Orgel (eds.), *Patronage in the Renaissance* (Princeton University Press, 1981).

THE COURTIER'S SKILLS

On the literature of courtliness, see Ruth Kelso, *The Doctrine of the English Gentleman in the Sixteenth Century* (University of Illinois Press, 1929), Daniel Javitch, *Poetry and Courtliness in Renaissance England* (Princeton University Press, 1978), and Frank Whigham, *Ambition and Privilege: The Social Tropes of Elizabethan Courtesy Theory* (University of California Press, 1984).

Derek Attridge examines experiments in classical metre in *Well-Weighed Syllables: Elizabethan Verse in Classical Metres* (Cambridge University Press, 1974). Ch. 5 of Hallett Smith, *Elizabethan Poetry: A Study in Conventions, Meaning and Expression* (Harvard University Press, 1952) looks at 'Poetry for Music', as does Bruce Pattison, *Music and Poetry of the English Renaissance*, 2nd edn. (Methuen, 1970), and the more specialized accounts of Diana Poulton, *John Dowland*, 2nd edn. (Faber, 1982) and Joseph Kerman, *The Elizabethan Madrigal: A Comparative Study* (American Musicological Society, NY, 1962). On Sidney and politics, see Katherine Duncan-Jones, *Sir Philip Sidney* (Hamish Hamilton, 1991) and Blair Worden, *The Sound of Virtue: Philip Sidney's Arcadia and Elizabethan Politics* (Yale University Press, 1996).

IMAGES OF ELIZABETH

On Elizabeth's reign, see Simon Adams, 'Eliza Enthroned? The Court and its Politics', in Christopher Haigh (ed.), *The Reign of Elizabeth I* (Macmillan, 1984). Elizabeth's images have been extensively discussed, from E. C. Wilson's *England's Eliza* (Harvard University Press, 1939) through Frances Yates, *Astraea: The Imperial Theme in the Sixteenth Century* (Routledge & Kegan Paul, 1975), Sir Roy Strong, *The Cult of Elizabeth: Elizabethan Portraiture and Pageant* (Thames & Hudson, 1977), Philippa Berry, *Of Chastity and Power: Elizabethan Literature and the Unmarried Queen* (Routledge, 1989), to Susan Frye, *Elizabeth I: The Competition for Representation* (Oxford University Press, 1993). Jean Wilson has collected and analysed four *Entertainments for Elizabeth I* (D. S. Brewer: Rowman and Wittlefield, 1980).

Louis Montrose has written two important essays on Elizabeth— ' "Eliza, Queen of Shepheardes," and the Pastoral of Power', reprinted in Kinney and Collins, *Renaissance Historicism* (see Ch. 4, above) and '*A Midsummer Night's Dream* and the Shaping Fantasies of Elizabethan Culture: Gender Power, Form', reprinted in M. W. Ferguson, M. Quilligan, and N. J. Vickers (eds.), *Rewriting the Renaissance: The Discourses of Sexual Difference in Early Modern Europe* (University of Chicago Press, 1986). Richard McCoy discusses *The Rites of Knighthood: The Literature and Politics of Elizabethan Chivalry* (University of California Press, 1989) and Alan Young, *Tudor and Jacobean Tournaments* (George Philip, 1987). Mervyn James examines 'English Politics and the Concept of Honour, 1485–1642' in *Society, Politics and Culture* (Cambridge University Press, 1986), which includes his essay 'At the Crossroads of the Political Culture: The Essex Revolt, 1601'.

DISILLUSION

On literary patronage, see Phyllis Sheavyn, *The Literary Profession in the Elizabethan Age* (1909), 2nd edn. rev. J. W. Saunders (Manchester University Press, 1967); E. H. Miller, *The Professional Writer in Elizabethan England* (Harvard University Press, 1959); Michael Brennan, *Literary Patronage in the Renaissance: The Pembroke Family* (Routledge, 1988) and *Patronage in the Renaissance* (listed above). On the impact of Seneca and Tacitus, see essays by Malcolm Smuts in *Culture and Politics in Early Stuart England* (listed above), and by J. H. M. Salmon in *The Mental World of the Jacobean Court* (also listed above).

THE COURT OF KING JAMES

There are some excellent accounts of the culture of James's court, including Malcolm Smuts, *Court Culture and the Origins of a Royalist Tradition in Early Stuart England* (University of Pennsylvania Press, 1987), *The Mental World of the Jacobean Court* (which has an essay on the court of Queen Anne by Leeds Barroll), Graham Parry's *The Golden Age Restor'd* (see Ch. 6 above), and essays by Blair Worden, Kevin Sharpe, and J. Newman in *Culture and Politics in Early Stuart England*. David Starkey, *The English Court from the Wars of the Roses to the Civil War* (Longman, 1987) describes the layout of the palace at Whitehall and includes essays by Pam Wright and Neil Cuddy on the courts of Elizabeth and James (respectively).

Sir Roy Strong has written on *Henry, Prince of Wales, and England's Lost Renaissance* (Thames & Hudson, 1986) and David Lindley on *The*

Trials of Frances Howard: Fact and Fiction at the Court of King James (Routledge, 1993). J. Sharpe has an essay on ' "Last dying speeches': Religion, Ideology and Public Execution in Seventeenth-Century England' in *Past and Present*, 107 (1985). Alastair Bellany writes on the libels against Buckingham in *Culture and Politics in Early Stuart England.*

THE COURT PERFORMED

Albert Tricomi gives an account of *Anticourt Drama in England, 1603–1642* (University of Virginia Press, 1989). The masque has been extensively discussed, but Stephen Orgel's *The Illusion of Power: Political Theater in the English Renaissance* (University of California Press, 1975) is still the best starting-point. David Lindley (ed.), *The Court Masque* (Manchester University Press, 1984) provides a useful collection of critical essays; see also the essays by Jerzy Limon in *The Mental World of the Jacobean Court* and Martin Butler in *Culture and Politics in Early Stuart England.* Margot Heinemann's account of Middleton's *A Game at Chess* in *Puritanism and Theatre* (Cambridge University Press, 1980) can be supplemented with Jerzy Limon's *Dangerous Matter: English Drama and Politics in 1623/4* (Cambridge University Press, 1986).

Chapter 9

Andrew Gurr has written authoritative and enjoyable accounts of the Shakespearean playing places, audiences, and players in *The Shakespearean Stage, 1574–1642*, 2nd edn. (Cambridge University Press, 1980); *Playgoing in Shakespeare's London* (Cambridge University Press, 1987), and *The Shakespearean Playing Companies* (Oxford University Press, 1996). On censorship, consult Richard Dutton, *Mastering the Revels: The Regulation and Censorship of English Renaissance Drama* (Macmillan, 1991); on the theatres' anomalies, see Stephen Mullaney, *The Place of the Stage: Licence, Play, and Power in Renaissance England* (University of Chicago Press, 1988), and on the dialectical character of the drama, Joel Altman, *The Tudor Play of Mind: Rhetorical Enquiry and the Development of Elizabethan Drama* (University of California Press, 1978). See also Louis B. Montrose, *The Purpose of Playing: Shakespeare and the Cultural Politics of the Elizabethan Theatre* (University of Chicago Press, 1996).

A COMMERCIAL THEATRE

R. A. Foakes, 'Playhouses and Players' gives a useful summary (including the Rose excavations), in A. R. Braunmiller and Michael Hattaway (eds.), *The Cambridge Companion to English Renaissance Drama* (Cambridge University Press, 1990). Commercial aspects of the theatre are discussed in the first two chapters of Douglas Bruster, *Drama and the Market in the Age of Shakespeare* (Cambridge University Press, 1992). Henslowe's account books are included in Carol C. Rutter's *Documents of the Rose Playhouse* (Manchester University Press, 1984).

Three volumes in a series describe Elizabethan plays in performance, Michael Hattaway, *Elizabethan Popular Theatre* (Routledge, 1982); Peter Thomson, *Shakespeare's Theatre* (Routledge, 1983), and Keith Sturgess, *Jacobean Private Theatre* (Routledge, 1987). On the children's companies, see Michael Shapiro, *Children of the Revels: The Boy Companies of Shakespeare's Time and their Plays* (Columbia University Press, 1977).

OPPOSITION

Jonas Barish has examined *The Anti-theatrical Prejudice* (University of California Press, 1981); see also Laura Levine, *Men in Women's Clothing: Anti-theatricality and Effeminization 1579–1642* (Cambridge University Press, 1994), Jean Howard, *The Stage and Social Struggle in Early Modern England*, and Stephen Orgel's *Impersonations* (both listed under Ch. 3, above).

THEATRICAL ILLUSION

Alan C. Dessen discusses *Elizabethan Stage Conventions and Modern Interpreters* (Cambridge University Press, 1984).

COMEDY

On genre, see Barbara Lewalski (ed.), *Renaissance Genres: Essays on Theory, History, and Interpretation* (Harvard University Press, 1986). Still useful as starting-points for thinking about Renaissance drama are A. P. Rossiter, *English Drama from Early Times to the Elizabethans* (Hutchinson, 1950) and Madeleine Doran, *Endeavours of Art: A Study of Form in Elizabethan Drama* (University of Wisconsin Press, 1954). On classical background, see Leo Salingar, *Shakespeare and the Traditions of Comedy* (Cambridge University Press, 1974). Modern approaches to comedy are often influenced by Mikhail Bakhtin's,

Rabelais and His World, trans. Helene Iswolsky (1968; Indiana University Press, 1984).

TRAGEDY

On the classical background, see Gordon Braden, *Renaissance Tragedy and the Senecan Tradition: Anger's Privilege* (Yale University Press, 1985). J. W. Lever considers *The Tragedy of State* (Methuen, 1971); Jonathan Dollimore, *Radical Tragedy: Religion, Ideology and Power in the Drama of Shakespeare and his Contemporaries* (Harvester Wheatsheaf, 1984; 1989) and Catherine Belsey, *The Subject of Tragedy* (see above, Ch. 3).

Conclusion

Anne Righter, *Shakespeare and the Idea of the Play* (Chatto & Windus, 1962) explores Shakespeare's use of theatrical metaphor. Peter Burke, *Popular Culture in Early Modern Europe* (Maurice Temple Smith, 1978) looks at efforts to repress popular culture, and Leah S. Marcus, *The Politics of Mirth: Jonson, Herrick, Milton, Marvell and the Defense of Old Holiday Pastimes* (University of Chicago Press, 1986) looks at some literary treatments of this subject.

Index

OXFORD

MORE OXFORD PAPERBACKS

This book is just one of nearly 1000 Oxford Paperbacks currently in print. If you would like details of other Oxford Paperbacks, including titles in the World's Classics, Oxford Reference, Oxford Books, OPUS, Past Masters, Oxford Authors, and Oxford Shakespeare series, please write to:

UK and Europe: Oxford Paperbacks Publicity Manager, Arts and Reference Publicity Department, Oxford University Press, Walton Street, Oxford OX2 6DP.

Customers in UK and Europe will find Oxford Paperbacks available in all good bookshops. But in case of difficulty please send orders to the Cash-with-Order Department, Oxford University Press Distribution Services, Saxon Way West, Corby, Northants NN18 9ES. Tel: 01536 741519; Fax: 01536 746337. Please send a cheque for the total cost of the books, plus £1.75 postage and packing for orders under £20; £2.75 for orders over £20. Customers outside the UK should add 10% of the cost of the books for postage and packing.

USA: Oxford Paperbacks Marketing Manager, Oxford University Press, Inc., 200 Madison Avenue, New York, N.Y. 10016.

Canada: Trade Department, Oxford University Press, 70 Wynford Drive, Don Mills, Ontario M3C 1J9.

Australia: Trade Marketing Manager, Oxford University Press, G.P.O. Box 2784Y, Melbourne 3001, Victoria.

South Africa: Oxford University Press, P.O. Box 1141, Cape Town 8000.

PAST MASTERS

General Editor: Keith Thomas

SHAKESPEARE

Germaine Greer

'At the core of a coherent social structure as he viewed it lay marriage, which for Shakespeare is no mere comic convention but a crucial and complex ideal. He rejected the stereotype of the passive, sexless, unresponsive female and its inevitable concommitant, the misogynist conviction that all women were whores at heart. Instead he created a series of female characters who were both passionate and pure, who gave their hearts spontaneously into the keeping of the men they loved and remained true to the bargain in the face of tremendous odds.'

Germaine Greer's short book on Shakespeare brings a completely new eye to a subject about whom more has been written than on any other English figure. She is especially concerned with discovering why Shakespeare 'was and is a popular artist', who remains a central figure in English cultural life four centuries after his death.

'eminently trenchant and sensible . . . a genuine exploration in its own right' John Bayley, *Listener*

'the clearest and simplest explanation of Shakespeare's thought I have yet read' Auberon Waugh, *Daily Mail*

THE OXFORD AUTHORS

General Editor: Frank Kermode

THE OXFORD AUTHORS is a series of authoritative editions of major English writers. Aimed at both students and general readers, each volume contains a generous selection of the best writings—poetry, prose, and letters—to give the essence of a writer's work and thinking. All the texts are complemented by essential notes, an introduction, chronology, and suggestions for further reading.

Matthew Arnold
William Blake
Lord Byron
John Clare
Samuel Taylor Coleridge
John Donne
John Dryden
Ralph Waldo Emerson
Thomas Hardy
George Herbert and Henry Vaughan
Gerard Manley Hopkins
Samuel Johnson
Ben Jonson
John Keats
Andrew Marvell
John Milton
Alexander Pope
Sir Philip Sidney
Oscar Wilde
William Wordsworth

THE OXFORD AUTHORS

BEN JONSON

Edited by Ian Donaldson

Ben Jonson's literary reputation with his contemporaries rivalled, and perhaps surpassed, that of Shakespeare. This edition presents the full texts of Jonson's two most popular comedies, *Volpone* and *The Alchemist* and of his commonplace book *Discoveries*, his *Conversations with William Drummond of Hawthornden*, and all his non-dramatic poetry. To this is added a generous selection of songs and poems from the plays and masques, and a number of poems doubtfully attributed to Jonson.

THE OXFORD AUTHORS

SIR PHILIP SIDNEY

Edited by Katherine Duncan-Jones

Born in 1554, Sir Philip Sidney was hailed as the
perfect Renaissance patron, soldier, lover, and
courtier, but it was only after his untimely death at
the age of thirty-two that his literary achievements
were truly recognized.

This collection ranges more widely through
Sidney's works than any previous volume and includes substantial parts of both versions of the
Arcadia, *A Defence of Poesy*, and the whole of the
sonnet sequence *Astrophil and Stella*. Supplemen-
tary texts, such as his letters and the numerous
elegies which appeared after his death, help to illustrate the wide spectrum of his achievements, and the
admiration he inspired in his contemporaries.

WORLD'S CLASSICS SHAKESPEARE

'not simply a better text but a new conception of Shakespeare. This is a major achievement of twentieth-century scholarship.' Times Literary Supplement

Hamlet
Macbeth
The Merchant of Venice
As You Like It
Henry IV Part I
Henry V
Measure for Measure
The Tempest
Much Ado About Nothing
All's Well that Ends Well
Love's Labours Lost
The Merry Wives of Windsor
The Taming of the Shrew
Titus Andronicus
Troilus & Cressida
The Two Noble Kinsmen
King John
Julius Caesar
Coriolanus
Anthony & Cleopatra

WORLD'S CLASSICS SHAKESPEARE
HAMLET
Edited by G. R. Hibbard

Hamlet's combination of violence and introspection is unusual among Shakespeare's tragedies. It is also full of curious riddles and fascinating paradoxes, making it one of his most widely discussed plays.

Professor Hibbard's illuminating and original introduction explains the process by which variant texts were fused in the eighteenth century to create the most commonly used text of today. Drawing on both critical and theatrical history, he shows how this fusion makes *Hamlet* seem a much more problematic play than it was when it originally appeared in the disparate early texts.

This is a 'theatrical' and highly practical edition for students and actors alike.

WORLD'S CLASSICS SHAKESPEARE
THE MERCHANT OF VENICE
Edited by Jay L. Halio

What was Shakespeare's attitude to Semitism? The introduction to this edition of *The Merchant of Venice* opens by addressing this vital issue raised by the play, and goes on to study the sources, background, and date, including a discussion of Sigmund Freud's essay on 'The Three Caskets'.

Professor Halio interprets the play's contradictions, inconsistencies, and complementarities, especially as these relate to the overarching theme of bonds and bondage.

The text, based on a fresh examination of the early editions, is presented in modernized spelling and punctuation. Unfailingly lucid and helpful, this is an ideal edition for students, actors, and the general reader.

WORLD'S CLASSICS SHAKESPEARE

AS YOU LIKE IT

Edited by Alan Brissenden

As You Like It is Shakespeare's most light-hearted comedy, and its witty heroine Rosalind has his longest female role.

In this edition, Alan Brissenden reassesses both its textual and performance history, showing how interpretations have changed since the first recorded production in 1740. He examines Shakespeare's sources and elucidates the central themes of love, pastoral, and doubleness. Detailed annotations investigate the allusive and often bawdy language, enabling student, actor, and director to savour the humour and the seriousness of the play to the full.

WORLD'S CLASSICS SHAKESPEARE
MACBETH
Edited by Nicholas Brooke

Dark and violent, *Macbeth* is also the most theatrically spectacular of Shakepeare's tragedies. This fully annotated edition reconsiders textual and staging problems, appraises past and present critical views, and represents a major contribution to our understanding of the play.

In his introduction Nicholas Brooke relates *Macbeth*'s changing fortunes to changes within society and the theatre and investigates the sources of its enduring appeal. He examines its many layers of illusion and interprets its linguistic turns and echoes, arguing that the earliest surviving text is an adaptation, perhaps carried out by Shakespeare himself in collaboration with Thomas Middleton.

WORLD'S CLASSICS SHAKESPEARE
ALL'S WELL THAT ENDS WELL
Edited by Susan Snyder

Usually classified as a 'problem comedy', *All's Well That Ends Well* invites a fresh assessment. Its psychologically disturbing presentation of an aggressive, designing woman and a reluctant husband wooed by trickery won it little favour in earlier centuries, and both directors and critics have frequently tried to avoid or simplify its uncomfortable elements. More recently, several distinguished productions have revealed it as an exceptionally penetrating study of both personal and social issues.

In her introduction to *All's Well That Ends Well*, Susan Snyder makes the play's clashing ideologies of class and gender newly accessible. She explains how the very discords of style can be seen as a source of theatrical power and complexity, and offers a fully reconsidered, helpfully annotated text for both readers and actors.

WORLD'S CLASSICS SHAKESPEARE
HENRY V
Edited by Gary Taylor

Henry V, the climax of Shakespeare's sequence of English history plays, is an inspiring, often comic celebration of a young warrior-king. But it is also a study of the costly exhilarations of war, and of the penalties as well as the glories of human greatness.

Introducing this brilliantly innovative edition, Gary Taylor shows how Shakespeare shaped his historical material, examines controversial critical interpretations, discusses the play's fluctuating fortunes in performance, and analyses the range and variety of Shakespeare's characterization.

ILLUSTRATED HISTORIES IN
OXFORD PAPERBACKS

THE OXFORD ILLUSTRATED HISTORY
OF ENGLISH LITERATURE

Edited by Pat Rogers

Britain possesses a literary heritage which is almost
unrivalled in the Western world. In this volume, the
richness, diversity, and continuity of that tradition
are explored by a group of Britain's foremost literary scholars.

Chapter by chapter the authors trace the history
of English literature, from its first stirrings in Anglo-
Saxon poetry to the present day. At its heart towers
the figure of Shakespeare, who is accorded a special
chapter to himself. Other major figures such as
Chaucer, Milton, Donne, Wordsworth, Dickens,
Eliot, and Auden are treated in depth, and the story
is brought up to date with discussion of living
authors such as Seamus Heaney and Edward Bond.

'[a] lovely volume . . . put in your thumb and pull
out plums' Michael Foot

'scholarly and enthusiastic people have written inspiring essays that induce an eagerness in their readers to return to the writers they admire' *Economist*